Reporters Who Made History

Reporters Who Made History

Great American Journalists on the Issues and Crises of the Late 20th Century

STEVEN M. HALLOCK

PRAEGER
An Imprint of ABC-CLIO, LLC

A B C CLIO

Santa Barbara, California • Denver, Colorado • Oxford, England

Library of Congress Cataloging-in-Publication Data

Hallock, Steven M.
Reporters who made history : great American journalists on the issues and crises of the late 20th century / Steven M. Hallock.
p. cm.
Includes bibliographical references and index.
ISBN 978-0-313-38026-6 (hard copy : alk. paper)—ISBN 978-0-313-38027-3 (ebook) 1. Press and politics—United States—History—20th century. 2. United States—Politics and government—20th century. I. Title.
PN4888.P6H33 2009
070.92'2—dc22 2009019952

14 13 12 11 10 1 2 3 4 5

This book is also available on the World Wide Web as an eBook.
Visit www.abc-clio.com for details.

ABC-CLIO, LLC
130 Cremona Drive, P.O. Box 1911
Santa Barbara, California 93116-1911

This book is printed on acid-free paper

Manufactured in the United States of America

For Joanne

Contents

Foreword

Some things you just never forget.

One of the most vivid—and chilling—for me was a spring day in 1982, when I was fishing from a canoe on a farm pond with another doctoral student at Indiana University. As we caught panfish and bass, I mentioned that I had recently read Michael Herr's *Dispatches,* which was about his time as a war correspondent in Vietnam, and had found it to be so riveting that I couldn't put it down. My friend surprised me by saying that after his Army tour in Vietnam had ended, he had gone back for about a year as a newspaper correspondent and had known Herr well, and they were still friends. In fact, two weeks before, Herr, who was wandering around the country, stopped by his house unannounced and spent a night. We talked for a while about the book, which I strongly believe should be required reading for every mass communication student because of its mesmerizing writing as well as what it says about being a journalist, and then he stunned me: "If I could, I'd go back to a war in an instant."

"You're crazy," I replied incredulously.

"No," he answered quietly. "Ever since I left Vietnam, everything has been dull."

In many ways, that sentence summed up Herr's experience in Vietnam, too. He shunned the relative safety of Saigon, preferring instead to hop on a military helicopter to join the Marines, who were called "grunts," at dangerous jungle outposts. He saw horrific things. He continually worried about being injured or killed, but it was such an adrenalin rush when he survived to see another day that he did not want to leave.

I relate that story because it fits in perfectly with Steve Hallock's book. As he notes, the 10 ground-breaking journalists he interviewed for the book have a *calling,* just as my friend had a *calling* in the Vietnam War. They are fascinated to their very core by journalism. As a journalist, you experience a great rush when your incredible curiosity leads you to see historic things, interview interesting people, and bring great stories to the attention of large audiences. You love simply calling yourself a journalist and going after bad guys, and you firmly believe in the righteousness of the First Amendment to its very core. As the saying goes: "Write hard, die free!"

And maybe when you finally die, you will be so proud of having been a journalist that you will want a tombstone that simply has your name, the years that you lived, and the epitaph that was used after the last paragraph of telegraph stories in the Civil War to show that the story had been sent: -30-. The end! But it was a hell of a ride! And if those who see their tombstone realize what -30- means, they will know that they passionately practiced a noble profession just as those profiled in this book have done.

Yes, journalism is a *calling,* and this valuable book shows why. But there is so much more to this book than simply that. Like any good historian, Steve puts the journalists' lives and stories they covered into context by talking about what was going on in the country as they grew up and prompted them to become writers or broadcasters. Because of that, you have a better understanding of them, including how they became journalists and the factors that shaped their stories, their broadcasts, and ultimately their lives.

The importance of understanding the times in which they worked was brought home to me in 1979 when I was a graduate assistant at Indiana University for a course in journalism history. On a test, the professor asked students to name one of the times when President John F. Kennedy angrily lashed out at press coverage. Although almost every student had been born before Kennedy became president, one student said he did not like the coverage of the Pentagon Papers case (which was seven-and-a-half years after Kennedy died), and another said he did not like the press coverage when he bombed Japan (the two atom bombs were dropped more than 15 years before he was president). And then, in one of the most imaginative and humorous historical answers that I have ever encountered, one student said Kennedy did not like the coverage of his assassination.

This book is good for a number of reasons. First, it reminds readers of the significant events that have happened in the United States since 1950. As someone who has taught journalism in college, I have found that many of the students have a deep curiosity about these events, but they do not necessarily make an effort to find out about them unless they have to. Therefore, I require my journalism history students to read *All the President's Men,* and many of them have thanked me because, for the first time, they really understand the Watergate scandal. Steve's book will not only introduce readers to Watergate, but it will also acquaint them with such divergent stories as the Vietnam War, the Black Panthers, the civil rights era, and U.S. presidents from Dwight D. Eisenhower through Bill Clinton. The students have heard about these events and important figures but they probably do not know much about them, and the stories of the reporters who covered them are mesmerizing tidbits of information that students are bound to appreciate—and may even spur them to learn more. One can only hope.

The book is also important because it shows how reporters tackled important stories, the challenges they faced, and the things that they thought about as they wrote and broadcast. In other words, readers are frequently right there with them *in the trenches,* so to speak, as the action takes place. That is a mesmerizing place to be because readers and viewers can feel the excitement of the hunt for great stories, the disappointment as leads sometimes fail to pan out, and the sudden twists and turns in a story that takes a reporter in a new direction that he or she never imagined.

Finally, it should not be overlooked that Steve's taped interviews with the 10 extraordinary and well regarded reporters in this book are invaluable as primary historical documents. For a historian researching any of these journalists, the interviews may provide information that exists nowhere else. He is to be applauded for doing this because, in time, it will be impossible to interview these great heralds of history.

Steve's sources also make some fascinating observations about where journalism has been in the last half of the 20th century and where it is headed. Like some of these individuals, I spent a number of years working on daily newspapers, and we came out of it fascinated by the rapidly-changing technologies and how these innovations were affecting the profession. For example, when I started working on newspapers in 1963, I typed my stories (with carbons) on manual typewriters, and they were set in the backshop as hot type. Over the next 13 years, I moved to electric typewriters, and then, for about six months, the copy was scanned until the day came when we went to VDTs (video display terminals). The computer age was suddenly upon us, and that meant we were now using cold type, which resulted in downsizing the number of printers in the backshop and all but ending a 90-year national run of the use of Linotype machines. And even more importantly, VDTs suddenly set back the deadline for stories by a staggering 45 minutes. Those were valuable minutes in gathering more up-to-date news. But that did not mean that computers were the best thing to come along since sliced bread. Suddenly, it became so easy for reporters to write stories almost without thinking about it and make last-minute changes if they needed to, that the quality of the news stories clearly declined from the precomputer era. When I started on manual typewriters, reporters paid more attention to the style and content of their news reports because changes were more difficult to make.

Meanwhile, over the last 40 years, other technologies have been equally staggering in their impact on the profession. Satellites made it possible to go live from anywhere in the world, and lighter, portable broadcasting equipment made it more difficult for the military to manage the press and turn reporters into *hotel warriors*. That was the term that originated in a famous book about the first Gulf War, when reporters were virtually shut out from covering combat areas and able to report only what their military handlers wanted them to report. So, they virtually covered the war from their hotels. And now the Internet is shaping journalism rapidly. Reporters have more information at their fingertips than ever before, including blogs that shape what they write and raise intriguing questions about journalistic ethics—and the exact definition of a journalist. We can bemoan the changes brought about by these new technologies, but there will be no returning to the old days. And more technological marvels are undoubtedly right around the corner. They will unquestionably affect the press in profound ways that cannot be imagined, and about all that we can be sure of is that we will always need reporters who will challenge authority and tell the public what it needs to know—as those chronicled in this book have done.

In other words, people will continue to find reporting a *calling*, not because it pays more than most other jobs (it does not) and not because it is a job with regular hours (it is not in many cases, particularly as a sportswriter, which is how I started out). Rather, it is not only a job that gives us a chance to make a difference in society and to occasionally help people, but it is also much more challenging and thought-provoking than most other fields of endeavor.

Like Steve, I never covered the big national stories on the four papers that I worked on full time. But as a reporter, I rode with the Blue Angels (the Navy's acrobatic airplane team), I hunted coyotes and rattlesnakes on the West Texas plains, I rode a go-kart 90 miles an hour, I went to a gay Valentine's Day party, I watched flooded houses fall into Lake Ontario as the water rose in the spring because of the snow melt, I toured a nuclear power plant and saw the eerie blue glow emanating out in a circle from spent fuel rods hanging in a radioactive pool of water, I was threatened by a gunman who did not like a story I was writing, and I interviewed famous people such as jazz trumpeter Louis Armstrong, baseball Hall of Famer Satchel Paige, and hydrogen bomb designer Edward Teller.

I would not trade those experiences for anything. Working as a reporter taught me how to write; it made me less naïve, less conservative, and far tougher; it turned me into someone who could operate calmly under extreme pressure and oblivious to distractions; and it made me incredibly curious and interested in knowing new things. Those are traits that have stood me in good stead for my entire life, as a reporter, a college teacher, and as a journalism historian. So, I have never regretted working as a reporter, just as the 10 legends profiled in this book clearly have no regrets. Steve has performed a real service by allowing us to read about them, and to learn from them.

—Patrick S. Washburn
Ohio University

Preface

During my first job as a reporter covering high school football and then county government at a small daily newspaper on the wintry cold plains of southwestern Wyoming, a colleague and I used to meet at week's end at a downtown bar after the paper had been put to bed about 11 P.M. There we would tell stories of our adventures of the day or the week—tales of sources who had delivered good information or who had misled us, of an editor's mangling of our copy, of a reader's complaint on the telephone.

This pattern continued at my next newspaper, a larger daily in west Texas on the Mexican border. After our 11 P.M. deadline, my fellow reporters and I drove across the Rio Grande, to bars where we drank inexpensive Mexican beers and listened to U.S. rock 'n' roll on the jukeboxes while we told the same kind of stories, which have come to be known in newspaper jargon as *war stories*. Some of these tales are exaggerations of journalistic feats, certainly; but mostly they are remembrances of the daily and weekly triumphs of newspaper reporters, spiced with occasional sojourns into yarns about editors, fellow reporters and escapades of long ago.

Many of these war stories actually are tales of war. It is difficult to find a long stretch of years during my career, or during the careers of the older reporters and editors I've met over the years, when the United States has not been involved in some kind of military operation. In my own lifetime, they have included wars in Korea, Vietnam, and Iraq, and military skirmishes in the Middle East, South America, and Europe. Alongside these battles was the nearly half-century Cold War, which on occasion threatened to escalate into nuclear war, during a period of time lasting from the end of World War II to the fall of the Soviet Union at the end of the 1980s.

Journalistic tales of covering these wars found their way to the bars, dinner tables, and living rooms of reporters gathering after deadline to weave yarns of adventure, intrigue, lousy pay, and dastardly editors.

This book is my attempt, spurred by a passion for journalism and a great interest in history and in the folks who made it and wrote about it, to look at the tumultuous last half of the 20th century through the words and memories of the reporters who covered it. Journalism, despite its faults—instances of fabrication and plagiarism, too-heavy reliance on unattributed or unidentified sources, frequent arrogance—remains a noble calling. It is, to me and other colleagues, truly the Fourth Estate, erected on a foundation of truth and a belief that truth, if not wisdom, will eventually emerge from an unfettered, competitive marketplace of ideas—that an unbridled news industry keeping watch over government and business is essential to a thriving democracy. Atop this foundation is a mission of not only informing the public and carrying out the traditional watchdog (or what some have termed a guard dog) role, but also of holding up an independent societal mirror, and of simply entertaining and informing readers and audiences.

Besides carrying out this mission, though, the press has provided a national album and record, of sorts, an archived remembrance of things past—particularly, for this book, of a dynamic and remarkable 50-year era. Gathered here are the reminiscences of 10 print and broadcast journalists, a few of them who likely shared drinks together and exchanged war stories sometime over the years. Their recollections of events, trends and news reported over the last half of the 20th century for major U.S. news organizations and broadcast outlets do include some real war stories. But there is a lot more, ranging from politics to sports and entertainment. The stories they tell in this book are true accounts. They are history, or, as former *Washington Post* publisher Phil Graham reportedly said of journalism, these reporters and countless others produced the first rough drafts of history.

This book is an attempt to collect some of these stories into a sort of U.S. history doubling as a history of journalism from 1950 to 2000, a period that saw the United States emerge from World War II as one of the two most powerful nations on Earth. These 10 remarkable journalists, the first rough-drafters of history, witnessed and reported on the major news events that shaped this period. This book is not intended as a comprehensive, all-inclusive, date- and event-specific chronological presentation of U.S. history during this period. Rather, it is a scrapbook of journalistic productions combined with their authors' recollections and thoughts about some of the people and news events that comprise the collection. Where possible, it uses the original first-hand reports of the correspondents. Lacking access to those, I sought out stories and broadcasts of the journalists' news organizations that produced the coverage of these events or people. And I mined their personal accounts of the period from their memoirs and autobiographies.

Careful consideration went into my selection of the journalists interviewed for the book. This was no random sampling; it was deliberate. A priority in my selection was to compile a strong but diverse cross section of journalists and platforms from the period: print, broadcast and wire service journalists, men and women, and a mix of racial and cultural backgrounds. I interviewed the 10 journalists during the spring and summer of 2006. For each session, I used a notebook, a tape recorder and, for backup, a digital recorder. During my nearly three decades as a print journalist, I have admired the writing and broadcasts of the journalists in this book. My original list of interviewees was larger than the 10 here; but these final 10 were all first choices. Other journalists I selected were too busy or otherwise committed to participate; some chose not to respond to my queries. Had they participated, I simply would have expanded my work to include them.

In addition to the biographical questions, my interviews comprised three major subject categories. One category was what the interviewees considered to be the major news stories of the half century—sort of a journalistic top-10, if you will—in the following subject areas: foreign affairs, politics, legal issues or trends, military/defense, business, crime, science, medicine, sports, artistic/entertainment trends, and the major cultural or societal shifts of the half-century. This category, relying on oral history exclusively, makes up the book's first chapter, which serves as an overture to set the themes and topics taken up throughout the body of the book.

The second category of questions was ordered by decades and their major topics and events. I divided the half century by its five decades and assigned two journalists to each decade for in-depth questioning from a list of prepared questions, plus whatever stories or topics they wanted to bring up. This category included archival research of the reporters' or their news organizations' coverage of some of these specific stories; reliance on some of the journalists' memoirs, especially sections pertaining to the particular subject area; and an oral history of the journalists' recollections of and opinions about these stories and the people in them. I included in these chapters observations of news events, along with newspaper ads, from their hometown newspapers on the days that the journalists were born and listings of national and some major international news events from a historical archive for the years they began their reporting careers. The purpose was to provide contextual background—the cultural mood of the nation and society around them at these times. This narrative category comprises the book's next five chapters.

Because this book is about journalism as well as history, the third category of questions focused on the subject of how journalism has changed since the end of World War II, and where journalism is heading. Topics for this category, the subject of chapter 7, included the journalists' thoughts on how the news business has changed technologically and in method; how journalistic competition has changed, along with the nature of news and news agendas; how the altered ownership of news organizations, such as mergers and buyouts (concentrated ownership), and the decline in the number of daily newspapers and in circulation and network audiences, has affected journalism and the nation; how new platforms such as cable television and the Internet have affected the news business; how reader and audience needs and demands have altered the news business; and the journalists' thoughts about the future of journalism.

Finally, in conclusion, I offer my own thoughts on these subjects in an afterword.

Some of the journalists profiled in the following pages were gypsies of sorts, moving to large, national markets from regional ones. Some were pioneers, women, and minorities wading into an industry dominated by white men. Most were idealists, seeking an opportunity to make a positive mark on society; indeed, readers will detect an adversarial voice in some of their comments and coverage in their zeal to bring about change or to right a wrong. Others adhered strictly to the notion of objectivity, which became popular with the rise of advertising-supported journalism and the decline of media competition. The lure of adventure and a simple love for the craft of writing drew others in an era when clacking typewriters and bulky cameras and sound gear marked them for what they were: recorders of the first drafts of history. Evidence of the march away from that traditional equipment can also be seen in the journalists' remembrances of the events and stories, from notebooks, pay phones, and glue pots to miniaturized recording devices, cell phones, and computer screens and printouts.

A list of the journalists, and the decades they represent in this book, follows.

1950s

Former *New York Times* columnist Anthony Lewis, winner of two Pulitzer Prizes, one for the *Washington Daily News* in 1955 and one for the *New York Times* in 1963, was born in New York City in 1927. He earned a BA with a concentration in English in 1948 at Harvard College, where he was editor of the *Harvard Crimson*. He is author of *Gideon's Trumpet; Portrait of a Decade: The Second American Revolution; Make No Law: The Sullivan Case and the First Amendment;* and *The Supreme Court and How it Works: The Story of the Gideon Case.* He edited *Written into History: Pulitzer Prize Reporting of the Twentieth Century from the New York Times.* I interviewed him in his Cambridge, Massachusetts apartment.

Helen Thomas, a long-time correspondent for United Press International who became the first female wire service White House bureau chief, began covering the White House during the Kennedy administration. She was born in Winchester, Kentucky, raised in Detroit, and graduated with a degree in English from Wayne State University, joining United Press in 1943. She is the author of *Thanks for the Memories, Mr. President: Wit and*

Wisdom from the Front Row at the White House; Front Row at the White House: My Life and Times; and *Watchdogs of Democracy?: The Waning Washington Press Corps and How it Has Failed the Public.* She was writing a syndicated political column at the time this book was written. I interviewed her in a small conference room at the Hearst Corporation headquarters in Washington, D.C., where she kept an office.

1960s

60 Minutes correspondent Morley Safer was born in 1931 in Toronto, Ontario. He began his career as a newspaperman before joining the Canadian Broadcasting Corporation and then, in 1964, CBS News, for which he covered the Vietnam War. His six decades of journalism have earned him numerous awards, including a Lifetime Achievement Emmy, a George Polk Memorial Career Achievement Award and the Robert F. Kennedy Journalism Award. He also has claimed twelve Emmys, three Overseas Press Club Awards, three George Foster Peabody Awards, two Alfred I. DuPont-Columbia University Awards, two George Polk Memorial awards and the Paul White Award. He is author of *Flashbacks: On Returning to Vietnam.* I interviewed him in his *60 Minutes* office in Manhattan.

Earl Caldwell, born in Clearfield, Pennsylvania, in 1935, developed his newspaper reporting skills at his hometown newspaper, *The Progress,* before moving on to larger newspapers and landing at the *New York Times.* There, he covered such major stories as the assassination of Dr. Martin Luther King, Jr., the race riots of the 1960s and the street riots in Chicago during the 1967 Democratic National Convention. His coverage of the Black Panther Party during the 1960s made him the focus of a key U.S. Supreme Court ruling that the First Amendment does not protect reporters from revealing confidential information regarding their sources. In 1979, he became the first African American journalist with a regular column in a major daily newspaper, the *New York Daily News.* He is author of *Black American Witness, Reports from the Front,* which is a collection of his newspaper columns. As this book was being written, Caldwell, whom the Robert C. Maynard Institute for Journalism lists as a founding director, hosted Pacifica Radio's "The Caldwell Chronicle" and was Hampton University's Scripps Howard endowed professor of journalism. I interviewed him in his Manhattan apartment.

1970s

Ben Bradlee, former executive editor of the *Washington Post* who oversaw the coverage by reporters Bob Woodward and Carl Bernstein of the Watergate scandal that led to the downfall of former President Richard Nixon, was born in Boston in 1921. He graduated from Harvard College with a major in classical Greek literature and joined the Office of Naval

Intelligence, working as a communications officer during World War II. After the war he helped launch the *New Hampshire Sunday News* and then joined the *Washington Post* in 1948, a newspaper he returned to after a stint at the Office of U.S. Information and Educational Exchange followed by a position at *Newsweek* magazine. He is author of *A Good Life: Newspapering and Other Adventures; That Special Grace;* and *Conversations with Kennedy.* As this book was being written, Bradlee maintained an office at the *Washington Post,* where he was interviewed.

Georgie Anne Geyer was born in 1935 in Chicago; she graduated from nearby Northwestern University's Medill School of Journalism in 1956. The recipient of a Fulbright Scholarship to the University of Vienna, Geyer joined the *Chicago Daily News* in 1959 as a society reporter before moving to the news desk and then becoming a foreign correspondent reporting on revolutionary movements in Latin America. She was the first Westerner to interview Iraqi president Saddam Hussein, who was one of a long list of foreign leaders she has interviewed. Other names on the list include Yasser Arafat, Anwar Sadat, King Hussein, Shimon Peres, the Ayatollah Khomeini and Fidel Castro. Geyer, who speaks five languages, became a syndicated columnist in 1975. She is author of *Americans No More; Buying the Night Flight: The Autobiography of a Woman Foreign Correspondent; When Cats Reigned Like Kings: On the Trail of the Sacred Cats;* and *Guerrilla Prince,* a biography of Fidel Castro. I interviewed her in her Washington, D.C. apartment.

1980s

Syndicated columnist Ellen Goodman, born in Newton, Massachusetts, in 1941, earned a degree in modern European history at Radcliffe College in 1963. She entered journalism immediately after graduation, joining *Newsweek* magazine as a researcher, moving on to the *Detroit Free Press* as a reporter in 1965, and then landing at the *Boston Globe* in 1967. There, she started her column, which was syndicated by The Washington Post Writers Group in 1976. Goodman, winner of the Pulitzer Prize for commentary in 1980, is author of six column collections: *Paper Trail: Common Sense in Uncommon Times; Close to Home; At Large; Keeping in Touch; Making Sense;* and *Value Judgments;* and of *Turning Points,* dealing with women's changing family roles. She coauthored with Patricia O'Brien *I Know Just What You Mean: The Power of Friendship in Women's Lives.* I interviewed her in her suburban Boston home.

National Public Radio senior correspondent Juan Williams was born in Colon, Panama, in 1954 and moved with his family to Brooklyn in 1958. He graduated from Haverford College in 1976 with a degree in philosophy, then joined the *Washington Post* as an intern. That turned into a 21-year stay at the paper as a White House correspondent, editorial writer and columnist. Williams then turned to broadcasting and earned an Emmy for television documentary writing. His articles have appeared in *Newsweek, Fortune,* the *Atlantic Monthly, Ebony, Gentlemen's Quarterly,* and the *New Republic.* His books include *Thurgood Marshall: American Revolutionary; Eyes on the Prize: America's Civil Rights Years 1954–1965;* and *Enough: The Phony Leaders, Dead-End Movements, and Culture of Failure That Are Undermining Black America—and What We Can Do About It.* As this book was being written he was also a contributing political analyst for the Fox News Channel and on Fox News Sunday. I interviewed him at his NPR office in downtown Washington, D.C.

1990s

Washington Post and nationally syndicated columnist David Broder was born in Chicago Heights, Illinois, in 1929 and earned bachelor's and master's degrees in political science from the University of Chicago. His first newspaper job was as a reporter at the *Pantagraph* in Bloomington, Illinois, and he also wrote for *Congressional Quarterly,* the *Washington Star* and the *New York Times* before joining the *Washington Post* in 1966. The winner of the Pulitzer Prize for commentary in 1973, Broder has been a regular panelist on NBC's *Meet the Press, Washington Week in Review,* and CNN's *Inside Politics.* He is author of *Democracy Derailed: Initiative Campaigns and the Power of Money; Behind the Front Page: A Candid Look at How the News is Made; Changing of the Guard: Power and Leadership in America;* and *The Party's Over: The Failure of Politics in America.* He is coauthor of *The System: The American Way of Politics at the Breaking Point,* with Haynes Johnson; *The Man Who Would be President: Dan Quayle,* with Bob Woodward; and *The Republican Establishment: The Present and Future of the GOP,* with Stephen Hess. I interviewed him in the lunch room of the *Washington Post* in downtown Washington, D.C.

Public Broadcasting Service correspondent Judy Woodruff was born in Tulsa, Oklahoma, in 1946 and earned a degree in political science at Duke University. A broadcast journalist all of her career, she has worked in all three of the major television platforms: network, cable and public. Woodruff was NBC's chief White House correspondent from 1977 to 1982 and also covered Washington for the *Today* show during that time. She joined PBS in 1983 and hosted *Frontline,* where she stayed until 1990 and also reported for *The MacNeil/Lehrer News Hour*. She was host of CNN's *Inside Politics* from 1993 to 2005, returning to PBS in 2006 to work on a documentary project on young people and their thoughts about world events, titled *Generation Next: Speak Up, Be Heard*. She is the author of *This Is Judy Woodruff at the White House.* Woodruff is also a 1997 Emmy winner in the news and documentary category and a recipient with Bernard Shaw of the 1996 CableACE Award for best anchor team and of the CableACE Award for best newscaster in 1995. I interviewed Woodruff at her office in the MacNeil/Lehrer Productions headquarters in suburban Washington, D.C.

These first-drafters of history worked (most of them are still at it) during a period of time that one of them, during an interview session, called a golden period of U.S. journalism. They covered the United States and the world during a time that historians will likely look back on as the age of the American empire. While I don't think the United States deliberately invaded other nations for the sole purpose of empire-building during this time, the United States was a major world power that certainly played a large role—militarily, economically, and culturally—in Europe, Asia, South America, and Africa. The influence of the United States spread throughout the globe after World War II. The stories of the past half century, the era of these 10 journalists, are remarkable: manned travel to the moon, intercontinental missiles armed with bombs capable of destroying entire cities and inducing a global nuclear winter, doctors removing beating hearts from human beings for transplanting to other human beings, the eradication of crippling and fatal diseases and lengthening of life expectancy, paved roadways connecting cities to mountains and oceans, irrigation of deserts that sprouted glistening skyscrapered cities, the peaceful removal and replacement of a presidential administration, cultural upheavals that include expanded civil rights, altered sexual mores and artistic expression.

They covered or witnessed:

- The flame of the global Cold War;
- The fires of racial rage and the ensuing fight for civil rights;
- The controversies of an undeclared and lost war in Asia;
- The protests and love-fests of a generation bent on changing the nation and the world in a decade of political upheaval and assassination;
- The historic resignation of a scandal-plagued president;
- The planting of the seeds of Islamic fundamentalism and terrorism in the Middle East;
- The swinging of the American political pendulum to the right in reaction to the New Deal and the Great Society;
- The emergence of family and women and the human condition as a full-blown news beat;
- The rise and fall of a new Democrat who became president to usher in a new political era of bipartisan bickering and centrist cooperation before his impeachment over matters relating to sex and alleged, though unproven, political scandal;
- Predecessors to the wire-tapping and other law-enforcement efforts to detect terrorist activity today, to appeals to bipartisanship to deal with bona fide national emergencies, and to political scandal that seems so rife in the modern era but really is no more pronounced than in years past.

These journalists covered the rising international star of this nation—and some might argue that they are witness to the beginning of its decline. In his book, *Are We Rome? The Fall of an Empire and the Fate of America, Van-*

ity Fair editor at large Cullen Murphy suggests some interesting, and troubling, comparisons between the corruption and decline of Rome to eerily parallel situations in the United States. Other scholars and historians have put forth similar warnings and comparisons. If this nation is indeed in decline, speculation best left for more qualified commentators in other forums, these journalists have been front-row observers—a cadre of correspondents who entered the field, as will be seen in the coming pages, because they had a desire to do good and to leave a worthwhile mark on the world, and an overwhelming sense of adventure.

Whether or not the nation is in decline, these correspondents and reporters have participated in a style and era of journalism that is on the wane as new platforms, technologies, and methods arise, as old platforms, technologies, and methods wane. Newspaper and broadcast foreign bureaus have been shut down, newspapers shuttered—as this is written, the Chicago Tribune Company is in bankruptcy proceedings, the *Seattle Post-Intelligencer* has ceased daily publication, as has the *Tucson Citizen* in Arizona of its daily print edition, the Minneapolis *Star Tribune* has filed for Chapter 11 bankruptcy protection, and Denver's *Rocky Mountain News* has closed. And broadcast outlets have been splintered and quilted. These phenomena have contributed to a severely altered, if not diminished and weakened, media community to the point that the traditional media role of providing oversight of government, business, and society has become dangerously compromised.

I bring to this book my own experience, of nearly three decades, as a daily newspaper journalist during the era highlighted in this book; I lived first-hand, if not the specific events and stories detailed in this book, a shared experience of the times and of the evolving newspaper industry. So the stories and memories of this book also are mine. And they are the nation's. As the citizens and voters of this country comprise its politics, its pastimes, its disappointments, its hopes and dreams, it is the readers and listeners who are the audience—the focus—of these journalists' work. In the same way that music cannot be enjoyed without ears or paintings seen without eyes, the works and thoughts of these journalists would be meaningless without the subway readers, the living room television viewers, the automobile radio listeners, or the bedroom Internet surfers they serve; this is where their impact and importance are found.

In light of the woes of journalism and the media today, from declining audience and financial distress to lapsed watchdog responsibilities and credibility gaps, it is important to recognize and chronicle the achievements of journalism on behalf of recorded history and of providing timely checks on governmental abuses and corrections of societal flaws. The following pages are an attempt to do that.

—*Steve Hallock*

Acknowledgments

Numerous people helped me research this book and connect with the journalists I interviewed. They include Inell Willis of the *New York Times* op-ed page, Kathie Kerr at Universal Press Syndicate, David Andrukonis, Tahira Hayes, and Zoe Pollock of the *News Hour with Jim Lehrer,* Carol Leggett of Ben Bradlee's office at the *Washington Post,* The Paley Center for Media (formerly the Museum of Television and Radio) in New York City, Stephanie Graves of Morris Library at Southern Illinois University Carbondale, and Angelena Turner at the Clark Public Library in Winchester, Kentucky. I also want to thank my in-laws, David and Jimmie Juarin, for hosting me while I conducted research in Washington, D.C. And I want to thank the journalists who graciously gave their time and shared their thoughts.

CHAPTER 1

Onto the World Stage

Watergate. Sputnik. Free Speech Movement. McCarthyism. Cuban Missile Crisis. Monica. Berlin Wall. Détente. Single words or phrases, like news story or photo slugs, evoke eras, themes, and emotions. The scenes that the first historians of the last 50 years of the 20th century covered play in the head like sound and image artifacts.

Some of the memories—call them half-century scrapbook entries—are grainy, like the black-and-white videotapes we see in our minds as we recall certain events. Dallas motorcade. My Lai. H-bomb. Chicago riots. Moon landing. Others play back in sharp color with stereophonic soundtrack. Flower power. Motown. King shot. Silent majority. Ali wins.

As the scent of a lilac prompts childhood remembrances in a Proust epic, names from our history evoke emotional responses ranging from pride to anger, from hope to despair. They spark mind newsreels unraveling through the episodes of the years. Eisenhower. Stalin. Parks. Bobby. Fidel. Lennon. Johnson. Nixon. Mao. Ginsberg. Carter. Sadat. Montana. Reagan. Gorbachev. Sinatra. Warhol. Bush. Saddam. Sontag. Clinton. Milosevic. Mantle.

The catch phrases and slogans—do your own thing, different strokes for different folks—resonate in the differing reactions each of us experiences to these recollections. Trickle-down economics. Mutual assured destruction. Make love not war. The Great Society. Contract with America. The Silent Majority. The in crowd. Black is beautiful. Peace with honor. Hell no we won't go. Evil empire. Whip inflation now. Ask not what your country can do for you. Groovy. Power to the people. Give peace a chance.

The affluent society. Far out. Jail-no-bail. Eighteen-and-a-half-minute-gap. Star wars. I like Ike.

These cultural snapshots are simplified symbols of a 50-year national drama of complexity, one that wove brutal civil rights and war protests with socially and politically defining legal decrees, that saw U.S. politics and culture shaped by ground-roots networking and theatrics, all accompanied by a folk, jazz, blues, and rock-infused soundtrack and enhanced by technological changes that speeded and greatly enabled communications and artistic renderings of these movements. And the media didn't only mirror the tidings of the half century. From the communist witch hunts of McCarthyism to the televised bloodletting of Vietnam, to the black-and-white satellite images of missile silos in Cuba, to the leaked Pentagon Papers that bared the failure of an Asian war, to the investigative journalism that brought down a corrupt president, and to the televised crumbling of the Berlin Wall that was a metaphor for the eroding Soviet bloc, the nation's newspapers and broadcast media not only chronicled but sometimes helped set in motion the events that saw the United States emerge from World War II as the dominant military and cultural superpower by the end of the century.

The 10 journalists interviewed for this book brought different reactions and varied interpretations to the events and trends they identified as the major news stories or issues—the news slugs—of the period from 1950 to 2000. In response to the author's questions about the news categories identified in the preface to this book, many of them often agreed on what comprised the major stories of the era. But they frequently framed them differently. For example, the Vietnam War was seen by some of them as a political story because of the effect it had on domestic politics and policies. Others, though, saw it as the major military story of the period, though certainly not a positive military achievement. Some saw the rise of the United States as an international player during the Cold War years following World War II as a foreign affairs story, while others considered it a political story. Some framed the U.S. Supreme Court's landmark *Brown versus Board of Education* decision and the civil rights movement as a political story, while others placed it in the legal category or saw the civil rights movement as a major societal or cultural shift in the nation. Some journalists considered the Cold War to be more of a political or military story than one in the domain of foreign affairs. For some, computerization and the rise of the Internet were business stories; others saw the computerization of America as a scientific development. Where one journalist saw the Watergate scandal as a major crime story, another saw a big political saga. Television also fell into multiple categories—societal shift, arts and entertainment trends, while a couple of journalists deemed the development of the medium as so dynamic that it deserved placement in both of these categories.

During interviews in their homes and offices, the journalists tended to speak more at length about events and issues in their areas of special interest, while they were inclined to tread lightly in areas in which they had little interest or felt less informed. For example, syndicated columnist Georgie Anne Geyer, who spent much of her career as a foreign correspondent, spoke in some detail on issues involving world affairs. Other columnists whose careers focused more on politics and domestic issues, such as the *Washington Post*'s David Broder and the *New York Times'* Anthony Lewis, gave more attention to topics dominated by Washington-centered politics. Former United Press International correspondent and now-columnist Helen Thomas simply had no comment or interest regarding the topic of sports.

The respondents tended to bring some of their own cultural background, ethnic makeup, or gender to some of the issues, particularly those focusing on the major social or cultural trends of the era or in their opinions regarding sports or legal issues. Or they differed in contextualizing, some naming a specific athlete or sport in response to the question about major sports issues, others discussing sports in larger social terms such as the integration of black athletes into the nation's games. Still others offered a world view as opposed to a domestic focus on some issues. Morley Safer of CBS News' *60 Minutes,* for example, framed many of his comments with an international flavor. "I always considered myself no matter what I was covering a foreign correspondent," said the Canadian-born journalist. "And that's how most reporters should view their work."

It was sometimes difficult for the journalists to distance themselves from more recent events, such as the war in Iraq undertaken by the George W. Bush administration, and more current happenings in science, medicine, and communications—areas in which some of them discussed issues and events that have dominated headlines since the turn of the new century, such as cloning, stem cell research, and Internet blogging.

Yet, despite differences in category, framing, and background, the journalists agreed in their identification of many of the major issues and movements of the era, such as the shift in the South from a Democratic bastion to one claimed by the Republicans, the importance of the civil rights movement and its gains, the cultural and political effects of the Vietnam War and its fallout, and the huge impact of television, be it as a business or entertainment phenomenon, on American society. The following pages list the categories discussed during the interviews and the journalists' analyses of what they identified as the major stories, issues, and trends from 1950 to 2000 within each category.

POLITICS

Four writers cited the related trends of the civil rights movement and the shift of power in the South from the Democrats to the Republicans as the dominant political movement in the United States from 1950 to 2000. One spoke in more general terms of the shift away from the liberalism of the 1960s to conservatism. One cited an economic issue, the rising debt of the United States to foreign nations, particularly Asian countries, as a worrisome political trend, while another referenced the changing dynamic of imperialism and the decline of colonialism. Other topics falling into the political realm were the Watergate scandal, the Cold War, and the statesmanship of Nikita Khrushchev and President John F. Kennedy in averting nuclear war, while one reporter cited the assassination of Kennedy and the resulting political fallout.

"The major political story without a doubt is civil rights," said National Public Radio senior analyst Juan Williams. He cited the 1954 *Brown versus Board of Education* decision in which the U.S. Supreme Court outlawed public school segregation. The decision, Williams said, was "a legal issue, but then the political fallout is just tremendous, everything from national resistance on the part of the Southern governors to the shift that we see take place after the civil rights laws.

"We've seen huge political arguments over busing, affirmative action," Williams continued during an interview frequently interrupted by sources telephoning with information during a sultry late afternoon interview in his downtown Washington, D.C. NPR office. "In many ways, the Vietnam War protests were modeled on the kind of protests that took place in the civil rights era, and that has huge political implications as well."

Former *New York Times* columnist Anthony Lewis, who wrote and edited a book on the subject of the civil rights movement, *Portrait of a Decade: The Second American Revolution,* similarly cited the Brown decision and "the empowerment of blacks in the South and the resulting complete transformation of the Southern vote from Democrats taking it for granted to Republicans taking it for granted."

Interviewed in his Cambridge, Massachusetts book-filled apartment on a cool spring morning, Lewis recalled President Lyndon Johnson's comments when signing the Civil Rights Act of 1964. "This is going to turn the South Republican, and it did. And the ability of blacks to vote in the South, much more important than what I just described, the rise of Republican power. The fact that blacks were elected sheriff and mayor and congressmen all over the South was a great achievement, and a transforming achievement, overdue but wonderful."

David Broder, over a cup of coffee in the *Washington Post*'s employee cafeteria, expanded on Lewis' observation about the political power shift in the South, which "moved the South from being the bedrock Democratic coalition to being the bedrock Republican coalition."

The alteration in political alignment, Broder said, obviously had to do with race. "But it also involves changing economics of the country and a lot about the leadership of the two parties during that period of time. When I came to *Congressional Quarterly* in '56, Congress was dominated by a conservative coalition, conservative Democrats, mostly from the South, and Republicans. There were progressive Republicans, like in New England and the states that bordered Canada; they worked with older

Democrats to pass civil rights legislation. But the dominant coalition was the conservative coalition which ran fiscal policy and almost totally dominated Congress, except for the first two years that Lyndon Johnson was the president."

Former *New York Times* reporter Earl Caldwell sat at a dining room table in his Manhattan apartment overlooking the Hudson River, and New Jersey beyond, the morning after his weekly radio program and cited what he called the "story of race."

"When I say the story of race, what I mean is if you look back, everything that we say we stand for in America, without our civil rights movement it's a lie. . . . Another thing about the movement is, Martin Luther King, Jr., about having a movement where you say we're not going to blow up any buildings, we're not going to have any chains and guns, we are going to do it nonviolently. It was inspiring. I mean when you just think about it, there was the music, it was everything. To me there was nothing greater.

"I would argue that it was this great movement of people that changed the laws of this country. I hear people in Eastern Europe singing 'We Shall Overcome.' My God, this movement inspired people all over the world."

For *Boston Globe* and syndicated columnist Ellen Goodman, the nation experienced during this 50-year period a brief flirtation with liberalism and progressivism that turned out to be false expectations as the conservative shift cited by Lewis and Broder took bloom, but not only in the South.

"I think for a long time I thought that the progressive politics were the way of the future and we were just moving onward in that direction," she said of the Kennedy and post-Kennedy era of the antiwar, civil rights, and women's movements as she ate a bowl of cereal in her suburban Boston kitchen. "I didn't realize it was a blip on the landscape. Not a blip, but a cycle, half of a cycle. So I think, and that's probably age-related, because when you're young you tend to have a shorter time frame and so you see things going in a much more linear way, and then as you get older, you see the cycle. . . . You see things differently, but it's also true of what's happened in the country.

"Well, there was a progressive direction, and it got what John Irving called 'undertowed,' and there has been a conservative retrenchment, withdrawal, and the country is now very polarized, even though there's a lot more overlap than people acknowledge. It really wasn't until the '80s that we began to see that 'oh wait, this isn't an automatic, progressive direction.'"

Syndicated columnist Georgie Anne Geyer put an economic spin on the political trends of the half century, while Safer viewed the political topic through an international prism.

The United States having gone from a country "that was solid financially to one that is in hock to the Chinese and Asians, I think that's what I would say," said Geyer in her Washington, D.C. apartment filled with statuary and souvenirs from her world travels. "We had a country that came out of a depression, waged a war, and came out the wealthiest country in the world, and now it's frittered away its wealth. If the Chinese were to call in all of our debts we'd have no place to go."

Safer, interviewed in his CBS office, discussed old-world imperialism and how it changed, from colonialism fading out to the rise of a new kind of imperial movement in an era that saw an international push for liberation.

"Those fifty years included most of the major national liberation movements that happened in the world," he said as he exhaled cigarette smoke from behind his cluttered *60 Minutes* desk. "All of Africa decolonized virtually, partitioning in India in 1950, '51, Israel more or less, the decolonization of Eastern Europe by the Soviets, so it was genuinely the end of the imperial era and the birth of a new kind of imperialism"—one that included American adventurism abroad.

The assassination of President Kennedy, the Watergate scandal, and the rise of U.S. influence during the Cold War topped the political category of stories for Public Broadcasting Service correspondent Judy Woodruff, former *Washington Post* executive editor Ben Bradlee, and Thomas.

Kennedy's murder "shook up politics" Woodruff said in her office at MacNeil/Lehrer Productions outside of Washington, D.C. "You still had a Democrat in the White House after that, but in the modern day . . . you had an enormous reaction to it." She also cited Vietnam—"a political story because we're still reacting to it in the ways we make decisions about international policy in this country."

The botched burglary of the Democratic Party office in the Watergate complex and the resulting cover-up that led to the 1974 resignation of President Richard Nixon topped Bradlee's list of the half century's political stories.

"Its influence was a political impact much more than a criminal impact," said the editor, who oversaw the *Washington Post*'s investigative reporting that broke the Watergate story, during an interview in the office he maintains at the *Post*.

For Thomas, the rise of the United States to superpower status and the leadership role it took internationally was the dominant political theme after World War II.

"The world looked to us, and we're calling most of the shots," she said in a conference room outside of her office in downtown Washington, D.C. "And we did win the Cold War, sixty years of Cold War, by keeping our carbine dry, essentially. . . . We won it by blue jeans, the Pope, black music, Voice of America, exchange students, exchange teachers, there was a peaceful way to try to reach two giants facing each other who could have wiped out the world."

She saw Nikita Khrushchev, the leader of the Soviet Union during the Cuban Missile Crisis of 1962, as a hero of the U.S.-Soviet confrontation over the Soviet Union's installation of nuclear missiles in Cuba.

"He had the courage of cowardice," she said, "when he made a deal with Kennedy, and let Kennedy save face, and he pulled his missiles out of

Cuba, openly, and six months later we pulled ours out of Turkey, very surreptitiously. It was a graceful moment, each one had been in war, they knew the horror of war, and the option was to blow up each other, and each cared more about humanity and mankind and stepped back. They both blinked, literally. They had the statesmanship; they don't have that today.

"He was a very colorful man," she said of Khrushchev. "But at least he had the grace to care more about humanity. I mean, the military on both sides were pushing each side to catastrophe, our military was pushing Kennedy to go into Cuba."

FOREIGN AFFAIRS

A couple of the issues that arose during the journalists' discussions of political trends—wars hot and cold—recurred with other journalists when the subject moved to foreign affairs. For six of them, the post-World War II Cold War, followed by the fall of the Berlin Wall and crumbling of the Soviet bloc, was the dominant foreign affairs story of the latter half of the 20th century. Three of them spoke in more general terms of the arrival of the United States as a major player on the international stage and the difficulties of adjusting to the role of international player and leader—a role that two of them rued as a gradually diminishing one of lost opportunities and lowered international reputation. Two journalists had a larger, more international take on the foreign affairs stage, one citing what he saw as a troubling trend of rising tribalism and the other the rise of black awareness in Africa, a development that also carried tribal implications.

Geyer more than any of the other journalists was in her own arena on this subject. She discussed at length attempts by U.S. policy-makers to institutionalize the world, through such venues as the Marshall Plan, the United Nations, the North Atlantic Treaty Organization, and the World Trade Organization, "in its own style. The style and institutions of America became the style of the world."

Peaceful attempts to expand American influence, such as the U.S. Information Agency, Radio Free Europe, and the Voice of America, were undercut by war and foreign military adventurism, she argued.

"These wars were killing us. Killing us. We got over Vietnam, with horrible losses, but then we would go into another one. It was staggering."

Geyer said the 1980s brought a different attitude. "You could feel when Reagan took over, partly because of him, partly because of history, things began to change in the early '80s, you could feel the Cold War was beginning to end, you could feel that the Soviet Union was failing. . . . You could see the Cold War was melting."

And then came the collapse of the Soviet empire. She was in Berlin two weeks before the fall of the Berlin Wall in 1989. "I was at the anti-Communist rallies, at city hall in East Berlin, and all of the Communist officials were there, and the demonstrators were making fun of them, and I said to myself, 'it's over, it's over,' and I took a plane from East Berlin to Yugoslavia, because I said 'now, the next period is going to be disintegration of these multinational states.' You should see my interviews with the top Communist officials, and they all confirmed it, and Tito had died, and as the state goes down the politicians would hang onto ethnicity to keep their power. The next stage was not the euphoria at the end of the Cold War or the euphoria of the Soviet Union falling, but we went very directly into the Balkan wars, which nobody knew how to handle at all."

The fall of the Soviet empire was a lost opportunity, she said. "It seems very sad to me that the '90s could have been the end of World War II again if you'd had an Eisenhower, and a Marshall, and those kind of men, and I think we did have them in the first Bush administration. I liked Father Bush, I liked (Secretary of State James) Baker, I liked (National Security Adviser Brent) Scowcroft, but then the Clinton administration came in with no ability to grasp this, and suddenly we went into one of our historic moments of who would be our enemy now, we had no enemies. . . . The world had changed."

History repeated, Geyer said, as the nation's leaders following the collapse of the Soviet Union replayed past patterns. "Americans always go through that phase, reconstruction after World War II, after the Civil War, doing away with the military after World War I. Instead of building up in the '90s, it seems to me that we tore apart our institutions, and now the institutionalization seems torn apart internally, and I don't know that it can be built up again, I don't know that another administration (after President George W. Bush) can do that."

Woodruff, Williams, and Bradlee agreed that the Soviet Union's dissolution was the major foreign affairs story of the period—"just because of the profound effect," Woodruff said.

Added Williams, summarizing the rapid, almost systematic falling apart of the Soviet bloc in terms ironically analogous to the domino theory that Vietnam War strategists used to cite in justifying that war: "Essentially you start the second half of the twentieth century involved in a Cold War and the Cold War aftermath of World War II, a Cold War that encompassed both Korea and Vietnam as struggles, democracy trying to hold back the spread of communism and influence of the Soviet Union, then all of a sudden you start to see the Soviet Union crumbling, and then you see the Berlin Wall fall in 1989, and subsequently then the struggles in all of the satellite states and all of the Slavic states around the Soviet Union, all of the former republics."

Bradlee saw the collapse as great foreign affairs theater. "The rise and fall of communism was a huge, huge story, for the whole century, I mean it started to rise at the end of the first half of the century, but it imploded, and that was the great drama."

For Thomas, the foreign affairs scenario of the half century was, as alluded to by Geyer, the rise of the United States on the world stage. Coming out of its prewar isolationism, she said, "suddenly we became a great nation with a full sense of responsibility to our fellow nations, what we were going to become. We began to grow, mature, and realize what our position in the world could be toward our fellow man." She cited the United Nations and other diplomatic advances such as the SALT (strategic arms limitation treaties) nuclear containment pacts between the United States and the Soviet Union. "Having one treaty after another for disarmament, those are the things that struck me."

Goodman shared Geyer's disappointment over the decline of U.S. stature in foreign affairs and diplomacy. "The reputation and the view of America in the world has tragically declined, so now young people are told not to backpack with American flags," she said. "Certainly over this long period, the American reputation declined from the postwar high."

But foremost in Goodman's mind in the foreign affairs category was the trauma of the Cold War. "I grew up in the duck-and-cover era, and there are so many different things to say about it. People tend to look back with nostalgia to an era when we all were so secure, and that's just not true. The era of my childhood, how many people of our generation had nightmares about the end of the world, or the atom bomb, so our generation grew up with fear, a designated enemy, rather than a more confused enemy. If people feel nostalgia for the good old secure days, it's because they were children, it's not because it was true, because it wasn't true."

Again, Safer applied a broader, internationally tinged viewpoint to the issue, discussing the rise of tribalism in the world community, and Caldwell joined Safer with his own international interpretation, discussing the independence movements in Africa—also a form of tribalism in that these African movements were largely on behalf of black nationalism.

"This is something I felt strongly about for the last twenty years maybe, maybe fifteen, and that is the descent into tribalism that's happened in the world," Safer said. "We're witnessing every day of the week a real descent into tribalism, we're reverting back to our earliest days." Safer cited the violence in Ireland, the Balkans, and the Middle East, but "not so violently here in terms of the Christian rectitude that's going on."

"I'm not trying to be philosophical about it in a grandiose way," he said, but "look at East Timor, look at what's happening in parts of China, what's happening and continuing and going on and on in Pakistan and Kashmir. Afghanistan never stopped being tribal, Iraq never stopped being tribal; we ignited the fuse to the horrible explosion that continues today. That is the big story, I think, and it's never been covered that way."

The big story for Caldwell, though, was the struggle for freedom by blacks in Africa, particularly South Africa. "The whole movement for freedom of the people in Africa was not only a tremendous story, it had these tremendous heroes, led by Nelson Mandela, who to me was one of the most remarkable men in human history. So many of the things that we say we believe, he embodied, but to me, this movement in Africa is huge."

LEGAL ISSUES

Many of the journalists were succinct on this topic, summarizing it in single sentences or brief observations. But one of them, Geyer, had no opinion on the subject other than to rue what she saw as the lack of respect for privacy and press rights by the administration of President George W. Bush. Again, this perhaps reflected the journalists' relative interest in this issue as opposed to other topics such as politics or foreign policy. Long familiar themes having to do with empowerment and civil rights, such as desegregation (*Brown versus Board of Education*) or privacy rights as they relate to a woman's right to seek an abortion (the 1973 U.S. Supreme Court *Roe versus Wade* decision that laws banning abortion were unconstitutional on privacy grounds), emerged. But some of the journalists also traveled new thematic routes that included the legal rights of those charged with crimes, and the protection of journalists' confidential sources.

For most, though, the court-ordered desegregation of public schools and the ensuing civil rights movement was the dominant legal event of the half century, and a few of them said so pointedly. Broder's succinct response to the question was: "The great civil rights revolution"; and Thomas' emphatic statement regarding the Brown ruling was: "Absolutely, without a doubt. A transforming event."

Bradlee mentioned the 1971 Pentagon Papers case, in which the Supreme Court upheld the right of the *New York Times* and the *Washington Post* to publish the government report detailing United States involvement in the Vietnam War, before naming the Brown decision as the major legal story of the period.

"I mean, the Pentagon Papers was a great press versus power story. I don't know how to subdivide it, perhaps it doesn't fit comfortably into one category. But race was just, everywhere you turned there was race, and that was an enormous story," he said, segueing into a remembrance of his friend, John F. Kennedy. "God, I can remember the night that Jack Kennedy made some speech, and it was the first time he'd talked about civil rights, and he came back and he said he just wondered why it took so long to tackle that story. I mean, it's been around for years; you know, it's been around since long before the Civil War."

Williams also cited Brown, placing the decision into the context of others who also dealt with empowerment—of women, of the press, and of race.

"The other key decision that I think people live with is *Roe v. Wade,*" he said, "and some people might throw in things like the Pentagon Papers, you and I as reporters would be sensitive to that one. I think people might look at Bakke (the 1978 Supreme Court decision striking down university admission quotas intended to bring more minorities into higher education while upholding the legality of affirmative action). Bakke was in a way the afterbirth of Brown. It didn't say that you can segregate, but it did say you don't have to, it's illegal to give someone a spot" in a university based on race.

The reverberations of *Roe versus Wade* are still being felt, he said. "You've got to tie it into conservative religious movements that have played such an important part in American society and American politics, and many of those people have made *Roe v. Wade* and abortion the signal issue . . . in a way that I think escaped people who are at the so-called elite newspapers and institutions in the country. I think it was a very primal appeal, a populist appeal to people."

Goodman likewise alluded to the long-term effects of *Roe versus Wade,* along with other issues affecting gender and reproductive rights.

"Obviously, the ones that have interested me the most professionally, the ones that I've written about the most, have been the courts' involvement in reproductive rights and bioethics in general and the way the court has been drawn into whole areas that didn't exist," she said, also citing DNA evidence and stem cell research. "There are all these things that the court has been drawn into that certainly the framers of the Constitution had no idea of specifically and yet laid some foundations for the way that we could deal with these. But those issues that came to the courts just plain old didn't exist. Whole new legal realms and, of course, the whole area of women's rights, which I've followed, obviously, in my work and in life, you know there were many groundbreaking moments. Of course, there's also the aftermath of civil rights decisions."

Safer cited the entire civil rights movement as the primary legal issue, and he framed it as a phenomenon unique to the United States.

"I don't know that there's been anything comparable in any major or even not so major power as that cultural change in this country, which was only because of legal decisions," he said. "It was not a kind of osmosis of any kind, the culture was not changing because it was trying to be better or fair, it was the law, and for the most part the law was obeyed, and I cannot think of a situation in any other country in history, at least in my knowledge of history, where legal decisions so radically changed a society with a minimum of violence. I'm sure there are a lot of black Americans who will disagree about its effectiveness, and I suppose if I were a black American I would disagree with that view, but looking at it as a foreign correspondent, I think it's a remarkable story. I really do think it is."

Lewis said he also would vote for the Brown decision before citing another case as perhaps vying for the most important legal case of the half century, one having to do with voting rights.

"I have a personal reason, in agreement with Chief Justice (Earl) Warren, that the most important decision by the Supreme Court was not Brown, but Baker against Carr, the reapportionment decision, and its follow-up holding that every state legislature had to be districted according strictly to population . . . ending the corrupt, rotten boroughs when they dominated most of the legislatures," Lewis said in reference to the 1962 decision involving reapportionment in a Tennessee county that established the right of the federal judiciary to decide reapportionment cases. The columnist said he had written about the subject while studying law, "and it was published in the *Harvard Law Review,* calling for the Supreme Court to intervene, which it had declined to do previously, and miraculously the court decided to do so."

Woodruff also cited Brown, Roe and the Pentagon Papers, but not after first naming the 1966 *Miranda versus Arizona* decision, in which the court ruled that police must advise suspects of their legal rights. "I know enough criminal attorneys that they would talk about the rights of defendants, the Miranda ruling, it had a huge effect on our criminal process."

Caldwell offered a unique take on the question, one relating to his own legal experience. As a reporter for the *New York Times* during the 1960s, Caldwell was asked by the Nixon Justice Department to provide information that he had obtained from confidential sources about the Black Panthers, whom he was covering for the *Times.* He refused, and the matter went to court, where he won in an appeals court before the U.S. Supreme Court ruled, reversing the lower court, in a 5–4 decision in 1972 on behalf of the government. That ruling sparked the creation of numerous state shield laws allowing reporters to protect their confidential sources, and it is the root of a continuing debate today about the issue of source protection and calls for a national press shield law.

"Because of my own experience in journalism, it will always be that the biggest legal thing is that when I was a reporter coming out of Clearfield, Pennsylvania, trained by old, committed newspapermen, taught what your ethics are, what you stand for, what the separations are," he said. "By the time I get to the *New York Times,* the government, the federal government, the government of the United States, the FBI: 'You're out there with these Black Panthers, you hear what they're saying, we want you to be an undercover operative for us.' And when I tried to explain that I can't do it, they insist that 'you will do it.' To me that was humongous, but there was this wonderful fellow named Anthony Amsterdam who took this case. I didn't even understand, truly, all of the civil rights movement was based on constitutional law. But this guy came to represent me and black journalists in that period and fought this case to the Supreme Court. I think we truly won it, but they stole it from us. Legal? That's where I come in, that period with that case."

MILITARY

The Cold War experienced great cross-categorization, listed by some journalists as a foreign affairs issue, by others as a political story, and by some as a military story. Some cited the fact that the United States and Soviet Union were able to avoid nuclear war, while others identified the war in Vietnam, which was a proxy war between the Soviets and the United States in the larger Cold War, as a major military issue. One journalist discussed the social and political effect of the Cold War in the United States, and two others spoke about the changes in the U.S. military that emerged following World War II and the Vietnam War.

Lewis labeled nuclear weaponry and the avoidance of its use during the Cold War as the significant military story. The nuclear threat is one that he sees as a continuing problem in the world.

"Well, the half century includes the hydrogen bomb. That's pretty important, and the Soviet explosion of one (in 1955)," he said. "Nuclear weapons are so much a part of our lives now, you hardly think about them, and yet there they are, fifty-thousand nuclear weapons in the world, any one of which, if started, someone would reply and then it would be all gone. We used to be very frightened of that, there was this whole period when people dug out shelters. We don't do that now, but there they are. So let's put nuclear weapons and their development right up there with Vietnam (as a military story)."

Broder pondered the question for a moment, then suggested that Vietnam might be the top military story. "I'm hesitating because in some ways it never happened, which was nuclear war that everybody feared was on the horizon," he said.

Thomas invoked the sheer terror of the Cold War, the nuclear threat and the policy of mutually assured destruction, which deterred the use of nuclear weapons because of the fear of nuclear retaliation.

"The buildup of the Pentagon and the dominance, really," she said. "I think that the whole question of having what we thought was our nuclear dominance and then realizing that we didn't have it at all. And then working to achieve some sort of equivalence, what Churchill called the sublime irony of mutual destruction, constantly negotiating with the Soviet Union in terms of our nuclear armaments, and everyone realizing that each side could blow each other up and blow up the world."

Goodman agreed with Lewis about the continuing threat of nuclear war and shared his relief that the Cold War "never became a hot war. The fact that we were able to avoid a nuclear war, which still seems to me a miracle. It can't last indefinitely. . . . If you build it, they will use it."

For others, the Vietnam War and, for one journalist, foreign interventionism in general topped the military stories of the half century. Bradlee recalled that he lost a cousin in the Korean War but nonetheless labeled the war in Vietnam a bigger story.

"I covered wars," he said. "I covered the war in Algeria, which was a real war. I didn't do Saigon. I went to Vietnam, but not during the French part of Vietnam, and only on the periphery of the American part, it was in the '70s." Vietnam, he said, was "a big story, big story. Militarily, it amounted to a pile of beans because we didn't save it from the Godless communists, and we didn't prove anything except our inability to influence those events." Still, he said the Vietnam War "was the dominant military story of the second half century, I think it was bigger than Korea."

Woodruff also referred to the fact that the United States lost the war. "It had such an effect on the psyche of the country, on politicians; it affected their willingness to have America involved in the rest of the world. Didn't it affect for years the way the Pentagon bought, and ordered, new weapons systems, and their whole strategic thinking? I mean, that's my sense of it. When I talk to generals, they talk about how Vietnam affected the thinking for years and years to come. It was only when (former Defense Secretary Donald) Rumsfeld came in in 2000 and 2001 before 9/11 that he started thinking seriously . . . about streamlining."

Williams' answer to Woodruff's question would be yes, the war did affect the nation's military and diplomatic strategy for years to come, including the perception that the U.S. military had been weakened and become disrespected and that "authority had been undermined in the country." The result was felt in the nation's politics years later, he argued.

"I think that's really the basis of so much of (President Ronald) Reagan coming back, I think that the whole notion of being proud of the U.S. military and believing in the power of the U.S. military."

The end of the military draft also became an important factor in long-lasting post-Vietnam War diplomacy and military decisions, Williams said. "I think the all-volunteer Army, and then you move forward and you come into questions of how we use force as the world's superpower, a superpower that's been chastened by the Vietnam experience. When I think about, for example, in the '80s, how controversial it was for the U.S. to get involved in Grenada, today that would be like a pimple, given the involvement in Afghanistan and Iraq, but that was a huge controversy."

Williams suggested that hesitation to use military force, an attitude with its roots in the Vietnam War, helped bring about the Iran-Contra scandal of 1986, in which Reagan administration officials played a role in the sale of weaponry to Iran with the proceeds used to arm the Contra anti-communist rebels (Sandinistas) in Nicaragua.

"Iran-Contra was an attempt again not to use military force, and we had so many secret involvements in Central America, the Sandinistas, that whole theory, I think that was a reluctance to use military force, at least publicly, to engage in, and a preference to practice covert operations," Williams said. "And then you come into the '90s and there's a huge shift under the first President Bush with regard to the Gulf War and the occupation of Kuwait by Saddam Hussein and the notion of people like Colin Powell and General (Norman) Schwarzkopf, those guys standing up there and saying we're going to cut it off and kill it . . . and showing you pictures of smart bombs and all of that. That was the new era, and I think that was 'We are not in Vietnam, we know exactly what we're doing, we're using force, we're using force in a surgical way, and we're not going to go into Baghdad, we're going to stop.' This is all as a result of our experience in Vietnam, so I think if you are trying to perceive for that latter half of the twentieth century sort of the formative military experience, without a doubt, to my mind it's Vietnam."

It was Vietnam for Caldwell also, but in a different way. The veteran New York journalist discussed the war in terms of the political and social effects it had on the nation, including the antiwar riots and protests the war and the military draft spawned.

The story, Caldwell said, "was more the movement against the war, the way the people and the country began to just say that their own government was wrong and you have to stop your own government. I mean that was pretty heavy duty, because even within the civil rights movement, when we were saying the government was wrong, and that was in the latter part, and that was caught up on the war. You had Stokely Carmichael (the civil rights leader who coined the phrase 'black power') and (H.) Rap Brown (justice minister of the Black Panther Party). But I think that whole Vietnam thing was another huge piece of it."

The story for Safer went beyond Vietnam to U.S. intervention overall.

"The biggest military stories are these disastrous interventions by the United States. Vietnam. Totally disastrous military intervention. Iraq. Absolutely disastrous military intervention," he said, bringing the question into modern times. "I think the biggest military stories are the two major military debacles by this country."

Geyer also brought the issue into the 21st century, regarding the military subject in the context of the changes in the U.S. military over the course of the half century and what she saw as its dismal state today.

The military, she said, went "from a highly institutionalized military of World War II and afterwards to one today that is very split up. Special forces, all kinds of special militias, contractors who do not have any responsibility . . . or any kind of rules of combatancy or noncombatancy, who are all over Iraq. I worry greatly about the privatization of the military; I think this is really, really serious."

SCIENCE

Journalists are notoriously atechnical, nonmathmatical, and science-challenged, so it should come as no great surprise that these 10 journalists did not talk at length about the scientific breakthroughs of the half century. They did, however, agree on a common theme: the major scientific achievements of the period had to do with the expansion of our universe—space exploration—or research in the opposite, smaller, direction involving atoms and cells.

Goodman discussed both directions.

"I suppose you're supposed to say that we went to the moon," she said in response to the question. "You know, we went to the moon, and then what? We're getting a much greater, and maybe more humbling, sense of our place in the universe, with the Hubble and telescopes and a sense of a larger and larger universe. I think the major scientific advances have been outward and downward, what's bigger and what's tinier. I think probably it's been as powerful in terms of changing the way people view their place in the universe as, say, Darwin in the nineteenth century, the twentieth century has changed the way that those of us who are scientifically attuned see our place in the world."

For the columnist, the issue is tied into human identity. "And don't forget the environmental, the way science has looked at and analyzed the environment. Just who are you?"

She then offered a brief synopsis of the scientific history of the world before moving on to an indictment of the reticence of scientists to engage in political debate.

"I'm not going to do a thirty-second sound bite from Copernicus to the Hubble (telescope), but the centrality of the human being and the Bible, and you move on and on and on and then you get to Darwin and learn we weren't all created 'as is,' maybe we adapt and evolve and then you get beyond that. And with that, the incredible resistance to science. To me, one of the great science stories is the resistance—the creationists—and the way scientists . . . they have had this wonderful notion, 'the truth will out,' so in some places in America, Darwin is controversial. Where are all the scientists who are politicians? And don't give me (former Republican U.S. Senator from Tennessee) Bill Frist, please."

Woodruff also cited exploration of areas vast and tiny. "Space, space exploration, it's either space exploration or it's in the other direction, it's the atom in some way," she said. "You know, it's either understanding the universe better or understanding the smallest or the biggest. They go together, so it's understanding, it's physics, we've already come to the end of my ability to talk about it."

For Broder, tiny trumped space. "Learning about the basics of human biology, cellular structure, and DNA and the whole ability to manipulate some of that tiny little beginning of life is the most striking thing in science."

Ditto for Geyer, who cited genetic research. "It seems to me the whole DNA thing," she said.

Space exploration, though, topped the list for most of the other journalists.

"Going to Mars, exploring the universe, space," Thomas said, referencing both unmanned and manned space ventures. "We've been to the moon, people might even be traveling to the other planets in this century."

"For me, because I was born in 1954, Sputnik and the whole excitement of the first man walking on the moon," said Williams. "Watching that on TV, that was just thrilling. And then you have everything from the Concorde to jet travel. That's a big change."

Caldwell was early in his journalism career, in Lancaster, Pennsylvania, when John Glenn orbited Earth in 1962. "That had a big impact on me because it was that period in America of John Kennedy, and even though there were no black people in it then, it was an American thing, that had a big impact on me."

Two of the journalists listed computer technology as the major scientific achievement of the era, citing its contribution to communication and research.

"I guess the computer would be science," Lewis said. "The Google phenomenon, it is virtually amazing."

"I suppose you would have to include the instant communications and miniaturization of information. I don't know how much good it's done us, hasn't made us much smarter," Safer said, chuckling. "It's given us more information and much less wisdom."

Bradlee, without citing a specific achievement, expressed marvel at the speed of scientific breakthroughs. "All you have to know is this wonderful fact, that there's more discovery in one year of science than there has been in all the other previous years. That's true every year. I've heard that, I don't know if it's true or not, and who's counting? But I mean, my God, the changes in science, in medicine."

MEDICINE

Medical issues or advances had personal significance for two of the journalists: Caldwell, who lost a close relative to brain cancer, and Bradlee, who had a bout with polio as a child. He, and the majority of the journalists, cited the Salk polio vaccine as the major medical story of the half century; others listed the scourge of cancer, the AIDS threat, and genetic research.

"I have a great interest in the polio vaccine," Bradlee said of the medical breakthrough announced by Dr. Jonas Salk in 1955. "It was big. It was big. Of course, you know I have a characteristic of not being, um, it's said of me that I don't worry enough, even while I was with my legs in braces and corset on, I didn't worry about being paralyzed. I didn't. And it turns out that I was right. It turns out I didn't have to worry about it, I wasn't paralyzed permanently. But Jesus, if I was still pulling myself around on pulleys and my legs in braces, I'd be worried about it."

Bradlee spoke at some length about his experience with the disease.

"Polio was like a bad cold when you get it, you have a headache and you have a temperature, and then all of a sudden you don't have a headache and you don't have a temperature," he said. "But you don't move very well, and the doctor comes in and starts up here and goes down to your toes to see what you can move and what you can't, and they get a very precise picture of what muscles are damaged, but they don't know what to do about it, and never did. For a polio victim, there was never anything that they could do, give you a few exercises, but they couldn't fix anything. If your arm was paralyzed it was paralyzed, they could put it in a sling and forget about it."

He saw the disease afflict his friends and classmates. "You know we had this epidemic at my school, a hundred-eighty-five kids, and twenty-two or twenty-three kids got it, and it was an absolute perfect example of the disease, in that group, one died, three or four were permanently paralyzed, you know, had their legs in a brace or a neck in a brace or an arm in a brace for the rest of their lives. About five of us spent a good part of the summer paralyzed in some form, and the rest of them went around and just said, 'hey.'"

The end of polio in the nation was also seen as a major medical story by those young enough to have avoided it.

"The end of polio. I think that's pretty big," Williams said, "something this generation can't appreciate, because we just don't know."

"The Salk vaccine, there is no question," Safer said. "I was a young reporter when that story broke. I remember when I was working in London (Canada) and some of the senior guys drove down to Michigan to cover the press conference that we knew would be the announcement of the Salk vaccine. Without question, given that when I was a kid in the '30s the epidemic after epidemic every summer of polio, and kids dying and at least three or four kids in every class in braces. So to me that was a most extraordinary breakthrough, to have a disease like that you can actually stop, not just some mild prophylactic that sometimes works and sometimes doesn't. This works. So that obviously was an extraordinary scientific breakthrough."

Thomas agreed before citing the medical community's failure to find a cure for cancer as one of the period's most important medical stories, along with a couple of other medical trends.

"I think raising the awareness of health problems," she said. "I think that more and more people are healthy and we have much more awareness of what can be done. . . . Having forty-seven-million people without health insurance."

Broder, though, saw the story of cancer less as one of failed medical technology and more one of advances made. "I think the whole ability to diagnose chronic illnesses and come up with answers for almost all of them now, including some forms of cancer, is probably the biggest story."

Cancer struck Caldwell's family suddenly and devastatingly when his sister was diagnosed with a brain tumor, and the experience remains vivid in his memory.

"I'd never seen anybody go through what she went through," he said. "And now I see it all the time. Cancer, and what it's doing to people. After my mom died, (my sister) said she wasn't feeling good, and she went to the doctor. The doctor said, 'you've got a tumor and you're dying.' He told her, 'you'll be dead in six months,' and she was as healthy as a horse, taking care of all the family homestead. And I said, 'how can that be?' There was nothing they could do, but the first thing they did is they took her to Pittsburgh for a cancer operation, open her up, 'nothing we can do,' sew her back up and she never recovered from that. Then they started giving her this chemotherapy, radiation, and it just made her, every day, the treatment made her look less and less like a human being until, wow, even the people who loved her said they hoped she would die because no one should have to go through this."

Columnists Lewis and Goodman spoke of the medical beat in more general terms, citing progress in diagnoses and treatments.

"Medicine has been utterly transformed in my lifetime, from a palliative," Lewis said. "Medicine in 1950, even as late as that, had one significant nonpalliative development, which was sulfa drugs developed in the war, and penicillin. But since then, we've had pills for everything, and it's really medicine. Pills actually make you better. They don't just make you feel better or deaden the pain. There are cures for all kinds of things. Revolutionary medicine. Those fifty years were different than all of recorded history before."

Lewis had a personal anecdote, a recent test he'd undergone for a kidney ailment. The test, he said, "tells you about six different things. It's amazing. They put things through and it comes out on a computer form, and it's all there on the computer. Unheard of, not just fifty years ago but ten years ago."

Likewise, Goodman testified to progress she's seen in the half century, including a phenomenon none of the other journalists noted: organ transplants.

"Somebody practicing medicine fifty years ago, if you were plunked down there right now, if he were an internist you might really like him because he would come and make a house call and hold your hand and give you the only thing that helps anyway, which is Aspirin. But if you're having cardiac surgery, you definitely would want him to go back to training. It's a huge, huge change. The technical ability. I'm no doctor, but you know all the changes that have come about in terms of what's done surgically and what we can fix. When I was at the (Detroit) *Free Press,* that was the time if I recall that Ann Arbor did its first kidney transplant. And I think it was still only twins at the time. So you fast-forward from that."

BUSINESS/ECONOMICS

The majority of the journalists saw globalization and stock market trends as the major economic stories of the period, while a couple of them cited computerization and its impact on buying and communications as the most significant story on the business beat. Instead of driving from store to store or to the mall, consumers could instead literally let their fingers do the shopping on the computer keyboard. Some reporters also cited a couple of trends they saw as negative business stories: corporate greed and the weakening of the labor movement.

Lewis gave a one-word response to the business question: globalization. Broder and Safer agreed; but each interpreted globalization differently. Broder focused his comments on domestic effects, of corporations "no longer orienting themselves basically to national boundaries, but thinking of markets and supplies and manpower on a worldwide basis, and all of the side effects of that, including the weakening of the labor movement dramatically in this country."

Safer, though, framed his response in more international terms, specifically, the economic rise of China.

"The end of the century was the beginning of serious globalization and the rise of China," he said. "I mean, the rise of China in economic terms, and that's what I think is really fascinating, to watch what is happening to China. The Chinese slipping back into sanity after the Cultural Revolution and the craziness that went on, and quite successfully when you think about it, making this kind of transition, which was all done by the old hacks in the Communist Party, into a capitalist economy.

"I agree with all the pressure that people are trying to put on China in terms of civil rights and so on, but that is going to happen, there is no doubt in my mind, if they want to maintain this duality or some kind of control while they exercise a rampant capitalism, it's going to have to change and to change incrementally. But what I don't think people quite understand is that incrementally it's very quickly, the increments will come one upon the other."

Williams offered a multiple-choice answer, led by the stock market climbing to an all-time high of 10,000 in 1999. "A major event," he said, especially after "the bad times. It wasn't a depression, but the recession of the late '70s and early '80s, and then Reaganomics and what a contrast it is, things never got to the point, as I said, of depression, but we had high unemployment, and we had high inflation, so it looked like things were teetering."

Woodruff also cited a stock market event, but a low rather than the high referenced by Williams. "I think about the stock market crash of 1987," she said. "It certainly was a major story, and it had a profound effect on the market and the Federal Reserve."

The business trend for Goodman was the expansion of consumer power thanks to the Internet.

"The economy and business has gone from producing stuff in this county, manufacturing stuff," she said. "The big change has been in computers and the Internet in terms of how we relate, how we do business. We do business on the Internet. Certainly people still go to the marketplace, but not anywhere nearly as much as they did. All of the technology, there has been a huge change to the culture and the community. Everything from somebody walking around with iPods and not paying attention to other people, buying their stuff over the Internet and not at their friendly neighborhood marketplace, or maybe not so friendly neighborhood marketplace."

Caldwell, though, viewed computerization as a major advance in our ability to communicate with each other—a development that he said needs to be expanded to the international level.

"From the very beginning, I always saw the change in technology as being a humongous thing because it was a great equalizer," he said. "The Internet, it means you push a button, you can talk to all of the country at the same time. It's an enormous thing that still isn't being fully utilized as it ought to be. It's the same thing with African Americans, to me it's outrageous that with this technology we've got that you don't have one site on there where you're speaking to the world. I see that in terms of the business, to me this all hooks together, you succeed in that and it will have tremendous affect on economies."

Geyer and Thomas expressed dismay over the rise of corporate greed and the decline of business ethics.

Geyer likened this phenomenon to the negative effects of the privatization of the military, "where all the corporate executives don't seem to feel any responsibility toward the country at all. There were always scandals, but today it seems that there's nothing but scandal. Commercialization of everything. One night on (the) Biography (Channel) I saw the story of J. C. Penney, and he said, 'I have 2,000 partners,' and the Penney's stores were each run more or less independently, and that was the original Protestant ethic of this country, and that's gone."

Similarly, Thomas expressed dismay over "the whole idea that you take over a company to destroy it and destroy its liabilities and so forth, wipe out the pension, bottom line, the emergence of, I mean, putting a halo on greed. I think that business does not realize . . . I am sorry to see the demise of unions, the killing off of unions by Reagan"—a reference to the busting of the air traffic controllers' union by the former president.

Bradlee framed the issue purely in journalistic terms: business as a newspaper beat is of growing importance.

"I began to get interested in it as I began to realize how important economics were," he said. "I took economics at Harvard as a duty, and I'm sure I got a C-minus if I got that." Bradlee said he came to see the importance of business, and covering it, over the years, first during his stint at *Newsweek* and then as executive editor of the *Post.*

"It was after you deal with things like taxation and unemployment and unions and stuff like that that you realize how important the economy is. Wage rates, prices, it's such a part of society, that there came a time that I could never be an expert on this, but you'd better damn well pay attention to it. You know when I came over to the *Washington Post,* the very first person that I brought over from *Newsweek* was a man called Bart Rowen, who was the *Newsweek* economic correspondent, and he was terribly good. He knew it like the back of his hand. I knew that he was good, but I didn't understand everything that he was . . . Don't let it out, but it's true, (as an editor) all you need to know is what you don't know."

CRIME

In a half century of political assassinations, riots, and political protest, the bombing of the Alfred P. Murrah Federal Building in Oklahoma City, the O. J. Simpson murder case, the kidnapping of newspaper heiress Patty Hearst by the Symbionese Liberation Army, one trend—increasing crime in the cities—drew the bulk of attention of these journalists. Two of them focused on specific issues of urban crime, such as illegal drug use and the accompanying spate of handgun use by young people involved in the drug trade, along with domestic violence and rape, while another cited the white flight to the suburbs that left behind cities of minorities and urban poor, and neighborhoods rife with crime. On the issue of minorities and crime, one correspondent linked crime to another issue: education and training. She blamed the failure of American society to train young blacks as a contributor to crime.

Again, as in other topics, the journalists displayed remarkable variance of focus and context on the subject, from viewing the crime issue as one that experienced no "dramatic" change during the half century (Broder) to one who saw a telling change in the court system's dealings with criminals thanks to the Miranda decision (Woodruff), which provided "another arrow in the quiver for defense attorneys and defendants to make the case before the court." A couple of journalists took the discussion beyond violent crime into the arena of white collar and political crime.

Urban crime, though, dominated the discussion. Bradlee at first suggested that crime is a constant component of the human community that "just goes with society, and I suppose it always has." But he then cited a particular kind of crime problem associated with urban culture: the mob. "You know gangsters and organized crime. I think that's an important story. You know, they never won, they never took over, they never took over a government. They had their moments certainly, and they achieved great power in certain cities, but they never took over, I mean you could never talk about any part of America being a criminal society, at least I don't think of it as that way."

Williams, who had worked for Bradlee's *Post* as a reporter and editorial writer before moving into broadcasting, identified urban crime—abetted by white flight—as the primary story of the half century.

"Crime became the number one problem in cities like New York, Boston, Washington," he said. "One of the huge developments we haven't touched on is the development of the interstate highways, designed by

Eisenhower, and you have an interstate system, plus you have white flight from inner-city schools and you have horrible crime in the big cities."

Geyer lamented the link of minorities to violent, urban crime that she believed could have been avoided.

"I think one of our great victories was civil rights. But one of the great failures to come out of civil rights is that we didn't train the young black males," she said. "That was the failure of civil rights, that we did not carry that into really intensive training, particularly for young black males. Young black females are doing very well, ironically."

Asked if that failure translated into high crime rates among the black population, she said, "Oh yeah. And it didn't have to be, they don't have to be criminals."

Goodman also talked about crime and its relationship to demographics and ethnicity in cities; but she saw a major change during this era in how crimes and victims are identified and treated.

"What strikes me about crime is not just merely the crime waves, crime goes up, crime goes down," she said, "and the lingering reality of crime in the inner cities and what it means to families and the ability of a child to go out on the playground and play. Those things are very real, but one of the things that strikes me over the last half century are the things that became crimes that nobody had even noticed, or that had a very different cast to them, just in terms of my own interests and career."

She cited domestic violence as an example of this changing societal attitude. "In the '50s, in the early '60s, if a policeman was called on a domestic violence case it was 'oh, it's just a husband and wife case.' Domestic violence, when I was a young reporter, when it was a black crime, a black-on-black crime, it was hardly a crime, you know, it was only when it was a black-on-white crime that it was a crime."

Rape was another example of how perceptions of the crime and victim changed, she said. "It had to be a stranger, it had to be an assault, and you had to be a virgin, virtually, for rape to be a crime. You couldn't be a husband, the rapist couldn't be a husband, but you know, it certainly couldn't be what we now call date rape. One of the things that's really interesting to think about in the last half century is hate. We now have acknowledged violence and social destruction as crimes that we didn't even pay attention to."

The phenomenon of urban drug abuse and the accompanying rise of handguns on the streets struck Caldwell as what he called "an uninvestigated story."

"The worst thing I have ever seen in my life, the biggest crime, was this whole thing with this crack that was brought into all these cities across America," he said. "I've seen things that were just unreal. And then with that, bringing these guns and putting these guns into the hands of these kids."

Caldwell mentioned a trip he'd made to Africa and the violence he witnessed there. "I was struck by, they were having an election in, it was

Rhodesia then, Zimbabwe now, and every day the Brits would come in, and they were the colonizers, and they'd come in and see what had happened the night before, and 'oh, forty-seven people hacked to death, the bus was burned,' they would describe the crimes, there was a beating with axes, and they would describe it, but in the end maybe six people were shot, they weren't really armed, they didn't really have the weaponry."

He said remembering that violence made him think about the urban violence in the United States, "where it used to be that kids were making zip guns, but suddenly somebody was putting serious weapons in their hands and they were driving people out of these neighborhoods. I remember going into those communities, and people would say 'how did you get up here,' and I would say 'I got the car service to come over.' 'How you getting home?' 'I'm going out to the corner,' and they'd say 'you can't do it.' 'What do you mean I can't do it?' They'd say, 'you don't know the kind of thing that's going on out here, it's different.' I'd say, 'nobody's going to bother me.' 'But these people don't even know you.' And they were telling me about the way these things were changing, about these drug runners, and you'd begin to see it and I was very fearful of it myself. To me the biggest story of crime was this whole huge thing with the drugs."

It was drugs also for Safer—but in a bigger, international way. He likened the world's drug trade to the globalization of business and linked it to the financial support of terrorism.

"An argument could be made that the drug trade was the business model for the huge corporate enterprises that now regard the world as a world without boundaries," Safer argued in a September 2006 e-mail. "The drug trade also accelerated and financed the trade in terrorism. From the IRA, to Hezbollah, Al Quaeda, et al. From the poppy fields of Afghanistan and the Bekaa Valley in Lebanon to the poisoned streets of America, Soviet Union/Russia, Thailand, Japan, France, Britain, et al."

The Watergate scandal, cited elsewhere by other reporters as a political or legal story, drew Thomas' nomination as the top crime story of the period. She also cited the Iran/Contra scandal; clearly, Thomas viewed the political crime of the era as the major problem.

"Watergate was certainly a defining moment, and when a president is forced to resign," she said. "White collar crime. Abuse of power."

Lewis also talked about politics and its relation to crime, but in a different context: the politics of crime and what Lewis rued as the tragic result of crowded prisons due to uniformly rigid sentencing and an overemphasis on harsh punishment instead of treatment and prevention.

"I think the sad trend or the trend I regret the most has been the politicization of crime, Nixon's War on Crime," he said. "The result, unchanged trend continuing is savage sentencing and Congress passing sentencing minimums, and jails overflowing and the War on Drugs with a similar result. You know. The United States has by far the most severe sentences of any Western country and the last one with capital punishment, and so in general I think that's a regrettable thing."

SPORTS

The games and pastimes of a society can say a lot about its culture by way of the attention given over to after-hours interests and hobbies. They offer evidence of the emphasis a society might put on sportsmanship and competition, on entertainment as business and as a pleasure in relation to other interests; and they reflect how society adapts to cultural change such as integration of ethnic minorities and women into society.

As in other categories analyzed in this chapter, the journalists tended to categorize the major sports stories based more on big-picture trends and issues than on specific games, individuals, or teams. The breaking down of color barriers, from blacks and Hispanics in baseball to Muhammad Ali, *nee* Cassius Clay, championing the black athlete as a social and political icon for his race, was one of the leading themes in this category. So was the commercialization of sports, from huge television contracts to the professionalization of college athletics. Interestingly, two of the female journalists had little, or nothing, to say on the subject—Geyer made passing reference to the problem of steroids, while Thomas dismissed the subject, claiming "absolutely no interest." Goodman, though, took the subject into a different arena, that of exercise.

Like Geyer, Williams mentioned the scandal of steroid abuse, as he cited two developments in sports that stood out for him.

"One is the growth of sports on television and in specific the National Football League, which is I believe our most popular sport in the United States. But that growth takes place in the latter half of the 20th century, the billion-dollar TV deals that lead to these huge salaries and the sort of what I consider the perversion of sports into a money enterprise as opposed to the virtue of the athlete. Plus, you have all of the scandals in college sports that come from these big TV contracts. And then you have Major League Baseball, which struggles to get into that arena, and part of that corruption is the biggest sports scandal in the latter half of the 20th century, which is the steroids scandal. People bulking themselves up to hit massive homeruns, superhero types."

The second development Williams cited was the popularity of "oddball things like professional wrestling, which is a TV studio production. And it's not a sport, it's entertainment, but it is in the guise of two people competing, athletic competition, it's made-for-TV. And then you look at developments like in boxing, pay-per-view, which comes in the latter half of the 20th century, certain sports that can't cut it anymore as mass entertainment on television but carve their own niche."

Bradlee likewise cited the growth of professional sports.

"We're a bunch of jocks in this country, great interest in sports," he said. "I bet you that statistically, half the people in the world don't read a sports section. I don't think that many women care about sports. My wife doesn't read the sports section, and she is extremely well-informed and as bright as hell. She'll pick it up if suddenly she notices that people are talking about sports."

Echoing Williams, Broder referenced the increased variety of spectator sports that have become available to the viewers.

"When I grew up we had baseball, football, hockey, and basketball, and that was about it, and track," he said. "And now there are forty different sports that you access on television and follow it all by yourself."

Safer talked eloquently at some length about the sport he still considers to be America's game, baseball, and about the influence of Latinos on the game.

"The extraordinary effect of Latin America on the United States' national sport, that's a wonderful story," he said. "I happen to love baseball, I love it at every level, including the aesthetic level, because all of the movements of baseball are human movements, unlike basketball or football, which are inhuman movements; they're therefore Amazons and monsters and things that normal people can't do. One of the reasons for baseball's continued popularity is we can imagine ourselves making that catch, or hitting that homerun, even though we are incapable of doing it, we can imagine ourselves doing those things. And the movements are all graceful."

Baseball, for Safer, is a metaphor for the continuum of life. "Baseball at its best is a noncombat sport and has the beauty of not being against the clock, it's like life, it goes on, it can just go on and on. All of those movements, all of those steps to the dance, to the ballet of baseball, were considered American, North American. And it turns out that it had this extraordinary effect on the game when these young, super bright athletes from Santo Domingo and Mexico and Venezuela, and you name it. So that obviously is one of the great sports stories."

But Safer rued, with Geyer and Williams, the rise of performance-enhancing drugs: "And on the delicate side, steroids, in all of sports, when cheating became the norm, whether it was in a professional sport or so-called amateur sports. Chemicals."

Lewis also remembered baseball fondly, particularly some past Yankees teams; but he shared with Williams and Broder an observation about the commercialization of sport, a phenomenon Lewis saw as emblematic of problems in society in general.

"I grew up with the New York Yankees," he said, "the teams of '37, '38, '39. They won the series twelve games in a row, three years they won four to nothing. Since then, the commercialization of sports has proceeded apace."

Lewis cited a recent book by a former Harvard dean, Harry Lewis, *Excellence Without a Soul: How a Great University Forgot Education,* which he said deals with problems in U.S. society.

"He has a chapter on sports in which he concludes that the amateur ideal of American sports is completely phony and we ought to just let people get paid, because this so-called purity is a fake."

Woodruff also mentioned amateur sports as a major phenomenon of the period, but in a more positive way.

"The rise of college basketball, March Madness," she identified as her choice for major sports story of the half century. "I'm sure there are some others, but I don't think college basketball was so popular in the first half of the 20th century. Football certainly was."

Another important trend for her, though, was in the integration of minorities into sports at the amateur and professional levels.

"I'm thinking of Hank Aaron, the color barrier, I would say that's been a huge, a huge effect on sports. All the sports are now so clearly integrated, basketball, football, golf, and even boxing, I guess."

It was boxing—specifically, a boxer—that drew Caldwell's interest, for reasons that transcended sports.

"Ali was different," Caldwell said of Muhammad Ali, the multi-titled heavyweight champion. "He was Cassius Clay when he came into my life, but by then, I wasn't a kid in the mountains. By then, in the 1960s, I was emerging at the top as a reporter. Not just me alone, but a generation of us who were black were breaking though in the major newsrooms. Black America was changing. Indeed, a whole black consciousness movement was rising. And we, the black reporters, had this story in our hands. Boxing had always been a big thing in my life. For me, back to the time of Joe Louis. In our black/Italian neighborhood, Joe Louis gave us standing. He was the champion. But Joe's story turned sour. He got beat. He went broke. He became another sad story of boxing and the black man. But with the '60s came the time of black nationalism and Malcolm X, and the torch being passed to a new generation."

It was an era of rising black identify of which Ali was symbolic for Caldwell and others.

"We had our own music, the Motown sound. We looked different, Afro hair styles. We had new demands, black power, and language, 'by any means necessary.' And we were breaking through in a lot of places, and into this came Cassius Clay. He was magical. In many ways, he was this new black man rising. He was good, he could fight, but more than that, he could talk and he would sass white folks and by himself took 'black is beautiful' to another level. I wasn't a sportswriter. I didn't cover him. But he became central in my life. I was a huge fan as he rose to win the championship."

Ali came to stand for more than black power though. When he refused to be drafted into the U.S. military, he crossed racial lines to join with white Americans who had stood up to deny the war.

"This is a hero figure of mine standing up for what he believes is right," Caldwell said. "He puts it all on the line. He is not afraid of anything: losing the title, his wealth, and even going to jail. And as it would happen, I would come almost right behind him to be faced with my own confrontation with the power of government. Ali had made it easy for me. Of course, I would not spy on black people. Ali had set the standard. He inspired me. He inspired all of us. To fight against the Justice Department's demands became a cause. And we got strength from Ali. He was so much more than a sports hero. He was about being a man and standing up and being strong. We called him 'the greatest.'"

For Goodman, the sports issue of the half century was not spectator sports, but participatory athletics, which was a unique sort of integration in itself—a phenomenon in which folks who once were not athletic took up a sport or exercise regimen.

"Probably just the explosion of the average person's involvement in exercise and sports," she said. "If you look at the biggest change, it used to be that you played sports in college and then you didn't. You played sports in high school, and then you didn't. And it was mostly men who were playing and the women who were cheerleaders. And now you look at everybody, in some fashion, exercising. Fitness is the greatest sport in America at the moment. I can track my own sports. I have been an athlete, more or less, and as I've gotten older, from all kinds of sports to tennis and squash, through knee surgery, to golf. But walking, and you know, Yoga. It's probably those things that are more common."

ARTS/ENTERTAINMENT

Commercialization, a broadening and lowering of artistic standards, and technological change marked the journalists' remembrances of an era that experienced developments that included the so-called British invasion of rock 'n' rollers; the shrinkage of big-screen, domed movie palaces to small, mall-centered film venues, and advances that saw the development of transistorized portable radios and digital sound.

Arguably, the most remarkable of these technological marvels was television, which brought current events, films, theater, variety shows, and other popular fare into the living room. Television's presence in this section as an arts and entertainment phenomenon of the half century as well as in other categories of this chapter lends it a cross-disciplinary importance that suggests it might have been one of the most important contributors to cultural change of the era. At the end of the century, the rising popularity of the Internet as an entertainment and information medium indicated that it was poised to replace television as the most important technological change of the period.

A few of the journalists cited the stage, fine arts, and dance as areas of improvement, while others deplored entertainment genres that have vulgarized the arts or that were often incomprehensible.

Television journalist Woodruff and newspaper columnist Broder shared the view that television was the primary artistic and entertainment story of the half century.

"The reason I keep coming back to television is because it really has changed the way we get information," argued Woodruff. "It's changed our base."

"The ways in which people can access information and entertainment," said Broder. "I'd certainly put television into that category. And now all of the wonderful stuff with the Internet and all of the other electronics."

"Television, television," said Bradlee, who then cited the Internet as a replacement for television, much as many news consumers switched from newspapers to televisions for their information during the first three decades of the half century. "Television was, well I didn't know anybody who had television before the '50s," he said. "It's disappearing, not disappearing, but it's being replaced, and when they talk about the decline of newspaper audiences, readership, the decline of people who are watching television for news is precipitous. They've lost a third of their . . . those big network news stations, NBC News has only two-thirds of what they had at their peak. They're (consumers) picking it up somewhere else, they're picking it up on the Internet."

For Williams, television was only part of a larger phenomenon of entertainment consumers staying at home, a trend that took in music and games.

"I think home entertainment was a huge development," he said. "I remember in the '80s buying a thing called Pong (electronic ping pong), and to think of what we have today, this entire industry of sports and video games, all that, that is a huge social shift, the whole big home theater, the development of cable television, the development of satellite radio, all those things that came toward the end of the 20th century were a major cultural development, I think."

He also cited changing music and listening tastes.

"In terms of music, I would guess hip-hop. I'm amazed hip-hop is number one, is the best-selling music in America," he said. "It didn't exist before the 1990s. And talk radio has been a phenomenon in the '90s, mostly conservative, but talk radio is a powerful format, and I think the forerunner of what we now see at the start of the 20th century: the blogs, and that whole sort of private-niche conversations of people."

Goodman framed the topic in terms of journalistic agendas and career choices.

"Arts and entertainment has occupied a larger and larger space in people's lives, if I can do that rather than say Michael Jackson," she said. "That there are so many choices, and people spend so much time in the general realm, and it's such a huge part of the economy now, and a lot of the young people who would once go into journalism or go into writing are now making their own little documentaries, videos . . . it's just become huge."

Thomas and Lewis saw the era as one of advances in the higher cultural arts, primarily theater and dance.

"I think some of the great plays by Arthur Miller really had an impact on our society, like *Death of a Salesman,*" Thomas said. She also cited Jerome Lawrence's and Robert E. Lee's *Inherit the Wind,* a play based on the Scopes monkey trial of 1925 that opened on Broadway in 1955. "I think that in theater, there was a tremendous contribution, and also music and arts have always had an impact on every era."

Lewis saw a significant rise in the popularity of dance.

"My own prejudice would be that dance has made a great breakthrough in American life in those fifty years," he said. "Go back to 1945, there was very little dance in the American scene, a little bit, Martha Graham, but it's now very big, there are dozens of dance companies and a lot of audience. I like dance a lot, so I'm prejudiced."

The other trends, he said, "have been in things I don't care for: popular music, rock, and the modern forms of music I'm completely deaf to; rap I find completely incomprehensible, they could be talking Afghani for all I know; hip-hop, I don't even understand it."

He prefers the popular music "of the old kind. Cole Porter, (George) Gershwin, wonderful. But today it just passes me by, and I have to say that my classical music taste stops in about 1850 as well. I'm pretty much an old fogey when it comes to music, and my real interest is supported by what goes on in Boston in early music."

Geyer and Safer saw a more discouraging trend in the arts, one tending towards vulgarity and banality.

"Vulgarization. Just a general vulgarization," Geyer said. "I'm not prudish at all, but some of the things I see on television make me extremely unhappy, I'd like to break somebody's neck. And these things go out to the rest of the world. You imagine what a Muslim in Lebanon thinks, and this is being foisted on them."

Classical music has declined, she said, but musicals seem to be holding their own.

"We have a lot of good theater, it comes down mostly to television, but also radio. It's hard to ever find a radio show where you can take the music, where I can stand it. And this is all that Americans are hearing."

Safer called the period a "relatively stagnant" time for the visual arts.

"The biggest shift in the visual arts, I think, was the near-death of aesthetics, because standards have fallen so drastically," he said, "and the rather graceless use of technology and calling it art, whether it's video art, which is a joke, I think. What is the difference between visual art and television? Beats me, honestly. I think, and I'm not going to mention any names because some of them are my friends, but the artist as deep thinker who hires people who actually make art, to do their work for them, and that's become very common and continues as we speak. So I think it's the near-death of craft."

Mediocrity has become "standard" in popular music, Safer said. "For the most part, it has not been a great period for the arts. It's interesting. It's probably one of those periods, when you think of fifty years and some of the dreadful things that have happened in those fifty years. The previous fifty the worst things were, the better the art became, so Picasso's *Guernica* was what came out of despair, and despair usually creates great art. All of the despair of the last fifty years has produced some of the most mediocre art that we've had."

For Caldwell, the music was the thing, and it was a good thing—especially black music.

"I love music, and in my life, every period of my life, it's been framed by this music. A lot of it comes from the black experience. Some of it was presented to America by artists who were white, a lot of them weren't the first to record this music, a lot of it was first recorded by blacks (rhythm & blues). To me, if you go into the 1960s, and I'm thinking of Marvin Gaye, think Motown. If you take that music from that period, to me almost like the second half of the century, music dominates."

In Africa, Caldwell noticed that a lot of jazz is played, "whereas here, you don't really . . . the major jazz station here is a station over in Newark, WBGO, we don't even have a major jazz station in New York City, which is very hard to understand."

Music, Caldwell said, played a large role in American culture of the period, especially in communicating the spirit of minorities.

"I see the impact the music has had in America, every aspect of American life and how it's really widened it out," he said. "The music is everywhere. I'm proudest perhaps of what black people have done in music, and in their arts. I mean, James Baldwin said one writes out of one thing and one thing only, one's own experience. I think that's true with everything."

The same concept of writing from one's own experience also held for the writing of Pulitzer Prize-winning playwright August Wilson. Citing the play *Fences* in particular, he said: "It was really introducing and telling America stories about what happened to black people," he said.

CULTURAL/SOCIETAL SHIFT

For most of the journalists, the major shift of the era centered on empowerment, from blacks moving more into society's mainstream to women gaining more career and economic opportunity to the sexual revolution and gay rights. Other categories assessed by the journalists, primarily legal and political, played a role in these broader societal shifts, phenomena that in themselves gained the focus of some of the journalists.

Bradlee, Williams, and Caldwell all cited the story of race as the arena in which the major cultural shift of the period occurred. For Bradlee, the answer was a succinct one-liner: "I suppose integration. America's battle with race is a huge story."

Williams and Caldwell put a more personal spin on this question, framing improved race relations and political and social gains for minorities, primarily blacks, in terms of what they witnessed and experienced.

"In my mind, I just don't think that a kid like me standing on the street corners in the '60s and working for a major radio operation like this (NPR) or a TV operation (Fox) or *The Washington Post* would have been possible for a black person," Williams said. "You could work at some black newspapers at the time, like the *Amsterdam News* or the *Pittsburgh Courier,* but in terms of major white-owned and operated news operations, that just didn't occur, so I think that's a major shift that I feel personally."

Empowerment of females also ranked high with Williams.

"I would say the feminist movement is huge," he said. "Now, it's an odd one for me, I say this almost clinically to you, as someone who reads history, I know it happened, but I grew up with a very strong mother. My father, I often think of my father as sort of a dashing larger-than-life figure." But the person who was the leader in his house, he said, "was my mother, and so when I hear about people viewing women as less intelligent, less able, I'm like 'are you nuts?'"

The change in racial relations, Caldwell said, was the obvious answer to the question of major societal shift during the era. Beyond that, though, he cited the shift of American society to a more conservative political attitude. In particular, he discussed his experience covering election night in Rochester, New York, during the 1960s. He had been assigned to cover the Republicans on one particular night.

"This was the mid-1960s, but you had these people who were talking this conservative thing, and they were on the fringe, it was almost like they were nonexistent, they were just nothing," he said. "To me the most amazing thing, and I always tell people that things are possible if you work at it because these people, now they run the government. They've gone from being way out there to being the center. The way America's changed, this whole conservative movement that's taken over the country. A lot of it I don't consider to be conservative, but that's what they call it. To me, we up there in the mountains of Pennsylvania were the true conservatives. I didn't see growing up there that there was any racial component in it, maybe I'm looking at it too narrow, but we were conservative in our values, God-fearing, hard-working, believed that education was a way up and believed in judging people, truly as King said, because they were hardworking people, family people, strong, just strong American-valued people. To me that was the true conservative. These people now, I don't consider them true conservatives. But to me and politics, it's just the way that they have come to dominate the country."

Lewis also cited political change, considering the political shift in America as one that has brought about greater, divisive, partisanship and taken the nation into a less respectful political mood.

"The growth of partisanship, the hard-edged partisan politics we have today," he said. "(Syndicated columnist) Ann Coulter says the widows of people killed on 9/11, they're happy their husbands died and all that stuff, things that people say that would have once been regarded as revolting and unacceptable in the living room, and in general the society is much less respectful than it was. I regret that. I think politeness and humanity are good qualities, and it's a much more hard-edged society, meaner, nastier, negative."

Asked why he thought American politics had taken this turn, Lewis cited President Richard Nixon.

"Nixon was an exemplar of a trend of politics that says the only thing that matters is winning," he said. "It's the Vince Lombardi rule transported to life. Winning is all that matters, and that's much worse than it used to be. Moderation is out, extremity is in."

But, the former *Times* columnist said, the nation's citizens have seen general improvement in their economic status.

"There are many better things," he said. "People are much better off than they were, I mean infinitely better off. Even the ones in the middle who have been taking a beating in the (George W.) Bush years are much better off than they were forty or fifty years ago."

Yet another reference to television as a major story or development arose in this category, cited by two journalists.

"Because of the effect it had on bringing us all together in terms of what we've seen and what we've heard, and the way it's just homogenized our exposure to entertainers," said Woodruff in explaining her choice of this informational and communications medium and of the larger developments in information technology. "Now I'm thinking I should be naming all the other bits of technology that bring culture together, to homogenize our culture. Because of television you have people who gather around the water cooler and talk about *American Idol*. I don't think I'm putting my finger on it, though. It's bigger than that. Hollywood. It's certainly not in the direction of the classics, in terms of the great literary or musical classics, it's in the opposite direction. We're much more celebrity-focused and Hollywood-focused, you know, what's on the big screen and what's on the small screen, and clearly the Internet is changing that."

Woodruff, involved during the period of this interview in a national project on the attitudes of American youth, said her interviews with youngsters revealed their heavy usage of emerging technologies, such as the Internet and iPods, for their musical entertainment. Their view is if it's something important, it will come to them, she said.

"Their cell phone. They'll see it on the Internet. Or somebody will say something. They don't feel the need to go find the news. Now, to some extent that reflects what young people the generation before them thought, you don't start paying attention to the news until you have a stake in it. Young people have never been high consumers of newspapers.

"So we're clearly moving beyond television," she continued, but "for that last half of the twentieth century, I would say television."

Broder also cited the influence of television on U.S. culture as "very high" before shifting his focus to changing gender relations—"the fact that women no longer feel that they are second-class participants either in marriage or in the job market."

Goodman agreed with him on this issue, seeing empowerment of women as the major cultural shift of the period.

"I can't help but think that probably the biggest social change in my lifetime has been women's roles, it's just from the single defined appropriate role for women being mothers and being at home to this diverse notion of choices, to a much wider spectrum" said the columnist, who has focused much of her journalistic attention on gender and family issues. "That has changed so much, it's changed the economy, it's changed families, it's changed child bearing, it's changed relationships between men and women, I think it's probably the biggest social change that I know about."

For Thomas, the sexual revolution took in more than women; it also included gays and lesbians.

"Sexual revolution, in every sense of the word," she said. "From the '60s on, I think the whole transformation of freedom, more freedom for, and certainly the feminist movement made great strides, women went into all the fields, there was more acceptance of them, and men certainly felt freer in the way they dressed, and so forth. The sexual revolution, people living together without the benefit of marriage, also the gays being liberated, being able to come out."

Geyer and Safer differed from their colleagues on this question, focusing their comments on the role of Americans in their own society and in the world—and not necessarily in a positive way.

"We've gone from a country largely unified, culturally homogeneous, not ethnically or racially, but a country that had a strong sense of itself, particularly after World War II, and coming out of the depression, and it was very, very clear to people what it was to be an American," Geyer said. "Citizenship was considered a privilege. We were a kind of natural outcome, we represented things that other countries might strive for, but we did not impose it. The founding fathers made that very clear, you don't impose it, you try to set an example, to today a country . . . where it's not clear at all what it is to be an American."

Geyer rued what she saw as a trend in the country away from national pride toward ethnic differences playing a more prominent role and toward an estrangement of U.S. citizens regarding national foreign policy.

"Within twenty years we'll have a Mexican separatist movement that is so strong that almost anything could happen," she said. "I see just any number of disconnects."

She moved into the current century and the nation's mood regarding the war in Iraq.

"There's a disconnect between the people and the military, they're volunteers," she said. "People say, 'well they're volunteers, they volunteered for it.' Their patriotism is to me very false, it's a patriotism of 'oh yeah, we're proud of them.' I see disconnects on every level. Most people, I go around the country, they don't even talk about the war, they're really not that interested in it. The only thing I can say is the country is just seriously disconnected, on all levels."

Safer framed the question in terms of the change of cultures internationally because of U.S. social and cultural influences, what he termed a sort of cultural imperialism.

"The most important cultural shift is the effect in the world of what the Europeans call American cultural imperialism," he said, "so that there isn't a country in the world where kids do not wear blue jeans, chew gum, listen to the same music. The most watched television station in the world is MTV, so what does that tell you about a cultural shift? MTV, in God knows how many languages, including Chinese, at least 400 million people watch MTV. This is quite a cultural shift."

CHAPTER 2

The '50s of Anthony Lewis and Helen Thomas: Reds and Blacks and Peace

> We tend to be a bit nostalgic about the past, and anything that's forty years old, many of the rough edges have worn off. But it certainly wasn't a wonderful time for the blacks, or the black population. They had a rough time. It was a much more racist country, much more anti-Semitic, it seemed doubtful that a Catholic would be elected president; there was one Catholic on the Supreme Court when I started noticing it, today there are a majority of Catholics on the Supreme Court and nobody cares. So I don't think it was perfect by any means. It was an earlier day, and it had some qualities to recommend it, but I don't think it was wonderful.
>
> —Anthony Lewis

Abraham Chasanow, a civilian Navy employee, had been a worker in good standing with the Hydrographic Office for almost 23 years when he was suspended and then wrongfully fired as a security risk. A young Anthony Lewis was on the story for the *Washington Daily News* when Chasanow met with newspaper reporters in April 1954 to tell them he was seeking reinstatement to his job, which he had lost "despite a hearing board's strong finding that he should be cleared."

The charges against the 43-year-old Chasanow, Lewis wrote, were for "dealing with some suspect persons with whom he had allegedly associated"—including "known communists." Chasanow denied to reporters that he was "any kind of a radical."[1]

The nation was in the throes of McCarthyism, a plague of anticommunist witch hunts led by Republican U.S. Senator Joseph McCarthy of Wisconsin, who accused hundreds of government employees and officials

Anthony Lewis. © Anthony Lewis. Used by permission.

of belonging to or sympathizing with communists. Lewis was one of a handful of reporters, including CBS news correspondent Edward R. Murrow, who investigated the communist-connection allegations and stood up to the red-baiting tide.

In response to the Chasanow firing, Lewis put together a series of stories on the case in which he told the story of "a small man, a most ordinary man" who was purchasing a house in Greenbelt, Maryland, who belonged to the Lions, and who had a wife involved in the community's Red Cross and Community Chest. The series, which won Lewis his first of two Pulitzer Prizes, included:

- An in-depth interview with Chasanow, who answered each of the charges against him;[2]
- An analysis of Navy documents dealing with the case and revelations of a chilling government search of his office desk that gave him the feeling "people are crawling out of the woodwork;"[3]
- Testimony from coworkers who stood "openly by" the accused man, including signing affidavits on his behalf;

- Testimony from neighbors indicating that the work of the two agents investigating Chasanow was shoddy, including the Greenbelt chief of police's comment that he considered "those two fellows to be rank amateurs in the field of security investigations;"[4]
- Interviews with town residents indicating that the root of Chasanow's difficulties may have been in his work as an attorney for the Greenbelt Veterans Housing Corp. that angered some of the development residents, and a profile of Chasanow and his family, in which they revealed fear and stress from the government investigation. "At first you don't want to talk on the telephone," Chasanow told Lewis. "You don't want to say hello on the street. It's an awful feeling."[5]

Lewis' series cleared Chasanow, who was reinstated to his job; and these stories set the thematic stage of the red scare, civil rights, and U.S. Supreme Court coverage, that would become one of the major beats of the future newspaper reporter and columnist who was born in the nation's largest city and its cultural center on March 27, 1927. The United States of that period was near the end of the roaring twenties era of prohibition, gangsters, and economic boom that preceded the Great Depression. A 20-pack of Lord Salisbury Turkish cigarettes could be had for 18 cents, and discriminating motorists could purchase a Willys-Knight Six for $1,295 to $1,495.

The dispatches that day in Lewis' hometown newspaper, the *New York Times,* included a story on a substitute Brooklyn public school teacher who had been dismissed for teaching evolution to his seventh-graders;[6] and a music review transmitted to the newspaper by wireless reported that a Beethoven fete had opened in Vienna. "Beethoven was not made to put his best musical foot forward in this," the correspondent opined.[7]

But the big news of the day was contained under a banner headline on the front page that read: "Foreigners Flee From All Yangtse Points; More Bloodshed Feared As Red Flame Spreads; 1,500 More Marines To Go At Admiral's Call."[8]

The civil war just beginning in China was between the Kuomintang (KTM), led by Chiang Kai-shek, and the Communist Party of China, led by Mao Zedong.

"While American refugees from Nanking began arriving in Shanghai today, after the carnage of the past few days there," reported a dispatch datelined Shanghai, "American naval, military and consular authorities here agree that the situation throughout nearly all China is very grave, and they expect further bloodshed.

"The casualties at Nanking, so far as known, include one American and one Englishman, both doctors, and one Japanese sailor killed; four Americans and several other foreigners wounded and injured by bullets or beatings."[9]

In Shanghai, refugees told of their adventures.

"Harrowing tales of escapes from death at the hands of Cantonese soldiers inflamed against foreigners were related today by Nanking refugees arriving at Shanghai on the steamers Kungwo and Wenchow," the newspaper reported. "The refugees totaled 220.

"Mrs. John K. Davis, wife of the United States Consul, was still shaken by the ordeal. She told of the flight of Americans, including herself and her two children, from the Consulate, where the Cantonese threatened to kill all foreigners. Mrs. Davis and her children arrived with nothing save the clothes on their backs. She displayed a bottle of cough syrup given to her by an officer on the Kungwo, saying, 'Here's my baggage.'"[10]

The fighting had repercussions worldwide. In England, a Chinese official warned that the trouble in his nation had only just begun.

"Reuter's Shanghai correspondent quotes 'a particularly well-informed high official' as declaring:

"'We are only at the beginning of the trouble in China. The real thing is only now beginning.'"[11]

The Chinese civil war reportage centered on a theme, communism, that would come to be a big one during a newspaper career that began in 1948 when, armed with a bachelor's degree with an English concentration from Harvard College, Lewis set out to work toward his goal of becoming a newspaper editor.

"If possible, THE editor," he would recall in his apartment nearly 60 years later. "If I had an ambition, it was to be the editor of the *New York Times*, the top editor. I didn't say that to anybody, and it was very remote, it was like saying I was born in a log cabin and I would like to be president."

Lewis knew by high school, the Horace Mann School in New York, that he wanted to be a journalist, "but I think I started thinking about it in grade school. I think it was the glamour. You know, not literally the movies, Jimmy Stewart coming in with his hat on and typing out the story '*Herald* exposes corruption.' It just seemed like it was glamorous, I'd have to say, it's ego fulfilling, your name is on the byline. I'm being slightly cynical, because I've always thought it was something where you could do good and expose wrong."

The nation offered plenty of glamour and wrongs to be righted for a journalist entering the newspaper trade in 1948, and New York City had all the culture a young journalist and classical music fan such as Lewis could want. This was the year that the U.S. Columbia Record Company released the first LP (long-playing record) to preserve on vinyl disc such new works as Richard Strauss' *Four Last Songs* or Dmitry Shostakovich's *Violin Concerto No. 1.* On the theater beat, Tennessee Williams won the Pulitzer for *A Streetcar Named Desire;* and in the cinema, John Huston released two films, both Humphrey Bogart vehicles: *Key Largo* and *The Treasure of the Sierra Madre.* The new medium of television, with sets in one million U.S. homes by 1948, showcased such cultural and entertainment possibilities as a British Broadcasting Corporation production of *Hamlet,* which won the TV Society's Silver Medal. Ed Sullivan's *The Toast of the Town* was aired by the Columbia Broadcasting System. In publishing, Norman Mailer's *The Naked and the Dead* fictionalized the adventures of U.S. soldiers in World War II, Irwin Shaw published *The Young Lions,* Ezra Pound published *The Pisan Cantos* as part of the poet's *Cantos,* and the homosexuality of Gore Vidal's protagonist in *The City and the Pillar* raised controversy. Truman Capote published his first novel, *Other Voices, Other Rooms,* and William Faulkner published *Intruder in the Dust.* U.S.-born poet T. S. Eliot won the Nobel Prize for Literature.[12]

International and domestic political events continued to feature the East-West tensions and civil rights themes of Lewis' life and career. The Soviet Union in June blockaded road and train traffic between Berlin and the West, leading to an airlift of supplies into the British and French zones of the city that had been divided into quadrants following World War II. Two months later, the Soviets halted diplomatic relations with the United States, claiming that two visiting teachers had defected while U.S. officials argued the educators had been kidnapped.

At home, the U.S. Supreme Court in March upheld separation of church and state in a major ruling against prayer in public schools, and Congress passed the Marshall Aid Act, establishing payment of $5.3 billion to help in European recovery following World War II. Symptoms of the red scare could be found in congressional approval of funding for the Voice of America to beam radio propaganda broadcasts to foreign countries, including those ruled by communist governments. In July, 12 leaders of the Communist Party of the United States were indicted by a federal grand jury on charges of urging the overthrow of the U.S. government; and in December, Alger Hiss, a former official in the U.S. State Department, was indicted on a charge of lying to a federal grand jury related to alleged espionage activity.

The courts and executive branch in 1948 also laid some of the groundwork for the looming civil rights activism of the 1950s. The U.S. Supreme Court ruled in May that the federal government could not foster private discrimination. Also, the high court ruled that inhabitants of exclusive housing districts could not refuse to sell their houses to blacks, and the justices ordered that whites-only law schools must admit black applicants unless equal black law school tuition was provided. And in a major civil rights decision by the White House, President Harry S Truman ordered the desegregation of U.S. armed forces.

Lewis fell short of his goal of sitting in the editor's seat at the *Times,* settling instead for winning two Pulitzer Prizes for journalism, the second as a pundit for the newspaper he had wanted to edit. He arrived as a columnist at the *Times* through a circuitous route from New York to Washington to New York to London, then back to New York.

The *Times* hired Lewis straight out of college; he'd worked there as a copy boy during summers while at Harvard. The newspaper started him in the Week in Review section, which featured in-depth wrap-ups of the week's major news.

"I was very bad at it," he recalled. "I sojourned on for four years, and then the editor said 'you're not getting anywhere. Go.' So I was fired in a gentle way."

He joined the Adlai Stevenson presidential campaign of 1952, then was hired, with the help of a friend, by the *Washington Daily News*. He returned to the *Times* in 1955, hooking up with the man he took as his mentor, chief Washington correspondent James Reston, to cover the Supreme Court.

"I went to London, I became a columnist," Lewis recalled. "Completely surprising. And it was only when I became a columnist, and I was offered a job as foreign editor, and I turned it down, because I realized that I liked writing better than editing."

The major themes that would dominate his writing during the 1950s, Lewis would recall, were "the red scare. Race. Those are the two biggest things in my life. I was involved in both. Those are the two dominant crises."

With the communists victorious in China and the Soviet Union securing its Iron Curtain grip on Eastern Europe, the communist bogeyman thrived in the United States, with good reason, based on some of the headlines of the era. One case that garnered a lot of attention was that of Hiss, a State Department adviser to President Franklin D. Roosevelt at Yalta, who in 1950 was convicted of perjury, drawing a five-year prison sentence. Whittaker Chambers, a writer and former Soviet spy who had defected, testified before the House Committee on Un-American Activities that Hiss was a communist and had spied for the Soviet Union. The spying charge could not be proven, but Hiss was found guilty of lying to a grand jury about his involvement with a communist spy operation.

Another spy saga that garnered national attention was the case of Julius and Ethel Rosenberg, accused of being members of a Soviet spy clique. The trial included the claim that electrical engineer Julius had sent a rough sketch of the atomic bomb to Russia. Questions about whether the couple were guilty circulated for years after they were executed.

"Julius and Ethel Rosenberg, defiant to the last, paid with their lives for betraying their native land," read the *Washington Daily News* in a June 20, 1953 story datelined Sing Sing Prison in New York. "Executioner Joseph Francel sent 16,000 volts of electricity thru their bodies shortly before sundown last night. Julius went first."

The Rosenbergs refused to the end to trade for their life secrets of a Soviet spy ring which officials fear may still be operating.

The husband and wife were executed against a backdrop of world-wide agitation unequaled since the Sacco-Vanzetti case of the 1920s. The demonstrations reached such fever pitch in Paris that shooting broke out and one man was wounded.[13]

The backdrop for this period of U.S. history, though, would be McCarthyism, the primary impetus behind the raging anticommunist fervor of the time. Lewis doggedly reported on the fallout from the Wisconsin senator's activities. In a January 1954 story, he reported that "the President said there were 2,200 against whom the Government had some derogatory information and against whom it intended to move. That is, he said there was some doubt about them."[14]

In a story that detailed the chilling atmosphere in the nation's capital, Lewis later that month wrote that President Dwight D. Eisenhower said he would consider honorable discharges for employees "who leave Government service under normal conditions, so that neighbors and friends will not suspect them of being security risks." Lewis reported Sarah McClendon "of Texas papers told the President at his press conference today that she knew a man who was afraid to tell anyone he had left the State Department because people might think he was disloyal. She suggested the honorable discharge idea."[15]

The next month, Lewis reported that the administration of President Eisenhower had ordered all departments to categorize their security removals into four areas "depending on the type of information in their files: suspected subversion, perversion, past convictions, and all others."[16]

Meanwhile, in congressional action reminiscent of the red scare earlier in the 20th century and foreshadowing government-approved wiretaps against anti-Vietnam War demonstrators later in the century and suspected terrorists early in the 21st century, the House of Representatives was undertaking yet another assault on the nation's citizens and their privacy three months after the resignations of thousands of government employees reported by Lewis' newspaper.

"The House was expected to approve today the Administration's 'anti-traitor' bill, which would permit wire-tap evidence to be used in prosecuting subversives," the *Washington Daily News* reported in April 1954. "A number of Democrats insist that use of wire-tap evidence should be permitted only by a Federal court order.

"Wire-tapping itself is legal now. But the Supreme Court has ruled that evidence so obtained cannot be used in Federal crime cases. The Administration measure would let the Government use evidence obtained by tapping phone lines in the prosecution of alleged traitors, spies, saboteurs and seditionists."[17]

That summer, though, saw the beginning of McCarthy's decline, as Lewis covered the Army-McCarthy hearings for the *Washington Daily News*. A couple of excerpts indicate the tenor of the proceedings.

"Roy M. Cohn returned to the stand at the Army-McCarthy hearings today and fenced with sub-committee counsel Ray H. Jenkins over some

Army testimony in connection with Army charges that Mr. Cohn used extreme pressure in efforts to obtain favored treatment for Pvt. G. David Schine, former McCarthy aide," Lewis and colleague Neil McNeil wrote early in June 1954.

The dispatch reported the sparring between Jenkins and Cohn, during which Cohn produced a stack of legal files in a cardboard box; the exchange underscored the tense mood of fear and distrust that permeated the hearings.

> "Mr. Cohn remarked at one point that he thought some of the papers in the box should not be shown to Army Atty. Joseph N. Welch, because they referred to 'investigations of his clients.'
>
> "Mr. Welch got the floor a few moments later and remarked that his 'very few' clients might be watching on television and be worried by this remark. So far as he knew, Mr. Welch said, none of his clients had anything to do with the McCarthy committee.
>
> "'I wish you would say something that would make my few, little clients feel better,' Mr. Welch pleaded."[18]

Ten days later, McCarthy was at it again, leveling charges of communist sympathy against government officials.

"Sen. Joseph R. McCarthy (R., Wis.) said today that he personally overheard Army Counselor John G. Adams offer Roy Cohn information about communists in the Navy," Lewis reported with Don May. "The Wisconsin senator began testifying as to issues in the Army-McCarthy hearings today. He took the stand yesterday and testified at length, but only about his ideas on the menace of communism in general."

> Sen. McCarthy ran thru a long series of actions which the McCarthy side has charged to the Army. He agreed with testimony already given by Mr. Cohn, adding very little to the charges already brought out at the hearings.
>
> This morning's session was an anti-climax to yesterday's fireworks, when Army Counsel Joseph N. Welch said he had "never really gauged" the Senator's "cruelty and recklessness."[19]

That latter statement had come in response to McCarthy's allegation that Welch's assistant had once belonged to a "communist front," the newspaper reported, to which Welch had responded, "I think until this moment I never gauged your cruelty and recklessness . . . I wish it were in my power to excuse you, but your forgiveness will have to come from someone else . . ."[20]

The hearings bared the senator's empty crusade and reversed the McCarthyism tide. By the end of the year, the steam had run out of the McCarthy anticommunist campaign. The senator had been censured, changing the congressional body if not the senator himself, Lewis' newspaper reported.

"The censure of Sen. Joseph R. McCarthy may not change his 'alley fighting' ways, but it could have profound effects on the future of the Senate, the Republican Party and possibly on the Junior Senator from Wisconsin," the newspaper reported.

"The split marked off the pro and anti-Eisenhower wings of the party as much as the pro and anti-McCarthy factions and assured the President that he will have to deal with a Senate minority divided right down the middle," the report continued. "By contrast, the Democrats were pulled together by the censure vote as they seldom have been in recent history. Not one Democrat bolted his party's line on key roll calls."[21]

The historical and political context of the time helped fuel the rise of McCarthyism, Lewis would later recall. "There was a lot of pressure, a lot of fear, you know the Hiss case. We were afraid of spies, and there were spies, so you had some reason. It took an extreme form and in many cases a ludicrous and unconstitutional form, but it wasn't without some reason."

In retrospect, Lewis had his own opinion about the major spy cases. The Rosenbergs, he maintained, were guilty. "There were spies in the nuclear program. But the worst was not the Rosenbergs but Klaus Fuchs. He was a British spy, he came over to New Mexico and was part of the whole Oppenheimer team (developing the atomic bomb), and he gave the Russians everything. He was a real spy. He wasn't executed. The British did still have capital punishment, but he eventually got out, he wasn't even given a life sentence."

Hiss, Lewis said, may not have been guilty but was a victim of the spy and anticommunist hysteria of the time. "I've come to a rather detached view that he did do some things. I've yet to be persuaded that they were very serious, but that he was a liar and deceptive I've no doubt, I think he was. It was very hard then. I went to the trial a few times, and he didn't look like a bad guy, and Chambers did. Chambers was a mess."

Lewis told a story of the Prothonotary Warbler, a tale of an obscure bird that linked Chambers and Hiss.

"Unknown to Hiss," Lewis recalled, "Chambers in a closed session of the House Un-American Activities Committee, (Richard) Nixon's committee, had said that he'd taken a trip up the Potomac with Hiss to show what good friends they were, and they were looking for birds and had seen a rare bird, the Prothonotary Warbler. And then testifying publicly later, not knowing about this Chambers testimony, and denying that he'd known Chambers at all well, Hiss somehow mentioned that he'd seen the Prothonotary Warbler."

Such were the details of spies and accused spies and American paranoia in which the seeds of McCarthyism were planted—with the help of a lackadaisical press corps, in Lewis' eyes.

"In the nineteenth century and the eighteenth century, there was no pretense of objectivity in journalism," he recalled. "The point of newspapers was to have a point of view, like European newspapers today. Then, the new cult of neutrality arose, and journalists became stenographers."

The reporters, Lewis said, "blandly just printed Joe McCarthy saying 'I will reveal tomorrow the reason that John Foster Dulles is a secret communist,' and they just put that in the paper without any framework indicating that he'd said things like that a hundred times before, none of which ever panned out. So it taught them a lesson; news is not just stenography."

But then, Lewis said, the reporters discovered that McCarthy was using them.

"I give credit to two journalists and myself as a rather distant third because I was working for a much less prestigious newspaper, the *Washington Daily News.* Philip Potter of the *Baltimore Sun* and Murrey Marder of the *Washington Post* got the goods on McCarthy, and they began following him around like bloodhounds, and they wrote down whatever he said and then they put in the context, and people gradually realized—not (Edward) Murrow, but they did it before Murrow did. They didn't just say 'this guy's a scoundrel,' they just put it in the context and let the reader see that for himself. And their example was eventually followed by the *New York Times* and others."

What drove him in his reporting of the Chasanow case, Lewis said, was a sense of right and wrong. The case vindicated what Lewis would identify as a type of watchdog journalism that requires reporters to move beyond the popular objectivity of the day.

"All the time I was a reporter, for the *News* and then for the *Times,* I really had views, I wasn't a colorless, bland, uninterested guy who just took notes and then regurgitated them," he said. "I was in favor of Abe Chasanow, right? I really thought it was wrong, and I was there to right a wrong. There never was a less radical man than Abe Chasanow, I assure you that. And there's some poetic justice. His son Howard became the chief judge of the highest court of Maryland, and his daughter-in-law is a federal district judge in Maryland. And his daughter was the food writer for *The Washington Post.*"

The dark fog of McCarthyism rolling through post-World War II Washington was not a unique phenomenon, Lewis pointed out. It was but the latest version of a cyclical occurrence of suspicion and fear of unknown or radical political movements that threaten the status quo.

"It's an endemic element in American society," he said. "It goes way back to 1798 and the passage of the Sedition Act by the Federalist Congress and signed by John Adams. The political argument for it was that it was needed to stop French Jacobin terror from coming into the United States. Well, the real reason was to defeat pro-Jefferson editors in the runup to the election of 1800. That's what they wanted to do, and that's what they did, but the cover was we've got to fight these, keep these terrorists out, left-wing terrorists. In World War I, (President) Wilson sent up another sedition act, which was enacted and prosecuted people for absurdities, twenty years in prison for throwing leaflets from the tops of buildings in New York. In the twenties, many states passed anti-syndicalism laws, anticommunist laws, a lot of people were put in prison in the 1920s, '30s, the Dies Committee, the first House Un-American Activities Committee under Martin Dies of Texas. It's not a new thing, it's through our history, every time there's something that's perceived as a threat."

This list continued as Lewis, from memory, reeled off a roster of wrongs committed against civil liberties and against members of organizations and groups that included immigrants—"Remember Wilson's attorney general arresting thousands of immigrants in the night, shipping them out of the country? Wilson was a terrible president, in civil liberties terms, a disaster.

"You know," he continued, "this country has a violent history, and a lot of it is left-right and seeing the left as a radical revolutionary threat to the stable order. After the war (World War II), why was it? I suppose because the Russians seemed like a threat. They were very powerful, a large country which had sabotaged freedom in Czechoslovakia and seized Hungary and Romania, Yugoslavia a little different, but in essence there were reasons for fear. And then when the Russians got nuclear weapons, that was further reason, much underlying the fear of their power."

Eisenhower, in Lewis' view, shared some of the political guilt in the scourge of McCarthyism. For example, he said, Eisenhower had initiated the government security system in response to the communist scare blowing through the nation like an icy wind from the Cold War.

But though Eisenhower was slow in responding to McCarthy, Lewis said, "he probably was right because he was waiting until he could really grab him, which he did. And, if you remember toward the very end of *Goodnight and Good Luck,* the movie, there's Eisenhower reading off a statement. It's a wonderful statement about the American way, which he really believed in, he really more than once said without naming McCarthy that attacking people without giving them a chance to defend was rotten and not the American way."

The other major domestic crisis of the decade Lewis identified was the race problem that spawned civil rights and civil liberties confrontations and violations from the beginnings of the institution of slavery to well past the 1950s. The nation's race problem has been its single most abhorrent scar, Lewis recalled.

"Millions and millions of American human beings were mistreated, brutalized, discriminated against, killed, for a very long period, from the seventeenth century until Brown (the 1954 U.S. Supreme Court decision that desegregated public schools), and it hasn't ended yet. It got better, much better, nobody should be mistaken about that. I think the modern-day revisionists who say Brown should have been decided the other way are completely nuts. But some bad things go on, we all know that there's still racial discrimination in different parts of the country, but the grip of it on our society, the distorting effect on everybody and everything was so profound for such a long period, there's just nothing like it."

Lewis documented the history of the *Brown versus Board of Education* Supreme Court ruling in *Portrait of a Decade: The Second American Revolution,* a compilation of *New York Times* articles and his own writing and reporting. The book lays out the legal and social history leading up to the historic decision, pointing out that the ruling did not arise from a nation suddenly aware of the injustices against the blacks but that it came out of a legal cauldron that had been boiling for some time. A primary factor behind the decision, though, was the 1953 appointment by Eisenhower of Earl Warren to replace Chief U.S. Supreme Court Justice Fred M. Vinson, who had died.

This change, Lewis wrote,

> made a real difference in the way *Brown v. Board of Education* looks to history. Chief Justice Vinson's inclination was to carry on the approach of the Texas Law School case, further tightening up the standard of equality within the separate-but-equal doctrine. In short, he thought it was not the time to challenge segregation *per se;* the most he was likely to have done was to say that the Negro pupils here did not have real equality. The indications were that he might have carried one or more of his colleagues with him, and there is reason to believe that at least two members of the Court were inclined to put the whole issue to Congress . . .
>
> Unanimity was the most striking aspect of the actual decision when it came down on May 17, 1954. Chief Justice Warren delivered the opinion; there was no dissent, not even a separate concurrence.[22]

In that decision, in which Warren and the justices concluded "that in the field of public education the doctrine of 'separate but equal' has no place," the chief justice wrote:

> Today, education is perhaps the most important function of state and local governments. . . . In these days, it is doubtful that any child may reasonably be expected to succeed in life if he is denied the opportunity of an education. Such an opportunity, where the state has undertaken to provide it, is a right which must be made available to all on equal terms.[23]

But real change in the nation's schools was slow to come. Lewis' colleague at the *Times,* George Barrett, described in an excerpt from the book the events in Clinton, Tennessee in September 1956.

Late one Friday night in August, Barrett wrote, a stranger in town sat down at a telephone booth in a local drug store and began telephoning local residents saying: "The niggers got to be pulled out of the high school. We're calling a meeting—you'd better come." That call initiated a period of community terror, despite what Barrett described as the intention of community leaders "to guarantee a smooth and peaceful transition to school integration."

Barrett described the stranger, a man named John Kasper, a 26-year-old New Jersey resident, who organized the "Seaboard White Citizens Council" and began staging public demonstrations, including prayer meetings, "against the Negro." On Monday, August 27, 12 black teenagers entered Clinton High School despite Kasper's telephone calls to white parents warning against allowing their children to attend the same school as blacks. A federal district judge enjoined Kasper from interfering with court-ordered desegregation, but on Saturday night a mob of 3,000 "shrieking, laughing, cursing, fun-making, blood-hunting men and women and youngsters" gathered at the courthouse, "banging on one Negro's car as he turned accidentally into Main Street, slashing his tires, then suddenly putting friendly shoulders to the car to help him get it started again."

As the riot fumed downtown, a group of citizens organized a small, armed band and went into town to confront the mob. Battle loomed. A local lawyer tossed four tear-gas grenades into the crowd, and then 110 state highway patrolmen arrived at the scene, dispersing the rioters. The National Guard came to town the next day.

"'What happened to us is going to happen to a lot of communities when they try to integrate,'" one resident told Barrett. "'Some towns down here are going to make mistakes that we—maybe just by accident—didn't make, and they are going to lose law and order, and back down before the mob.'"

"If Clinton has demonstrated any lesson that can be learned by other states also accepting the challenge of integration," Barrett wrote,

> that lesson is: Keep a microscopic eye and strong arm on the professional agitator, and mobilize the responsible elements of the community, once the courts have made their decision, to stand up firmly to the race haters. Communities like Clinton have shown that a few resolute civic leaders can have much more combined strength than they may suspect.[24]

Events in Clinton also signaled that despite the efforts of some to repel the looming civil rights movement, it had arrived, and it would take in more than the rights of black children to be educated in desegregated classrooms. It would also be about sipping coffee at a lunch counter and easing into an empty bus seat up front by the driver instead of in the rear.

The bus seat issue, one of the more notorious battles of the civil rights movement, had occurred the previous year. Lewis' book recounts the narrative of 43-year-old Montgomery, Alabama seamstress Rosa Parks' defiance of local segregation laws when she refused to give up her bus seat to a white man on December 1, 1955. She was ordered to trial, and the incident sparked a bus boycott by black riders, who comprised most of the city bus system's riders—and this largely peaceful movement spawned the rise to national notoriety of its young leader, the Rev. Dr. Martin Luther King, Jr.

In February of the following year, King and about a hundred of his supporters were indicted, charged with conducting an illegal boycott, sparking a meeting the following night described in Lewis' book by *New York Times* reporter Wayne Phillips.

One after the other, indicted Negro leaders took the rostrum in a crowded Baptist church tonight to urge their followers to shun the city's buses and "walk with God."

More than two thousand Negroes filled the church from basement to balcony and overflowed into the street. They chanted and sang; they shouted and prayed; they collapsed in the aisles and they sweltered in an eighty-five-degree heat. They pledged themselves again and again to "passive resistance." Under this banner they have carried on for eighty days a stubborn boycott of the city's buses. The boycott has brought criminal charges against Negro leaders; and tomorrow those arrested are to be arraigned in Circuit Court. The Negroes have been called on to stage at that time a "prayer pilgrimage day"—to give up the use of automobiles and taxis and walk the streets in protest.[25]

King was convicted in March, fined $500, and ordered to pay another $500 in court costs. He refused to pay and was sentenced to a year and a day in jail instead, after which the reverend agreed to pay a total of $500 and the other cases were dropped, Lewis wrote. Following a series of legal battles, and with the boycott continuing, the U.S. Supreme Court, citing the Brown case, unanimously struck down bus segregation as a violation of the U.S. Constitution. The ruling ended the bus boycott, as reported by the Associated Press in a dispatch filed from Montgomery on December 20.

Dr. Martin Luther King, Jr., urged the gathering to patronize the buses but warned against violence. "This is a time when we must evince calm dignity and wise restraint," Dr. King pleaded. "Emotions must not run wild. . . . If we become victimized with violent intents, we will have walked in vain and our twelve months of glorious dignity will be transformed into an eve of gloomy catastrophe."[26]

Lewis' book includes the following summary of the Montgomery event by the *Times'* Phillips, citing the non-violent method of protest that King had adopted from Indian leader Mahatma Gandhi:

By emphasizing the Christian virtue of "love thine enemy," the boycott was made a mass movement of passive resistance—though it took months for the Gandhi similarity to be recognized. And by preaching the protests in their churches and mass meetings they gave it the dynamism of a religious crusade, bringing to bear the strongest emotional force in the Negro community.[27]

Still, the battle waged by white supremacists against the basic rights of black citizens persisted. One of the uglier episodes of the 1950s occurred in Little Rock, Arkansas, a community that Lewis described in his book as a "city of the New South, a middle class, moderate town with an enlightened mayor (Woodrow Wilson Mann), congressman (Brooks Hays) and newspaper (the Arkansas *Gazette,* edited by Harry Ashmore)." The state, Lewis wrote, already had integrated education at the university level, "and Governor Orval Faubus had never been a race-baiter; indeed, his election had been considered a liberal victory. The federal courts had approved a desegregation plan, it was to begin with the senior high schools in the fall of 1957—specifically, with the admission of a few Negro children to Central High School on Tuesday, September 3, 1957."[28]

Nonetheless, the night before school began, the governor announced on television that carrying out the ordered integration would be impossible the next day and said he was ordering National Guardsmen to the school to act "not as segregationists or integrationists but as soldiers."

"The Guardsmen," Lewis wrote, "acted as soldiers on the side of segregation. They were there the next morning, two hundred and seventy of them, and on the advice of the School Board no Negro child appeared." And when nine black students tried to attend the following morning, a waiting crowd greeted them, and a National Guardsman barred the door.[29]

The governor's challenge to the federal government brought a slow response from the Eisenhower administration, Lewis wrote, prompting an initial comment from the president that "you cannot change people's hearts merely by laws" but a stronger warning to the governor the next day: "The only assurance I can give you is that the federal Constitution will be upheld by me by every legal means at my command." This was followed by legal proceedings that included the government asking a federal judge to enjoin the governor from interfering with the school's integration. Still, the Eisenhower administration balked at answering force with force.

"It is all very well to discover a statute that would allow the President to send an army into Little Rock," Lewis quoted a government dispatch to the *New York Times.* "But no responsible person in or out of government thinks this would advance peaceful acceptance of the Supreme Court decision in the South. The one certainty about the Administration's plans is that there is no desire for an open test of strength."[30]

The situation lasted for several more days, heading toward violent mob confrontation after the federal judge granted the government's request for an injunction and the school was opened a couple of weeks later. The National Guard was gone, replaced by a crowd of "hysterical" townsfolk who forced the nine black children away from the school, prompting the local police to intervene. Finally, three weeks after the crisis had begun, the president ordered federal troops to the scene.

"For the first time since Reconstruction, federal troops were sent into the South to protect the rights of Negroes," Lewis wrote. "Eisenhower ordered one thousand paratroopers to Little Rock and placed ten thousand members of the Arkansas National Guard on federal service to put down the mob."[31]

On September 25, the nine black school children entered Central High School, under the supervision of federal troops, which stayed on the scene for the remainder of the school year. This case prompted yet more U.S. Supreme Court deliberation, in response to a lower federal court decision granting the Little Rock school board a two-and-one-half-year suspension of the integration plan because of community resistance.

Meeting in special session on August 28, 1958, the court heard the arguments and then issued its ruling on September 29, just over a year after the initial encounter, rejecting the suspension of the desegregation plan. "Law and order are not here to be preserved by depriving the Negro children of their constitutional rights," said the court opinion.[32]

So, school and bus desegregation did not come to this country easily, despite court rulings and presidential orders upholding them. The rulings and orders obviously did not end the bigotry, the hatred, or the violence. For example, during the year following the Brown decision, Lewis reported in his book three instances of lynchings of blacks in Mississippi—"the first in this country since 1951. One victim was a fourteen-year-old Negro boy, Emmett Till, who had been accused of whistling at a white woman."

The book goes on to describe another Mississippi lynching, in 1959, of a 23-year-old man, Mack Charles Parker, who had been accused of raping a white woman. The case became stymied in the local court system, with a judge in his charge to the jury blaming the recent Supreme Court rulings for the lynching.

"He referred to the Court as that 'board of sociology, sitting in Washington, garbed in judicial robes,'" wrote Lewis about a case he described as throwing "unusual light on the quality of Mississippi justice." According to Lewis' report, U.S. Attorney General William P. Rogers called the case "a travesty on justice . . . flagrant and calculated." Rogers took the case to a federal grand jury, but with the same result. "On January 14, 1960, the jurors said they were 'unable to arrive at any true bill,' having found no 'basis for prosecution in the case.'"[33]

Clearly, much work remained on the nation's civil rights front as the 1950s ended. But the decade had experienced some progress. The Brown decision, Lewis would recall a half century later, told black Americans in the South "that law, morals and the Constitution were on their side, so they could go into battle with the cross of Jesus going on before, and they did. The kids, the sit-in students, that was very soon after Brown, the ones who sat in at lunch counters, it wasn't school segregation, it was a completely different subject, the right to eat at a counter at Woolworth's, literally, Woolworth's, but they were inspired by it, and I have no doubt that Brown was absolutely fundamental in empowering King, everything. Dr. King wasn't school desegregation, but he was the voice."

Asked what might have happened in the country without the ruling, Lewis said "something would have happened eventually, because the notion that this country could go on massively, and it's a very large part of the country, like 40 percent of the public school children in the country, that could not go on indefinitely."

Despite his appointment of Warren to the court, Eisenhower did not endorse the justices' decision, Lewis said.

"He didn't believe in it, didn't agree with it, thought the Supreme Court was wrong. That's what I think. I cite in the book the fact that he changed the government's brief in the Brown case, he changed it to write in that—this was the brief for the second Brown decision, the brief on implementation—he added it should be slow not only because of the difficulties but because after all the law had approved it for so long, and I think that was expressing his view (that) it shouldn't have been changed or, if changed, by legislation. But that would have taken how many more years before a Southern filibuster could be overcome? People forget, you couldn't change things by legislation. It was a nice idea, but it wasn't going to happen."

But while Lewis continues to believe that the race issue was one of Eisenhower's weaknesses, he credits the former president for his leadership in other areas, including exercising restraint in the face of Soviet aggression in Europe. Asked, for example, if the Soviet quashing of the 1956 Hungarian uprising against Soviet rule might have fueled McCarthy's anticommunist scare at home, he said yes, "and yet, there's an irony when you say that. People on the extreme right, not just McCarthy but much broader than McCarthy, had been denouncing Eisenhower for being, uh, what was the phrase at the time, détente, for détente with the Soviet Union and saying we should be more aggressive and prepared to take military action to push them back. But when the moment came, of course we didn't have military action. Eisenhower would have no more dreamt of sending troops into Hungary than he would have dreamt of dropping out of a dirigible. It was crazy, and the policy ideas were crazy. You couldn't do that. We were in a nuclear standoff. You couldn't invade countries in the Soviet bloc. So there is a certain irony in it. Their (the right-wing voices) policy proved to be a paper tiger, and yet, as you say, they quite rightly said this demonstrates what a lousy, regressive country the Soviet Union is and how you can't trust communism."

The Eisenhower legacy, Lewis said, was peace.

"Like many others, I have a much higher regard for Eisenhower in retrospect than I did at the time. I think I probably went to every Eisenhower press conference, or most of them, and I thought of him as bumbling, unprepared, often uninformed and very bad on race for reasons already discussed.

"Much of that time I was writing for a national paper," he continued, "and I would go to the press conference and then run out of the room to a telephone and just from notes, my hand-written notes, because this took place in the Indian Treaty Room in the Executive Office Building, there were no computers, there were no recorders, there was nothing, just your little pad of paper. I would dictate a top for the second edition every day, and my effort was to make something meaningful out of the often disjointed and garbled remarks of Eisenhower. Then when I later read the transcript, I thought 'gee, I really improved him a little.' But now that I look back on it, I've come to believe the pro-Eisenhower critics who say that underneath this sort of mangled syntax he really knew what he was doing and was avoiding provocative remarks, and so I respect that. I continue to think that he missed the boat on race."

Eisenhower's predecessor, Harry S Truman, earned much higher marks from the columnist on the race issue coming into the decade: "The ending of segregation in the armed forces and the endorsement of civil rights legislation. It didn't pass then, but it was very important to get the presidency behind it."

But the country was ready to move in a different direction after Truman, Lewis said.

"Democrats had been in power since 1933, nearly twenty years," he said, citing Eisenhower's status as a war hero and the nation's desire to "get past the stringencies of the war and go back to normalcy, as Harding said. Eisenhower didn't use that term. Actually, the irony of that is that it wasn't that different. In many ways, despite the sense of change because of the long time the Democrats were in, there wasn't that big a change. It wasn't like George W. Bush after Clinton. Foreign policy was unchanged, absolutely unchanged. You have Eisenhower dedicated to NATO and the alliance, all the things Truman had set up Eisenhower was a hundred percent for; he'd been a NATO commander, and the one thing that changed was simply that he was able to end the Korean War. I think by being a new broom he was much more effective in ending that war, as I think another president would be in ending the Iraq war, difficult as that is. The foreign policy didn't change and domestic policy didn't change that much; it was more conservative, but it was nothing like the total radicalization of policy under George W. Bush. It was a different age, a less partisan age."

It was a difficult decade all-in-all, Lewis said, because of issues that included the racial confrontations, the Cold War, the domestic red scare, and the Korean War.

"The Korean War was a pretty bloody war," he said. "Probably a necessary war, unlike the present one (Iraq). We tend to be a bit nostalgic about the past, and anything that's forty years old, many of the rough edges have worn off. But it certainly wasn't a wonderful time for the blacks, or the black population. They had a rough time. It was a much more racist country, much more anti-Semitic, it seemed doubtful that a Catholic would be elected president; there was one Catholic on the Supreme Court when I started noticing it, today there are a majority of Catholics on the Supreme Court and nobody cares. So I don't think it was perfect by any means. It was an earlier day, and it had some qualities to recommend it, but I don't think it was wonderful."

But the nation ended the decade as a better place, Lewis said. "Probably, yes, but thanks in substantial part to the Supreme Court of the United States."

* * * *

We had been an isolationist country and had no idea of what we would become in the world, a major, major superpower. And certainly all the publishers all thought that the GIs who went in as buck privates, even with college educations, would come out and want to come back to $24-a-week jobs in the news business, and they came back as colonels, majors, and they had learned about everything, an explosion of new ideas and everything in technology had come out of the war. So it was a very exciting time, and you could see America just growing and becoming really giant.

—Helen Thomas

Helen Thomas thought the comment was off the record when she complained to a reporter from the *Daily Breeze* of Torrance, California, about President George W. Bush.

"He is the worst president in all of American history," Thomas was quoted in the 2003 remark that made the veteran United Press International correspondent a news figure instead of a news reporter. Indeed, when she was

Helen Thomas. © King Features. Used by permission.

late for an interview appointment with this author in the summer of 2006, it was because she was being interviewed by a broadcast journalist in her Washington, D.C., office regarding the fallout from her comment about the president.

Earlier that year, during a March interview with Cable News Network's Wolf Blitzer on the same subject, in which she conceded that she had "sort of" apologized to the president for the remark, she resumed her criticism of the president. She accused the Bush administration of "encouraging all of the horror that's going on" in Iraq following the U.S. invasion of that country. "In this case, in the case of the president and his cohorts, I think they have really spread war throughout the Middle East. They have really encouraged all of the horror that's going on. We have killed so many innocent people."[34]

During her 2006 interview with this author, asked if she regretted her "worst president" comment, she chuckled and then said no. She said she couldn't take back words that never should have been printed, but: "I do think that there's a lot of room for improvement in this administration in terms of, when you reach the top of the mark, there ain't no other place to go; it seems to me, you'd want to do the right thing. A president, everything is done for them, what else do you need except to do the right thing? I mean, to not even be able to explain why you've been in a war after three years? Is it because the explanation is not acceptable?"

All fair game for a straight-news-reporter-turned-columnist, who revealed in a 2002 speech at MIT that after censoring herself "for 50 years when I was a reporter," she now wakes up as a columnist and asks herself: "Who do I hate today?" She added, in comments that served as a warning of her looming all-out battle with the Bush administration that would cost her her longtime front-row seat at presidential press conferences: "I have never covered a president who actually wanted to go to war. Bush's policy of pre-emptive war is immoral—such a policy would legitimize Pearl Harbor. It's as if they learned none of the lessons from Vietnam."[35]

And it was all quite a change in attitude toward the presidency from a columnist/correspondent who would remember the first president she had covered far more fondly. "I'll never forget the Kennedy inauguration, the excitement, the new life, the New Frontier, the great hopes," she recalled that summer of 2006. "He gave us hope."

Unlike the state of war with Iraq during the latter days of Thomas' career, the United States was at peace when she was born in Kentucky on the fourth day of August 1920. Warren Harding was promising a return to normalcy if U.S. voters would send him to the White House; indeed, all was normal in Winchester, Kentucky, on that humid Wednesday—partly cloudy skies were forecast for that night, and rain was probable for Thursday. But while the nation was at peace, her hometown *Winchester Sun* reported on its front page that day ominous tidings of European events that would foreshadow the foreign policy debates that would dominate much of Thomas' career: the communist menace. The *Winchester Sun* documented the bloody military engagement between Soviet Russia and the Second Polish Republic in the Russo-Polish War, as Lenin tried to expand the Bolshevik revolution into neighboring states in his desire to reclaim Poland and other lands lost to Germany in World War I.

"MUST EVACUATE WARSAW IN NEXT THREE DAYS SAID," proclaimed the headline. "According to Military Experts Capital Must be Moved in Short Time."

The story, by the Associated Press, told U.S. readers that British and French military experts believed the Polish capital must be evacuated and government headquarters moved, "probably to Crakow." According to the dispatch, "Russians now are thirty miles from Warsaw."[36]

By mid-August, however, the Polish forces surprisingly won the Battle of Warsaw. Hostilities ended with the signing of the Peace of Riga treaty in March 1921,[37] and all was well on the anticommunist front for the time being. Nonetheless, the war, though relatively brief, was eyed warily by a U.S. populace concerned over the revolution in Russia and its possible effects on Europe and the rest of the globe—even in the small rural community of Winchester.

Pressing domestic issues concerned the nation as it entered the Roaring Twenties and a decade of Republican Party rule after voters had spurned the policies of wartime president Woodrow Wilson. Other stories of the *Winchester Sun*'s front page that day were of the economy, agriculture, and booze—specifically, the lack thereof, thanks to prohibition. The headlines announced that heavy selling had brought the price of wheat down by 14½ cents, United Mine Workers President John Lewis ordered 3,400 Kansas miners to end their strike and return to work, and a platform submitted to state Democratic officials sought modification of the Volstead Prohibition Enforcement Act.

Thomas was not long for this Kentucky burg, though. Thomas's family moved to Detroit in 1924, and it was there, at the age of 12, that she first told a family friend of her intentions to be a reporter. "I wanted to be a great one," she remembered in her autobiography 67 years later. "It's a goal I still aspire to."[38]

The thrill of a byline in her high school newspaper confirmed her decision. "I was a sophomore at Eastern High School in Detroit and my English teacher liked a story I'd written and had it published in the school newspaper, *The Indian*," Thomas wrote in *Front Row at the White House: My Life and Times*. "Seeing my byline for the first time was an ego-swelling event, and soon afterward I joined the staff of the paper. I loved the ambience, the collegiality and the just plain fun of putting out the weekly. Printer's ink was in my veins, I decided, and I became dedicated to the proposition that this was the life for me."[39]

Thomas stayed in Detroit to earn her English degree at Wayne University and wrote for the college newspaper, *The Daily Collegian,* before succumbing after graduation in 1942 to the lure of Washington, D.C., a reporter's city, during World War II. "With the United States fully engaged in the war, I decided Washington was the only place I wanted to be."[40]

Following a stint as a hostess in a downtown restaurant, Thomas was hired by Scripps-Howard's *Washington Daily News* as a copy girl earning $17.50 a week. Her responsibilities included "fetching coffee for the editors in the morning; sometimes I even made the coffee. But I guess I would have swept the floors if they told me to. As far as I was concerned, I was working in journalism."

Female reporters in those days, Thomas wrote, "more often than not were relegated to the society pages." But, she added, they "were beginning to be moved into news beats as more and more men were drafted. After a few months I too was 'promoted' to cub reporter, assigned to cover local news."[41]

> Being in a newsroom was like having my every dream as a student come true. Watching great newsmen and newswomen perform under deadline pressure with the presses rolling was a heady experience. Listening to the headline writers argue over the right word was bracing.[42]

At the age of 22, Thomas had arrived in 1942 at the political capital of the nation as a reporter and, with the serendipitous timing of the war, as a female reporter covering traditionally male beats. A year later, with the recommendation of *Daily News* managing editor Aubrey Graves, Thomas joined the reporting staff of the United Press (later United Press International), earning $24 a week. The job would last 57 years and would include coverage of the FBI, Capitol Hill and, in 1961, the White House. She was named the first female wire service White House bureau chief in 1974, a post she held until her resignation in 2000, following the acquisition of UPI by News World Communications. She then became a columnist for King Features Syndicate.

Washington, D.C. in 1943 was still the city of President Franklin D. Roosevelt, who was in the midst of the second major crisis of his four-term presidency: fighting the Nazis in Europe and the Japanese in the Pacific in World War II—a war that many credit with helping the United States overcome the first big crisis of the Roosevelt years, the Great Depression. But the war also brought depression-like sacrifices. That year, the Roosevelt administration ordered the rationing of canned food, meat, fat, cheese, and shoes; the nation undertook a massive recycling campaign of rubber, metal, silk, nylon, tin cans, and fat.[43] Women were making progress in other fronts that year. Congress approved the establishment of a female division of the U.S. Marines; this followed the civil conscription of women into the German army. Congress also authorized the withholding of federal income taxes from salaries and wages by employers. The federal government took over the operation of soft coal mines after striking miners refused back-to-work orders. At the end of the year, to avoid a railroad strike, Roosevelt ordered the seizure of the nation's railroads by the federal government. Gas rationing began at year's end.

Artistic developments also gained some headlines in 1943. Pablo Picasso used a bicycle seat and handlebars to fashion *Bull's Head* while his contemporaries Jackson Pollock painted *The She Wolf,* Henry Moore sculpted *Madonna and Child,* and Arshile Gorky painted *Garden in Sochi.* French existentialist Albert Camus published *The Myth of Sisyphus;* his existential comrade Jean-Paul Sartre published *Being and Nothingness,* and his play *The Flies* had its debut in Paris. German writer Herman Hesse published *The Glass Bead Game;* American writer Ayn Rand published *The Fountainhead;* U.S. novelist William Saroyan published *The Human Comedy;* and American journalist Walter Lippmann published *Foreign Policy: Shield of the Republic.*

In the movie houses, Lassie, played by the male dog Pal, came home in a film starring Roddy McDowell and Elizabeth Taylor while Joseph Cotton and Teresa Wright starred in Alfred Hitchcock's *Shadow of a Doubt. For Whom the Bell Tolls,* adapted from Ernest Hemingway's novel, opened in the United States and starred Gary Cooper and Ingrid Bergman.

But the dominant story was war. Roosevelt and British Prime Minister Winston Churchill met in Casablanca in January, where they agreed to step up the bombing of Germany and to invade Sicily. They called for the unconditional surrender of the Axis powers; at the end of the month, the German 6th Army surrendered to the armies of the Soviet Union at Stalingrad, the Japanese gave up organized resistance to U.S. forces on Guadalcanal in February, British and U.S. forces began 24-hour bombing of Germany later that month, and in March, U.S. bombers defeated the Japanese navy and air force in the Battle of the Bismark Sea, followed by the retaking in May of the island of Attu from the Japanese. In July, U.S. and British forces landed in German-occupied Sicily, and Hitler ordered the cessation of offensive efforts on the eastern front. That August, Roosevelt and Churchill, meeting in Quebec, agreed to defeat Germany before Japan and to plan for a May 1944 invasion of France. The collapse of the Axis continued in September with the signing of an armistice between the Allies and the Italian government of Marshal Pietro Badoglio, who succeeded the fascist dictator Benito Mussolini. In November, Roosevelt and Churchill informed Soviet leader Joseph Stalin of the plan to invade France the following year, a move that would be the beginning of the final march toward the defeat of the German army.

With the allied victory came a new mood in America as the 1950s began. Thomas remembered in her office more than 50 years later an upbeat change in the psyche of the nation.

"I think it was just so glad the war was over," she said, "that they could get on with their lives. No one in this country had any concept of the growing pains, of what we would become after World War II. We had been an isolationist country and had no idea of what we would become in the world, a major, major superpower. And certainly all the publishers all thought that the GIs who went in as buck privates, even with college educations, would come out and want to come back to $24-a-week jobs in the news business, and they came back as colonels, majors, and they had learned about everything, an explosion of new ideas and everything in technology had come out of the war. So it was a very exciting time, and you could see America just growing and becoming really giant."

But just five years after the United States and its allies achieved military victory against the Axis powers, two new wars were on, one hot, one cold, both lasting for decades and both featuring a new enemy: communism.

The Korean War, begun June 25, 1950, until hostilities were suspended with a cease-fire on July 27, 1953, officially has not ended yet; a state of armistice continues as this book is written. The war, technically between North and South Korea, was a proxy battle between the communist People's Republic of China, with technical support and arms assistance from the Soviet Union, and the West, primarily the United States.

Much as the politics of the Vietnam War were to trouble Presidents Lyndon Johnson (playing a key role in his decision not to seek re-election) and Richard Nixon in the 1960s and early 1970s, the Korean War and differences over how to fight it dogged President Harry Truman, who had brought a successful end to World War II. In particular, Truman differed with General Douglas MacArthur, commander of the United Nations forces in the Korean conflict, over whether to expand the war into a larger military confrontation with Communist China.

MacArthur initially had permission from the brass to carry the war into North Korea as far as the Yalu River, which formed the border between Communist China and North Korea, prompting Chinese intervention in the war and forcing a fallback of UN forces. The general sought permission to bomb Chinese bases in Manchuria, which Truman refused.

Following a successful amphibious maneuver at Inchon in September 1950, MacArthur pursued retreating North Korean forces all the way to the Yalu. Washington and UN backers of the American campaign warned against expanding the war. MacArthur, whose proposed strategy in the Korean War included the use of nuclear weapons, publicly criticized Truman's stance on the war. The president subsequently removed MacArthur from command, a decision that sparked political furor in Washington.

"New U.S.-UN moves to seek an end of the Korean War are expected to follow the discharge of Gen Douglas MacArthur," reported Thomas' United Press agency on April 11, 1951. "President Truman early today dismissed the General of the Army from all Far East commands on charges of failing to support the U.S. and UN policy."

It was the end of a long military career that included service in World War I and World War II, followed by the general's being placed in charge of the occupation of Japan following World War II.

"The dismissal paved the way for the revival of an important policy statement expressing UN willingness to seek a cease-fire and the statement is expected to be made in the near future by Mr. Truman in the name of the UN allies," continued the United Press dispatch. "Removal of Gen. MacArthur was a key part of the swiftly developing strategy. Allied unity in the Korean war had been headed for the rocks before the President discharged Gen. MacArthur. The General's criticism of policy-handling of the war had struck fear in the 13 other nations fighting under the UN banner that the General wanted to extend the war to China."[44]

A story the same day datelined Tokyo characterized MacArthur's headquarters as "stunned" and quoted one GI as calling Truman's decision a "low, God-damned blow."

"Informed sources said afterwards that Gen. MacArthur reiterated to Mr. [U.S. Army Secretary Frank] Pace his previous requests for more U.S. and other United Nations troops and for a freer hand in fighting the Chinese Reds—generally interpreted as a request to strike at China proper at least by sea and air."[45]

Meanwhile, in Washington, the *Washington Daily News* reported talk of impeachment.

"Angry Republicans today raised threats of impeachment against President Truman—and possibly Secretary of State Dean Acheson—within hours after the President fired Gen. Douglas MacArthur from his Far Easter commands," reported the newspaper. According to the report, House Republican Leader Joseph W. Martin Jr. emerged from a secret meeting, involving House and Senate Republican leaders speaking by trans-Atlantic telephone with MacArthur, to demand a congressional investigation into Truman's foreign policy. Martin also announced that the conference attendees agreed "that the Congress should have the complete views of Gen. MacArthur and he should be invited to return for that purpose forthwith.

"In addition, the question of possible impeachment was discussed."

Some key Democrats, however, including House Speaker Sam Rayburn, rallied behind Truman. MacArthur, Rayburn told reporters, "in his insubordination was not being helpful" to the administration's and the UN's efforts on behalf of peace.[46]

Truman survived the congressional uprising, and, following the cease-fire in Korea, the nation relaxed into its post-World War II peace mode under the Dwight Eisenhower administration, until Middle East turmoil sparked a U.S. military undertaking in that historically troubled region. The president in 1958 decided to send Marines to Lebanon, in support of the pro-Western Lebanese government of Christian President Camille Chamoun five years after the United States orchestrated a successful coup that installed a new government in Iran under the rule of Shah Mohammad Reza Pahlavi. Eisenhower's decision followed a Muslim rebellion in Iraq that brought about the overthrow of a pro-Western government there. The UPI reported Soviet Union condemnation of the Lebanese operation.

"President Eisenhower announced today that more than 5000 U.S. Marines have landed in Lebanon to protect 2500 American lives and help defend that revolt torn land against aggression," announced the lead paragraph of the story, carried by the *Washington Daily News,* on the Middle East crisis. While assuring the American public and the world that the troops had not been sent "as any act of war," Eisenhower "linked the U.S. action directly to the bloody overthrow of the Iraq government by pro-Nasser rebels in Baghdad."[47]

Democratic leaders backed the Republican president's decision, presenting a unified political stance to the international community.

"Senate Democratic Leader Lyndon B. Johnson said 'Americans will certainly unite when the security of the free world is imperiled,'" the report continued. "House Democratic Leader John W. McCormack said 'there was no other course to take but a course of appeasement.'"[48]

The report also relayed speculation that American troops might continue on into Jordan. "The U.S. position is that Jordan is part of the Arab Union with Iraq, and that a member of the United Nations has a right under the charter to defend itself and to call on its friends for help.

"King Hussein of Jordan has assumed full powers in the Arab Union in the absence of his cousin, Iraqi King Feisal. Reportedly, King Hussein has called on the U.S. for military assistance as has Lebanese President Camille Chamoun."

The dispatch continued: "The heads of state of Iran, Pakistan and Turkey met secretly in Ankara, Turkey to consider action in support of King Feisal of Iraq. Military action was considered a possibility by the three surviving members of the pact."[49]

The Soviets, meanwhile, asked the United National Security Council "to order them out immediately," the UPI reported. "Soviet Ambassador Arkady A. Sobolev, who sought to delay today's crucial Council meeting until the revolutionary Iraq regime could get a representative here, denounced President Eisenhower's action in sending the landing parties into Lebanon."[50]

American troops left the region three months later. But the Cold War also played out in the Western Hemisphere during the decade, spurring involvement by the Eisenhower administration in Latin America, in the form of a CIA-backed coup of the democratically elected government of Guatemala in 1954. The operation, prompted by U.S. fears that the policies of Guatemalan President Jacobo Arbenz Guzman were communist-backed, foreshadowed U.S. foreign adventurism that would last the rest of the century and spill into the current one, often involving Middle Eastern and Latin American countries.

Many of these foreign military and intelligence operations were aimed at countering the Soviet and communist threat that fostered a pervasive fear in the nation. The menace was personified by Soviet leader Nikita Khrushchev, a blustery, bald-headed Communist Party veteran known for histrionic scenes of threat and anger. Khrushchev displayed this famous temper in the winter of 1956 when he told a group of Western diplomats in Moscow that "we will bury you."

"Western envoys walked out on Communist Party Leader Nikita S. Khrushchev last night for the second time in two days when he gave them another tongue lashing and said God would be on the communist side if 'we believed in the existence of God,'" the United Press reported on November 19. "'We will bury you,' Khrushchev told the Western diplomats at a reception at the Polish Embassy to mark the signing of a Soviet-Polish agreement giving Poland the right to pursue an independent course of communism.

"'If you do not like us,' the vodka-drinking Khrushchev told the American, British and other envoys, 'do not accept our invitations, and do not invite us to yours.'

"The red-faced Khrushchev delivered his bitter tirade at a reception given for Polish communist-leader Wladyslaw Gomulka," the report continued. "'Things are going very well with us. If we believed in the existence of God we would thank him for it.'"[51]

Three years later, the Soviet leader met U.S. Vice President Richard Nixon at the July opening of the American National Exhibition in Moscow. There, the two engaged in what would become known as the "kitchen debate."

"Vice President Richard M. Nixon and Premier Nikita Khrushchev clashed head-on today in a heated informal debate climaxed by Khrushchev's charge that Mr. Nixon was trying to threaten him," UPI reported. "'We will answer your threats with threats,' Khrushchev stormed in an exchange watched by a crowd of startled spectators as the two men toured the American Exhibition here."

The debate became more heated and ominous; the UPI offered a verbal-blow-by-verbal-blow account.

"In one of the more bitter exchanges, Khrushchev warned that 'we have means at our disposal which can have very bad consequences'—an apparent reference to Russia's nuclear weapons.

"'We have too,' Mr. Nixon retorted.

"'But ours are better. If you want to compete,' Khrushchev shot back belligerently."

The debate wound down with accusations regarding how the argument began.

"Again Mr. Nixon said he did not quite understand how the conversation had shifted so quickly to such hard terms.

"Khrushchev answered, 'You started it. You wanted indirectly to threaten me.'

"In spite of the sharp temper of the exchanges, Khrushchev said, 'We want peace and friendship with America and all other nations.'

"Mr. Nixon said, 'We also want peace, but I don't think that the cause of peace can be served by reiterating the point you have brought up.'

"Khrushchev replied, 'but you challenged me. Let us argue fairly.'"

The incident ended with Nixon urging in a speech opening the exhibition that the two nations' "great differences" should be "settled at the conference table and not on the battlefield"—an urging that presaged the spirit of détente he would promote during his presidency a decade later.[52]

Americans had valid reason to fear the military might of the Soviet Union, the former ally of the United States in World War II that transformed into the nation's Cold War nemesis in the postwar years. Four years after the United States dropped atomic bombs on Hiroshima and Nagasaki to end World War II, the Soviets tested their first nuclear bomb. Then, in 1955, they exploded a hydrogen bomb; the so-called nuclear club was no longer one of exclusive membership. Equally frightening, though, was the realization that the Soviet Union had devised a means for delivering this awful weaponry to the United States beyond conventional jet bombers, as demonstrated by the launch of the Sputnik satellite.

"Russia has won the race into outer space by launching the first earth satellite and a triumphant Moscow broadcast today hailed the victory as the first stage of projected flights to the moon," the United Press reported on October 5, 1957.

But it was not possible flights to the moon that troubled American observers so much as it was the military implications. The same dispatch reported several paragraphs later that the launch "bolstered Russian claims to be the first to have perfected an intercontinental ballistic missile for it might well have taken such a missile to launch the satellite on its flight around the world every 95 minutes—about 15 times a day."

Beyond the perceived military threat, the launch also brought the Soviet Union a significant public relations victory in the ongoing propaganda battle that marked much of the Cold War. The article concluded: "The United States had done 90 percent of the talking about earth satellites.

"Russia, it turned out, had done 100 percent of the performing."[53]

The Soviet Union about the same time made clear that it would use its military muscle when it deemed such action necessary. Its putdown of the Hungarian Revolution in1956 provided the evidence.

"This is free Hungary's last hour," the *Washington Daily News* front page of November 5, 1956, reported in a story datelined REBEL HEADQUARTERS, SOPRON, Hungary (Sunday afternoon). "Soviet tanks are advancing on this final link with the Western world. All surrounding towns have fallen. The Russians are about 5-½ miles outside the city, converging from the east and south. It is now about 2:55 P.M. At noon they were reported 15 miles away. They are moving slowly, confidently and methodically, cleaning out machine gun nests and capturing resistance leaders in every village along the way."[54]

A day later, the United Press reported that the rebels were hanging on, but barely.

"Hungarian freedom radios went back on the air today after hours of silence with new appeals for aid in the desperate struggle Nationalists still were waging against the conquering Russian army," reported the dispatch. "Fighting still raged in Budapest where Russian artillery on the heights of Buda were reported wiping out nests of freedom fighters in Pest, according to the monitored radio reports."[55]

The sealing of the Iron Curtain around Hungary was reported by the United Press four days later.

"Hungary Communists refused today to admit thru the Austrian border western medical aid into Hungary for bleeding Budapest," the story said. "Communist guards blocked an international Red Cross convoy of 15 trucks carrying food, medical supplies, doctors and nurses. They halted the convoy at the border crossing point at Klingenbach on the road to Sopron."[56]

Americans watched angrily and fearfully as the Soviets squelched the Hungarian democratic uprising, knowing that little could be done, considering the nuclear umbrella that protected the Soviet Union.

The 1950s, though, had their upside. On the medical front, Dr. Jonas E. Salk's polio vaccine had been successfully tested, according to a report by Dr. Thomas Francis Jr., a professor of immunology at the University of Michigan, who had directed a study of the vaccine. The medical community applauded the breakthrough, according to Thomas' wire service.

"The Salk anti-polio vaccine today was pronounced safe and effective," reported the United Press in a story datelined Ann Arbor, Michigan, April 12, 1955. "The long-awaited results, hailed immediately by the American Medical Association as 'one of the greatest events in the history of medicine,' showed the vaccine was 80 to 90 percent effective.

"The vaccine works."[57]

The 1950s also saw what many consider to be the major civil rights story of the era, the court-ordered desegregation of public schools, known legally as the *Brown versus Board of Education of Topeka* decision by the nation's highest court.

"The Supreme Court ruled today in an historic decision that racial segregation in public schools is unconstitutional," reported the *Washington Daily News* on May 17, 1954. "Speaking for a unanimous court, Chief Justice Earl Warren said education must be available to all on an equal basis.

"The decision is probably the most important in United States race relations since the famous Dred Scott decision of 1857, which held that a Negro was not a citizen. The Civil War reversed that decision.

"Because of the wide ramifications of the decision, formulation of specific decrees will be delayed until further arguments have been heard."[58]

As American troops were patrolling South Korean highways in an uneasy armistice and the nation's African Americans were hailing their civil rights victories, American drivers were heading to the suburbs on new superhighways, assisted by the massive construction of roads initiated by Congress and the Eisenhower administration. The president in 1956 signed a highway bill that would cost an estimated $32.9 billion.

"The 13-year construction program includes a 41,000-mile interstate highway network to link every state and most state capitals," the *Washington Daily News* reported in June.[59] The system would link inner cities to suburbs, and the migration of middle-class Americans to the outskirts of their cities was under way.

"I think everyone was seeking their little plot and their little place of their own," Thomas would recall 50 years later. It was a time when Americans wanted to put the sacrifices of World War II behind them. "That was natural, that people thought they were deprived, and rationing, and so forth, and I think when you embark on a time of peace, you retreat to your homes and your communities, to buy your homes and to do things. Things were a lot less expensive, people were glad to settle down and bring the boys home, and you were glad you were alive."

The new highways enabled middle-class office workers and executives to easily motor to downtown jobs and then to return to their manicured green lawns and barbecue patios far removed from the increasingly black neighborhoods of the city proper.

"There was suburbia, and there was a big retreat from the cities where there was a lot of racial conflict," Thomas recalled. The Supreme Court's Brown ruling opening up public schools to minorities was a primary spark of the white flight to the suburbs. It also produced one of Thomas' most vivid memories of the era.

"I suppose something that really struck me indelibly was being the lowest person on the telephone pole, again, a kind of gofer," she recalled of the day of the Brown ruling. "I was sent over to help out the team, they had a real top team there, knowing the decision was going to be handed down, not knowing what the decision was, but that was the most thrilling moment of my life, when they came down the chute, the pneumatic chute, the decision, and the reporter, named Lou Cassels, who later became our religious editor, he pulled it open and called in the flash . . . and I must say that it was a thrilling moment."

She recalled that she had no idea at the time of the impact on the country, "the ripple effect of really, really going after racial discrimination and eliminating this terrible blot. It didn't really eliminate it for years and years, but the impact of that, it was one of the most thrilling moments."

But the war in Korea, the smoldering Cold War, U.S. adventurism abroad—all were troubling backdrops to the domestic tranquility. In retrospect, Thomas said of the first president of that decade, history has judged that Truman acted correctly in his decision to oust MacArthur.

"I thought Truman was right," she said. "I think he had to put MacArthur in his place. MacArthur went to the Yalu River on his own, he had been warned and warned and warned, 'if you go to the Yalu River, the Chinese are coming into the war.'"

But the Korean War was discredited, she said, along with its Asian successor, the Vietnam War. "Both didn't have the real support, the country was split on both wars, there was not the full backing on the Korean War, especially after 1951. Truman had to practically throw in the towel. . . . All we had was an armistice, but we never had a peace treaty."

Nonetheless, Truman's legacy, despite the calls for impeachment, was intact, thanks primarily to the sum of his post-World War II policies, she said: "The Marshall Plan, the Truman Doctrine (a policy announced in 1947 aimed at containment of the Soviet Union), and drawing the line against communism and also saying that our country had to help rebuild Europe, and we did."

The policy of containment adopted by the Truman administration was followed by the more aggressive stance against the Soviets by Eisenhower's Secretary of State, John Foster Dulles, who played a key role in the formation of the Southeast Asia Treaty Organization. The hard line was sometimes a difficult one, as the Hungarian crisis demonstrated. "There was a thought it might touch off a third world war," Thomas said. "It was a very, very disheartening time, and I think that's when we really realized that we really had a strong enemy in terms of the Soviet Union, and that it did have expansionist ends."

Relying on the threat of massive retaliation as a counter, she said, "was dangerous. . . . It stoked up the Cold War. I think that it really put everybody on edge, the constant threat."

Dangerous—and frightening, though Thomas said she was not afraid personally.

"The school kids were told to get under the desks," she recalled, describing the air-raid exercises that U.S. educators conducted in the nation's classrooms during the era. "I think it had an impact all right. Once the Soviet Union got the bomb, it was a transforming event for all of us, for the country, in terms of the way we did things."

The beginning of the space race, she added, was an exciting competition, but "also frightening, because people thought, well, the Russians are ahead of us. It was a very competitive era, and I think it was kind of fraught with danger. And we thought we were going to be beaten."

She spoke the words slowly—"We will bury you"—as she recalled Khrushchev's threat. "It was shocking, it really was. Of course, we buried them, literally. There is no Soviet Union left today."

The meddling by the Eisenhower administration in Latin America, she said, was a mistake.

"I thought it was horrible. Wrong, wrong, wrong. We were deposing democratically elected governments because they were leftist. I thought it was wrong. I think it was very detrimental to us." Noting that the United States had intervened in other nations' affairs "a lot before that," Thomas said such involvements set the stage for the nation's future troubles, particularly in the Western hemisphere. "There were very landmark moments when we built a lot of hatred for ourselves in Latin America when we should have been extending an olive branch and helping them."

Nonetheless, the postwar peace of the Eisenhower years would be the enduring part of his legacy, she said: "World War II, commander in chief, D-Day. As a president, I think having eight years of basic quiet, and of keeping our powder dry."

Eisenhower had been a good president, Thomas said, "on foreign policy. But not domestic policy. Foreign policy, he knew war too well, and he was a man of peace. And he sought peaceful ends. In terms of domestics, he was very pro-business, and he wasn't even strong versus the board of education (the Brown decision) or anything else, and he was very reluctant to send troops to Little Rock" when that state's governor, Orval Faubus, in 1957 ordered the state National Guard to stop black students from enrolling in a city high school.

As the decade ended and Eisenhower steered toward the exit ramp of his presidency, the nation was heading toward a generational change, a new political regime led by a younger chief executive—one who had seen military action during the war but who also represented a rising tide of Americans and political leaders. The election of John F. Kennedy brought an end to the decade of Eisenhower's peace; but it also saw the emergence of the nation as an international superpower and the stoking of a Cold War that would last for another three decades. This transition from the Republican Eisenhower administration to the Democratic reign of the Kennedy team, besides marking a change in national direction, also took Thomas down a new journalistic path in her assignment to the White House.

"I was forty years old and beginning what has become my life's work: covering the presidency," Thomas wrote in her autobiography. "I think Merriman Smith—'Smitty' to all—and Al [Spivak] knew, as did the UPI brass, that covering the Kennedys would be a seven-days-a-week, twenty-four-hours-a-day proposition. It seemed that the nation and the world were captivated by this group of young firebrands who were going to change the world."[60]

She wrote in her autobiography of her first encounter with the senator whose presidency would mark the beginning of her long career of covering U.S. presidents for United Press International. It was an unremarkable meeting during a remarkable time involving two remarkable people: a president who would represent a new generation and style of American leadership and a reporter who would represent the emerging female journalist on the American media stage.

She recalled meeting Kennedy as the two were departing a party at the Pakistan embassy during the 1950s. The "young senator from Massachusetts offered me a ride home," she wrote. "He was pleasant and charming and friendly enough, and we made small talk. He dropped me off at my apartment, and the next day, my friend Eleni Epstein called and asked for my assessment.

"'He's kind of dull,' I told her. What *was* I thinking?

"After the Kennedy victory, the White House was where I wanted to be. When I think of the battles endured at the press club, getting to cover the White House was easy. I just started showing up every day, and to their credit and my gratitude, UPI's White House bureau chief Merriman Smith and his colleague Al Spivak never turned me away."[61]

The nation at the end of the decade, Thomas recalled, "was better in the sense of we knew the possibilities of what we could be. We were growing, but I think we didn't have any concept of what we would become. It was very defensive, and everything was containment. Trying to contain the Soviet Union was the whole motivation.

"I think we were ready for a change, certainly when Kennedy came in. I think we had had too much of Eisenhower, it was a pretty passive society. I think the younger generation wanted to move, change."

NOTES

1. "Anthony Lewis, 'Risk' Fired by Navy Asks Public to Help," *Washington Daily News,* April 15, 1954, 5.
2. Anthony Lewis, "Many Things Hinge on Navy's Case Against Greenbelt 'Risk,'" *Washington Daily News,* April 16, 1954, 3.
3. Anthony Lewis, "You Get the Feeling People Are Crawling Out of the Woodwork," *Washington Daily News,* April 19, 1954, 5.
4. Anthony Lewis, "Rank Amateurs in the Field of Security Investigations," *Washington Daily News,* April 20, 1954, 17.
5. Anthony Lewis, "Find Compassion in Your Heart," *Washington Daily News,* April 22, 1954, 8.
6. "CHARGES EVOLUTION COST HIM JOB HERE," *New York Times,* March 27, 1927, 6.
7. Richard Aldrich, "Beethoven Fete Opens In Vienna," *New York Times,* March 27, 1927, 23.
8. "FOREIGNERS FLEE FROM ALL YANGTSE POINTS; MORE BLOODSHED FEARED AS RED FLAME SPREADS; 1,500 MORE MARINES TO GO AT ADMIRAL'S CALL," *New York Times,* March 27, 1927, 1.
9. Frederick Moore, "Shanghai Attack Planned," *New York Times,* March 27, 1927, 1.
10. AP, "REUGEES TELL OF FLIGHT," *New York Times,* March 27, 1927, 1.
11. AP, "SAYS TROUBLE IS ONLY BEGUN," *New York Times,* March 27, 1927, 2.
12. Milestone listings for 1948 for this paragraph and those that follow taken from Neville Williams, *Chronology of World History Volume IV: 1901–1998/The Modern World* (Santa Barbara, CA: ABC-CLIO, 1999), 383–93.
13. Jack Woliston, United Press, "Rosenbergs Die in Electric Chair," *Washington Daily News,* June 20, 1953, 3.
14. Anthony Lewis, "Some of 2200 Don't Know They're Risky," *Washington Daily News,* January 13, 1954, 3.
15. Anthony Lewis, "Honorable Discharge for Govt. Workers?" *Washington Daily News,* January 27, 1954, 3.

16. Anthony Lewis, "Administration May Reveal Even More on Security Risks," *Washington Daily News,* February 18, 1954, 3.

17. United Press, "House Is Expected to O.K. Wire-Taps," *Washington Daily News,* April 7, 1954, 7.

18. Anthony Leis and Neil McNeil, "Cohn and Jenkins Fence at Hearings," *Washington Daily News,* June 1, 1954, 3.

19. Anthony Lewis and Don May, "McCarthy Accuses Stevens & Adams," *Washington Daily News,* June 10, 1054, 3.

20. Ibid., 39.

21. Jack Steele, Scripps-Howard, "Censure Changes Senate, if Not Joe," *Washington Daily News,* December 3, 1954, 3.

22. Anthony Lewis and the *New York Times, Portrait of a Decade: The Second American Revolution: A First-Hand Account of the Struggle for Civil Rights from 1954–1964* (New York: Random House, 1964), 28.

23. Ibid., 29.

24. Ibid., 37–42.

25. Ibid., 72–73.

26. Ibid., 76.

27. Ibid., 72.

28. Ibid., 47.

29. Ibid., 47–48.

30. Ibid., 48–49.

31. Ibid., 55.

32. Ibid., 67–68.

33. Ibid., 210–14.

34. "Bush Suggests U.S. Troops May Be in Iraq Through 2008; Interview With Helen Thomas," CNN The Situation Room, March 21, 2006. http://transcripts.cnn.com/TRANSCRIPTS/0603/21/sitroom.03.html (accessed April 18, 2006).

35. "Journalist Helen Thomas condemns Bush administration," Massachusetts Institute of Technology news office, http://web.mit.edu/newsoffice/2002/thomas-1106.html (accessed April 18, 2006).

36. "Must Evacuate Warsaw In Next Three Days Said," *Winchester Sun,* August 4, 1920, 1.

37. The New Encyclopaedia Britannica, Macropaedia, Vol. 25 (Chicago: 1923), 953.

38. Helen Thomas, *Front Row at the White House: My Life and Times,* (New York: Scribner, 1999), 17.

39. Ibid.

40. Ibid., 24.

41. Ibid., 28.

42. Ibid., 29.

43. Milestone listings for 1943 for this paragraph and those that follow taken from Neville Williams, *Chronology of World History Volume IV: 1901–1998/The Modern World* (Santa Barbara, CA: ABC-CLIO, 1999), 340–46.

44. United Press, "UN Due to Seek Truce; Mac Home in 3 Weeks," *Washington Daily News,* April 11, 1951, 3.

45. "'. . . This Has Been His Finest Hour,'" *Washington Daily News,* April 11, 1951, 3.

46. "GOP Weighs Impeachment," *Washington Daily News,* April 11, 1951, 3.

47. "President Announces Marines Have Landed," *Washington Daily News,* July 15, 1958, 3.
48. Ibid.
49. Ibid.
50. "Reds Demand U.S. Ouster," *Washington Daily News,* July 15, 1958, 3.
51. UP, "Khrushchev Would Thank God—if He Thought There Was One," *Washington Daily News,* November 19, 1956, 7.
52. UPI, "Khrush Shouts, 'You're Trying to Threaten Me!'" *Washington Daily News,* July 24, 1959, 3.
53. UP, "Reds Launch Satellite; Moon Next, They Say," *Washington Daily News,* October 5, 1957, 3.
54. Ludwell Denny, Scipps-Howard, "Eye-Witness at the Front: '. . . THIS IS THE END OF FREE HUNGARY . . . ,'" *Washington Daily News,* November 5, 1956, 1.
55. UP, "Rebel Resurgence Reported," *Washington Daily News,* November 6, 1956, 3.
56. UP, "Hungarian Reds Stop Mercy Convoy," *Washington Daily News,* November 10, 1956, 3.
57. UP, "Salk's Vaccine is 'Safe and Effective'," *Washington Daily News,* April 12, 1955, 3.
58. "HIGH COURT BANS SEGREGATION IN PUBLIC SCHOOLS," *Washington Daily News,* May 17, 1954, 1.
59. "Ike Leaves Tomorrow," *Washington Daily News,* June 29, 1956, 7.
60. Helen Thomas, "Front Row at the White House," 55.
61. Ibid., 55.

CHAPTER 3

The '60s of Morley Safer and Earl Caldwell: War and Protests and Assassinations and Civil Rights

> I am not one of the people who believes the disillusionment of the war came because of television. I think the disillusionment of the war came because the country could never explain to the people why they were at war. . . . I've heard people say that if World War II had been televised we never would have stuck the course. That's bullshit. I think there was a pretty strong determination by most people in this country, not all, that this really was a war of survival of the most important things we hold dear, to put it in simple terms, including of our own democracy.
>
> —Morley Safer

The black-and-white footage opened with a scene of a U.S. Marine using a cigarette lighter to set fire to the thatched roof of a Vietnamese hut. CBS correspondent Morley Safer, wearing camouflage fatigues, looked into the camera as a Vietnamese peasant stacked logs behind him.

"This is what the war in Vietnam is all about," the 33-year-old Safer reported on August 5, 1965. The peasant, dressed in black, a gray goatee sprouting from his chin, babbled to Safer in Vietnamese. The reporter held a smoldering cigarette in his left hand; his gear was slung over his shoulder. Smoke rose from the hut.

"The old and the very young. The Marines have burned this old couple's cottage because fire was coming from here. Now we walk into the village and see no young people at all."

In the next clip, Safer was belly-down on the ground next to a Marine, thrusting a microphone into the Marine's face as the Marine watched the scene.

Morley Safer. © CBS News. Used by permission.

"Have you seen action like this before, Marine?"

"No, I haven't. Not like this I haven't."

The Marine's voice had the higher, softer timbre of a young man. He chewed gum as he answered Safer's questions and watched the aftermath of the village's burning.

"Did you set fire to these houses here?" Safer asked.

"No, we were just off to the left. . . ."

"Were you getting fire from them?"

"Somewhat, not too much, just a little sniper fire."

Next came a voiceover by Safer as the footage showed soldiers cleaning up and inspecting the ruins, wrinkled peasant women sobbing and grasping their children, villagers trekking down the road out of their homes, under the direction of Marines.

"If there were Viet Cong in the hamlets, they were long gone, alerted by the roar of the amphibious tractors and the heavy barrage of rocket fire laid down before the troops moved in. The women and the old men who remained will never forget that August afternoon."

Finally, as the report passed the one-minute mark, Safer did his stand-up, looking into the camera.

"Today's operation is the frustration of Vietnam in miniature. There is little doubt that American firepower can win a military victory here, but to a Vietnamese peasant whose home means a lifetime of backbreaking labor, it will take more than presidential promises to convince him that we are on his side. Morley Safer, CBS News, near the village of Cam Ne."[1]

Twenty-five years later, Safer, in his memoir of the Vietnam War, offered his retrospective of the village burning in a first-person piece of war reporting that captured, blow-by-blow, the destruction of a village.

We hear a few distant "bap-baps," the unmistakable signature of automatic weapons. Then from all around, the echoes doubling the effect, there is an enormous "whoosh!" of fire and the deeper thumps of outgoing mortar rounds and rockets. To my immediate right a marine is down . . . farther down the line shouting then screaming to cease fire. The closest wounded marine is writhing in pain, still conscious. He's been shot in the buttocks; farther down I see medics treating the two others, one wounded in the buttocks, the other in the back. There can be little doubt that we have been hit by so-called friendly fire.

The soldiers entered the village of Cam Ne, Safer wrote. He was greeted by a "black-toothed old woman" who "runs, surprisingly gracefully, toward me, tears streaming down her face, hands outstretched, pleading."

As people stumble out of houses, marines, some with flame throwers, others using matches, yet others with Zippo lighters, begin systematically to set fire to each hut. The villagers are in shock. A few run to flaming houses to rescue valuables, a plastic bag of rice, a dog that had been tied to a post. Not a pet, an evening meal. But mostly the people just stare.

Safer and his two crew members entered an alley, where they witnessed villagers with hands in the air being moved out by Marines. They came across four Marines crouched outside a house, three of them aiming their rifles at the structure. A lieutenant ran up to them.

"What's happening?" he asks.

"We heard voices from that hootch," a private says.

The lieutenant empties a magazine from his automatic rifle into the house, and bits of dried mud and thatch go flying.

Now the voices are very clear, but not like human voices at all. A wailing sound, high and clear, followed by a chorus of keening and the rattling sound of a baby crying, but it is almost an animal sound.

"Torch it," the lieutenant says. The private with the flamethrower rises from the ditch, thick gloves holding the nozzle waist high. The three of us cannot believe what is about to happen.

Then the lieutenant ordered the marines to hold off. He shouted instructions in Vietnamese to the house, ordering the inhabitants to come out or be killed. Safer's Vietnamese cameraman, Ha Thuc Can, approached the hut and talked to the inhabitants, urging them to come out.

> Now there is silence. The marines, emboldened by Can's almost casual stroll to the doorway, leave their cover and join us, standing, rifles aimed at the doorway. In the half-darkness inside are some shattered cooking pots, two or three cots, and a hammock slung against a side wall. The cooking fire is smoldering, whatever was in the pots has doused most of the fire. Next to the fire a crack begins to widen in the dirt floor. As the trapdoor rises, ancient eyes appear, then a nose, mouth, and wispy beard. A marine switches on a flashlight, and an old man steps out onto the dirt floor, hands clasped over his head, then two children, then a young woman holding a baby. The baby is crying. The mother is holding a filthy bloody cloth to its side.
>
> The lieutenant orders the family to get out, to join the others on the main path. They stare at him . . . now all of them have placed their hands over their heads.
>
> Can retrieves the camera, and we three are wired together again. The marines move back about twenty feet with us. The flamethrower belches like some eager dragon, and the house is consumed.[2]

Cam Ne, Safer reported in his book, "was part of the fortified hamlet program that the United States had urged the Diem government to undertake." The Marines, he wrote, "had been requested by the province chief, who wanted the hamlet punished for nonpayment of taxes. This was discovered months later."[3]

The fallout from Safer's report included an angry telephone call from President Lyndon Johnson to CBS President Frank Stanton, in which Johnson accused Stanton of trying to "fuck" him; it included allegations by Secretary of State Dean Rusk that Safer had "ties to the Soviet intelligence apparatus;" it included, Canadian-born Safer wrote, the questioning by Johnson's press secretary, Bill Moyers, of why CBS was using "foreigners" to cover the war, "a Canadian and a Vietnamese?"[4]

"It's interesting," Safer mused in his memoir. "One story I came upon in the most routine way, a story offered up by the marines themselves, became, to some people anyway, symbolic not only of the war but also of the coming of age of television. Proof that the road to glory or damnation may often be paved with no intention at all."[5]

CBS News credits Safer's coverage of the burning of the village of Cam Ne by U.S. Marines in 1965 with changing "America's view of the war and . . . war reporting forever."[6] The report, depicting one of the down sides of the war, the U.S. military committing questionable acts against Vietnamese civilians, presaged future reporting of the war that included not only body counts and Pentagon and administration official statements of progress and lights at the end of tunnels, but also reportage of atrocities committed by the U.S. military. It was a prelude, broadcast into Americans' living rooms, to such stories as Seymour Hersh's November 12, 1969 report of the March 16, 1968, My Lai massacre by U.S. soldiers of hundreds of unarmed Vietnamese civilians, including women and children.

In the jungles of Vietnam, Safer found the adventure of war that he had imagined as a youth contemplating a career in journalism. During his time there during the 1960s, in what former CBS News President Fred Friendly would later call "Morley Safer's war,"[7] the television correspondent found the journalist's adventure of war—along with the tragedy of it, the senselessness of it, the thrill of it. He found it in the aftermath of U.S. B-52 bombing raids, in the mutilated bodies, in the tunnels in which the Viet Cong soldiers carried on a guerrilla war against American GIs more accustomed to fighting on beachheads, in the brothels that served soldiers on weekend R&R, in the cities teeming with the odors of Vietnamese cooking served alongside the aroma of decaying limbs and dying young men.

This was the sort of experience that Safer, the future CBS *60 Minutes* correspondent whose reporting would come to be known by millions of Sunday night American television viewers, had sought, that he had read and heard as a youth—the work of Ernest Hemingway and Edward R. Murrow. Growing up in Toronto during World War II reading war novels and newspapers, Safer decided early what he wanted to do with his life.

"During the war, I was an eleven-, twelve-year-old, you read the paper, you read the paper seriously," he reminisced from behind his cluttered *60 Minutes* desk in Manhattan. "I decided that's really what I wanted to do. A romantic job. I was a great reader as a kid. I read Hemingway and all of that and, I think, even younger, reading the dispatches from the war. I mean, in that period in Canada, the war was the topic in all of our lives. The country had been at war since 1939, so it was *the* event. There was no question, the streets were practically empty of men except for the ones in uniform. The war writing, the sense of adventure, the wonderful datelines that those stories carried, you know."

But though World War II would be the driving force of Safer's formative years, his nation and the world was at peace when he was born in November 1931. The pressing issues of the day were the communist peril and the worldwide Great Depression. Indeed, the day after his birth, the lead story on the front page of the *Toronto Daily Star* of November 9 (no *Daily Star* archives were available for the day of his birth, Sunday November 8) was continuing coverage of the trial of a group of nine alleged communists. They were accused of using "'illegal methods' of operating the Communist party of Canada, stressed by the crown in quoting from Communist literature." The alleged communist leader, Tom Ewen, denied the charge, though he admitted that sometimes aliases were used to conceal identities.[8]

On page two, the newspaper reported in connection with the trial that four "young girls" had been arrested by police and charged with vagrancy "allegedly for soliciting money for the defense of the Communists on trial.

"No evidence was taken, and Miss [Fanny] Kalin and Miss [Nellie] Fistel were released on $1,000 bond. The other two were remanded for a week in custody. Bail was fixed at $500 each."[9]

In tidings of the depression, representatives of the Lakeview Ratepayers' and Workers' Association protested the 30-cent hourly pay rate for unskilled labor on Toronto Township projects, while "another deputation of 25 farmers from the north end wanted to know why they should be billed in their taxes for unemployment relief. The Lakeview men asked that every unemployed man be assured $16 per week."[10] In Oshawa, Toronto Comptroller James Simpson in a "stirring address before a large congregation at King St. United church" challenged the Christian church "to co-operate with labor to search for a better economic and social system than that existing at present in order that the human race might progress along the principles laid down by Jesus Christ. . . .

"With 520,000 unemployed in Canada, Controller Simpson declared there is much radically wrong with the present economic system whereby immense wealth is controlled by a few thousands . . .

"'There is nothing wrong with capital, it is the use to which capitalists put capital,' Controller Simpson asserted."[11]

The newspaper's ads offered depression-era Toronto consumers three tins of Campbell's tomato soup for 25 cents, a pound of fresh creamery butter for the same price, and for after-dinner sleep, a four-piece Malcolm bedroom suite "of massive construction, having figured walnut veneer fronts, well matched," for $112.[12]

Despite his early upbringing during the depression years, it was not money that lured 19-year-old Safer to journalism as an untrained, inexperienced reporter at the Woodstock, Ontario newspaper and then the *London Free Press* a couple of years later; it was love of the craft.

"I don't think you can do that anymore, unless you were some kind of whiz kid, which I wasn't," he said of his start as a general assignment reporter without the benefit of a journalism school or training. "You did everything, sports to culture to local politics. I just enjoyed doing the work, even though I didn't get paid very much. Liking to write came a little bit later. I liked getting my teeth into stuff.

"I just felt so lucky to be doing the work," he added. "I really did. I liked it. I didn't know anybody else who was a journalist, which was kind of fun, to not be doing what everyone else was doing. I hated school pretty much, obviously."

Leaving college after trying his hand at higher education for only two weeks, Safer was schooled by tough editors, he said.

"All the editors I had in the first couple of jobs in Woodstock, in London, Ontario, in Reuters in London, the *Oxford Mail* where I worked for a while, all the editors were just real sons of bitches," he said. "And those are the best editors anybody could have. They were tough. I mean, very demanding, and you knew if you got even the mildest praise, you had done extremely well because they're not generous in their praise."

It was a journalistic era when newspaper city rooms often were the training grounds for reporters to learn their trade before crossing over to broadcast networks or into the media of magazines or books—the route that Safer traveled into a broadcast career with the Canadian Broadcasting Corporation (CBC) that took him abroad, to Europe, Africa, the Middle East, Asia, before he hooked up with CBS News, the foremost broadcast news medium of the 1960s.

"I can't say I had a serious mentor, but Charles Collingwood, whom I worked with in London, in Vietnam, and in Eastern Europe, became a good friend," he said. "I worked with all of the Murrow boys, as they were called. I was with that last generation of people who crossed over in that period. Alex Kendrick in London, Charles Collingwood, Winston Burdett, Eric Sevareid. So I was very lucky in that sense. It was the golden age in broadcast news, and those guys represented it, probably more than any group of people.

"You know, I'm seventy-four years old," he continued, "and I've been traveling on somebody else's nickel all of my life, practically. I've done some interesting stories, been about everywhere in the world, lived in some fascinating places."

But he was on his own nickel as a young reporter in 1950, entering a post-World War II world with echoes of the communist scare of his infancy. In June that year, communist North Korea would invade South Korea, touching off a conflict that would last three years and that would presage the much more protracted Vietnam War, another proxy war fought by agents of communist China and the Soviet Union and of the Western democracies. And at home, renowned editorial cartoonist "Herblock" that year would create the term "McCarthyism" based on the accusations of communist sympathies brought against U.S. government officials and others by the Wisconsin demagogue, Republican U.S. Senator Joe McCarthy. The red scare pervaded every corner of the nation, as the U.S. Congress enacted the Internal Security Bill requiring communist organizations to register with the government and outlawing the hiring of communists by defense contractors.[13]

Much of the red paranoia was based in fact. In January, Alger Hiss was convicted of perjury in connection with his alleged membership in the Communist Party; in February, the Soviet Union and communist China entered into a 30-year treaty alliance; in March, atomic scientist Klaus Fuchs was sent to prison for giving atomic secrets to the Soviets; in April, the Soviets shot down a U.S. Flying Fortress bomber, claiming it had entered their air space; in July, President Harry S Truman asked Congress to approve a large military budget to give the nation the capability to respond to the communist threat; and in November, communist Chinese troops joined with North Korea in the Korean War. Tensions heightened when, in December, Truman ended U.S. trade with communist China and declared a state of emergency in the nation after United Nations forces suffered defeats.

U.S. citizens found their escapism from this new war and the red menace in films that included *All About Eve, Father of the Bride, Harvey, Rio Grande,* and *Sunset Boulevard.* For those inclined to more literary escapism,

C.S. Lewis published *The Lion, the Witch and the Wardrobe;* Isaac Singer published *The Family Moskat;* Carl Sandburg published *Collected Poems;* and Hemingway published *Across the River and into the Trees.* Science fiction fans were treated to Ray Bradbury's *The Martian Chronicles.*

And in the world of journalism, newspapers continued their financial dominance over broadcast as it was reported that newspapers took in $2.1 billion in advertising by U.S. businesses, compared to $605 million for radio and $171 million for television—numbers the young journalist Safer likely did not pay much attention to as he began his journalism career but that would have great bearing on both of his media of choice as the second half of the century progressed.

The communist threat, the Cold War, and U.S. military involvement in Asia would continue to dominate the news as Safer developed into a seasoned journalist at the CBC and then CBS during the 1960s. It was a decade that would see the Soviet Union erect a wall to divide East Berlin from West, the United States and the Soviets on the brink of nuclear war during the Cuban Missile Crisis, the assassination of the nation's youngest president and then of his brother, and the political descent of a Democratic president, who championed the rights of minorities and the poor, because of an unpopular war.

Safer was in Europe, more precisely in Berlin, when the Soviet Union in 1961 erected the wall and barbed wire that sliced through the city, dividing the free West sector from the communist East sector. Though he wasn't with CBS at the time, that network provided stark broadcast coverage of the wall that became a symbol of the East-West standoff during the height of the Cold War during President John F. Kennedy's visit to Berlin in June 1963. Accompanied by voiceovers from Douglas Edwards and correspondent Daniel Schorr, the CBS cameras showed the young president arriving in his motorcade, getting his first view of the "wall that separates East from West Berlin." He shook hands with a British officer in the British sector. He climbed a platform and, flanked by military officials, he gazed at the wall as the wind blew his famously thick hair and the camera panned to the "very real curtain."

The West Berliners gave the president a hero's greeting. "Never within memory has the city of Berlin given any man such a reception as it poured out today to John Fitzgerald Kennedy," intoned the voiceover.

> Nowhere in the world has the president ever been greeted with such massive enthusiasm. More than a million people clamored and cheered and threw confetti as Mr. Kennedy made his way around the city for seven and a half hours. He's gone now, already in Ireland, where tomorrow he'll visit his ancestral home. But in Berlin, he was so carried away by the reaction of the people that he told them that, in spirit, "*ich bin ein Berliner.* I am a Berliner."

The cameras and microphones captured that moment, as thousands waved and spilled into the side streets. The president looked out on the vast throng, waved to them as the cheering continued—the chant of "Kennedy . . . Kennedy . . . Kennedy." He beamed his famous broad Irish smile.

"I am proud to come to this city as the guest of your distinguished mayor who has symbolized throughout the world the fighting spirit of West Berlin," Kennedy told the mob. He spoke of his pride of being in the city "during its great moment of crisis" and vowed to return "if ever needed"—a promise that prompted cheers from the crowd. He then set forth the theme of the Cold War era.

"There are many people in the world who really don't understand, or say they don't, what is the great issue between the free world and the communist world," he said.

> Let them come to Berlin. There are some who say that communism is the wave of the future. Let them come to Berlin. And there are some who say in Europe, and elsewhere, we can work with the communists. Let them come to Berlin. And there are even a few who say that it's true that communism is an evil system, but it permits us to make economic progress.

He paused and spoke the words slowly, first in German, then in English, enunciating them carefully. "Let them come to Berlin."

The president then made of Berlin a symbol of the larger struggle and of the hope that he and his presidency inspired.

> What is true of this city is true of Germany. Real lasting peace in Europe can never be assured as long as one German out of four is denied the elementary right of free men, and that is to make a free choice. In eighteen years of peace and good faith, this generation of Germans has earned the right to be free, including the right to unite their families and their nation in lasting peace with good will to all people. You live in a defended island of freedom, but your life is part of the main. So let me ask you as I close, to lift your eyes beyond the dangers of today to the hopes of tomorrow, beyond the freedom merely of this city of Berlin or your country of Germany, to the advance of freedom everywhere, beyond the wall, to the day of peace with justice, beyond yourselves and ourselves, to all mankind. Freedom is indivisible, and when one man is enslaved, all are not free. When all are free, then we can look forward to that day when this city will be joined as one, and this country, and this great continent of Europe, in a peaceful and hopeful globe. When that day finally comes, as it will, the people of West Berlin can take sober satisfaction in the fact they there were in the front lines for almost two decades. All free men, wherever they may live, are citizens of Berlin, and therefore, as a free man, I take pride in the words *Ich bin ein Berliner.*

This was a period of broadcast journalism that lent ample air time to reporters and cameras to tell a story, to provide background and context. The CBS report included footage of the building of the Berlin wall two years before.

"On August 13, 1961, the communists stemmed the human tide from East Berlin by building the Berlin Wall," noted the voiceover as the footage showed wire fencing being erected, a soldier tossing an object over the fence to the western side, followed by citizens being doused with hoses.

"From the start there was violence, a communist soldier hurls a smoke bomb at the jeering, protesting crowd on the other side, more trouble, and water is sprayed on the people who cannot stand to see their city grimly divided by what is first called a Chinese wall and which later comes to be known as the Wall of Shame."

Accompanied by scenes of East German soldiers pushing against crowds of people at the barricade, the reporter described a "panicky rush" of people to leave the Eastern sector during the last 24 hours the passage was open. The cameras, filming in grainy black and white, captured the dull eyes and forlorn faces on the other side of the wall.

"But now the escape route is cut off, and so is hope. . . . East and West Berliners look at one another across the wall and shout a few words with their tears."

More footage, of workers erecting the barrier. "Where civilians once walked to freedom, only soldiers patrol. The wall keeps getting more formidable. Heavy anti-tank barriers are installed behind the wall at seven key points. It's reported that [Soviet leader Nikita] Khrushchev himself once conceded that the wall is an ugly thing."[14]

Safer was there when it was built. In the security of his CBS office, he told his story of his own experience with East-West hostilities, which for him became a bit warmer than Cold War rhetoric.

"I was arrested in Berlin the day the wall went up," he said. "I was over the night before. There was another Berlin crisis going on, every couple of months in the '60s, and I went over. You could just casually go to East Berlin, you had to go through a checkpoint, and I'd gone over with a friend to have a drink and dinner in East Berlin, just to look around. It was a pretty miserable place, and I came back at about 11 o'clock I guess, and I noticed a lot of activity. I couldn't see."

Turns out something was going on, alright. Safer, an early riser, had his radio on the next morning at about 6 A.M., "and there were bullets going. I grabbed my cameraman, and the wall then was just barbed wire and stuff, and cement barricades, and we were shooting on the other side, and we went around the bend and there were about forty Russian tanks that were not hidden but very carefully placed around the bend about, I guess, half a mile inside East Berlin, and we started to shoot, and I looked to my left and I saw this military motorcycle with a sidecar, and this German guy driving it with a Russian colonel in the sidecar who was pulling out his revolver. And then a truck pulled up behind us."

The soldiers ordered Safer and his cameraman to stop what they were doing, grabbed them and forced them into the back of the truck. They drove them to a prison building and ordered them to empty their pockets. They took his money but left him his cigarettes and then put Safer and the cameraman into a cell with a group of prisoners who had been rounded up for questioning. Safer said they held him for a day and a half.

"A guy slapped my face. What happened was, I knocked on the door and said I wanted to go to the john. There was a metal door with a slide, so he opened the slide, and I told him, so he calls his buddy to come and open the door, and he walks with me, and as I walked into the door, I wanted a cigarette. There was a no-smoking sign, so wham, he slapped me in the face, and then he pointed to my cigarette pack and said 'hmm,' took half my cigarettes, left me the other half and then let me go in and smoke a cigarette. He wanted to let me know, I guess, who was boss. But the questioning was all very casual; the thing that intrigued them more than anything was the number of stamps on my passport and they wanted to know what each stamp represented, why I was in Ghana, why I was in Jordan, why I was in Egypt."

But it was an event more than a year after the building of the Berlin Wall that slapped Americans with the stark realization of the tensions and dangers of the Cold War, and of the fact that it could easily turn hot. On October 22, 1962, CBS News preempted its regularly scheduled program, *Stump the Stars,* to allow President Kennedy to address the nation on the subject of the installation by the Soviet Union of nuclear missiles in Cuba, just 90 miles away from the United States' Florida coast.

Wearing a dark suit, sitting at a desk with two desk microphones, and with the stars and stripes of the American flag televised in black and white behind him, the president told an anxious citizenry of the latest development in the Cuban Missile Crisis.

"Within the past week, unmistakable evidence has established the fact that a series of offensive missile sites is now in preparation on that imprisoned island," said the president, reading from a prepared text, looking up to gaze straight into the camera that represented the eyes of America. "The purpose of these bases can be none other than to provide a nuclear strike capability against the Western Hemisphere."

Kennedy then outlined the steps he was taking to deal with the Soviets, including a military quarantine of Fidel Castro's Cuba. All ships bound for the island, "from whatever nation or port," containing cargos of offensive weapons would be turned back, "but not denying the necessities of life, as the Soviets tried to do in their Berlin blockade of 1948." Also, Kennedy warned, "it shall be the policy of this nation to regard any missile launched from Cuba against any nation in the Western Hemisphere as an attack by the Soviet Union on the United States requiring a full retaliatory response upon the Soviet Union."

As reported by Douglas Edwards, the Kennedy directive included searching and sinking, if necessary, ships of any nation carrying offensive weapons to Cuba. Edwards added that Soviet-bloc ships were at that moment on their way to Cuba, and that Kennedy had urged Khrushchev to withdraw from the "abyss of destruction."[15]

The Soviet leader did withdraw, ordering the ships to turn back, averting a potential nuclear war, as reported by CBS correspondent David Schoenbrun six days later. Wearing a double-breasted suit, his head bald, and sporting a William Powell moustache, Schoenbrun reported from the desk backed by pulled drapes that served as the CBS News set that:

Nikita Khrushchev today did precisely what President Kennedy has been asking him to do ever since this crisis began. He ordered the dismantling of Soviet missile bases in Cuba under United Nations supervision and the return of the rockets to the Soviet Union, and he dropped the demand he made only 24 hours earlier for the dismantling of NATO missile bases in Turkey in return. Khrushchev made his decision known in a letter to the president. . . . Strange as it seems, the president of the United States like any ordinary citizen, learned of Khrushchev's decision from a radio broadcast.

Noting that translators were working on the text, Schoenbrun told his audience that the language of the letter "is quite extraordinary. Nothing like this has ever been seen since the start of the Cold War, indeed not since America and Russia were allies against Germany has a Soviet leader written in such warm and friendly terms to an American president.

"Esteemed Mr. President," the letter begins, "I have received your message of 27 October, 1962. I express my satisfaction and gratitude for the sense of proportion and the understanding of the responsibility borne by you at present for the preservation of peace throughout the whole world which you have shown. I understand very well your anxiety and the anxiety of the people of the United States in connection with the fact that the weapons which you describe as offensive are in fact grim weapons. Both you and I understand what kind of weapons they are."

As the report continued, the broadcast cut to footage of Kennedy arriving at church that morning, "as usual," in a black limousine. Surveillance of Cuba was continuing, Schoenbrun reported, "as is the general alert posture of all American forces at home and abroad." This was followed by footage of Press Secretary Pierre Salinger standing before a bank of microphones, reading from the text of the president's statement:

I welcome Chairman Khrushchev's statesmanlike decision to stop building bases in Cuba, dismantling offensive weapons, returning them to the Soviet Union under U.N. verification. This is an important and constructive contribution to peace. We shall be in touch with the secretary general of the United Nations with respect to reciprocal measures to assure peace in the Caribbean area. It is my earnest hope that the governments of the world can, with a solution to the Cuban crisis, turn their urgent attention to the compelling necessity for ending the arms race and reducing world tension.[16]

The two superpowers had averted nuclear war. Safer was on assignment in Europe, for the CBC in a Soviet-bloc nation, during the Cuban

Missile Crisis. He recalled it in one brief, but chilling, recollection of a moment—one that evoked the anxiety and fear that many Americans experienced during that week when aircraft, in Safer's case Soviet fighter jets, happened to scream above them in a blue autumn sky.

"I remember I was doing a story in Poland. I was doing a stand-up of something in Warsaw, and we stopped, and a squadron of MiGs came over practically at treetop level as we were doing this report, and I remember thinking when I heard those jets, 'I hope they're not ours.'"

Just over one year later, only months after the president's visit to the Berlin Wall, the nation experienced one final crisis involving this president: his assassination on November 22, 1963, in Dallas. CBS News interrupted the soap opera *As the World Turns* to bring the first bulletin to its viewers. The words "CBS News BULLETIN" were superimposed on a black screen as an announcer gave the news.

> In Dallas, Texas, three shots were fired at President Kennedy's motorcade in downtown Dallas. The first reports say that President Kennedy has been seriously wounded by this shooting. More details just arrived. These details about the same as previously, President Kennedy shot today just as his motorcade left downtown Dallas. Mrs. Kennedy jumped up and grabbed Mr. Kennedy. She called "Oh no," the motorcade sped on. United Press says that the wounds for President Kennedy perhaps could be fatal. Repeating, a bulletin from CBS News, President Kennedy has been shot by a would-be assassin in Dallas, Texas. Stay tuned to CBS News for further details.

The official word that Kennedy had indeed died came from Walter Cronkite. The newscaster, dressed in a crisp white dress shirt, dark tie, his collar buttoned down, put on a pair of thick, black-rimmed glasses to read a piece of paper that had just been handed to him.

"From Dallas, Texas, the flash, apparently official, President Kennedy died at 1 P.M. Central Time"—Cronkite glanced at the clock on the wall in the CBS newsroom—"two o'clock Eastern Standard Time, some 38 minutes ago."

Interspersed among the reporting was a still of the president in the car, slumped, his wife trying to hold him. Cronkite paused and appeared to be trying to gather himself. He tightened his lips. "Vice President Lyndon Johnson"—Cronkite cleared his throat—"has left the hospital in Dallas, but we do not know to where he has proceeded, presumably he will be taking the oath of office shortly and become the 36th president of the United States."

A few days later, the nation still stunned by the murder of the president, correspondents Charles Collingwood and Dan Rather narrated a CBS News special about the assassination and its aftermath. The cameras showed a motorcade moving slowly through the crowd, following a meandering course to give a maximum number of citizens a "chance to see the chief executive." The crowd was 14 to 15 people deep; others watched from windows and the streets. Confetti filled the air, throngs applauded the president, "and further downtown, one man was watching whose purpose was not to welcome the president, but to murder him. Several floors above the cheering crowds, a man waited with six-point-five rifle. The motorcade moved leisurely down Main Street, where the crowds were the heaviest." Then, something happened. The crowd suddenly panicked; black-and-white footage showed people fleeing Main Street, hundreds of backs of people surging away.

"Terse, excited messages crackled over the radio system of the Dallas Police Department."[17] Officials, cops, scampering, cars speeding. Fast. Like that, the president gone.

Like all North Americans who were alive then, and old enough to form memories, Safer could remember precisely where he was and what he was doing the day of the assassination of President Kennedy: in Ghana, on assignment. He had been out to dinner with a couple of aid workers.

"We got back to the hotel, and I noticed that the hotel's flags were flying at half staff. I couldn't understand what the hell was going on, so walking in I said to the night guy at the desk, why the flags at half staff? He said, 'oh, your president Kennedy has been murdered.' I said, 'what?' He said—you know how people tend to put stories like that, how rumors spread, and they always put them in the wrong context—and he said, 'yes, he was murdered in your House of Parliament by somebody in the opposition.' Which makes no sense."

Safer and his dinner companions went to the U.S. aid office, down to the basement.

"They had a big transmitter and receiver, and we listened to the Voice of America, which was using its own stuff and plugging into all the networks, CBS included, and we were there when they announced that the president was dead, sitting down in the basement. It's just one of those things you don't forget. I was in shock."

Safer went to the U.S. embassy the next day, to pay his respects.

"Somebody at the desk said 'hold on a minute, I think maybe the ambassador will want to see you.' Not that he knew me; I was a Canadian correspondent, and he said he just wanted to talk to somebody, and we just sat there and had coffee for a couple of hours. He was in tears."

Nearly four and a half years later, another Kennedy was down—just after having taken a key Democratic presidential primary contest. Robert Kennedy, Democratic senator from New York, "had just won the crucial California Democratic presidential primary," reported Dan Rather in a CBS retrospective of American political assassinations. "He was looking forward to a hard fight for his party's nomination at the Democratic convention in Chicago."

The scene shifted to color footage of the younger Kennedy, who had been his brother's attorney general, making his victory speech in California: "We are a great country, a selfless country, and a compassionate country, and I intend to make that my basis for running over the period of the next few months. My thanks to all of you and now it's on to Chicago and let's win there."

Immediately following this scene came footage of Kennedy on the floor, his right hand and wrist covered with blood, two men cradling his head in their arms and hands. As Rather narrated, the screen displayed black-and-white stills, along with audio of the people tending to the victim and trying to manage the scene: "Look out for the gun . . . OK . . . all right . . . got the gun, got the gun . . . OK hold on to the guy, hold on to him." Followed by a black and white photo of the suspect being held, his hair dark and curly, his eyes small beneath thick black eyebrows, a shadow of beard stubble smudging his cheeks and chin.

"The man, who turned out to be a Palestinian refugee named Sirhan Sirhan, was quickly subdued," Rather reported, "but not until he had emptied all eight chambers of his .22 caliber weapon. Senator Kennedy died a day later."[18]

Safer remembered what the two Kennedys stood for, the possibilities and hope they offered.

"I think there's no question that he was part of a generation of Americans," he said of President Kennedy. "I should think anyone in their twenties or even late teens at that time really felt a sense of possibilities for the country. And I think his early death and the way he died was just devastating disillusionment for that generation and subsequent generations. That sense, in the best sense of the real mission the country has, was a positive, beneficial message and example for the world, and particularly for itself."

It was the same despair with Bobby Kennedy.

"The sense of loss came much later when you realized that Bobby, here was a man who had so fundamentally changed his own view. He was really, he was the Kennedy who could have made a real difference to the country because he was willing to think, contemplate the intrinsic unfairness in life in this country and was prepared to do something about it."

But hanging over the political assassinations and racial turmoil in America like a dark, treacherous cloud during that decade, was the Vietnam War. This was a conflict that crossed the American political spectrum, beginning with assistance, advisement, and training lent to South Vietnam by the Eisenhower and Truman administrations, inherited and escalated by Kennedy and, after him, Johnson and then Richard Nixon. As Fred Friendly had suggested, it also was a war that became Safer's beat for CBS, which he joined in April 1964. He opened the network's Saigon bureau in 1965 and did two tours of duty there, earning several awards.

The war coverage produced stark memories for the young journalist. In his memoir, Safer recalled two things happening one day in Vietnam as he accompanied U.S. troops after a B-52 bombing raid. One was a mortar round that had fallen short, killing one person and wounding two or three others. The other was the sights and smell of the remains of the sortie.

"The stench was beyond all belief," he wrote. "The bombers had gotten very lucky. One bomb had cratered a command bunker. The maggots had already taken over. Farther along there was a pile of bodies near a cooking fire."

It was an eerie scene. The bodies, he wrote, were "perfectly intact North Vietnamese regulars. Fully uniformed, some of them had their pith helmets still in place. They must have been killed by the blast or pressure. I recall thinking they looked much larger, stouter than most Vietnamese. The internal gases, of course, were beginning to swell the bodies."[19]

A North Vietnamese combatant Safer interviewed during his return to Vietnam two and a half decades later remembered the B-52 raids as the worst of his wartime experiences. Asked if the fighting had been what he expected and if he had been prepared for it, Professor Nguyen Ngoc Hung responded to the correspondent: "For the fighting, yes . . . but not for the B-52s."

"There is nothing that can prepare you for that," said Hung, whom Safer described as "the delicate young man who did his duty. He put down his books; put on rubber tire sandals—' Ho sandals'; picked up his Kalashnikov, the standard issue AK-47 assault rifle and three clips for it, a bayonet, three grenades, a water bottle; and strapped on a fifty-five pound pack that included a poncho and hammock but mainly contained rice to eat along the way and started walking South with orders to kill as many Americans and their puppets as possible."

The difficulty in understanding the war, Safer wrote, was comprehending "the idea of duty to a country that is waging a war of stubbornness . . . a war being fought, once you get past the slogans, to prove you can whip technology with sandals, and incidentally a million or so lives."

For Hung, Safer wrote, "'liberation' seems the least of it. The profoundly unliberated walk as much as a thousand miles to liberate the equally unliberated, to kill them when necessary, and to kill perfect strangers who've flown thirteen thousand miles to do the same."

But there was nothing, Hung told Safer, that could prepare him for the onslaught of the B-52s, an experience he recalled in surreal detail.

> "The first time they came I remember the place went absolutely silent. Normally there was some kind of aircraft around if we were anywhere near a battle. It was a wonderful day, not a sound, nothing but birds and insects, and I remember watching bombs fall, and they seemed to fall slowly, and they grew bigger and bigger. And we were fascinated because they took on different shapes as they fell. And then there was nothing; we could hear nothing or see nothing. The dust and the smoke were everywhere . . . it was night in the middle of the day. Two of my closest friends died."

The hard part, Hung said, was burying his friends. "Mark the grave with something and then keep moving. If the helicopters were around, you could not even do that. The worst was the B-52. After the B-52 raids you go around and gather up the bits, the pieces of the bodies, and you try to bury them."[20]

The same year as Cam Ne, 1965, Cronkite paid his first visit to Vietnam. Safer played a role in opening Cronkite's eyes to the "other" side of the war, the side the military brass did not want the famous television correspondent to see.

"The ancient military practice of dulling the brains of visitors with endless briefing, using opaque military jargon, and strings of incomprehensible map coordinates, supported by sports metaphors and locker-room optimism did not succeed in making him a believer," Safer wrote. "He was too skeptical, too savvy, and had too sensitive a shit-detector to be taken in."

But he also had Safer as a guide.

"His itinerary was designed to keep him away as much as possible from correspondents and others permanently based in Vietnam who were considered to be naysayers," Safer wrote.

> It did not entirely work. I managed to arrange at least two meetings to counter the lies and bogus optimism that had been so carefully orchestrated for him. One was with an army officer based in the Iron Triangle for two years who slipped into Saigon clandestinely and met with us in the Continental Palace Hotel. In terse but emotional language he catalogued the disaster to come. "With a million men here, we still would not win," he said.

The other was with a CIA officer, not yet completely "disillusioned with the war and its conduct but, nevertheless, hobbled by confusion and disenchantment, by the corruption of the military junta he was helping to keep in place and dejected by the ignorance and self-imposed blinders of the State Department and the Pentagon. 'They don't even read the cables that do not support the cockeyed idea of the moment,' he complained."[21]

While Safer's report on the torching of Cam Ne may have marked the beginning of the televised and newspaper coverage that turned American opinion against the war, it was the Tet Offensive three years later, Safer wrote, that lost Cronkite and, in Johnson's view, the war.

"After his [Cronkite's] broadcast from Hue, when he suggested that the only rational way out of Vietnam was to negotiate, Lyndon Johnson allegedly said, 'If we've lost Cronkite, we've lost the war,'" Safer wrote.[22]

While the war effort was failing, though, Johnson was finding political success on other fronts at home. This included not only the programs of Johnson's Great Society agenda and his war on poverty, such as Medicare and Medicaid, but also significant progress on civil rights.

The same year that Safer was in the jungles of Vietnam reporting on the war, the president offered his vision of the Great Society in his State of the Union address, broadcast by Safer's network to the nation. Johnson's agenda included programs to help the poor, the disenfranchised, and the environment.

"Our first aim remains the safety and well-being of the people of our own country," the president declared as the camera panned to the Kennedy brothers, Robert and Ted, in the chamber, and then to Johnson's wife and daughters.

To reach that goal, Johnson offered to Congress and the American people a list of proposed legislation that included initiatives in education, urban renewal and crime-fighting, environmentalism, ensuring voting rights for minorities, providing better health care for the needy and the poor, high-speed rail transportation, farm assistance reform, full employment, immigration legislation, and support for artistic endeavors—all with a balanced budget. Each item brought applause from the audience.

"We worked for two centuries to climb this peak of prosperity, but we're only at the beginning of the road to the Great Society," the president told his audience.

> Ahead now is a summit where freedom from the wants of the body can help fulfill the needs of the spirit. We built this nation to serve its people. We want to grow and build and create, but we want progress to be the servant and not the master of man. We do not intend to live in the midst of abundance isolated from neighbors and nature, confined by blighted cities and bleak suburbs, stunted by a poverty of learning and an emptiness of leisure. The Great Society asks not how much, but how good; not only how to create wealth, but how to use it; not only how fast we are going, but where we are headed. It proposes as the first test for a nation, the quality of its people. This kind of society will not flower spontaneously from swelling riches and surging power. It will not be the gift of government or the creation of presidents. It will require of every American for many generations both faith in the destination and the fortitude to make the journey. And like freedom itself, it will always be challenge and not fulfillment. And tonight we accept that challenge.[23]

In March of that year, the president took a major step toward meeting one of the goals on his list. CBS News covered his address to Congress on his proposed Voting Rights Act, in which he promised to send to Congress "a law designed to eliminate illegal barriers to the right to vote."

The major elements of the legislation would strike down restrictions to voting in all elections, federal, state, and local; establish a simple, uniform standard "that cannot be used to flout the Constitution"; provide for citizens to be registered by officials of the U.S. government if state officials refuse to register them; eliminate lawsuits that delay the right to vote, and ensure that properly registered individuals are not prohibited from voting.

"I speak tonight for the dignity of man and the destiny of democracy," Johnson said in his speech to both houses of Congress.

> I urge every member of both parties, Americans of all religions, and of all colors, from every section of this country, to join me in that cause. At times history and fate

> meet at a single time in a single place to shape a turning point in man's unending search for freedom. So it was at Lexington and Concord. So it was a century ago at Appomattox. So it was last week in Selma, Alabama. There, long-suffering men and women peacefully protested the denial of their rights as Americans. Many of them were brutally assaulted. One good man, a man of God, was killed. There is no cause for pride in what has happened in Selma. There is no cause for self-satisfaction in the long denial of equal rights of millions of Americans. But there is cause for hope and for faith in our democracy and what is happening here tonight.

Interrupted frequently by applause, Johnson, a gifted orator and savvy legislator, offered one of his more eloquent addresses in imploring Congress to join this cause.

"There is no Negro problem," he told his audience.

> There is no Southern problem. There is no Northern problem. There is only an American problem. And we are met here tonight as Americans, not as Democrats or Republicans, we are met here as Americans to solve that problem. This was the first nation in the history of the world to be founded with a purpose. The great phrases of that purpose still sound in every American heart, North and South. "All men are created equal." "Government by consent of the governed." "Give me liberty or give me death." And those are not just clever words and those are not just empty theories; in their name Americans have fought and died for two centuries, and tonight around the world they stand there as guardians of our liberty risking their lives. Those words are a promise to every citizen that he shall share in the dignity of man.[24]

The day after Safer's report on Cam Ne, on August 6, 1965, Johnson signed into law the Voting Rights Act. In tandem with the Civil Rights Act, which he had signed the previous year, Johnson's efforts on behalf of civil rights carried out the hopes of the Kennedy administration before him.

"Those were the most important years of the civil rights movement," Safer would recall four decades later. "The country changed enormously when you think about it, '60 to '70, it was a huge cultural change. No question the country got better, more opportunity for people who were deprived of opportunity."

But Johnson's political successes carried with them what Safer called the "asterisk" of the Vietnam War.

"Here was a president who for all his flaws had the necessary tools to do what Bobby Kennedy only dreamed about and John Kennedy could only dream about," Safer said. "And here Johnson could do it through conniving and wheeling and dealing and speaking the language and all of that."

The civil rights advances of the decade, Safer said, "was the most fundamental change. And yet, he was stuck with this monster on his back of Vietnam. He felt betrayed, I think. I don't know by whom, but he felt betrayed about that war. I don't think he ever believed in that war.

He was a man just utterly tortured by this monstrous war that he found himself in."

Safer, invoking the time-honored explanation by journalists that they are the messenger and not the message, dismissed suggestions that press coverage of the war contributed to the failure.

"I am not one of the people who believes the disillusionment of the war came because of television," he said. "I think the disillusionment of the war came because the country could never explain to the people why they were at war."

In this respect, he compared the Vietnam War to President George W. Bush's Iraq war.

"The difference being, in Vietnam the war was over when the parents were practically ready to demonstrate, because they were parents of a draftee army, everyone except the really dodger ones and clever ones had to serve. It really was a people's war in that sense, a largely draftee army. That won't happen in this one because most Americans don't know anyone who's been killed in Iraq, and that's really the difference.

"But in terms of the effect of television, I think it's generally exaggerated. I've heard people say that if World War II had been televised we never would have stuck the course. That's bullshit. I think there was a pretty strong determination by most people in this country, not all, that this really was a war of survival of the most important things we hold dear, to put it in simple terms, including of our own democracy. I think there really was a great sense of nation and a great sense of democracy, and this war has perhaps even less of a rationale than Vietnam."

* * * *

The change was coming, and I could see it with the music, I could see it with the ideas about this redevelopment, you could see it in politics. To me the '60s, that was the beginning, and also for me personally it was me leaving the mountains, not only coming into journalism but coming into these bigger markets and these bigger cities where you had this mix and everything, and so hey, the early '60s was like this breaking out in America and breaking out in all kinds of ways.

—Earl Caldwell

Moments before he was murdered, the Rev. Dr. Martin Luther King, Jr. was leaning over the green railing of the Lorraine Motel balcony in Memphis, Tennessee, chatting with Jesse Jackson, an associate who was standing in the court below. Jackson introduced King to Chicago musician Ben Branch, who was to perform at a scheduled rally that spring night, April 4, 1968.

"Yes, that's my man," said King, dressed in a black suit and white tie.

"The Rev. Ralph W. Abernathy, perhaps Dr. King's closest friend, was just about to come out of the motel room when the sudden loud noise burst out," *New York Times* reporter Earl Caldwell wrote in his dispatch from the scene of the assassination of the famed civil rights worker. "Dr. King

Earl Caldwell. © Maynard Institute. Used by permission.

toppled to the concrete second-floor walkway. Blood gushed from the right jaw and neck area. His necktie had been ripped off by the blast.

"'He had just bent over,' Mr. Jackson recalled later. 'If he had been standing up, he wouldn't have been hit in the face.'"

When he turned around, Jackson told Caldwell, who was in a nearby building when he heard the blast, "'I saw police coming from everywhere. They said, "where did it come from?" And I said, "behind you." The police were coming from where the shot came.'"[25]

Caldwell found himself in the midst of the biggest race story of the era, the violent end of the life of the leader of a nonviolent civil rights movement that had begun the previous decade, when King emerged in 1955 as a firebrand preacher who helped put together the Montgomery, Alabama, bus boycott during the Rosa Parks incident.

"The Rev. Dr. Martin Luther King Jr., who preached non-violence and racial brotherhood, was fatally shot here last night by a distant gunman who then raced away and escaped," began Caldwell's story, datelined Memphis, Friday, April 5. "Four thousand National Guard troops were ordered into Memphis by Gov. Buford Ellington after the 39-year-old Nobel Prize-winning civil rights leader died."

The city was put on curfew, Caldwell wrote, and sporadic shooting, fires, and thrown bottles and bricks were reported, followed by looting in the "Negro" districts that spread citywide.

"Police Director Frank Holloman said the assassin might have been a white man who was '50 to 100 yards away in a flophouse.'"

Police found a 30.06-caliber rifle a block from the scene of the shooting; Police Chief W.P. Huston said he believed it was the murder weapon and it would be turned over to the FBI.

"Dr. King was shot while he leaned over a second-floor railing outside his room at the Lorraine Motel. He was chatting with two friends just before starting for dinner," Caldwell wrote. "One of the friends was a musician, and Dr. King had just asked him to play a Negro spiritual, 'Precious Lord, Take My Hand,' at a rally that was to have been held two hours later in support of striking Memphis sanitation men."[26]

The story of King's assassination was one of a gallery of stories by Caldwell on the major political and social themes of the 1960s: the anti-Vietnam War demonstrations, the race protests, and the free-speech movement. Begun as a sports reporter in his small, western-Pennsylvania hometown, Caldwell's career would see him rise to become not only a national correspondent for the *New York Times,* but also the first African American to write a regular column for a major newspaper, the *New York Daily News.* His journalistic journey began as a detour in a career path for the young business student at the University of Buffalo who was seeking a future in insurance in Philadelphia before abruptly leaving school to try his hand at sports reporting back home.

Home was Clearfield, a community lush with big Italian gardens where Caldwell's father sold lumber, did landscaping, and bartered the pears grown on his own trees for grapes and other fresh fruit raised by neighbors. It was a town more concerned during Caldwell's childhood with the ravages of the Great Depression, followed by the sacrifices and peril of a world war fought in the Pacific and in Europe, than with the racial struggles and Vietnam War protests that would dominate much of his newspaper reporting in later years.

News of the depression dominated the front pages of the Sunday Pittsburgh and Philadelphia newspapers his father read when Caldwell was born on November 12, 1934. His hometown newspaper, the *Clearfield Progress,* carried similar fare, accompanied by datelines from far away; the events that dominated Clearfield's economic life were staged in Washington, D.C. and in the big cities of the East. The front page menu of the *Progress* on November 13, 1934, revealed a nation struggling to recover from economic blight after four years of unrelenting depression.

American economists and politicians saw signs of encouragement in the upward movement in the building trades, as evidenced by a boom in construction shares on the stock market, according to a front-page Associated Press article datelined New York. Another story, this one out of Philadelphia, announced the placing of an order for 57 streamlined electric engines intended "to be the most powerful electric passenger locomotives ever built in the world." The story's headline promised that 18 of the locomotives would be built in Altoona, Pennsylvania, with Erie and Philadelphia also feeling the positive effects of the order.[27]

In Boston, meanwhile, statistical expert Roger W. Babson suggested in a speech to the Advertising Club of Boston that President Franklin D. Roosevelt's administration should be followed by a coalition government that would mix the philosophies of both major political parties in dealing with the depression. "The Democrats are right when insisting on more equal opportunities and on favoring the plain people at the expense of the privileged few," said the speaker, adding: "The Republicans, however, are equally right in appealing for more rugged individualism and insisting upon rewards and punishments. The truth lies with a combination of both Republicans and Democrats."[28]

And in the South, a prominent Southern political leader, who would become a national demagogue challenging Roosevelt's policies, was strengthening his political hold on Louisiana. "Kingfish Huey Long," the newspaper reported, "tightened his dictatorial reins today for speedy enactment of his 'debt management' legislation." The legislation included bills establishing a two-year moratorium on personal debts and creation of state civil service for city police and fire departments and of a state bar association and a state narcotics law, "among other subjects."[29]

Economic hard times had some benefits, though, such as keeping prices low. The Quality Market in Clearfield offered "choice" T-bone steaks for 29 cents a pound and smoked hams for 21 cents a pound, while Jimmie's Fruit Market was selling California Sunkist oranges at 39 cents for two dozen.[30] And to carry shoppers to and from the market, Dorse Albert's line of used cars included a Chevrolet Coupe or an Erskine 6 Coupe, each priced at $45.[31]

Spurred by the hardships of the depression, Caldwell entered the University of Buffalo intent on pursuing business, which he studied for two years—long enough, he would recall, to learn "I had no business being a business student." Earning poor grades in all of his classes except those dealing with issues of insurance, Caldwell landed a summer job in Philadelphia, then was told he would have to go south and work for a black company because nobody would hire him in the North.

"Well, to me Alabama was the land of the bogeyman," he recalled more than half a century later. "I was just devastated."

So he returned home, where Caldwell was confronted with his father's rule: "You have to have a job. You're either going to school or you're going to be working or you're going to be in the Army." Caldwell went job hunting. Journalism appealed to him, based partly on his experience with newspapers read by his parents.

"One of the things my father always got was all of these papers, and the Italian across the street, he used to bring my father the Italian paper, so you had to pick up some of it. Also, my mom, and I think this was her way of testing me, what I was learning in school. At night, when it was her quiet time and she'd be reading the papers after dinner and everything, we'd be in the kitchen at the kitchen table, and I'd find an article, and I'd read it out loud."

Caldwell did more than read out loud, though; he studied the writing in a routine that would serve him as a journalist.

"I got into the habit, I would see something in the newspaper I really liked, I used to memorize it. I remember, at my second job, I was at Lancaster, it was in 1960 and Pittsburgh was in the World Series, and I was a sports writer down there at Lancaster and they sent me out to Pittsburgh to cover the first two games."

He met the *Washington Post*'s Shirley Povich and Hearst's Bob Considine at a World Series banquet there.

"The two of them were sitting together at this table, and I said to Mr. Povich, 'I thought that the story you'd written on Don Larsen's perfect game in the World Series was the greatest sports story I ever read.' I said that was one of the easiest stories for me to memorize. And he said, 'what do you mean?' and I said, 'well, if I liked the story, I memorized it.'"

Considine told the young reporter to stand up and recite the story.

"So I stand up there like a song, rattling it off, they were just bowled over by it, and Considine pulled up a chair and said 'tonight, you're going to sit and drink with us.' And there I was at the World Series."

Caldwell's mother, besides requiring him to read stories aloud, also became his first writing coach. After dinner, she would read out loud letters she had written to family members.

"I always liked that, and I wanted to get into writing letters. She showed me how to write letters and all that, so it was the beginning of me writing. But if you're reading a lot, it just dovetails right in, it goes with writing."

So it followed naturally that Caldwell, returned home from an insurance career cut short, would stray toward journalism on the streets of Clearfield.

"As it happened, there was a kid named Frank Cardon, a neighborhood Italian kid," Caldwell recalled. Growing up, Cardon had worked for the high school paper and had started his own newspaper, a mimeographed sheet for which Caldwell would write. When Caldwell returned to Clearfield looking for work, Cardon told him he could get him on at the local newspaper, the *Progress,* where Cardon read proofs, answered phones and wrote occasional sports stories.

"I loved sports," Caldwell said. "I said I'll do this for the summer, and by the end of that summer I was doing pretty good. I mean, I was learning how to do it, they liked me, and so I had to explain to my parents how it was better for me not to go back up there to Buffalo, that I wanted to stay home and do this."

So, in 1955, Caldwell settled in, for the time being at least, at the local newspaper. Current events in the nation and world had moved far beyond the depression and war tidings of his youth; major news events in the nation the year that Caldwell went to work for the *Progress* included civil rights issues that would define much of his journalism career. In May, the U.S. Supreme Court ordered the desegregation of state public schools "with all deliberate speed" in the *Brown II* ruling implementing the first Brown decision, and in December, Martin Luther King, Jr. formed the Montgomery Improvement Association in support of the Montgomery bus boycott. The court in November desegregated public parks and recreation facilities, and that same month the U.S. Interstate Commerce Commission banned segregation on interstate trains and buses. And noted historian C. Vann Woodward that year published *The Strange Career of Jim Crow*.[32]

The year opened up with the stoking of the domestic communist scare and McCarthyism stew when it was reported in January that the Eisenhower administration had dismissed thousands of federal employees between May 1953 and September 1954 because of suspected communist affiliations or connections; that same month the U.S. Senate voted unanimously to extend its investigation of communism in the United States.

The Cold War was in full force. In March, President Dwight D. Eisenhower endorsed the use of nuclear arms in the event of war, possibly in anticipation of the formal ending, in May, of the Allied occupation of West Germany. The Cold War heated up some in May when the Soviet Union annulled its alliance treaties with Britain and France in response to the ratification of the Paris agreement's inclusion of West Germany in the Western European Union. The Soviets then pieced together their own alliance, the Warsaw Pact—a treaty signed by the Soviet Union, Albania, Bulgaria, Czechoslovakia, East Germany, Hungary, Poland, and Romania. In September, the Soviets inked a treaty with East Germany, recognizing it as a sovereign state; and the next month, the Soviets strengthened ties with the globe's other communist superpower by signing an economic cooperation agreement with China.

Jonas Salk in April announced successful trials of his polio vaccine, and in the arts and letters community, Picasso painted *The Women of Algiers* while moviegoers enjoyed *Rebel Without a Cause* starring James Dean. C.S. Lewis published *The Magician's Nephew*, the sixth volume of *The Chronicles of Narnia;* Graham Greene published *The Quiet American;* and J.R.R. Tolkien published *The Two Towers*, the second volume of *The Lord of the Rings* trilogy. Vladimir Nabokov published *Lolita* in Paris following its rejection by U.S. publishers. And Tennessee Williams' *Cat on a Hot Tin Roof* made its debut in New York. This also was the year many credit with the birth of rock and roll; Bill Haley and the Comets popularized the music form with the release of *Rock Around the Clock*, featured in the film *The Blackboard Jungle* starring Glenn Ford, Anne Francis, and Sidney Poitier.

Caldwell, meanwhile, claimed the position of sports editor after his friend, Cardon, moved on to Lewistown. The owners of the *Progress* held the job for Caldwell when he did his six months for the National Guard after he was drafted by the military in 1957.

"I was very serious about being the sports editor of this paper," he remembered. "I liked it, and in that little town it was a very highly regarded position."

Caldwell was mentored at the *Progress* by editor George Scott, who stressed specificity of language to his young reporters.

"He used to have these meetings where he would bring all the staff together and tell us stuff about journalism. I can remember things he would say, I can remember, 'he wasn't hurt, he was injured.'"

One night a linotype operator showed Caldwell an ad from *Editor & Publisher* magazine for a newspaper in Lancaster seeking a reporter. The ad encouraged applicants to telephone collect, so he did, followed by an interview. The editor phoned six weeks later to offer the job.

"I'll tell you why it took us so long," the editor told Caldwell. "You're black, and nobody black ever came down asking for a job. If you would have come wanting a job as an elevator operator or something we could have hired you right away, but you wanted to be a sports writer. I had to check to see if there was any rule against it."

Caldwell left, with the blessing of Scott, who put in a word on behalf of Caldwell with a friend at the Lancaster newspaper, its chief political writer. Scott told Caldwell he didn't want to see him leave, but "that's a good paper you're going for. I want you to go down there."

The civil rights stories of the early 1960s were only headlines with faraway datelines as Caldwell covered sports for the *Intelligencer Journal*. But it would not be long before these stories became his stories; Caldwell's rise from Lancaster to the *New York Times* was rapid, taking him through Rochester, New York, on the way.

"Earl Caldwell had been perfectly content covering golf for the Lancaster, Pennsylvania, *Intelligencer Journal* when the civil rights movement suddenly made him, as a talented and experienced African American reporter, a hot commodity," wrote journalist Mark Bowden in a 2004 *Columbia Journalism* article. "A newspaper in upstate New York recruited him, and so distinguished was his reporting on race issues that almost four years later he was covering the most important story in the country for the *New York Times*."[33]

What Caldwell calls "the race story" caught up with him after he joined that upstate New York newspaper, the Rochester *Democrat and Chronicle*, when the editor sent him to New York to cover Harlem.

"They were trying to understand the story of race, and also it was exploding in a way," he recalled. "It culminated with them sending me to New York. A riot had broken out in Harlem, the first of the riots that were to really change America in the 1960s and eventually changed the complexion of the newsroom too. My paper sent me down to New York to write a 'can-it-happen-here' series. Big promotion on page one."

"The rioting in Harlem came in furious bursts," Caldwell would remember in *The Caldwell Journals*.

Rocks and bottles sailed from tenement roofs. Molotov cocktails exploded on streets littered with broken glass. Cops fired salvo after salvo into smoky, pitch-black skies. Police cruisers, sirens wailing, roared in pursuit of hit-and-run looters.

Crowds lined the streets, sometimes as many as a thousand people, all of them black and screaming, jeering, ducking, dodging and—when turned on by riot-weary cops—scrambling and running. And there we were, smack in the middle of it, with notebooks in hand, dashing at the heels of the crowds, observing the battles and trying as best we could to record it all.

Frenzied as it would be in those moments of battle, that's all they were, moments. They would rise like a storm and then, just as suddenly, dissipate. And with every inevitable lull in the action, attention turned to us. "Who are you?" people demanded. Some would reach for the press credentials that dangled from our necks.

We tried to explain ourselves. "We're press," we said. But that was not nearly explanation enough. "What press?" our inquisitors fired back.

In that back-and-forth, something that even we had not realized came into focus. Harlem cops and black residents had seen black reporters before. But almost without exception those reporters worked for black newspapers, mainly weeklies. This time we represented mainstream white-owned dailies and radio stations, a major first.[34]

Caldwell got to know Jimmy Breslin of the *New York Herald Tribune* during the riot coverage; Breslin introduced Caldwell to a *Herald Tribune* editor, and it was off to New York for Caldwell. After the *Herald Tribune* closed, and following his brief stay at the *New York Post*, the *New York Times* came calling. It was for this newspaper that Caldwell became a national correspondent covering not only "the race story" but also the free speech and student protest story—the '60s story, the one not about the war in Southeast Asia but the cultural wars at home.

Race riot was one of Caldwell's early beats at the *Times.* He filed a story from Cincinnati in June of 1967 about a riot there that injured 13 people.

"Ohio National Guardsmen with fixed bayonets were ordered into Cincinnati to join 900 policemen battling intense rioting that continued to sweep a large part of the city early today and spread to at least one suburban town," Caldwell wrote. "Forty-seven persons were reported arrested and at least 13 were injured in the second night of violence in Ohio's second largest urban center. One of the injured was reportedly a Negro man who was shot in the neck while sitting on his porch in the Mount Auburn section. Neither his condition nor his assailant was known immediately."

The story continued: "Police Chief Jacob Schott estimated that 'thousands' of teen-agers and young adults were storming through three of the city's sections hurling Molotov cocktails, smashing stores windows, looting and setting fires. 'There are so many marauding gangs now we just can't contain them,' Chief Schott said." [35]

Covering the riots, in New York and elsewhere, introduced Caldwell to a new racial dynamic—the freedom riders and other civil rights activities of the early '60s—that he had not experienced back home in Clearfield.

"When I got to New York, a lot of these kids who did these things gravitated to the Student Nonviolent Coordinating Committee," he remembered. "And as that piece of the civil rights movement sort of ended, a lot of them went to Washington, D.C., and a lot of them came to New York. These kids, I don't know whether it was by design or by accident, but they had a lot of impact, because they gravitated to a lot of those who are like myself, young, black . . . and we'd sit for long hours and they would give me Education 101 on that whole era of the movement, the freedom rides and all of those kinds of things that they were doing all across the South. It was funny how I didn't know them, didn't know those movements, even the March on Washington, until very late in the day."

In a think piece published in August of that 1967 summer of rioting, Caldwell wrote that the racial violence in cities across the country had "moderate Negro leaders groping to recapture their effectiveness. Their old alliances have been shattered. And, at least for the present, they are finding that they can only talk among themselves."

The piece continued: "This dilemma for the moderates comes at a time when they openly admit that they must have victories. They claim—with considerable justification—that the vast majority of Negroes have followed their leadership. And now they feel that the pressure is on them to show that they can produce."

As the moderates debated, Caldwell wrote, King was ready to try a different tactic. "He announced plans last week to 'dislocate' Northern cities with massive but nonviolent demonstrations of civil disobedience as a means of forcing Congress and President Johnson to respond to Negro demands. 'This is something like a last plea to the nation to respond to nonviolence,' he warned."[36]

The murder of King the next year accelerated the conversation over tactics, as Caldwell's coverage of the days following the assassination suggested.

"In those hours just after the assassination of the Rev. Dr. Martin Luther King, Jr., stunned witnesses stood around at the Lorraine Motel in Memphis, quietly debating the future of nonviolence in the civil rights movement," Caldwell wrote from Atlanta in April of 1968.

> "This movement is finished," a young Negro man said. "You can say that nonviolence ended right here."
>
> Others shared the same thought. The movement could not survive, they felt, without the charismatic leadership of Dr. King. "The movement," someone else said, "died with him."
>
> The next morning when the Rev. Ralph D. Abernathy came forward to accept the challenge as Dr. King's successor, their fears were only strengthened.

Mr. Abernathy had stood at Dr. King's side for years. And it was Dr. King himself who had made certain that if anything were to happen to him, it would be Mr. Abernathy who would step into his place. But Mr. Abernathy did not appear ready. He seemed unsure of himself and too hurt by the violent death of his friend to take up the challenge that was laid out for him.

But by the middle of last week, he was presenting another image. For the first time, he exuded confidence. He showed toughness and determination. And he also made it clear that no matter what anyone felt, he would not stand aside. "I don't have to tell that I am the leader," he shouted to an enthusiastic rally in Memphis that was celebrating the sanitation men's strike victory, "Baby," he said, "I am going to show you."[37]

Early in the next month, Abernathy was ready to lead the massive poor march on Washington, D.C., which Caldwell reported on from Montgomery, Alabama.

"A caravan of poor Negroes moving across the South on the way to Washington arrived tonight in the Alabama state capital, where a peaceful march was held in Negro neighborhoods," Caldwell wrote, adding that Abernathy had acknowledged the death, just the day before, of Alabama Gov. Lurleen B. Wallace. "But he added that 'just as the death of the Rev. Dr. Martin Luther King Jr. did not stop the Poor People's Campaign, neither will we stop because of the death of Governor Wallace.'"

Caldwell reported that nearly two thousand marchers walked behind Abernathy in the Montgomery march, and, "Tomorrow the caravan moves on to Birmingham, Ala., the third stop on the 14-day trip to Washington."[38]

Later that year, Caldwell's editors sent him to Chicago, the scene of the 1968 Democratic National Convention. The gathering drew not only Democratic Party leaders and delegates, it also brought the National Guard and some star antiwar protestors including the Rev. Jesse Jackson and singer and civil rights activist Harry Belafonte. Caldwell covered the tidings of the convention from the perspective of the race beat.

"Negroes on Chicago's South Side shouted angry objections today as troops moved into the city for duty during the Democratic National Convention," Caldwell wrote on August 25. "The activating of National Guardsmen and the calling out of Federal troops were compared by some with the Russian invasion of Czechoslovakia."

"The only difference," the Rev. Jesse Jackson told a boisterous rally of several thousand Negroes here this morning, is that he [Mayor Richard J. Daley] is too embarrassed to have them walk down the streets.

Harry Belafonte, the singer and civil rights activist, later drew long, shouting applause from the crowd when he suggested that the troops were in Chicago "to intimidate and provoke black people on the march for dignity."[39]

Four days later, Caldwell reported on the rioting and bloodshed that was to mark this convention for history.

"On the streets of the South Side today, Negroes continued virtually to ignore the Democratic National Convention," Caldwell wrote. "But they watched with interest as clashes between the police and young white dissidents became more intense.

"'I'm so glad it's the white ones out there raising hell,' an old man, who sat on a wooden crate at East 47th Street and Cottage Grove Avenue, said."

The man's attitude, Caldwell reported, was the dominant one in the black community. "'I want to see one of those National Guardsmen come at them with guns like they did us,' a teen-ager who stood in the doorway of Allen's Poolroom on East 51st Street, said."

As the antiwar protests and the Democratic Convention rioting took place seemingly in another world, another member of the black community welcomed the presence of the National Guard. She reasoned that the guard's battles with the rioting white protestors would divert attention from her and others involved with Operation Breadbasket, the Southern Christian Leadership Conference economic program that was boycotting and picketing the A. & P. supermarket chain.

"'As long as they can keep the Guard and the police tied up, I'm happy," Mrs. Beam said. 'If they are busy with them, they won't have time to arrest pickets and I'm interested in picketing A. & P.'"[40]

As the civil rights movement shifted away from King's methods to more direct and confrontational means, so did Caldwell's coverage. His editors assigned him a beat that would provide one of the most challenging, and learning, experiences of his career: the Black Panthers. The Panthers offered a radically different approach than what Caldwell had seen with King—a revolutionary socialist and educational response to white supremacy. Caldwell began covering the organization in New York before being assigned to the Panther and protest beat on the West Coast. His reportage included in-depth news features about the Panthers, such as a piece the newspaper published in September 1968 profiling young converts. The youthful blacks spoke of revolution and of change—dominant themes of the '60s.

"He was young and black and dissatisfied," Caldwell wrote of a 17-year-old boy "who wore his hair in the African style and had a spent rifle shell on a band around his neck."

The Panthers, Caldwell wrote, "offered change, and that was what he wanted. 'Change, change and by any means necessary' he said, quoting one of Malcolm X's favorite phrases."

A 27-year-old father of three children told Caldwell he'd dropped out of a chemical company's executive training program to join the local (Brooklyn) chapter of the Panthers.

"'We're young revolutionaries," the man told Caldwell. "We're revolutionaries and we're fighting a war.' He called it a war for the survival of black people. 'You have got to understand,' he continued. 'We're not fooling. We are sincere about this. We are ready to die for what we believe.'"

In Negro gatherings where racial matters are discussed the presence of the Panthers in their black berets, black leather jackets and black trousers has become increasingly evident.

But like many militant organizations, Panthers refuse to discuss their numbers.

"Numbers," they said, "are not important."[41]

The Panthers did not limit their revolutionary zeal to the office and the streets. They took it home and to their children in educational programs that included free breakfasts.

In a dispatch from San Francisco, Caldwell described an early morning scene in which second-, third- and fourth-graders arrived in a "shabby little whitewashed church" for a breakfast of eggs, pancakes, grits, sausages, bacon, toast, coffee, milk, and "sometimes" juice. It was part of a national breakfast and educational program that party Chairman Bobby Seale had once boasted to Caldwell fed more than 10,000 children a day in cities that included San Francisco, New York, Chicago, Detroit, Boston, Los Angeles, and Kansas City.

"At the back door of the church, sitting at a scarred wooden desk, Richard O'Neal, a 20-year-old member of the Black Panther party waits for the kids," Caldwell wrote. "'Free Huey,' the first youngster to reach the door shouts. The others follow. 'Free Huey. Free Huey. Free Huey.' O'Neal grins and raises a clenched fist. 'Right on, little brothers and sisters,' he says. 'Right on.'" [The "Free Huey" slogan was aimed at Huey Newton, the party's minister of defense, imprisoned in connection with the fatal shooting of an Oakland, California police officer.]

The shouts for Newton's freedom, though, are not the only slogans the kids have picked up during the breakfast meetings.

In St. Augustine's Episcopal Church in Oakland, Marsha Turner, a young Panther leader, led the youngsters in a song that had these lyrics:

"There's a pig upon the hill, if you don't shoot 'em the Panthers will." And: "They got Huey in the jail, they won't let 'em out on bail."

Marsha, a pretty, 16-year-old, yelled the lyrics and after each verse, as in the old Army march song, she would ask the kids to "sound off" and they would respond with the familiar shout of "Free Huey."[42]

Sprinkled in with Caldwell's coverage of the Panthers were other antiestablishment beat pieces, such as antiwar demonstrations and student protests. An August, 1967, Caldwell story told of plans for a massive antiwar protest in September intended to "shut down the Pentagon."

"Organizers of the demonstration—scheduled for Oct. 21–22—said they believed it would be 'the most serious antiwar protest in American history.'

"The National Mobilization Committee to End the War In Vietnam outlined plans for the protest at a news conference at the Overseas Press Club, 54 West 40th Street."

The demonstration, Caldwell reported, had the backing of several antiwar groups, including the Student Nonviolent Coordinating Committee, Women Strike for Peace, the Episcopal Peace Fellowship, the Congress of Racial Equality, "the so-called hippie community and a number of active peace groups."

"In its statement announcing the demonstration, the committee called on 'all Americans who oppose our Government's aggression in Vietnam' to converge on Washington 'for a direct, personal and collective confrontation with the warmakers.'"[43]

On the West Coast, Caldwell continued to report on the protest beat; one of the stories he filed from the San Francisco office was a piece on striking students at San Francisco State College planning to defy the college's acting president, Dr. S.I. Hayakawa.

Reporting that the students were refusing to cancel a mass demonstration scheduled for the next morning on the "troubled campus," Caldwell reported: "In taking their militant position, the students set the stage for what could be a violent showdown with college officials."

Hayakawa, Caldwell wrote, had banned rallies, marches, and demonstrations on the campus.

"But the students said angrily to their supporters in the Bay yesterday that their plans had 'not changed' and went ahead with preparations for a mass convergence on the campus."

Hayakawa threatened to bring in the police, but a member of the student Strike Support Committee, "an organization of white students who support the Black-Student Union and other minority groups in their 15 demands that prompted the strike," dismissed the threat.

"As far as we are concerned," he said, "we have the right to assemble and speak and we're going to exercise those rights whenever we feel it's necessary."[44]

Later that year, Caldwell filed another free-speech story, on a University of California faculty boycott in protest of the National Guard's gassing of hundreds of university students.

"Aroused members of the university of California faculty," he wrote in May 1969, "began a boycott of classes today on the Berkeley campus."

While the campus was calm, Caldwell wrote, "there was an unmistakable air of tension as hundreds of students milled about in the Sproul Hall Plaza.

"It was in the plaza yesterday that the gassing took place. A National Guard helicopter began sweeping over students, faculty members and other demonstrators shortly after Guard troops attempted to disperse the crowd that had gathered at the home of Chancellor Roger W. Heyns."

The previous day's violence, Caldwell reported, occurred following a funeral march for a 25-year-old man "who suffered gunshot wounds in a clash last Thursday and who died on Monday." That march apparently was in violation of emergency restrictions issued the previous week by then-Governor Ronald Reagan prohibiting rallies and assemblies.

"According to the police, 14 persons were injured yesterday and 101 were arrested. Since the dispute began here last Thursday 288 persons have been arrested.

"The confrontation here grew out of the official closing of a plot of university-owned land that had been improved by students and other youths as a 'People's Park.'"[45]

But the Panthers were Caldwell's primary focus, such as a July 20, 1969, article reporting on a gathering of whites and blacks urged by Panther leaders to unite for the cause.

"They came with long hair and in faded old Army field jackets, in bulky sweaters and in worn and ragged levis," Caldwell wrote. "Most of them were white; some were youthful hippies. The majority were students, and they came off the campuses fired with what they called revolutionary fervor."

> "Power to the people," they shouted. "Power to the people." They made it a chant and they used it again and again. When they did, their arms shot into the air with their fists clenched.
>
> Nearly 3,000 of these young people gathered last night in the Oakland auditorium. They came at the urging of the Black Panther party to put together what the party chairman, Bobby Seale, called "a truly united front against Fascism."[46]

Seale was one of several prominent leaders of the Black Panther party who were in jail or out of the country on December 4, 1969, the day the party's national chief of staff would be charged with threatening the life of President Richard Nixon.

Party leader Eldridge Cleaver had fled the country, even as his book *Soul on Ice* was enjoying best-seller status, to avoid a prison term for violating parole. Seale, cofounder of the party, was being held on murder conspiracy charges. Newton, the party's minister of defense, had been imprisoned the previous year.[47] And now, the 27-year-old David Hilliard, party chief of staff, had been "arrested quietly in downtown San Francisco by agents of the Secret Service" following a speech he had made the previous month to a throng of thousands during a Memorium Day peace rally at Golden State Park.

"According to evidence presented to a Federal grand jury," Caldwell reported for the *Times*, "Mr. Hilliard referred in that speech to President Nixon as 'the man that's responsible for all the attacks on the Black Panty party nationally.'

"Mr. Hilliard was quoted as adding: 'We will kill Richard Nixon.'"[48]

That threat was part of a radical agenda for a radical time, an agenda that Hilliard, in a separate interview with Caldwell, explained clearly.

"'We are special,' Mr. Hilliard said recently. 'We advocate the very direct overthrow of the Government by way of force and violence. By picking up guns and moving against it because we recognize it as being oppressive and in recognizing that we know that the only solution to it is armed struggle.'"[49]

The guns got the attention of the federal government, as the Panthers apparently desired; and Caldwell, sent by the *Times* to Oakland to cover the Panthers, had become a trusted reporter by party leaders and a conduit for national notoriety for the party. Bowden, writing in 2004 about the party and Caldwell's coverage, said there had been a lot of talk of guns at party meetings. He quoted Caldwell:

> Huey Newton was on trial for killing a police officer. There was talk of taking violent action if he were convicted. On my first night in Berkeley I went to the house of Eldridge and Kathleen Cleaver, Panther leaders, and I wound up with a group that was moving a large number of weapons to Oakland. I wrote the story. I just figured they mustn't read *The New York Times*. It didn't dawn on me until later that they *wanted* me to write about it. They wanted law enforcement to know that they were heavily armed.[50]

Caldwell's reporting would not only send a message to the federal government, it would also bring the government to him, in the form of a subpoena ordering him to testify before a federal grand jury in San Francisco looking into the Black Panthers' activities. That subpoena led to a constitutional struggle over the right of reporters to protect their sources that would land before the U.S. Supreme Court in 1972, which ended with the court ruling that the First Amendment did not protect Caldwell and other reporters from divulging sources. As a result of that ruling, which prompted the formation of the Reporters Committee for Freedom of the Press, a majority of U.S. states now have shield laws protecting reporters' from revealing their sources.[51]

Caldwell became fascinated with the Panthers, as a social movement, as a black movement; hip members of the black community taught him about different elements of blackness. Indeed, he said at his dining room table nearly 40 years later remembering his time with the Panthers, they helped teach him about the black movement, answered his journalistic curiosity about it.

"I used to be over there for hours and hours and hours," he said, "and my whole thing was, I'm always looking for the answer to this. We're both black, we're both about the same age, now why is it that you're running around here with the leather jackets and the guns and want to pick up the gun and I'm over here just as black as you are and I don't understand why you're doing this. What is it in our lives, and what is it you see that's so different, and I was wrestling with this, and you go back from that March on Washington to those early parts of it. I was always trying to find out, what is my role in this, and what am I supposed to see, and in the meantime I'm also committed and really believed in being a journalist. . . . The struggle for me through many of those years was to understand what black people had experienced, understanding that, what do we do, what is your role in this?"

He used to sit with the Panthers late at night, he said. "I never did understand all of their Marxist-Leninist rhetoric. I used to spend a lot of time trying to figure out with them what they were really prepared to do and where they were prepared to go. But when I began to really look at them, I would notice certain things. I'd get up with them at three o'clock in the morning and they'd be cooking breakfast for the kids, and they had their little breakfast for children program, and these kids would come in and they would feed them and then after they would feed them the kids were hollering and everything and they'd make them learn little drills, and then they would have all these little politics things and they'd tell them all the Black Panther stuff and everything, but in my life, in my going around I would see these kids coming out of these really poor homes. I'd know every single day of my life, before I left home and went to school, my mom cooked a really big breakfast for everybody every day, it was just like clockwork, there was a breakfast and a lunch and a dinner. I can't recall a single day that it wasn't that way. So they were looking at something and dealing with somebody that I was just learning about, these kids at the bottom where they don't have the home, where they don't really have anybody looking out for them, where they are going out in the morning with their bellies empty.

"Another thing was the police brutality issue," he continued. "I understood what they were doing, but I had no idea it was as pervasive as it was, all these issues with black people and the police. But I was very impressed with these guys who would go around at night, following the police, and they'd have a tape recorder, and a notebook like we carried, and the cops would stop a black person, they would get out and get the names of the witnesses and all this kind of thing, and of course the police didn't like it. But at the same time, I'd see this guy like Eldridge Cleaver. He seemed to me like an evil person, and I had read this book of his, he'd raped some women and came out of prison and he just seemed like he was a—he was different than so many of the guys that I would sit and talk to for hours and hours and hadn't been to prison, had come to the Black Panther party for so many different reasons.

"But I think that we were all struggling with where do we go, these young, black men in America in the 1960s. We had come off that civil rights movement era, that had these apartheid laws; that was all knocked down, you could vote, if somebody discriminates against you, it's illegal, but where do we go, how do we get there, what do we do, and the Panthers, I felt, were opening up my eyes to a lot of things."

But the Panthers also were reckless, Caldwell said.

"King said 'no, we don't have to pick up any guns or clubs or knives,' but the Black Panthers said 'no, we're going to pick up the gun.'"

It was the nonviolence, Caldwell said, that was King's mark on the movement and on the country. He cited a peaceful demonstration led by King in 1965 that helped bring about one of the more significant civil rights milestones in the nation's history, passage of the Voting Rights Act of 1965. The march was credited with spurring congressional action on the act, which President Lyndon Johnson signed into law within five months of the freedom march from Selma to Montgomery, Alabama, led by King despite violent opposition and legal delays. Caldwell's newspaper captured the mood and significance of the march, similar to so many of the nonviolent protests and demonstrations undertaken by King, on March 24, 1965:

> While two American astronauts orbited the earth at extraordinary speed in the skies far overhead, 300 other Americans were trudging slowly along U.S. Highway 80 in central Alabama.
>
> Predominantly Negroes of Alabama birth but including persons of both races, all religious faiths and every section of the nation, these travelers were on the third day of a five-day walk from Selma to Montgomery, the state capital. A cold rain was falling, but the walkers did not seem to mind. . . .
>
> A rural South in which Negroes can vote and hold office and lift up their heads as equal will be a new and very much better south. An America in which white and Negroes are freed forever of that ugly old burden known as "the race problem," freed of the weight of centuries of hatred and guilt and misplaced pride, will be a new and very much better America.[52]

"I believe that King's legacy is exactly what he said," recalled Caldwell, "that we do have the power, and we can change things, and that we don't have to pick up the gun to be successful to do that. I think King also saw that we could have an impact on these economic matters. I think King had a global vision, I think he began to let us know that we're not isolated as black people, we're not truly in a global sense even a minority. And I also think that King had a huge impact in convincing or showing or teaching us not to be afraid. Not to be immobilized by fear, to confront and to go up against these forces, even though he got killed doing this, as he said, had it written down, a man who is not ready to die for something is not fit to live. Plus, King also believed in and fought for, and his last great triumph was, the vote, and he saw that this vote of black people could be a great deciding thing. . . . I think King saw the potential more than any other person that I know. Even though we have the national holiday, I don't think we do enough studying of what King really said, what he really believed and what he laid out."

King's death did change the direction of the civil rights movement, despite the picking up of the nonviolent civil rights torch by Abernathy, Caldwell said. The new direction would mean more militancy and an alliance with the antiwar movement. Even King had been modifying his approach, Caldwell said. The rioting and antiwar movement had altered the protest template.

"That's why King said he was going to have this poor people's campaign. He was going to try a new, more militant brand of non-violent action against the government. And people forget that in 1968 King said the goals of the poor people's campaign were to guarantee a job and an income for everyone. Can you imagine someone arguing that today? It's astounding. But that was what King was arguing in 1968, and he said, 'we can do it, the first place is all the money is going to the war, stop that war, fight against that war and we'll bring that money home and we can do these things here.'"

The younger blacks, Caldwell said, were leaning toward more militant activities, including the actions espoused by the Black Panthers.

"So they were preparing to go another way, and King said, 'where you going to go, where's that going to lead you, how are you going to be successful that way?' That was the big issue, and if King doesn't get killed, I believe he would have had a very difficult time being the person of great influence with the younger black people because they were bound and determined that they were going off in a more militant way."

Caldwell's editor at the *Times,* Claude Sitton, had sensed a shift away from King's nonviolent tactics before King's murder and before the march on Washington, Caldwell recalled.

"He says to me, he calls me up to his desk and he says, 'King's lost control of his people, he can't go ahead with that poor people's campaign.' He said, 'if he goes forward with that poor people's campaign it's going to cause a bloodbath.' I believe Claude, in a way, was a genius. This was before Chicago, and I think Claude said the way that things were, that there was this explosion just waiting to happen. And Claude saw that if King takes all these black people to Washington, and they confront the police the way King wants to, there's going to be a bloodbath. As it happened, King got killed, the confrontation between these forces and the police took place in Chicago.

"It was changing, and it was bound to change," he continued. "When King was killed, the door was opened for it. To go and to pick up the guns."

The '60s, Caldwell said, saw a dramatic change in the politics and mood of the nation. It was a decade that began conservatively, coming out of the Eisenhower era of peace and prosperity, but that ended in a vastly different political and social mindset. He remembered a Ray Charles song, "What I Say," which was considered at the beginning of the decade to be one that would not be played in polite company.

"There was a big night club in Cherry Hill, New Jersey. Ray Charles played there, and people got up on tables, they had to stop it, couldn't let him play like that. I still think about that period. You know, it was really . . . this change was beginning to come, tear down the old, just tear it all down and build this new. They would tear down downtowns, tear down these things, and redevelopment. A lot of people look at it now and say it was a big mistake, but it was like this change. I think one of the things was that after the war, maybe it's because they had more money, I don't know, maybe they had a lot of money to do things, but there were these new ideas about the way things were, and people seemed ready, there was this change that people wanted to do. Part of it was Kennedy too, but the change was coming, and I could see it with the music, I could see it with the ideas about this redevelopment, you could see it in politics. To me the '60s, that was the beginning, and also for me personally it was me leaving the mountains, not only coming into journalism but coming into these bigger markets and these bigger cities where you had this mix and everything, and so hey, the early '60s was like this breaking out in America and breaking out in all kinds of ways."

And journalism was changing, too.

"The newsrooms had no blacks, but no women either. For a long period, the change was more emphasis on race, then the women's movement caught on and that became a major thing and they springboard right over the blacks. But I think that's what made it magical, everything was changing, it wasn't just the music."

By the end of the decade, Caldwell said, the mood of the nation had altered; the Vietnam War had fatigued the country, yet the people who had fought to end the war felt a sense of accomplishment. And assassinations had altered the nation's course dramatically.

"I always felt that the people who went through it, that they came out being better people and a feeling and a sense of accomplishment because they did put themselves on the line, and there were a lot of things that they turned away from," he said. "But there was this whole thing called drop out, and a lot of people dropped out, and the black people said 'yeah, but the white people can drop back in when they get ready to drop back in, you can't drop in,' and actually it did turn out that way. I knew a guy who was a leader of the Yippies, Jerry Rubin, and I was covering him and the radical politics of the '60s, and then I came to New York in the '70s writing a column, and he was on Wall Street. So there was a lot of that.

"But when you take the '60s, it was a time of a great advancement because you had a very liberal Supreme Court, and that meant a lot. You also had a time of racial progress, but the war screwed it up; I thought there was a national move to try to do something about poverty, about changing things for poor people, and some of these programs, like the Head Start program, the Black Panther breakfasts were brought into the public schools. Some of these were really great creative programs."

The nation ended the decade a better place, Caldwell said.

"Mind you, we had tremendous setbacks in the '60s, with these political assassinations. What kind of country would it have been if Bobby Kennedy, Jack Kennedy and Martin Luther King . . . leaders that people look back on, even Malcolm X is in there too, the way that he was changing and where he was going, there's no telling. We paid a horrible price there."

But while the nation was better, Caldwell said, the end of the Vietnam War early in the next decade also brought new problems, such as homelessness. He said that as an experiment one day when he was on his way to work to write his column, he decided to ask each homeless person on the street how that person had become homeless.

"I finally had to put my notebook away and quit talking to people because so many of those stories were going to people talking about Vietnam, they were actually soldiers in Vietnam and they came back, there was nothing for them, and they had injuries, they had mental problems, they had disconnected, and almost all of them were black. Well this was a legacy from that period."

NOTES

1. CBS Evening News, August 5, 1965.
2. Morley Safer, *Flashbacks: On Returning to Vietnam* (New York: Random House, 1990), 89–91.
3. Ibid., 92.
4. Ibid., 95–96.
5. Ibid., 96.
6. "60 Minutes: Morley Safer," CBS News Web page, http://www.cbsnews.com/stories 1998/07/09/60minutes/main13545.shtml (accessed May 4, 2006).
7. Morley Safer, *Flashbacks: On Returning to Vietnam*, 96.
8. "Didn't Preach force, Communist Declares," *Toronto Daily Star*, November 9, 1931, 1.
9. "Allege Girls Tried To Aid Communists," *Toronto Daily Star*, November 9, 1931, 2.
10. "Unemployed Seek More Pay As Farmers Protest Relief," *Toronto Daily Star*, November 9, 1931, 20.
11. "Church Must Help Labor Con. Jas. Simpson Declares," *Toronto Daily Star*, November 9, 1931, 20.
12. "Simpson's MARKET," and "VALUES for Tuesday shoppers" *Toronto Daily Star*, November 9, 1931, 16.
13. Milestone listings for 1950 for this paragraph and those that follow taken from Neville Williams, *Chronology of World History Volume IV: 1901–1998/The Modern World* (Santa Barbara, CA: ABC-CLIO, 1999), 401–11.
14. "The President at the Wall," CBS News Extra, June 26, 1963.
15. "U.S. Quarantines Cuba," CBS News Extra, October 22, 1962.
16. "U.S. Quarantines Cuba," CBS Washington Report, News Extra, October 28, 1962.
17. "The Four Dark Days: From Dallas to Arlington," CBS News, November 25, 1963.
18. "The American Assassins, No. 4," CBS Reports Inquiry, January 5, 1976.
19. Morley Safer, *Flashbacks: On Returning to Vietnam*, 32–33.
20. Ibid., 29–32.
21. Ibid., 109–10.
22. Ibid., 110.
23. CBS News Special Report: President Johnson: State of the Union Address, January 4, 1965.
24. CBS News Special Report: President Johnson: Address on Voting Rights Act, March 15, 1965.

25. Earl Caldwell, "Guard Called Out/Curfew Is Ordered in Memphis, but Fires and Looting Erupt," *New York Times,* April 5, 1968, 1.

26. Ibid.

27. AP, "Pennsy Locomotive Order Means Great Deal To Altoona," *Clearfield Progress,* November 13, 1934, 1.

28. AP, "BABSON SEES COALITION GOVERNMENT IN 1936 AS THE NATION'S PANACEA," *Clearfield Progress,* November 13, 1934, 1.

29. AP, "Football 'Senator,' Made By Huey Long, Keeps to His Books; Legislature a Real Circus," *Clearfield Progress,* November 13, 1934, 1.

30. "Quality Market," "Cal. SUNKIST ORANGES," *Clearfield Progress,* November 13, 1934, 3.

31. "Chevrolet's Used Cars!" *Clearfield Progress,* November 13, 1934, 6.

32. Milestone listings for 1955 for this paragraph and those that follow taken from Neville Williams, *Chronology of World History Volume IV: 1901–1998/The Modern World* (Santa Barbara, CA: ABC-CLIO, 1999), 445–53.

33. Mark Bowden, "Lowering My Shield: A Murder Case, a Subpoena, and a Reporter Ready to Go to Jail to Protect What He Knows. Why Did He Start to Feel Like a Dope?" *Columbia Journalism Review,* July/August 2004, http://www.cjr.org/issues/2004/4/bowden–shields.asp (accessed February 5, 2007).

34. Earl Caldwell, "The Caldwell Journals/Chapter Nine/Harlem: The Colony Converges," Maynard Institute Web Site, http://www.maynardije.org/news/features/caldwell/ (accessed February11, 2007).

35. Earl Caldwell, "Guard Is Called Into Cincinnati As Riots Spread," *New York Times,* June 14, 1967, 1.

36. Earl Caldwell, "And the Negro In the 'Black Establishment,'" *New York Times,* August 20, 1967, E3.

37. Earl Caldwell, "After King/His Deputy Carries On His Work," *New York Times,* April 21, 1968, E3.

38. Earl Caldwell, "Poor March Into Montgomery, 2,000 Following Civil Rights Leader," *New York Times,* May 8, 1968, 31.

39. Earl Caldwell, "Negroes in Chicago Object as Troops Move Into City for Convention Duty," *New York Times,* August 25, 1968, 77.

40. Earl Caldwell, "Chicago Negroes Stirred by Clashes Between Whites and Police, Not Convention," *New York Times,* August 29, 1968, 22.

41. Earl Caldwell, "Black Panthers: 'Young Revolutionaries at War,'" *New York Times,* September 6, 1968, 49.

42. Earl Caldwell, "Black Panthers Serving Youngsters a Diet of Food and Politics," *New York Times,* June 15, 1969, 57.

43. Earl Caldwell, "War Foes To Try To Shut Pentagon," *New York Times,* August 29, 1967, 12.

44. Earl Caldwell, "Coast Students Defy Protest Ban," *New York Times,* January 6, 1969, 31.

45. Earl Caldwell, "Faculty Boycott Is On At Berkeley," *New York Times,* May 22, 1969, 19.

46. Earl Caldwell, "3,000 Radicals, Most Whites, Open Panther-Led Unity Parley," *New York Times,* July 20, 1969, 43.

47. Earl Caldwell, "Declining Black Panthers Gather New Support From Repeated Clashes With Police," *New York Times,* December 14, 1969, 64.

48. Earl Caldwell, "Panther Charged in Nixon Threat," *New York Times,* December 4, 1969, 37.

49. Earl Caldwell, "Declining Black Panthers Gather New Support From Repeated Clashes With Police," *New York Times,* December 14, 1969, 64.

50. Mark Bowden, "Lowering My Shield: A Murder Case, a Subpoena, and a Reporter Ready to Go to Jail to Protect What He Knows. Why Did He Start to Feel Like a Dope?" *Columbia Journalism Review,* July/August 2004, http://www.cjr.org/issues/2004/4/bowden—shields.asp (accessed February 5, 2007).

51. Steve Hallock, "Monograph reminds reporters of their own rights," *The St. Louis Journalism Review* Vo. 35, 280, October 2005.

52. "Walk for Freedom," *New York Times,* March 24, 1965, 42.

CHAPTER 4

The '70s of Ben Bradlee and Georgie Anne Geyer: Scandal and Peace with Honor and Foreign Intrigue

> Pretty good. I mean it feels pretty good. I did my job, I think I did what I was put on Earth to do, which was to follow a good story to the end, and the fact that it was a Republican and that it was the president was more important to the general public than it was to me. I just sometimes worry that, is that going to be the big thing of my life? That's thirty-some years ago, and that sort of makes me sad, but I guess it is. I think as important as it was to me and to this paper, it wasn't all that important. It wasn't.
>
> —Ben Bradlee

Ben Bradlee folded his hands between his knees, lay his forehead on the desk, and uttered a "very private 'Holy Moly'" after Richard Nixon announced that effective at noon the next day, he would resign the office of president of the United States. That moment gone, Bradlee set about the business of getting out the next day's newspaper and its front page story summarizing the downfall of a presidency.

"It is no mean feat under great pressure to get the fruits of a 9:00 P.M. press conference into the first edition of a morning newspaper," he wrote in his memoir of that day. Then, the page one lead story written, the headline composed, "I dragged my weary bones down one floor to the composing room, not wanting to let go of the most important single newspaper edition I ever had anything to do with. George Kidwell was making up page one, and he made sure I had nothing to do except practice reading the lead type upside down."[1]

Ben Bradlee. © The Washington Post. Used by permission.

For this newspaper editor, the lead paragraph of the story on the front page of the *Washington Post* on August 9, 1974, had more meaning than for any other editor in the United States on that day.

> Richard Milhous Nixon announced last night that he will resign as the 37th President of the United States at noon today.
>
> Vice President Gerald R. Ford of Michigan will take the oath as the new President at noon to complete the remaining two years of Nixon's term.
>
> After two years of bitter public debate over the Watergate scandals, President Nixon bowed to pressures from the public and leaders of his party to become the first President in American history to resign.[2]

"We had no picture symbolizing the dramatic moment for the first edition," Bradlee wrote in his memoir more than 20 years later, "but we had White House photographer Ollie Atkins's remarkable, poignant picture of the president tightly clasping his daughter, Julie Eisenhower, before his resignation—played half the page wide and half the page deep—for the later editions."

The unraveling of the Nixon presidency had begun nearly two years before, when the *Post*'s managing editor, Howard Simons, got a call the morning of June 17, 1972, from Joe Califano, a former special assistant to President Lyndon Johnson, informing him that five men had been caught breaking into the Democratic National Headquarters in the Watergate complex and were to be arraigned that morning. Bradlee would write in his memoir:

> The best journalists in the world could be forgiven for not realizing that this was the opening act of the scandalous political melodrama—unparalleled in American history—which would end up with the resignation of a disgraced president and the jailing of more than forty people, including the Attorney General of the United States, the White House chief of staff, the White House counsel, and the president's chief domestic adviser.[3]

For the next two years, the *Post* and its two primary Watergate reporters, Bob Woodward and Carl Bernstein, would take the lead, often alone but with substantial help from other news organizations that included the *New York Times,* the *Los Angeles Times, Time* magazine, *Newsweek,* and later, CBS News. Finally, the U.S. Congress joined in the process of investigating and documenting the money and political trails of the Watergate story. The *Washington Post*'s online site, in a chronology that reads like a political scandal scrapbook, lists the important events and dates of the investigation as follows:[4]

- June 19, 1972: A Republican security aide is reported by the newspaper to be one of the five burglars; John Mitchell, the former attorney general now heading the committee to reelect the president, denies any link to the burglary.
- August 1, 1972: The money trail materializes. The *Post* reports that a $25,000 cashier's check, "apparently earmarked for the Nixon campaign," ends up in a Watergate burglar's bank account.
- September 29, 1972: The *Post* reports that Mitchell, while attorney general, controlled "a secret Republican fund used to finance widespread intelligence-gathering operations against the Democrats."

Bernstein had telephoned Mitchell for comment on the story at 11:30 at night, Bradlee wrote, prompting an angry outburst from Mitchell.

> "All that crap you're putting in the paper. It's all been denied. [Publisher] Katie Graham's going to get her tit caught in a big fat wringer if that's published. Good Christ! That's the most sickening thing I've ever heard. . . . You fellows got a great ball game. As soon as you're through paying Ed Williams and the rest of those fellows, we're going to do a little story on all of you."[5]

- October 10, 1972: The *Post* reports that the FBI established that the burglary "stems from a massive campaign of political spying and sabotage conducted on behalf of the Nixon reelection effort."

As the Nixon administration entered its rapid descent over the next couple of years, the newspaper would report the following events: former

Nixon aides G. Gordon Liddy and James W. McCord Jr. were convicted in late January 1973 of conspiracy, burglary, and wiretapping stemming from the break-in; top White House staffers H.R. Haldeman, John Erlichman, and Attorney General Richard Kleindienst resigned in April of that year, and White House counsel John Dean was fired; the Senate Watergate Committee on May 18, 1973, began nationally televised hearings investigating the scandal; Nixon's former appointments secretary, Alexander Butterfield, revealed in testimony in mid-July that Nixon had recorded all of his conversations and telephone calls; in late October, Nixon fired special prosecutor Archibald Cox and abolished the special prosecutor's office; in December, the White House was unable to explain an 18-and-a-half-minute gap in one of the subpoenaed tapes; in July 1974, the U.S. Supreme Court ordered Nixon to turn over tape recordings of 64 White House conversations; and later that month, the Houses Judiciary Committee passed the first of three articles of impeachment.

Bradlee in his memoir acknowledged the work of the other news organizations, but he singled out the importance of CBS News in joining the coverage as particularly important. In mid-October 1972, a colleague of Bradlee's from the editor's days at *Newsweek* telephoned to say that Walter Cronkite and CBS would be airing two pieces about Watergate on the *Evening News*.

"That was good news," Bradlee wrote, "because television had been generally unable to cope with Watergate, and national acceptance of the story had lagged accordingly. Probably because it would never be a visual story until the Senate hearings five months later, except for a few shots of Dan Rather and Nixon shouting at each other in press conferences."

> When the pieces finally ran (fourteen minutes on October 27, and eight minutes the next night), they had a powerful impact everywhere—on the *Post,* on the politicians (if not the voters), and on newsrooms outside Washington. Somehow the Great White Father, Walter Cronkite, the most trusted man in America, had blessed the story by spending so much time on it. . . . We were thrilled. No new ground was broken, but the broadcasts validated the *Post's* stories in the public's mind and gave us all an immense morale boost.[6]

The irony of the whole operation was the incompetence of the burglars. It was a story that happened almost by accident, Bradlee would recall from behind his tidy desk in his *Washington Post* office more than 30 years later.

"They were mere amateurs as criminals," he said. "They (the Nixon crowd) just listened to the wrong people. I don't think that was in Richard Nixon's training, he wouldn't have done that unless he'd been influenced by people who craved power and wanted to keep it."

The editor who would help topple a king, or at least an imperial Republican presidency, came into the world the son of proper Boston Republican parents, what he would call "a kind of a guilt by association." It was a family he characterized as "carelessly anti-Roosevelt" during the depression years.

"They didn't have great cause, the depression they didn't blame on Roosevelt, the recovery they gave him some credit, they just didn't like Democrats," he recalled. "The WASPs (White Anglo-Saxon Protestants) in Boston were largely Republican."

Bradlee's father, Frederick, served the party. "At the end of his life, he was a parole commissioner, and he was on some investigative commission, and he did some investigating for the Republican Party and the (Mayor James M.) Curley administration. You know, the bridges used to fall outside of Boston, apparently he (Curley) gave them to his pals who were contractors, and they didn't know how to build. It was not hard to be a Republican. Chris Herder, Cabot Lodge, that was his crowd. You know, not that high up in the social order, but those are the people, he knew them all, and liked them."

Republicans were in charge in Washington, leading the nation to what presidential candidate Warren Harding promised would be a return to "normalcy" following the Woodrow Wilson years, when Bradlee was born in Boston on August 26, 1921, on the cusp of the Roaring Twenties. It was a time of labor strife, of red scare. The lead story on the front page of the *Boston Evening Globe* that day reported a march by West Virginia coal miners to protest martial law declared by Governor Ephraim F. Morgan in response to a dispute over union organization, fighting that involved mine guards, police, and federal troops.[7]

Labor issues also had the attention of Washington, D.C. officials on this day, as the newspaper reported that a U.S. senator was calling on his colleagues to probe conditions of the nation's unemployed.

"Senator David I. Walsh today issued a statement, urging the Senate Committee on Education and Labor to make a thorough investigation of the unemployment conditions throughout the country, their cause and effect," read the dispatch from the nation's capital. "He would have the committee recommend as a remedy for the unemployment situation, public works, such as irrigation, reclamation, afforestation, road building, canal building, or any other steps of relief which seem logical."[8]

Prohibition, enacted the previous year, was in full force. Enforcement and violations prompted numerous newspaper stories, including one on the *Evening Globe*'s front page reporting the ordered destruction of confiscated spirits.

"Immediate disposition of liquors seized under the National Prohibition act on which storage charges are accruing, was ordered today by Prohibition Commissioner [Roy Asa] Haynes," the newspaper reported from Washington, D.C. "Instructions were sent to Federal prohibition directors and internal revenue collectors to request the United States attorneys in their districts to petition the courts for disposition orders for all seized liquors, automobiles, boats or other vehicles taken by the Government for violation of the prohibition laws."[9]

Bostonians then could buy a leg of lamb for 30 cents a pound, top round steak for 49 cents a pound, fish for 6 cents a pound and butter for 46 cents a pound.[10] And $5,500 would buy a three-family house—a commodity in demand among Eastern European immigrant families—on a corner lot in Medford.[11]

There was never a question, Bradlee wrote in his memoir, that he would attend Harvard. "My father had gone there. My grandfather had gone there, and many generations of Bradlees before him, a total of fifty-one, all the way back to 1795 with Caleb Bradlee. No alternatives were suggested, or contemplated, much less encouraged."[12] He finished his studies at Harvard in 1942, as World War II raged in Europe and in the Pacific, and on the day of his graduation he was commissioned as an ensign with eleven other "preppies"—"the first of our class to make it to war as naval officers."[13]

Bradlee had not yet seriously contemplated a career in newspapering, but during the war he toyed with the idea of teaching.

"A bunch of us in the war, toward the end of the war, we started talking about what the hell we were going to do," he recalled, "and wondered whether that (teaching) would be a way of influencing society in a good way."

At war's end, Bradlee decided that perhaps journalism might be where he could make his best mark. It was a notion he had first entertained as a teenager.

"The summer I was 15 and 16, my dad said, 'well, you gotta get a job,' and that was fine with me," he recalled. "And he said that he had met this guy who ran the paper in Beverly, Massachusetts, and the guy said that he'd take me on as a gofer. I don't think I was even as high as a copy boy. I got coffee, and I swept the office, and I wrote a few stories. But it was my father who sort of chose it for me, and I said that was great, and I did love it. I mean I loved it right away. I didn't want to be a teacher much after that. I mean, I gave it some thought, you know I thought what if you could find some person who was really going to revolutionize America, it would be wonderful to be his teacher. But it didn't suit my desire."

Journalism did suit the young war veteran's desire. Bradlee wrote in his memoir that he was sure he "wanted to do something that would make the world a better place, that would really make a difference."

He received an offer from the hometown *Boston Herald* as a beginning reporter earning 30 dollars a week, but that opportunity fell through because the newspaper's publisher was a distant cousin and hiring Bradlee would have violated the newspaper's nepotism policy. Bradlee then hooked up with some other war veterans who had decided to start a newspaper in Manchester, New Hampshire.

"We came up with the concept of an independent Sunday newspaper, the *New Hampshire Sunday News,* a four-section paper, wrapped in a four-page comic section, the only Sunday paper in New Hampshire," he wrote. "In those days there were successful independent Sunday papers in Wilmington, Delaware, Newark, New Jersey, and Bridgeport, Connecticut.

"And we were quickly successful—in circulation. We wrote about illegal stills, missing children, empty mills, polluters and pollution, and farm problems like brucellosis, since I was also the farm editor. Before long, we were selling more copies on Sunday than either the *Union* or the *Leader* sold daily."[14]

Bradlee had launched a career in 1946 that would take him from New Hampshire to a brief stay at the *Washington Post,* then to a stint with the government as a staffer for the Office of U.S. Information and Educational Exchange before returning to journalism for good with *Newsweek* and then back to the *Post,* for the duration.

He struggled during his first stop at the *Post.*

"I'm not a natural writer, I just wasn't," he said. "I had to learn it, and I had to learn how to keep the frills out and tell the story and to be simple and direct. Toward the end of my first tour at the *Post,* five years in, I began to be confident and felt that I could cover pretty much everything. They sent me to cover a trial, they asked where were all the quotes, the Q and A from the cross-examination. I said 'shit, I can't take notes that fast.' There were no transcripts made available as they became later, so I had to go to the shorthand school, or speedwriting, and when I had that down I knew that I could take good notes, maybe five years into the business. *Newsweek* was different because you were writing backgrounders for other writers, so often, if you were a foreign correspondent, you could write some eyewitness stuff that pretty much went in word for word, but if you were contributing to a situationer about NATO or something like that, I was never any good at that. I could write some reportage, but I was never an editorial writer, and I wasn't good at that either."

Bradlee finally felt he'd arrived as a reporter while working for *Newsweek* in Paris, and then covering the rebellion against the French government by Algerian guerrillas.

"I thought I wrote some pretty good stuff about (Pierre) Mendes-France when he came on the scene, as a real radical," Bradlee recalled of the French head of state, who opposed French colonialism and formed a government in France following its military defeat in Vietnam in 1954 and then negotiated an armistice with North Vietnamese communist leader Ho Chi Minh. "He was of the Radical Socialist Party, but he was neither radical nor socialist, but he was very distinctive, and he led kind of a revolution of the people who were sick of the revolving doors of the Fourth Republic. He was a great influence; I was really interested in him, and I think I described him well. Also, I think I wrote some good war stuff out of Algiers and Algeria, some good stuff about especially Algiers, the so-called *Pieds Noirs,* the black feet, people who were the natives and very conservative who tried to sort of sabotage the efforts of the French government even as reluctant as they were to embrace North Africa and embrace the Algerian natives who took over the country."

The world in which Bradlee began his journalistic career in 1946 was trying to recover from the carnage and atrocities of World War II. The judicial body of the United Nations, the International Court of Justice, was founded that year in the Hague, The Netherlands, and the UN established the International Refugee Organization. In Nuremberg, the International Military Tribunal returned verdicts establishing that individuals can be found guilty of war crimes and punished for crimes against international law. Nazi war criminals Joachim von Ribbentrop, Hermann Goering, and 10 other Nazis were sentenced to death in October, and Rudolf Hess, Walter Funk, and Erich Raeder were sent to prison for life. In Tokyo, the International Military Tribunal for the Far East opened its war crimes trial in April in proceedings that would lead to the indictments of former Japanese Prime Minister Hideki Tojo and 27 of his associates. In January, the first session of the UN General Assembly convened in London. And former British Prime Minister Winston Churchill launched the Cold War with a speech in March in Fulton, Missouri, in which he stated that "from Stettin in the Baltic to Trieste in the Adriatic an iron curtain has descended across the [European] continent."[15]

At home, President Harry S Truman announced a plan to increase workers' wages by a third, while Congress committed officially to a policy of full employment. In the early throes of the Cold War, Congress in May extended the military draft in response to Soviet Union activities in Europe. Truman in July signed a $3.75 billion bill of credit to assist Britain in its postwar economic recovery, and the U.S. joined 20 other nations in Paris to begin meetings aimed at drafting postwar peace treaties. In October, Truman ended price controls on meat, and in November, following a Republican takeover of Congress, Truman ended wage and price controls except for rent, sugar, and rice. On the last day of the year, a day after the UN Atomic Energy Commission approved a U.S. plan for the control of nuclear weapons, Truman proclaimed an end to war hostilities.

Ray Milland won a best-actor Oscar for *Lost Weekend* while Joan Crawford won female honors for *Mildred Pierce.* Alfred Hitchcock's espionage thriller, *Notorious,* opened in the United States, as did *Great Expectations, Gilda,* and the Christmas favorite *It's a Wonderful Life.* John Ford also released his landmark western, *My Darling Clementine,* and Humphrey Bogart played detective Philip Marlowe in *The Big Sleep.* Robert Penn Warren published his novel reportedly based on Louisiana demagogue Huey Long, *All the King's Men,* while Kathleen Winsor's *Forever Amber* was cleared of obscenity charges in Massachusetts. German novelist Herman Hesse won the Nobel Prize for Literature. The musical *Annie Get Your Gun* opened in New York, and Eugene O'Neill's *The Iceman Cometh* premiered at New York's Martin Beck Theater.

Events that the young journalist Bradlee might have noticed with some passing interest that year included the signing of a treaty of friendship and commerce between the United States and China, and the Soviet Union's progress toward development of nuclear weapons with the creation by Russian physicist Igor Kurchatov of the first Soviet atomic chain reaction. Both of these nations, and their proxy, North Vietnam, would play a major role in President Richard Nixon's foreign policy.

Indeed, one of the striking ironies during Bradlee's stint as editor during the Watergate years was the success by the Nixon administration in bringing an end to the Vietnam War as Nixon's presidency was failing. The administration was trumpeting a peace agreement with the North Vietnamese in January 1973, the same month of the Liddy and McCord convictions. It must have been some relief for the beleaguered president to announce the peace accord to the nation.

"President Nixon announced last night in a television address to the American people that 'we have today concluded an agreement to end the war and bring peace with honor to Vietnam and Southeast Asia,'" Bradlee's newspaper reported Wednesday, January 24, 1973.

> A cease-fire, which will be internationally supervised, will begin at 7 P.M., Washington time, Saturday, the President said.
>
> Within 60 days from Saturday all Americans held as prisoners in Indochina will be released and there will be the "fullest possible accounting" of missing in action, the President said.
>
> In the same 60-day period, all American forces will be withdrawn from South Vietnam. There are fewer than 25,000 American troops in Vietnam today.[16]

The looming cease-fire reported a couple of months earlier also came at an opportune time for the *Post*, Bradlee would write in his memoir—just after the *Post* had made the most grievous error of its Watergate coverage: the October 25, 1972 report, based on the use as a source of Nixon's Committee to Reelect chairman Hugh Sloan, identifying Nixon aide H. R. Haldeman as one of five men who controlled the secret Watergate slush fund. As it turned out, Sloan had not given this information to the Watergate grand jury, as the reporters had believed.

"Mercifully for us," Bradlee wrote,

> on the afternoon of October 26, Henry Kissinger gave a press conference at the White House to announce that "peace was at hand in Vietnam," and that gave us a little breathing room, since it occupied both the press and the Nixon administration. And after a long conversation with Sloan's lawyer, James Stoner, and a few more days of digging, the truth emerged (as Walter Lippmann so long ago promised it would); Haldeman did have control of the secret fund, despite all the technical denials, but Sloan had not testified to that effect in front of the grand jury. He hadn't told the grand jury about Haldeman's control, because the jury hadn't asked him about Haldeman's involvement.[17]

The Watergate scandal took one more bite out of the American consciousness after Nixon resigned, due to the decision by his successor, Gerald Ford, to pardon the former chief executive. Ford, who had been selected as vice president by Nixon to succeed the tax-scandal-ousted Spiro Agnew, announced in September 1974 a pardon for Nixon, freeing the former president of any worries regarding possible legal recriminations for his role in the Watergate break-in and cover-up. The pardon sparked controversy, including the decision by White House Press Secretary J.F. terHorst to resign in protest.

"President Ford yesterday granted former President Nixon a 'full, free and absolute pardon' for all federal crimes Mr. Nixon 'committed or may have committed' during his terms in the White House," reported the *Post*.

> Mr. Nixon promptly issued a statement from his home in California accepting the pardon and admitting he had made mistakes but not acknowledging any crimes.
> Mr. Nixon had not been formally charged with any federal crime, but Philip W. Buchen, Mr. Ford's counsel, told reporters at the White House it was "very likely" the former President would have been indicted without yesterday's action.[18]

The story noted that a federal grand jury had already named Nixon an unindicted co-conspirator, "at a time when there was less evidence of his involvement than is available today."

The Vietnam War and the Watergate scandal exchanged front-page attention and sometimes shared it throughout Nixon's first term; and they shared some similar news traits, including attempted cover-ups. The war produced a major, pre-Watergate, tiff between the Nixon administration and the press. The *New York Times* began publishing in June 1971 a series of stories, based on stolen government documents, outlining the history of U.S. involvement in the Vietnam War up to 1967. Dubbed the Pentagon Papers, the documents and ensuing stories included such revelations as the decision by the administration of President Lyndon Johnson, two months before the 1964 presidential election campaign and as advised by Johnson's Republican opponent, Barry Goldwater, to commence the bombing of North Vietnam. The bombing began three months after the election.[19]

As Bradlee's staff worked frantically to obtain a copy of the documents for the *Post*, Nixon's Justice Department had gone to court seeking to enjoin the *Times* from publishing further excerpts from the documents. The injunction was granted—the first time in U.S. history that such prior restraint had been granted, Bradlee wrote. Meanwhile, Bradlee's national editor, Ben Bagdikian, had obtained a copy of the documents for the *Post*. Bradlee struck.

"With the *Times* silenced by the Federal Court in New York," Bradlee wrote in his memoir, "we decided almost immediately that we would publish a story the next morning, Friday, the 18th, completing in twelve hours what it had taken the *New York Times* more than three months to do."

Following hours of debate, including argument with *Post* lawyers who wanted to hold the story because the court had enjoined the *Times* and thus there was "reason to believe publication would damage the United States," Bradlee, with a long-distance assist from lawyer Edward Bennett Williams, got publisher Katharine Graham on the phone. The lawyers made their pitch, Bradlee made his along with the fact that Williams supported his decision to publish—"'Well, Benjy, you got to go with it. You got no choice. That's your business.'" Graham ruled on behalf of publication.

Victory.

"What I didn't understand, as Katharine's 'Okay . . . let's go. Let's publish' rang in my ears, was how permanently the ethos of the paper changed, and how it crystallized for editors and reporters everywhere how independent and determined and confident of its purpose the new *Washington Post* had become," Bradlee wrote. "In the days that followed, these feelings only increased. A paper that stands up to charges of treason, a paper that holds firm in the face of charges from the president, the Supreme Court, the Attorney General, never mind an assistant attorney general. A paper that holds its head high, committed unshakably to principle."

The *Post* joined its competitor, the *Times,* in the courtrooms, fighting on behalf of publication. Seventeen days after the initial story appeared in the *New York Times,* the U.S. Supreme Court ruled for the right of the newspapers to publish the material.

"For the first time in the history of the American republic, newspapers had been restrained by the government from publishing a story—a black mark on the history of democracy," Bradlee wrote of the initial court rulings against publication. "We had won—sort of."

Seventeen years later, U.S. Solicitor General Erwin N. Griswold confessed in a *Washington Post* op-ed essay, wrote Bradlee, that the government's case against the newspapers "was a mirage," that he had never seen "any trace of a threat to the national security from the Pentagon Papers' publication. Indeed, I have never seen it even suggested that there was an actual threat."

Wrote Bradlee:

> We had no answers to those questions beyond recognition that the Cold War dominated our society, and realization that the Nixon-Agnew administration was playing hardball.
>
> We did know that the Pentagon Papers experience had forged forever between the Grahams and the newsroom a sense of confidence within the *Post,* a sense of mission and agreement on new goals, and how to attain them. And that may have been the greatest result of publication of the Pentagon Papers.[20]

Countering the president's difficulties at home, though, were some historic breakthroughs in relations with the nation's two primary post-World War II nemeses: the Soviet Union and communist China. The world experienced a thaw in the Cold War during a period of eased tensions between the United States and the two communist giants thanks to Nixon's historic visit to communist China and his pursuit of détente and arms control pacts with the Soviet Union.

In 1972, Nixon, whose political background had always boasted impeccable anticommunist credentials, visited the secretive nation of mainland China; it was a diplomatic breakthrough that became a worldwide media event.

"China's leaders turned the spotlight on President Nixon yesterday with unprecedented domestic press radio and television coverage, apparently calculated to communicate to the Chinese population the advent of a new era in Sino-American relations," the *Post* reported in a February 1972 story carrying a Peking dateline.

> The president was also given a significant signal of Chinese receptivity to a potential accommodation with the United States when he and his aides were accompanied to the theater last night by Chiang Ching, the wife of Communist Party Chairman Mao Tse-tung.
>
> In an extraordinary gesture, the official People's Daily today devoted its entire front page to the President's visit with a banner headline and a large photograph of Mr. Nixon shaking hands with Mao, who enjoys a god-like status here.[21]

That May, Nixon made history again as the *Post* reported on the president's Moscow meeting with Soviet Communist Party boss Leonid Brezhnev, during which the two leaders signed a nuclear weapons limitation agreement that had been a long time in the making.

"President Nixon and Soviet communist Party chief Leonid Brzhnev [*sic*] signed tonight a strategic arms limitations agreement that has taken two and a half years to negotiate and which both sides hailed as a historic step toward a more stable peace in the world," the *Post* reported.

> The agreement was signed in the Kremlin at 11 P.M. Moscow time (4 P.M. EDT) after President Nixon gave a dinner for the Soviet leaders at Spaso House, the home of the American ambassador.
>
> In his toast at the dinner, Mr. Nixon said that the agreement is "enormously important" and that he is convinced both he and the Soviet leaders want to be remembered in history "by the fact that we made the world a more peaceful one for all peoples of the world."[22]

Other foreign-policy issues of the decade's early years, though, were less favorable to U.S. interests. In the fall of 1973, the OPEC oil cartel nations shut off oil supplies, in response to pro-Israeli policies of the United States and in retaliation for the outcome of the 1967 Arab-Israeli war, in what has come to be known as the Arab oil boycott. The result was long lines at the gasoline pumps and allegations of fuel hoarding and price manipulation by the oil industry. The embargo and the damage it did to the American economy are almost lost in the historic swirl of Vietnam and Watergate; but this episode of Middle East-related foreign policy woes prefaced some major developments in the region and in U.S.-Middle Eastern relations.

"The Arab oil states meeting here on how to use oil as a weapon in the struggle against Israel decided today to cut back production of petroleum in an attempt to hurt the United States," the *Post* reported on October 18, in a Reuters wire service story datelined Kuwait.

They pledged a general production cutback of 5 percent a month, starting immediately, but indicated that only the United States would get less oil.

The oil ministers of 10 Arab countries meeting here said that oil production would be reduced by 5 percent every month, using September's production figures as a base, until Israel withdraws from the Arab lands it occupied in the 1967 war and restores the rights of the more than 2 million Palestinians who became refugees after the creation of Israel in 1948.[23]

Such was the world and the nation's capital—an angry Middle East and a nation weary of war and political scandal—that in 1977 greeted incoming President Jimmy Carter, a Democrat who rose out of the ashes of Watergate and the subsequent Ford presidency. Plus, there were new challenges, including an opportunity to mend some Central American political fences with a treaty that stirred controversy domestically but that was welcomed south of the U.S.-Mexico border, and an opening for a peace treaty in the Middle East.

Central America was a region plagued by incidents of U.S. military intervention, usually on behalf of so-called anticommunist initiatives aimed at guerrilla and rebel forces often supported by Cuba and the Soviet Union. In the case of the Panama Canal treaties, however, Carter took a step forward in positive relations in the region by returning to the Panamanian government a symbol of U.S. imperialism that reached back to the presidency of Theodore Roosevelt, who championed construction of the Panama Canal.

"President Carter yesterday signed the historic treaties that would transfer control of the Panama Canal—long a symbol of U.S. global power and technological prowess—to Panama by the end of the century," the *Post* reported on September 8, 1977.

As Carter and Panama's military ruler, Gen. Omar Torrijos, put their signatures on the Spanish and English texts of the two treaties, they were flanked by a Who's Who of presidents, prime ministers and cabinet officers from 23 other Western Hemisphere nations gathered at the Organization of American States headquarters here.

The treaties, Carter said, "mark the commitment of the United States to the belief that fairness, not force, should lie at the heart of our dealings with the nations of the world."

With these words, the President underscored anew his administration's determination to deal with all countries, large and small, on the basis of "mutual respect and cooperation."[24]

The next year, Carter brokered a major breakthrough in the Arab-Israeli stalemate in a peace deal, reached in September 1978, nearly five years exactly after the oil embargo. The settlement, known as the Camp David Accords, was announced after nearly two weeks of secret negotiations involving Carter, Egyptian President Anwar Sadat, and Israeli Prime Minister Menachem Begin; the pact demonstrated that willingness to negotiate and compromise can bring results even among ancient foes.

"The leaders of Egypt, Israel and the United States publicly announced last night their agreement on a framework for settlement of the 30-year conflict in the Middle East," Bradlee's newspaper reported on September 18.

Only the general terms of the accords were announced at a dramatic ceremony in the East Room of the White House that came as the climax to 13 days of tense negotiation at President Carter's Camp David Retreat.

The accords, which are in no sense a final resolution of the conflicts in the Middle East, were described as "frameworks" for agreement in the Sinai as well as in the West Bank and Gaza Strip. They were signed by Israeli Prime minister Menachem Begin and Egyptian President Anwar Sadat and witnessed by President Carter at 11 P.M.

If the Sinai accord is carried out on schedule, it will bring a final peace treaty and full diplomatic relations between the two nations by the end of the year.

The Sinai agreement provides the basis for a treaty which would return the region to Egyptian sovereignty under a program of staged withdrawal of Israeli forces. The other accord establishes a context for setting the status of the West Bank and Gaza during a five-year transitional period. It provides for withdrawal of the Israeli military government and establishment of a self-governing authority with what Carter described as "full autonomy."[25]

What many observers consider to be Carter's undoing came a year later, when Iranians seized the U.S. Embassy in Tehran over the U.S. government's relationship with and longtime support of the former, deposed, shah of Iran, an unpopular ruler who had long been seen as a puppet of U.S. foreign policy. The seizure included the taking of up to 100 hostages, which included members of the diplomatic staff.

"The United States yesterday expressed 'concern' about the takeover of the U.S. Embassy in Tehran," the *Post* reported on November 5, 1979, "but administration officials refused to comment on the demands of the Iranian militants that the deposed shah be extradited to Iran."

The takeover underscored the increasingly nagging problem that the presence of Shah Mohammad Reza Pahlavi in the United States has become. He currently is undergoing treatment for cancer at a New York hospital.

At least two recent bomb threats against a U.S. airline have been linked to demands for the shah's extradition, and Iranian demonstrators protesting his presence yesterday chained themselves to the crown of the Statue of Liberty in New York.

In addition, the issue shows signs of giving political ammunition to domestic opponents of President Carter. Republican presidential candidate John Connally yesterday blamed the embassy takeover on a policy of appeasement by the administration.[26]

The hostage crisis stretched into the next year. Carter suffered irreparable political harm in the spring of 1980, when a botched military rescue mission of the hostages resulted in the deaths of eight members of the U.S. military.

"The United States tried and failed to rescue the American hostages in Iran with a commando style raid in which eight U.S. crewmen were killed, the White House announced today," read the front-page story of the April 25 edition of the *Washington Post.*

The military operation, according to a post-midnight statement from the White House, was "aborted" because of an equipment failure, followed by a collision of two aircraft, at a remote desert location in which the eight were killed and others injured.

The American troops, including the injured, were then airlifted safely from the unknown staging site in Iran, according to the statement issued by White House press secretary Jody Powell.

The statement issued shortly after 3 A.M. said:

"This mission was not motivated by hostility toward Iran, or the Iranian-people, and there were no Iranian casualties. Preparations for the rescue mission were ordered for humanitarian reasons, to protect the national interests of this country and to alleviate international tensions."[27]

The hostages were released shortly after President Ronald Reagan took office in January 1981—after the political damage to Carter had been done.

Bradlee's memoir includes recollection of another incident, again tied to foreign policy in the Middle East, that shows an angry side of President Carter early in his presidency, in 1976, that might surprise some. Bradlee wrote that Woodward had come to him with a single-source report that a Middle Eastern head of state, later learned to be King Hussein of Jordan, was on the CIA payroll—"the dollar amount: about $1 million a year for twenty years. . . . The money was 'walking-around' money, not connected either to economic or military aid, which Jordan received regularly." The money, Bradlee wrote, had been used in various ways, including "to procure women, when Hussein was little more than a teenager, and to pay for bodyguards for his children when they were old enough to go to boarding school in the United States."

A second source was needed, Bradlee wrote, and the president soon obliged them with an invitation to the White House to discuss the story after the newspaper had sought comment on the report.

"We were there the next morning for an interview I'll never forget," Bradlee wrote. "To be in the Oval Office of the White House with the

President of the United States will always blow my mind. Carter had been president for less than a month, but looked totally comfortable, poised, friendly and hospitable. He was dressed in a pinstriped gray suit, and smiling. First, the president said, the story was true. (There was our second source.)

"Second, the president said, he had been briefed on the situation by former Secretary of State Henry Kissinger; third, the payments had stopped, and fourth, he said he couldn't make the case that others of his staff were making that the national security was involved.

"We had our story."

However, Carter had a request. He asked Bradlee not to run the story, but he then asked for 24 hours notice if the editor decided to go with the story. After much agonizing—"the president had been so straight, so decent, that it seemed almost impolite to print anything he did not want printed"—Bradlee wrote, he and his staff decided to publish the story. The reasoning: it was true; the public didn't know about this expenditure of tax dollars. Also, the president "would not say that national security was involved," and "effective oversight of the CIA lay somewhere between ludicrous and nonexistent. No one really knew what the spooks were up to."

The day after the story appeared, Bradlee wrote, he received a handwritten note from Carter on White House stationery. It read:

"'To Ben Bradlee,

'I think your publication of the CIA story as the Secretary of State was on his Middle East mission and about to arrive in Jordan was irresponsible.

'This is offered by way of editorial comment.

'Jimmy.'"

"I could understand why the president was upset," Bradlee wrote. "So was I. I felt we had gone the last mile to be responsible.

"When Powell told Carter that I was upset by his letter, the president replied, 'Well, fuck him.'

"And I could understand that, too."[28]

In retrospect, Carter's election, Bradlee recalled, likely was a national reaction to the Watergate scandal; and it likely was Carter's own inept handling of a foreign crisis, that of the hostages in Iran, that undid him.

"He was such a long shot; there were other Democrats" who seemingly had a better chance of winning the ticket, Bradlee said. "One forgets what a long shot he was. He was not on anybody's list of candidates for so long. He shot up from nowhere, and it's funny. He got so screwed by the withholding of the prisoners (hostages). If the prisoners had come back in the last six weeks of his administration, he might have been reelected."

The issues of the Middle East that resonated during the Carter presidency and of Ford and Nixon before him continue to plague the region, and U.S. presidential administrations, today—including oil's hold on

American politics and policy, noted Bradlee. The Arab oil embargo of 1973 was a prelude to the international oil politics of later decades, from the Middle East to Asia and Latin America.

"That was a tactic in the maneuvering between the Arab countries and the United States, and the free countries," Bradlee recalled of the Arab oil embargo. "You don't think it's (oil) got a hold on us now? Why didn't we learn anything from that? We went back to heavy usage. Oil companies are too strong. I mean the oil monopoly was too strong, politically, and they still are."

Bradlee conceded that the decade that ended with the Carter presidency and heralded the beginning of the Reagan Revolution likely ended with the country better off. As a journalist, he said, he does not think in terms of ten-year bites; he thinks of tomorrow.

But the president that history will most identify with the *Washington Post* editor will be Nixon. Bradlee revealed little in his memoir about his inner feelings regarding the disgraced president's resignation or the *Post*'s role in it. His writing on the subject almost seems like the notes of a journalist's routine, simply of covering this news story as part of a larger easel of governmental and cultural reportage.

"Newspapering deals with small daily bites from a fruit of indeterminate size," he wrote near the end of his chapter on Watergate. "It may take dozens of bites before you are sure it's an apple. Dozens and dozens more bites before you have any real idea how big the apple might be. It was that way with Watergate."[29]

But he did offer some thoughts on the Nixon presidency, including Watergate, during the 2006 interview in his office, giving the former president credit for his non-Watergate governance.

"I thought that Nixon ran the country, except for Watergate . . . you wouldn't put him at the bottom of the list of presidents of either party. I mean, he did what he did, and he did it. The trouble is, the second sentence in his obit is going to be that he's the first and only president of the United States to resign from office under duress.

"Watergate showed an essential flaw in his character, but as a president, the pluses of the Nixon administration were considerable. China."

The editor also credited Nixon for the policy of détente with the Soviet Union. "But of course, he also bore a certain amount of responsibility for events that forced the Soviets into doing it (the arms race). They felt they were defending themselves, probably. Nixon never wanted to conquer the world the way the commies did, I guess, at one point; he never came close."

Bradlee also credited the Nixon presidency for some of its domestic policies.

"The wage and price freeze that he did, and he did raise taxes initially, those are things you think of with a regulatory, Democratic kind of approach," he said, taking a jab at Republican antitax rhetoric. "Don't

I hear these politicians say that everybody raises taxes? Didn't taxes go up during the Eisenhower administration, didn't they go up under Reagan? He cut them for a while, but didn't he raise them again? If you cut income taxes, that's cutting taxes, but on the other end, if you force sales taxes, then you're raising taxes."

So, did President Nixon give the nation peace with honor, as promised by Nixon when he ran for the presidency?

"For a time," Bradlee said. "But my God, we're never out of a war, we never stay out, it seems to me. What do you mean 'honorably?' You can't tell the parents of the people who were killed in Vietnam that it was honorable. But we had to end it, just like we've got to end this goddam mess that we're in in Iraq. The history books will not say it was a great dishonor, I don't think."

In hindsight, Bradlee rued that the Ford pardon of Nixon ended the possibility of criminal proceedings against the disgraced president.

"I wish he'd gotten more out of it," Bradlee said of the pardon. "I wish he would, that someone had written an indictment of Richard Nixon, and he had said 'I was guilty.' I know why he (Ford) did it, ultimately, to help the country."

For the most part, Bradlee said, the Ford presidency was little more than a caretaking procedure. "There was no harm done in that presidency, and he's certainly one of the nicest people I knew who ever were president."

As for the other major press story of the decade, the Pentagon Papers case, the editor remembered it simply as "a great press versus power story."

Asked what if feels like, at the age of 84, to look back at the Watergate scandal and to realize he played a role in the undoing of a president, Bradlee said:

"Pretty good. I mean it feels pretty good. I did my job, I think I did what I was put on Earth to do, which was to follow a good story to the end, and the fact that it was a Republican and that it was the president was more important to the general public than it was to me. I just sometimes worry that, is that going to be the big thing of my life? That's thirty-some years ago, and that sort of makes me sad, but I guess it is. I think as important as it was to me and to this paper, it wasn't all that important. It wasn't."

* * * *

These were the days of what Richard Nixon called benign neglect. When Jimmy Carter came to power, during the '70s, the civil wars in Central America were forming. Seventy-nine was when the Sandinistas took Nicaragua, took Managua, and those were the years I would say we should be investing our time and diplomacy in Central America instead of in Vietnam. This was on our doorstep. This hemisphere, it seems to me, was most important to us.

—Georgie Anne Geyer

For a few minutes, as she was being driven from her interrupted meal to the interrogation center that night, held against her will in a speeding

Georgie Anne Geyer. © Bill Fitz-Patrick Photography. Used by permission.

car, Georgie Anne Geyer took a glimpse at her mortality. She felt a rare emotion: fear.

The foreign correspondent wondered: who knew the purpose of this excursion, or its outcome? What did they want of her?

"They" were the young revolutionaries of Angola, where a civil war had raged to establish a government that was to be a model of the new socialist order in Africa. They had grabbed her during a late-night dinner at her hotel, where she had been trying to arrange for passport transportation out of Angola. She had gone to the country days before to cover the trial of 13 captured mercenaries in connection with the civil war.

In her 1976 *Los Angeles Times* column describing the ordeal, written from the safety of Paris, Geyer recalled being driven "recklessly, at least 80 miles an hour."

> I saw we were headed toward the port, where the lights of ships pulsed and slid like silver across the water.
>
> This fleeting moment of beauty was broken as we sped into the old Portuguese "cuartel," an ominous cluster of scabrous, aged buildings from 1876 that were built in that special manner that anywhere in the world announced, "I am a prison." It was also their interrogation center.

> When they rushed me out of the car—and took all of my luggage too—I felt a sudden rush of fear that itself frightened me because it was so unusual for me. They might not even be the government. They might be any of the gangs that now terrorize Luanda. Were my own feelings racist? I thought about this. But no, it was that I didn't know Africa and thus had no idea of what to expect.[30]

During the interrogation, her captors accused her of writing lies in a column she had dispatched that described the role that Cuban fighters had played in the civil war.

"There are no lies there," she told the interrogators in the small, "almost quintessentially Humphrey Bogart upstairs room" of the building to which she had been whisked away before being put by her captors on the flight for Paris.

"'Why are you writing about Cubans anyway?' he demanded, his voice sharp and cold. 'You are in Angola.'

"I told him, partly in English, partly in Spanish and Portuguese, what he knew very well—that there is a great deal of interest in this new Cuban phenomenon in Africa and that everybody had written about them. The only thing that occurred to me to justify this, shall we say, excessive reaction was the fact that, since I speak fluent Spanish, I might have been the only journalist personally to interview them."

Later, as she awaited her flight out of the county, she experienced one of those instances when "one grasps the reality of the existentialist moment," Geyer wrote of that 2 A.M. wait for an airplane. "Now a strong radio in the office in the stillness of the early morning picked up Radio Cabo Verde, and we sat there snoozing and listening to 'You Belong to My Heart,' which sang its way suddenly out of my childhood and into this strange African night."

She waited four hours for the flight that would take her from Luanda, Angola, to Paris. And she pondered how she could make those in power in the revolutionary government that had evicted her understand her role as a journalist, that she had been "fascinated for years by the Angolan revolution and had started twice to go there. I wanted to tell them that I could never be a Marxist, if only because of the element of untruth inherent in it, but that I certainly sympathized with all peoples gaining their rights.

"Fourteen hours later, it was Paris in the spring. As I sit here in this bustling beautiful city, so different from the silence and emptiness of new Luanda, I know that I would give virtually anything to make them understand. I also know that there is nothing in the world that would make them do that."[31]

Angola was but one stop in a world full of brief stops for Geyer; it was but one of several posts of revolution, civil war, and sectarian battles that beckoned this itinerant journalist. The 1970s, which saw domestic strife at home during the Watergate scandal and the winding down of American involvement in the Vietnam War, was a decade of rebellion and uprisings in the Third World regions of Africa and Latin America, and of continued violence in the Middle East. The United States, or some of its citizens at least in the case of Angola, had a hand in it all.

This was Geyer's beat, this roiling turmoil that drew foreign correspondents with their pens and pads like a burning yellow patio light attracts gnats.

The childhood from which the captive Geyer years later would recall the tune "You Belong to My Heart" was spent in Chicago, where Geyer was born on April 2, 1935. The foreign affairs menu that would comprise her journalistic diet as an adult was secondary then to a major domestic crisis, the Great Depression. Indeed, on the day of her birth, her future newspaper published a front page editorial attacking President Franklin D. Roosevelt for what the *Chicago Daily News* considered abrogation of his sworn oath to uphold the Constitution of the United States. The specific action that drew the newspaper's ire was the withdrawal from the Supreme Court by the Roosevelt administration of a case testing the constitutionality of the National Industrial Recovery Act and the National Recovery Administration's regulation of business competition.

"If the president of the United States and the executive authority of the government itself openly and palpably seek to evade the terms of the constitution, or to sidestep a test of constitutionality in the court of final resort, what becomes of the hope vital to our future welfare, that a higher code of ethics will rule in private business?" the editorial asked.

> The people of the United States rely upon Franklin Delano Roosevelt to remember that the FIRST PROMISE he made as president of the United States to the people of the United States, with his hand resting upon an open Bible, was a promise to PRESERVE THE CONSTITUTION. Consequently, when any executive act is challenged upon constitutional grounds, it becomes his duty to have such questions determined by the court of final resort, as swiftly as possible, to the end that the CONSTITUTION SHALL BE PRESERVED. To attempt to exercise a dubious constitutional right, and at the same time deliberately and palpably to evade a prompt judicial determination of the question, challenges the FITNESS for public office of the individual who so acts, and is utterly destructive of the confidence which should attach to the man who exercises such great responsibility under a constitutional form of government.[32]

Another depression-related administration foray was the subject of an inside story, where the newspaper published a United Press dispatch concerning farm policy legislation along with a report on a court challenge concerning a previously enacted farm recovery law.

"Farm relief, vexing problem of every administration for almost a generation, arose today as a vital issue in New Deal legislation," the newspaper reported.

"The court heard closing arguments on the Frazier-Lemke farm mortgage moratorium law passed last year by congress," said the story. It then went on to inform readers that action concerning amendments to the Agricultural Adjustment Act of 1933 "giving the agriculture department wide licensing powers, was held up to permit reconsideration by the house agriculture committee."[33]

Elsewhere, the newspaper reported that the president had a busy agenda awaiting him on his return from a vacation cruise, including a recovery appropriations bill, possible problems with his Social Security legislation, and other labor-related measures.

"When President Roosevelt returns from his fishing vacation, about a week from tomorrow, he will be faced with the necessity of drawing the strings of his raveled New Deal together and clarifying its 1935 purposes to the public as well as congressional minds," Washington correspondent Paul R. Leach reported in an era during which the United States was experiencing sweeping political and economic change that would endure for the remainder of the century. A nearly $5 billion works relief bill likely would gain House approval, the correspondent predicted, but trouble loomed in other areas.

"The social security bill will be in house committee for another week at least and then be subject to bushwhacking on both legislative floors," Leach reported.

> The Wagner-Connery labor disputes bill and the Black thirty-hour week bill are in a tangle with the new Harrison NRA extension bill, with its provisions for settling labor disputes. Industry has without exception condemned both labor bills, and labor without exception has taken the other side, in committee hearings. Strike threats are becoming more and more ominous over the country. Better business indices of a month ago are either at a standstill or shaky.[34]

As the nation struggled with the depression, foreign affairs did draw some newspaper attention, as the seeds of the coming world war of the next decade were being sown in Europe. Displayed next to the editorial berating Roosevelt's NRA policies, United Press reported that French leader Pierre-Etienne Flandin "today sounded a cry of unity in France to face German rearmament and declared the army high command had decided to keep the French ring of steel fortifications on the frontier permanently garrisoned."

The wire service reported that Flandin had confirmed reports of troop movements close to the eastern border and quoted him warning the chamber of deputies about German rearmament.

"'To face this powerfully organized army, France must organize her security—first, by having a strong army; second by organizing military alliances for the preservation of peace.'"[35]

Meanwhile, Italian Premier Benito Mussolini, who would ally his county with Germany in World War II, was also urging cooperative efforts to stave off possible war. He issued a call for an alliance that, had events followed the course suggested by Mussolini, might have resulted in a different sort of Allied and Axis alignment in the coming war.

"Premier Benito Mussolini today demanded that France, Great Britain and Italy adopt a united course of action in face of possible war," United Press reported. "The forceful duce, tired of what he called 'the European diplomatic circuit' of statesmen's visits to each other, demanded that at their conference at Stresa April 11 the foreign ministers of the three allied countries unite for action."

As Flandin had evoked German rearmament, Mussolini made reference to the German law enacted the previous month reinstituting compulsory arms service. "'The foreign ministers of France, Great Britain and Italy will meet at Stresa,'" the dispatch quoted Mussolini. "'It cannot be said that these governments have been completely in unison in facing the German gesture of March 16. The Stresa conference should establish a common line of action in the face of certain eventualities such as warfare.'"[36]

Back in Chicago, Wallace Beery was starring in *West Point of the Air* at the Chicago theater downtown, while the Apollo offered *Gold Diggers of 1935* and the Roosevelt featured *The Whole Town's Talking*. But the depression did help keep prices down. Henry C. Lytton & Sons were offering fur scarves and capes for $3.25 per skin;[37] Marshall Field & Company was selling a table cloth and four chair pads for $2.95 and two pounds of Murphy's Oil Soap for 55 cents;[38] and men's topcoats were on sale for $12.95 at Mandell's.[39]

Chicago of the depression era was a world of political corruption, racial hatred, and Mafia operations that pushed Geyer toward a journalistic path. The city's residents, she wrote in her memoir, accepted "as natural" the corruption and bigotry. "It was this tribal morality that fed the growing flames of my hatred for injustice and my desire both to protect myself from this parasitical world and to fight it and to try to change it."

The Geyer family came through the depression, thanks to the hard work of Geyer's father, whose dairy operation thrived "off the sheer amount of blood and sweat he and my grandmother, 'Oma,' poured into it," she wrote. The young Georgie Anne Geyer came through the depression and the ensuing war with constant reading and a "literary dreaminess."[40]

She decided at the age of nine, she remembered in her Washington, D.C. apartment years later, that she was going to be a writer.

"I read everything, went to the library, I could do all my homework in class, and then I skipped two years in grammar school. I graduated when I was fifteen. I just loved the written word. I played piano in those years, did some acting," she recalled. "But really it was the writing, I wanted to be a great writer."

So she studied great authors, taking inspiration later, while attending the Medill School of Journalism at Northwestern University, from the likes of Thomas Mann and Vladimir Nabakov. Then she honed her writing skills at the *Chicago Daily News*, which hired her from Chicago's *Southtown*

Economist in 1959. She joined the *Daily News* staff with the intention of becoming a foreign correspondent.

"I was able, I think, to use newspapering for the kind of writing I wanted to do, because foreign correspondents have so much more leeway to write more creatively, particularly on the *Daily News*," she recalled. "We had this incredible legendary history there on the *Daily News*, and a wonderful atmosphere, without a lot of jealousy or resentment. Being a woman, they would send us out to do the sort of thing, like washing the hippopotamus' teeth one day at the zoo. My big coup was being a waitress at a Mafia wedding, which no one else had ever been able to break into. We had a quarter of the front page, 'Our Girl.' You'd have to be a little crazy when you're starting."

The *Daily News*, she wrote in her memoir, was considered one the nation's great newspapers when she signed on. "It was the 'reporter's newspaper.' Ben Hecht, Carl Sandburg, John Gunther, Ernest Hemingway—all of them and many more have passed through its generous and creative doors."

She said the descriptions of the newsroom by Hecht, who went on to co-write *The Front Page* based on his newspaper days, "held up still when I arrived forty years later."

"We were a newspaper tribe," Hecht had written, "of assorted drunkards, poets, burglars, philosophers and boastful ragamuffins. We were supermen with soiled collars and holes in our pants; stone broke and sneering at our betters in limousines and unmortgaged houses; cynical of all things on earth, including the tyrannical journal that underpaid and overworked us, and for which, after a round of cursing, we were ready to die."

The writers called themselves "simply 'reporters.' No, not even 'journalists' and certainly not 'media' or 'media celebrities,' good God!" Geyer wrote. "Nobody came into journalism in those days for power or to be celebrities; they came in because they wanted to write, or walk the streets, or booze around and raise hell with the world. But those reporters knew the city; they lived in it, not the suburbs, like the editors today, and they loved the city. It was our clay and we were its."[41]

But the city room she joined in 1959 was not quite ready for the notion of female hard-news reporters. "They had a quota of two women on the city desk in those days, one for education and one for sob stories," she reminisced in a 1979 column. "I broke the quota after a year and became the third. Before you knew it, I was in Peru, where nobody could tell me to go and cover a fire."[42]

So 1960, the same year that John F. Kennedy won the election that would make him the country's first Catholic president, marked Geyer's entry into the community of serious journalism. It was the beginning of a decade of rapid change: the stirrings of social upheaval in the United States included the founding of the Students for a Democratic Society in Michigan that January; a February sit-in staged by black protestors at a segregated Woolworth's lunch counter in Greensboro, North Carolina; a gathering of a thousand black protestors to pray and sing for equal rights in March at the Alabama statehouse in Montgomery; and the formation in April of the Student Nonviolent Coordinating Committee by southern black college students intent on registering black voters and staging sit-ins on behalf of racial equality.[43]

The communist scare, a carryover from the '50s, continued to flare, as U.S. Air Force Secretary Dudley C. Sharp in February warned the House Un-American Activities Committee of communist infiltration of the nation's clergy; in May, the Soviets downed a U.S. high-altitude U-2 spy plane, leading to a 10-year prison sentence for pilot Gary Powers, and in July they took down a U.S. RB-47 survey aircraft over the Barents Sea. Later that month, Soviet leader Nikita Khrushchev threatened nuclear war if the United States invaded Cuba. Meanwhile, demonstrators in San Francisco protested actions by the House Un-American Activities Committee, signalling "the beginning of radical action by students of the University of California, Berkeley."

In domestic politics, Richard Nixon and John F. Kennedy in September engaged in a series of televised presidential campaign debates, which analysts later would conclude hurt Nixon and helped Kennedy, even though radio listeners thought Nixon bested his Democratic rival. Two months later, Kennedy defeated Nixon in the closest popular vote in U.S. history to date, and Democrats kept control of the House and Senate. In April, California legislators enacted the nation's "first state-sponsored antismog bill."

Nearly 46 million Americans went to the movies each week in 1960, taking in such fare as Otto Preminger's *Exodus,* Alfred Hitchcock's *Psycho,* Stanley Kubrick's *Spartacus,* and Billy Wilder's *The Apartment.* Charlton Heston won a best actor Oscar for *Ben-Hur,* and Simone Signoret was named best actress for her role in *Room at the Top.* It was a productive year for the letters, as A.J. Ayer published his philosophy tract *Logical Positivism,* Isaac Bashevis Singer published *The Magician of Lublin,* Harper Lee published *To Kill a Mockingbird,* and John Updike published *Rabbit Run.* Anne Sexton published *To Bedlam and Part Way Back,* and Sylvia Plath published her poetry collection *The Colossus.* French poet Saint-John Perse won the Nobel Prize for literature.

On Geyer's future beat, the major foreign affairs stories of the year included the establishment of the Organization of Petroleum Exporting Countries (OPEC), dominated by Middle-Eastern oil-producing nations; Britain, France, the Netherlands, and the United States signed an agreement for economic and social cooperation in the Caribbean; the United States ended assistance to Cuba because of that island nation's leftist politics; and civil war broke out in the Congo Republic.

These regions of the world, Africa, the Middle East, and Latin America, would come to dominate much of Geyer's foreign affairs coverage of the 1970s. It was an era that saw the continued rise of third-world, anti-imperialist, and colonial sentiment by rebels and by independence-minded nations, and increased United States involvement, militarily and economically, in these arenas.

Geyer strolled onto this foreign affairs journalism stage for good following her first foreign adventure, covering the 1965 revolt in the Dominican Republic. After that her resume includes accompanying a band of guerrilla insurgents, camping out with them in the Guatemalan mountains, and being held captive by Palestinian commandos who mistook her for "the mysterious 'Israeli Blonde' who led a raid on Beirut."[44]

The *Daily News* assigned her to Washington as an op-ed writer in 1974, a position she left the next year to begin her own syndicated column for the Los Angeles Times Syndicate. It was primarily in this role that she interviewed many of the prominent figures of the dramatic foreign-affairs stories of the decade and covered the accelerated insurgencies of Latin America and of the continued boiling up of the Middle East. These stories included the rise of the radical Islamic political structure of the Arab world and the region's oil-centered international politics, the roiling territorial battles of Africa as it transitioned from a colonial region to tribal and local independence, and the struggles of a Carter presidency intent on a foreign policy based on human rights and devoid of armed intervention. Many of these figures and issues presaged the politics and tensions that would be found in these same regions early in the new century.

One of these foreign leaders was Iraq's Saddam Hussein. The correspondent, while still with the *Daily News,* managed a journalistic coup when she obtained an interview with the secretive leader in 1973.

"Saddam Hussein, the mysterious underground strongman of Iraq, was someone whom no one ever saw," Geyer wrote in her memoir. "He was the toughest of the tough, the most brutal of the brutal, also the best economic developer and the single most mysterious and unknown leader in the Middle East, in the most closed and unknown land. . . . I became the first American ever to lay eyes on this important man—afterward the American diplomats were dying to hear what the world's great terrorist leader was like."[45]

> No man in khakis, no Arafat in Arab headdress and olive drabs, Saddam Hussein was tall, dark, and erect, with beautiful black hair, a neat moustache, and eyes that were hooded much like the Arab falcons. He was properly dressed as a French count at court. Indeed, he was wearing a perfectly tailored pin-striped suit, his hand outstretched. Against the background of the gilded rooms of the palace of the kings, the last one of which was dragged through the streets until he died when the revolution occurred in 1958, the image was perfect. But it was certainly not that of the underground terrorist, which was the image he wanted to leave behind and which was what this interview was all about.[46]

Following Saddam's invitation to ask him any question she wished, Geyer queried him about his background as a terrorist for the Ba'athist Party before its rise to power under his leadership in 1962.

"He answered, 'Sometimes you have to do things for your party that you would not do yourself.'"

He was trying so hard to be, or to appear, open and frank. But all of my questions evoked only hooded responses—as hooded as those handsome but chilled eyes. After several hours, out of desperation I fished about in my mind for still another question. "When did you join the Ba'athist Party?" I asked, thinking to myself, "What a foolish question."

And now his entire demeanor and mien changed. All the friendliness, so carefully constructed to go with the gilded room, dropped away. He looked at me now with open and unmasked hostility. "I don't remember," he said.

He didn't remember the watershed event of his life? I puzzled over this for a long time. Why should that utterly innocuous question have affected him when nothing else did? Years later a knowing psychiatrist said to me, "But of course—that was the moment he became a terrorist."[47]

The correspondent learned that she had been granted the interview because this was a period when Saddam was trying to curry favor with the West. Iraq had that spring settled a longstanding problem regarding British-owned petroleum. "My presence and newspapers presented a small vehicle that could serve that purpose—and it was only by chance that the timing served mine."[48]

Four years later, after eight years of trying, Geyer got an interview with another prominent Middle Eastern terrorist, Palestinian Liberation Organization Chairman Yasser Arafat. The interview took place in the Beirut apartment of Arafat's secretary; the session surprised Geyer.

"For one thing, he was far less harsh in person than in his pictures," she wrote. "He smiled and laughed easily, his face expressive and his odd popish eyes cushioned by the pouches that lay underneath them. There was, of course, the heavyset body, the head scarf or *kaffiyeh,* and the self-conscious khakis. He looked like a cross between GI Joe and the Buddha."[49]

Arafat told Geyer that the PLO was undertaking a new direction, one of seeking "international legitimacy." "The 'international bandits' of the world were embarking upon an all-out program of diplomacy, to gain respectability in preparation for the formation of a 'Palestinian state,'" she wrote.

The formation of such a state, he told her, would solve the problems with Israel for the next twenty years.

"Why twenty years?" I pressed him, suspicious.

"From your questions," he answered, smiling a patient-impatient oddly avuncular smile, "I can understand that you are asking for guarantees for Israel. I only say twenty years because by that time I will be dead. Others will have to work out the future." He then went on to renounce terrorism and to approve enthusiastically the new contacts between PLO representatives and "any Israelis or Jews who recognize the Palestinian people."[50]

The interview began at 10 P.M. and ended four hours later. "Just before 2:00 A.M. he said that of course he could not *fully recognize Israel at this time*," she wrote, "throwing up his hands and saying, 'You are asking from the victim everything.'

"Yet I knew that he had in fact given to me in this curious interview an *implicit recognition.* On the side, his people told me they were thinking about de facto recognition of Israel in the first stage of settlement, with de jure recognition coming in the final stage."[51]

The Middle East during this period was entering a stage unprecedented in the bloody years since Israelis created their own state in the midst of their Arab neighbors in 1948. The peace process was in full swing, with players that included Egypt's President Anwar Sadat, Israeli Prime Minister Menachem Begin and U.S. President Jimmy Carter, who had made renewed peace negotiations a priority when he entered office in 1977. Geyer stayed on top of the scene with interviews and commentary that analyzed not only the emerging peace process but also the rise of Islamic fundamentalism in Iran and elsewhere that continues to seethe in the region today.

A 1977 commentary by the foreign correspondent found her writing from Cairo, where she witnessed rioting students on the streets in the wake of Sadat's negotiations with fellow Arab leaders centered on finding a peaceful solution to the differences with Israel and their support for a Palestinian state—such a state always, it seems, was at the center of any Arab-Israeli conflict.

"From my 12th-floor balcony at the Hilton Hotel over the Nile, I could see the city exploding," Geyer wrote. "Students and workers ran down the streets like packs of wild dogs, starting bonfires, clubbing cars and attacking police."

Relating a conversation she had with Egyptian writer Abdul Kuddous the evening before, Geyer raised the issue of Islamic fundamentalism and its role in the peace process.

"At the moment, what he (and many other analysts, including Israelis) see as the danger here is an amorphous civilian revolution based somehow around a renaissance of Islam," she wrote. "He sees so many of the Egyptians, aware that neither socialism nor capitalism has worked for them, returning to past spiritual certainties."

So while the main story in the region remained the peace initiative undertaken by Carter and his secretary of State, Cyrus Vance, she presciently observed, "the *really* big stories are those of the danger of internal disintegration, particularly here but also in the other Arab countries and even in Israel. . . . what Sadat, and perhaps other Third World leaders really face is the fact that, once the enemy without can no longer be conjured up to make people forget their misery, they will have to meet the true threats of the corrosive, deadly, not-so-easily defeated enemies within."[52]

Geyer again focused on Sadat and his role in the Camp David Accords peace process in a 1978 column warning that Sadat had just a couple of months to "get some real movement toward peace." She wrote that Sadat had emerged from the first three rounds of the process—winning the first round with his successful peace trip to Jerusalem, Begin taking the second round when he put forth his pace plan at Ismailia, and Sadat in the process of winning round three by holding Israel up to standards consistent with peace.

"And Round 4? That is the sad part. It will be played out in the Arab world. With the peace initiative finished, forces fighting for radicalization will come to the fore. In Israel, plans now are moving rapidly forward to cope with the new wave of Palestinian terrorism and internal upheaval," she wrote. "Because of Sadat's lonely quest, the Arabs will never be able to be looked at again as a monolithic unity that will never accept an independent Israel. They are now identifiable human beings to the West, not racial stereotypes. But the change in the perception of Israel is probably greater."

The key to success in the peace process she wrote, again with some prescience, would be the leadership and pressure brought on Israel by the United States and the Carter administration.

> As Sadat correctly sees it, the only element that could even possibly make a difference is the United States. But the Carter Administration, traumatized by the pressures put on it last spring by the organized American Jewish community, is terrified to exert the pressures that would uniquely secure Israel's future.
>
> That is why Sadat's trip here represented high tragedy with mediocre response. The visit was one of utter desperation, because Sadat knows, if Carter and the Israelis do not, that Round 4 is about to begin.[53]

Following the successful completion of the Camp David Accords in September 1978, Geyer set out to assess the mood elsewhere in the Middle East in typical Geyer world-beat fashion: by focusing on and interviewing leaders of countries in the region. One such piece featured yet another rogue terrorist, Libya's Col. Moammar Khadafy. At the age of 34, Khadafy was working to improve his image in the West, Geyer wrote, "as the hardest of the hard-liners," but was intent at the same time "on being taken seriously not only as a world statesman but also as the ideological successor to Chairman Mao" who was irate over the peace accords.

Describing a Khadafy interview with herself and other visiting Americans, Geyer wrote, "On terrorism, Khadafy, who is widely accused of harboring international terrorists, said, 'We want to redefine terrorism. We say that American fleets in our waters are terrorism. When the Americans refuse wheat to starving people, that is terrorism.'" And Khadafy offered more of his defiant stance regarding the United States. "On what

Libya might do in the angry Arab aftermath of Camp David," she wrote, "he said for the first time, 'We could join the Warsaw Pact and let the world go to hell. Who's responsible for that? The Americans. And if that leads to a nuclear confrontation, who's responsible? The Americans.'"

Khadafy's anger over Camp David, wrote Geyer, was shameful "to him and the other more radical Arabs because, at heart, they know that there is nothing they can do about it." The peace accord was seen by Khadafy as the final treachery. And yet:

> Much of the rhetoric was as flaming and flamboyant as ever, for the benefit of a small group of American politicians, scholars and journalists invited here for an extraordinary, first-time "Arab-American dialogue" to improve Libyan-American relations. But the fact of its very occurrence showed (1) that there is still hope for communication with the radical Arabs after Camp David, and (2) that the Libyan "revolution" is slowly coming of age.[54]

Geyer turned to Jordan's King Hussein for a beacon of hope following the Camp David Accords, writing a few days later that Hussein, long taken for granted by the West, could "mean life or death" to the accords. The king, she wrote following an interview with him, "seemed at times to be brooding over Camp David as a 'threat' to the 'Arab identity.'

"'Our ties to the past may be in jeopardy,' he said once. And, another time, he called Egyptian President Anwar Sadat's breaking away from the Arab world 'the biggest challenge ever faced in terms of our inner feelings.'

"This represents far more than anger, disgust or even humiliation over Sadat's actions," Geyer wrote. "As one prominent Western diplomat who knows the king well said, 'The new Hussein has been developing over the tragedies of the last few years. He is tired of the Hashemites (his royal line) being constantly vilified in history.'"

The columnist urged the Carter administration to take Hussein's sentiments seriously. "The conclusion that I have come to is that this is no time to take Hussein for granted," she wrote. "He is not playing for time, as Washington originally thought. He is deadly serious about his stance, and he will go to the Arab summit in Baghdad Nov. 2 and take full part in the anti-Sadat festival of hatred.

"Ironically, the 'Friend of the West' may now be the one, for totally unforeseen and unexpected reasons, to truly end all hope for the Camp David accords."[55]

Meanwhile, the germ of the Iranian revolution that would blunt President Carter's diplomatic Middle East coup at Camp David was growing in France, where Geyer found and interviewed the exiled Ayatollah Ruhollah Khomeini, who was plotting a holy war and a triumphant return to Iran following the ouster of the shah.

"Calls for 'holy wars' may have gone forth in ancient times from stranger places, but it is hard to believe," Geyer wrote in a column datelined Neuphle Le Chateau, France. "This simple French country town seems more at home with cows chewing cud.

"Yet it is from two little houses in this hilly, pastoral setting that the entire deadly war in Iran is being waged."

During the interview, the "dour holy man" told Geyer that he considered the war to be holy, "'and by that we mean for the sake of Islam and for the sake of God and for the liberation of our own people.'

"But when you get beyond this first traditional Islamic cry for vengeance against the shah, it becomes obvious that there is something new—and deeply confusing—about this movement that has rent historic Persia and the Western World."

That something new was the separation of the Iranian struggle from political or economic motives. This movement against the U.S.-backed shah of Iran was not aligned with socialism, as Libya's might have been, or with oil interests.

"Much has been said about the new combination of Moslems and Marxists fighting this war," Geyer wrote. "Yet the Ayatollah—an imposing, heavy-set man with a gray beard and strange, dark, expressionless eyes—told me without hesitation, 'Our aims and goals are different from those of Communists and Marxists. Our movement is based on Islam and monotheism, and they are against both of them. Thus there is no cooperation and compatibility between our movement and theirs. As for Russia, we are not concerned because a nation is raised to take command of her own affairs.'"

The unique aspect of the movement, Geyer observed, was its complete alienation from historical trends. "It is not old Moslem, not really socialist. It is strongly anti-shah and anti-foreign domination." She concluded:

> Blood and the sword, industrialization and banks without interest, modern public relations and ancient chants—these are the eerie new movement that may rule Iran. It is not what we first thought—an archaic Islamic movement. But what?
>
> My memory is caught and held frozen in my strange interview. At the end, as we all squatted on the Persian rugs, the holy man simply got up without a word and silently flowed out of the room. That same mystery, at least to us Westerners, informs the entire movement that may take over what the Carter Administration now considers the area at the "vortex of the international crisis today."[56]

The next year, Khomeini made his triumphant return to Iran to establish the new Islamic regime, still intact as this book is written, that would lead to the Iranian hostage crisis and to President Carter's greatest foreign policy disgrace and his fall from grace in the United States.

Half a year after the Camp David accords, Geyer again focused a column on Sadat in another exercise of prophetic journalism in which she warned that U.S. policy might be making the Egyptian leader into another shah—that is, a figure to be ridiculed and opposed by Arabs and

Islamic fundamentalists, because of his role in the Camp David peace agreement with Israel.

U.S. support of Sadat, including military arms to help him control the region in the post-Camp David era, could be "setting him up as a new 'American linchpin,' and presenting a clear and irresistible target for the hostile countries in the area," she wrote.

"The Administration wisdom, repeated in ever lower 'sotto voce,' is that, if we can get something signed, the moderate Arabs will, by the sheer force of fait accompli, 'come in,'" she observed. "But, when pressed privately on whether there will actually be 'succeeding steps,' the highest U.S. officials usually sigh and say, 'No.'"

The columnist then asked how U.S. interests or those of Israel would be served by a "separate peace" that, "in the view of Israel's inability to give any realistic autonomy to the Palestinians, is all that we can possibly get?"

"While it is not particularly dramatic, sometimes it is valorous to settle—at least temporarily—for the status quo, the old, frustrating but workable 'no war, no peace' formula."

> It would be better to have Egypt as a moderate bridge between America and Israel and the rapidly radicalizing other Arab states than to set it up as the next Iran, ostracized and under attack from its neighbors and from within, and thus unable to help anyone.
>
> If we cannot have an overall settlement—and we cannot—it would be better, though certainly less gratifying emotionally, to live for a while with the precarious though balanced present.[57]

Two-and-a-half years later, Sadat was assassinated by Muslim fundamentalists opposed to the peace he had forged with Israel following a government crackdown on radical Islamic fundamentalists.

In the Western hemisphere, meanwhile, U.S. foreign policy interests were stirred by the rising Third Worldism south of the American border. Geyer visited Mexico in March 1978, to interview President Jose Lopez Portillo, who described to her a nation "at its greatest crossroads since the revolution of 1910.

"'This country,' he said thoughtfully, 'is in a peculiar condition. On the one hand we must deal with the crisis. On the other hand, we must prepare ourselves to begin to administer an epoch of abundance such as this country never has seen.'"

The crisis was the dissolution of monetary and political stability under the established Institutional Revolutionary Party (PRI), which, Geyer wrote, Lopez Portillo was working to open up. The looming abundance was oil.

"Today, with the discovery of vast amounts of oil and gas—perhaps, it is quietly estimated, with reserves of as much as 120 billion barrels of oil, or about as much as Saudi Arabia has—Mexico could become the Garden of Eden reincarnated," Geyer wrote. But, she cautioned, the country's new president, a writer, professor, and "man of culture," had made no inroads in a problem that remains familiar to the hemisphere today, "the excruciatingly sensitive problem of illegal aliens who are fleeing Mexican economic problems. Here he is philosophical, but without answers." She added:

> What Mexico ought to do is resolve its economic problems in order to export products and services—and not men—to the United States, he said. But he points out that Mexico is the fourth-biggest import client of the United States in the world and that, while the aliens are a problem for certain sectors of the United States, they are a great solution for others, which need cheap labor.[58]

Farther South, Geyer witnessed the nascent Sandinista movement rising in Nicaragua from the outskirts of the earthquake-rattled Managua to challenge the rule of President Anastasio Somoza, who was holed up in "his carefully guarded 'bunker' in the National Guard camp in the city . . . as closed off as a Turkish pasha from his enemies, who are many."

"What has happened here," Geyer observed in March 1978, "is that different out-groups have gained enormously in social and economic terms in recent years, and are tired of being excluded and hounded from political life." She cited the "army of the opposition," otherwise known as the Sandinista National Liberation Front, "originally a group of young Marxists who last October, for the first time, broadened the 'army' to include democratic forces.

"It is growing in numbers, in esteem and in daring, even going so far, in the present state of anarchy, to march about publicly with its red bandanas."

The Sandinistas were originally a front backed by Cuban Premier Fidel Castro, she wrote; but by 1978 the movement had gained domestic support.

"What's more, there is considerable evidence, for the first time, of contact between the various guerrilla groups in Central America," she wrote. "There may even be a central command. So if the front becomes a broad army of opposition in Nicaragua, as it appears, it could be extremely important for all of Central America."

Gone, Geyer correctly concluded during that dawning of the successful movement to oust Somoza, was "the myth, for Americans, of an untroubled, sunny, happy-go-lucky Caribbean where people are happy under dictators while drinking rum in the sun."[59]

Indeed, a year later Nicaragua was in the hands of the Sandinistas, identified by Geyer in a follow-up column to the successful revolution as a movement dedicated to a Marxist state but also "a movement of many groups, most of them some form of social democracy or democratic socialism."

She quoted the young revolutionary leader, Daniel Ortega, "the only person on both the junta and the Sandinista directorate: 'This revolution has a *compromiso* with the entire country. That is about the national reconstruction, and we're going to comply with it. The most radical measures already have been taken—agrarian reform, nationalization of the banks, takeover of the Somoza properties and the evolution of the national guard.'"

The correspondent placed a big-picture prism on the revolution, giving it a world politic spin.

So what Nicaragua really uniquely reflects today is the new pluralism in the world. It is an international reflection of the kinds of pluralism within the United States and within other developing, complex countries.

Within this pluralism . . . it will not be ideological purity that will be rewarded in the Nicaraguan revolution but economic success.

That, and that primarily, is how and why the Nicaraguan revolution is indeed a "new-style revolution," and that is why it offers so much cause now for hope.[60]

Geyer saw little hope, though, in the Carter administration's handling of the turmoil and socialist-inspired movements against right-wing authoritarianism in Latin America. The president's human-rights-based policies, she wrote, while offering idealism and self-confidence, suffered from "self-righteousness, an absence of any historic understanding and . . . an appalling ignorance.

"The truth is that there is no real policy," she wrote in a March 27, 1978, column advancing the president's first trip to Latin America that week. "I could speculate that we have the worst Latin American policy in the 14 years that I have covered the area, but that would presuppose having figured out what the policy is."

She cited "governments in the process of revolution against dictators, in small, malleable countries like Nicaragua and El Salvador, or where there already is a planned return to democracy, as in Ecuador," where she said Carter's approach worked well.

But, she wrote, the familiar old "special relationship" with the region had not disappeared but had been "transmogrified. The new one is not based, as was Kennedy's, on similar interests or systems or even geography; it is based on the use of the new Big Stick, human rights."

As one diplomat long familiar with Latin America said, "The Carter people see no economic, military, strategic or political importance in Latin America. The only importance they do give it is in terms of showing what they can do in human rights.

So Latin America is now their whipping boy. Morality on the cheap. What they wouldn't think of doing with any of the world's big boys, they do unabashedly in Latin America.[61]

But the problem was not the intent so much as it was the lack of a recognition of realism in world affairs, Geyer suggested in her writings.

"Patricia Derian, President Carter's coordinator for human rights, is such a charming and sincere woman with such a right cause that you wonder why she has become such a target for criticism by so many," Geyer wrote in a July, 1978, column defining the president's human rights stance.

> When you talk for four to five hours with Patt Derian, as I have on two occasions these past two weeks, several themes seem to emerge. Primarily, she has, at least in her own mind, made the political distinctions others say she lacks. She sees the threat from and the differences between the "aberrant personality" (an Idi Amin), a totalitarian state (like the Soviet Union) and an authoritarian state (like Argentina or South Korea). She quite rightly sees terrorism as the greatest threat to human rights in the world.

However, Geyer argued some paragraphs later, Derian "is an absolutist who says she can see no situation on earth, even a horrible terrorist act or an 'invading army,' which would justify torture or something like nerve gas, even if we were to be wiped out. 'You just have to restrain yourself,' she says.

"I can't ignore the relativity of the world I see," Geyer wrote of her own attitude.

> Or the harsh reality of countries in dissolution. Or what even men of good will might be forced to do. Or the moral and structural differences between authoritarianism and totalitarians. Or that repression often does work.
>
> But the real difference between me and so many in this administration is a far more profound one: I believe in evil."[62]

The next year, Geyer again criticized Carter's foreign affairs policy for its lack of a realistic agenda that recognized the potential of military force.

"This president vacillates strangely between his all-out optimism and his all-out pessimism," she wrote of the president's 1979 State of the Union address. "It all seems to go back to the president's problem with dealing with power. His first—and perhaps fatal—mistake in his administration was to tell the whole world we would, in effect, never use military power again. Once you do this (and no clever diplomat ever does this, particularly if it's true), you neutralize all your other powers."

The president, she wrote, spoke of being a "beneficent influence in the world" and of using "subtle diplomacy," while overlooking "the harsh world of reality."

"This is why, in all of our negotiations recently, we have given so much more than we have got," she wrote. "The President seems to think that America today is limited by objective conditions in the world. That is where he is fundamentally wrong. We are limited basically by our own behavior and attitudes, so well exemplified in his speech."[63]

The president's "subtle diplomacy" was put to the test during the Christmas season in 1979, when the Soviet Union's armed intervention in Afghanistan heaped one more foreign policy problem on top of the ongoing Iranian hostage crisis. The Afghanistan foray began with a Soviet arms buildup in the region and would last a decade. The Carter administration officially protested the Soviet incursion three days after Christmas.

"The United States today protested to the Soviet Union its 'unjustified' military involvement in the Afghan coup and warned that it will have serious implications for future relations between the two superpowers," the *Los Angeles Times* reported. The second paragraph of the story, though, revealed just how "serious" the implications would be.

"But State Department spokesman Tom Reston reaffirmed the Administration's policy that the strategic arms limitation treaty should stand on its own and that it should be approved by the Senate."[64]

The line Carter decided to draw in the diplomatic sand was the 1980 Olympic games. The administration gave the Soviet Union a February 20, 1980, deadline to withdraw its troops or face a U.S.-led boycott of the summer games scheduled in Moscow. The deadline passed, and the Soviet troops stayed.

"The United States will not participate in the Moscow Summer Olympics since there is no sign the deadline imposed by President Carter for a Soviet troop withdrawal from Afghanistan will be met, State Department spokesman Hodding Carter III said today," the *Los Angeles Times* reported. The story added that the U.S. Olympic Committee had said in the past that it would honor the government's decision; and the president said that 23 nations had publicly announced they would not attend the games. Another 13, he said, had given private assurances that they agreed with the United States.[65]

The next day, the administration announced that its decision to boycott the games was "irrevocable."[66] More than 50 nations joined in the boycott.

While Carter's human rights agenda had a basis in his religious convictions, Geyer brought a sense of her own religiosity to her coverage. Her religious background was a frame of reference she sometimes used to interpret world events. She had seen the Catholic Church as playing a strong and proper role in world politics—a sentiment that she perhaps shared with the former president.

For example, she saw the experience of the Polish-born Pope John Paul II with communism behind the Iron Curtain as playing a crucial role in his dealings with communist and leftist states.

"The Pope has been criticized . . . for reacting to his own experience in Poland behind the Iron Curtain—because he knows Marxist governments in practice at first hand," she once wrote. "Instead of being criticized for this, that is precisely why he should be listened to."[67]

In Africa, she wrote of some Christian churches "becoming deeply concerned about the spread of Marxism." She wrote that she was "delighted" at the release of a letter by the Catholic bishops of Zambia who, with the support of some Protestant leaders, warned of "scientific socialism."

"Is it possible, I keep asking myself, that this represents the moment of turnabout in Christian attitudes toward the revolution?" she asked in her column. "It well may. Until now, the Christian churches in Africa have tended either to suffer their massive martyrdoms at the hands of the tyrants in the Ugandas and in the Equatorial Guinaes, or to back liberation movements without regard to ideology, only to be wiped out once Marxism came to power."

The letter brought her hope of a shifting attitude among the religious, one less tolerant of totalitarian, particularly leftist, movements.

"The World Council reports that, by the end of this century, Africa will have more Christians than any other continent. So it is a genuine sign of hope that the churches finally are responding both to the cries for justice and to the basic need for the one spiritual and preserving force that offers a decent future to suffering Africa."[68]

Similarly, she saw the church having an influence in the leftist revolutions of Central America. She observed in El Salvador that movements such as that of the Popular Revolutionary Group, "originally Catholic and Catholic-led, have been taken over at the directorate level by Marxists." In response, she wrote, Catholic Archbishop Oscar Romero, "who, more than any other, has been at the center of the revolutionary hurricane, is pulling back from those who have maintained that there is little real difference or conflict between Christianity and Marxism."

The phenomenon was not unique to El Salvador.

"But the incredibly rich and vivid story of the place of the church in Central American revolution does not end at the new situation in El Salvador," she wrote of the Sandinista movement in neighboring Nicaragua. In that country, she wrote, "the church hierarchy was and is deeply sympathetic to the Sandinista revolution but still retains its independence and its willingness to condemn the horrors of the old regime as well as the mistakes of the new."

What is evident, she concluded, "is that a reawakened Catholicism is taking a clear, vivid, unambiguous and enormously sacrificial role in the Central American revolution. It is comforting, however, that great leaders like Archbishop Romero are carefully defining the Christian role and keeping it within Christian ideals.

"It may also be that it is this new activist role of the church that will keep the revolutions here within democratic forms and free of Marxist totalitarianism."[69]

Besides her religion, Geyer also brought another personal touch to her reporting: her gender. This enabled her to discuss not only traditional news stories, such as African and Latin American revolutions, from a different viewpoint, but also less traditional subjects, such as women serving in the military, from a unique angle.

"I admit to being torn," she wrote in 1978 about women serving in the armed forces. She observed that general John K. Singlaub, who had recently spoken out in opposition to women engaging in combat, was worried that women in such a situation might "'have an adverse impact on the male soldiers. Men tend to be protective and, while we might educate a generation of men who do not have that attitude, it is my contention that as long as men have mothers, they tend to be protective of women.'"

Geyer argued that "there is not the slightest question that women can work perfectly well in combat, as women become the necessary core of the new military, it will become inevitable."

Yet, she found herself "burdened with some perhaps unworthy or even retrograde thoughts. In Washington, D.C., there is a statue that couldn't easily be constructed today. It was given by women to the men who stood back and let women and children leave the Titanic first. Behind this 'gallantry'—on both sides—was a very practical idea: that women and children represent the survival of society, that man's sexual roles is much more of a 'sometimes thing.'"

The woman who was a leader in bringing down the barrier to women foreign correspondents concluded: "What really concerns me today, however, is that it is now becoming 'women and children last.' So, at the root of my being, philosophically I admit to having a problem with women in combat. If we, too, become the killers, whom or what will they send in to civilize us?"[70]

So far as being a female journalist in what had traditionally been a male realm, Geyer recalls today that there also were different attitudes on that front then.

"I was the first woman correspondent of our time," she said. "I went to South America in 1964. By the time I went to Vietnam in '68, there were quite a few women. In Latin America it was a problem, because they'd never seen women in these roles, and they were macho men and wanted to take you dancing, for starters. But it was so much fun. Then I went to the Middle East, and I expected the same kind of problems that I'd had in Latin America, and it wasn't that way at all. I found in those days in the Arab world, in the Muslim world, Western women were like a third sex, and if we behaved ourselves and dressed reasonably, you covered your elbows and wore a slightly longer skirt."

In this new millennium, though, is a new attitude and reality. In today's world, not only are women soldiers and journalists treated equally—held hostage by terrorists, slain and wounded by enemy and terrorist combatants and angry governments—the attitudes toward all journalists, male and female, have changed.

When she was covering the revolutions and wars of the world as a foreign correspondent, she recalled, "we were noncombatants. We were recognized by the Geneva accords. Until Cambodia, even these irregular movements which I'd written so much about recognized that. The Viet Cong would let journalists go; sometimes they'd get killed, but if you were alive, they let them go. The Khmer Rouge was the end. And now, of course, the journalists have gotten to be more of a target. I've watched this whole thing. A lot of my friends who are in Iraq—I was just talking to a friend of mine who is there now—they don't presume that they as women have any protection. Neither do the men."

Of the historic Middle East peace accord and the diplomatic failure by the United States and moderate Arabs to follow up Camp David with a regional peace settlement, Geyer blamed domestic attitudes toward Israel, regardless of the political party in power in Washington.

"You get to the attitude of this country toward Israel and anything it does," she said, "you really couldn't have a solution in the Middle East so long as the United States is not a fair bargainer or negotiator, and we never have been. Not under anybody, not under any president."

U.S. support for Israel, she said, "is completely unthinking, so you can't negotiate."

Similarly, longstanding U.S. policy in Latin America during the Carter years and before reflected a recurring attitude of low status as far as Latin America was concerned, Geyer recalled.

"These were the days of what Richard Nixon called benign neglect," she said. "When Jimmy Carter came to power, during the '70s, the civil wars in Central America were forming. Seventy-nine was when the Sandinistas took Nicaragua, took Managua, and those were the years I would say we should be investing our time and diplomacy in Central America instead of in Vietnam. This was on our doorstep. This hemisphere, it seems to me, was most important to us."

Carter's focus on human rights, seen by some as his strength, Geyer saw as his primary weakness. She remained consistent in this assessment then, and now.

"I mean, I believe in human rights very strongly, but there are times when you have to ameliorate your beliefs," she said. "The Iran hostages was disastrous, and that is his weakness, and it was Clinton's too, not being able to use power effectively. The Iranians knew that, and they held onto the hostages until the day Reagan was elected. I can still see him on television saying those hostages are coming home. It was just like that."

Carter's foreign policy, she said, "very much" undercut his presidency.

No discussion of the Carter presidency would be complete without mention of the sense of religious mission this president brought to his governance. This element contributed to Carter's human rights agenda and to his basic decency, she believes, but also lent itself to an air of superiority in him.

"He's a very nice man," she said, "but he's also very rigid, and somewhat arrogant about his goodness. There's a look about him, he can be very humorous. As he's gotten older, he's gotten more humorous, but when I interviewed him in Panama once, when they were doing the canal negotiations, and that's the only time I really interviewed him, he was in that mode of the arrogant, very good. He said, 'well, turning the canal,' and his eyes became rather tight, rigid, 'turning the canal over to them will make them more equal.' That was very strange."

Also, strange, she said, was the president's treatment of the shah of Iran. After the Carter administration brought the shah to the United States following his overthrow, a decision she said was not a mistake in itself, she said she saw a capacity in the president to do "really nasty things (because) then he sent him to this island, which was a death warrant. First thing, I don't believe the shah had to fall."

Carter, she said, had no grasp of how to use his office.

"I was raised Catholic, and I like the church very much. We were taught always to witness for what is good, and I could see that in Carter very much, not to use power. That's why he's been a great ex-president, because he's witnessing."

NOTES

1. Ben Bradlee, *A Good Life: Newspapering And Other Adventures,* (New York: Simon & Schuster, 1995), 381–82.
2. Carroll Kilpatrick, "Nixon Resigns," *Washington Post,* August 9, 1974, A01, http://www.washingtonpost.com/wp-dyn/content/article/2002/06/03/AR2005033108821.html (accessed February 26, 2007).
3. Ben Bradlee, *A Good Life: Newspapering And Other Adventures,* 324–25.
4. "Watergate Chronology," washingtonpost.com, www.washingtonpost.com/wpsrv/onpolitics/watergate/chronology.htm (accessed February 26, 2007).
5. Ben Bradlee, *A Good Life: Newspapering And Other Adventures,* 330.
6. Ibid., 341–42.
7. AP, "Marching Miners Turned Back by Union Officials," *Boston Evening Globe,* August 26, 1921, 1.
8. Charles S. Groves, "Sen. Walsh for Public Work To Aid Jobless," *Boston Evening Globe,* August 26, 1921, 6.
9. "Orders to Dispose of All Seized Liquors," *Boston Evening Globe,* August 26, 1921, 1.
10. "Week-End Market Quotations," *Boston Evening Globe,* August 26, 1921, 2.
11. "Medford Three-Family," *Boston Evening Globe,* August 26, 1921.
12. Ben Bradlee, *A Good Life: Newspapering And Other Adventures,* 43–44.
13. Ibid., 59–60.
14. Ibid., 95–98.
15. Milestone listings for 1946 for this paragraph and those that follow taken from Neville Williams, *Chronology of World History Volume IV: 1901–1998/The Modern World* (Santa Barbara, CA: ABC-CLIO, 1999), 366–75.
16. Carroll Kilpatrick, "Pact to End War Reached; Cease-Fire, U.S. Pullout Set," *Washington Post,* January 24, 1973, 1.
17. Ben Bradlee, *A Good Life: Newspapering And Other Adventures,* 338–41.

18. Peter Milius, "Ford Grants Nixon Full Pardon, Says He Has 'Suffered Enough,'" *Washington Post,* September 9, 1974, 1.
19. Ben Bradlee, *A Good Life: Newspapering And Other Adventures,* 311.
20. Ibid., 311–23.
21. Stanley Karnow, "Chinese Press, TV Play Up Nixon Visit," *Washington Post,* February 23, 1972, 1.
22. Carroll Kilpatrick, "U.S., Soviets Sign Arms Treaty," *Washington Post,* May 27, 1972, 1.
23. Reuter, "Arabs to Cut Oil Flow to U.S.," *Washington Post,* October 18, 1973, 1.
24. John M. Goshko, "Carter, Torrijos Sign Panama Canal Treaties," *Washington Post,* September 8, 1977.
25. Laurence Stern and Jim Hoagland, "Leaders Concur on Framework For Settlement in Middle East/West Bank, Gaza, Sinai Are Covered," *Washington Post,* Monday, September 18, 1978, 1.
26. William Branigin, "Iranians Seize U.S. Mission, Ask Shah' Return for Trial," *Washington Post,* November 5, 1979, 1.
27. William Greider, "8 U.S. Dead as Rescue Try Fails in Iran," *Washington Post,* April 25, 1980, 1.
28. Ben Bradlee, *A Good Life: Newspapering And Other Adventures,* 424–26.
29. Ibid., 382.
30. Georgie Anne Geyer, "I Would Give Virtually Anything to Make Them Understand," *Los Angeles Times,* June 20, 1976, IV 1.
31. Ibid.
32. "Preservation, or Evasion—Which? Mr. President," *Chicago Daily News,* April 2, 1935, 1.
33. UP, "Supreme Court Cons Farm Relief Validity," *Chicago Daily News,* April 2, 1935, 5.
34. Paul R. Leach, "President Roosevelt Faces Many Problems on Return from His Vacation Cruise," *Chicago Daily News,* April 2, 1935, 7.
35. AP, "France Arms Frontier Forts as Defense Against Germans," *Chicago Daily News,* April 2, 1935, 1.
36. UP, "Il Duce Urges 3 Powers To Unite In Crisis," *Chicago Daily News,* April 2, 1935, 2.
37. "Kolinsky Conquest," *Chicago Daily News,* April 2, 1935, 2.
38. "Marshall Field & Company," *Chicago Daily News,* April 2, 1935, 5.
39. "Men! Sensational April Sale of TOPCOATS!" *Chicago Daily News,* April 2, 1935, 7.
40. Georgie Anne Geyer, *Buying the Night Flight: The Autobiography of a Woman Foreign Correspondent* (New York: Delacorte Press/Seymour Lawrence, 1983), 28–29.
41. Ibid., 39–40.
42. George Anne Geyer, "Whatever Happened to Lois Lane?" *Los Angeles Times,* February 4, 1979.
43. Milestone listings for 1960 for this paragraph and those that follow taken from Neville Williams, *Chronology of World History Volume IV: 1901–1998/The Modern World* (Santa Barbara, CA: ABC-CLIO, 1999), 491–503.
44. Beth Ann Krier, "A Correspondent Exercises Her Options," *Los Angeles Times,* April 7, 1976, IV1, and "2003 Les Brownlee Journalism Series," The Chicago Headline Club, October, 2003, http://www.medill.northwestern.edu/spj.brownlee/2003/event20031003_geyer.html (accessed April 8, 2007).

45. Georgie Anne Geyer, *Buying the Night Flight: The Autobiography of a Woman Foreign Correspondent*, 213–14.
46. Ibid., 214–15.
47. Ibid., 215.
48. Ibid.
49. Ibid., 192.
50. Ibid., 193.
51. Ibid.
52. Georgie Anne Geyer, "Middle East: the *Real* Enemies Are Within," *Los Angeles Times*, January 26, 1977, II 5.
53. Georgie Anne Geyer, "and Gets Ready for Round 4 of His Fight," *Los Angeles Times*, February 9, 1978, II 7.
54. Georgie Anne Geyer, "'New' Khadafy Is Still the Old Firebrand," *Los Angeles Times*, October 20, 1978, II 7.
55. Georgie Anne Geyer, "Jordan's King Hussein May Hold Camp David's Key," *Los Angeles Times*, October 25, 1978, II 7.
56. Georgie Anne Geyer, "A Pastoral Setting for the Mystery Force Behind Iran's 'Holy War,'" *Los Angeles Times*, December 13, 1978, II 7.
57. Georgie Anne Geyer, "Is U.S. Setting up Sadat as the 'New Shah'?" *Los Angeles Times*, March 1, 1979, II 5.
58. Georgie Anne Geyer, "Mexico's President Struggles With Its Corrupt System," *Los Angeles Times*, March 8, 1978, II 7.
59. Georgie Anne Geyer, "Nicaragua's Quake Goes On, Shakes Up Somoza's World," *Los Angeles Times*, March 16, 1978, II 11.
60. Georgie Anne Geyer, "Nicaragua's Update of Marxism by 'Compromise,'" *Los Angeles Times*, August 17, 1979, II 7.
61. Georgie Anne Geyer, "Latin America: Carterites' Whipping Boy," *Los Angeles Times*, March 27, 1978, II 7.
62. Georgie Anne Geyer, "Human Rights: Here Is the Noble Theory . . ." *Los Angeles Times*, July 2, 1978, VI 5.
63. Georgie Anne Geyer, "Carter Should Say What He Means, or Mean What He Says," *Los Angeles Times*, January 28, 1979, V 5.
64. "U.S. Protests Soviet Role in Afghan Coup," *Los Angeles Times*, December 28, 1979, I 1.
65. AP, "U.S. Says No to Olympics on Afghan Deadline Day," *Los Angeles Times*, February 20, 1980, I 2.
66. Kenneth Reich, "U.S. Says Games Boycott Decision Is 'Irrevocable,'" *Los Angeles Times*, February 21, 1979, I 1.
67. Georgie Anne Geyer, "In Mexico, the Pope Suffers a Misjudgment," *Los Angeles Times*, February 9, 1979, II 7.
68. Georgie Anne Geyer, "Churchmen Stand Up to African Left—at Last," *Los Angeles Times*, October 7, 1979, VI 5.
69. Georgie Anne Geyer, "Marx and Jesus—An Uneasy Alliance," *Los Angeles Times*, August 19, 1979, V 5.
70. Georgie Anne Geyer, "In Israel and U.S., Doubts About Women in Combat," *Los Angeles Times*, June 12, 1978, II 9.

CHAPTER 5

The '80s of Juan Williams and Ellen Goodman: Reagan and Fallen Empire and Values

> I think people wanted to feel good about themselves. We had been through Watergate, after Vietnam, and after the assassinations of the Kennedys and all that. The whole notion was that Reagan was sort of bright and sunny, and "Morning in America, and we're going to make this happen and believe in me." And he was not about apologies to Vietnam, apologies over race relations; he was about American triumphalism. So he was a very sort of enervating force in American life. I think people saw in him this sort of movie star looks and promise that everything is going to be OK. People would mock him, and journalists like me would say this guy reads from notes. People tell him what to do. But he had principles, and he had tremendous communications skills, which is what the presidency had become.
>
> —Juan Williams

Two-year-old Lance Hosmer and his four-year-old brother, Absalom, were asleep in the back of an old blue Chevrolet Malibu. A dirty stuffed duck hung from the rear-view mirror. A city cop knocked on the car window. The youngest of the boys started to cry.

"His mother and father quickly woke up, startled in the dark by the noise," reporter Juan Williams wrote in his *Washington Post* story, datelined Columbus, Ohio. "They asked what was wrong. The policeman told them they couldn't sleep in the park."

The parents told the policeman they had nowhere else to go, they had no money. The policeman insisted they would have to leave the park.

"That night the family slept uneasily on a side street in a strange neighborhood.

Juan Williams. © Duquesne University, Office of Multicultural Affairs. Used by permission.

"A few days later, after their money for food had run out, Lance wanted milk. Absalom watched as his father gave blood to get $8."

Some nights later, when Lance threw up from eating spoiled meat obtained in a food line, "his mother could only hold him. There was no money to pay a doctor."

It was the middle of the United States in the middle of the 1980s and the middle of a revolution—the Reagan uprising against the social programs of the New Deal and the Great Society. The statistics reported by Williams in his Columbus dispatch related a story of the wealthiest nation on the planet failing to provide for its neediest and youngest citizens—its children.

"One of every five American children under 18 and one of every four under six live in poverty," Williams reported. "There are more poor children in the United States than at any time since 1965, before the Great Society programs began.

"With most of the elderly buoyed above the poverty line by Social Security cost-of-living adjustments, children are now the largest age group in poverty; 37.6 percent of all the poor are children," Williams' story continued.

"'In 1985 affluent America, poverty is the greatest child killer,' said a report released by the Children's Defense Fund last week. 'More American children die each year from poverty than from traffic fatalities and suicide combined. Twice as many children die from poverty than from cancer and heart disease combined.'"[1]

The story was a remarkable contrast in framing from an opinion piece Williams had written for the *Post* four years before, at the beginning of the Reagan revolution. Then, the young writer told the story of another poverty-stricken American who, despite her difficulties, welcomed the Reagan administration's efforts to change the meaning and scope of government welfare.

"Cheryl Reese is all for Ronald Reagan. She likes his idea that poor people should get off welfare by getting to work. She agrees that it's too easy for poor people to live on welfare," Williams wrote of the Washington mother of two who was on welfare, collected food stamps, and lived in publicly subsidized housing.

> But instead of singing tributes to the compassion of a nation that cares for its poor, Reese, like Reagan, speaks of hate of welfare. It's for a different reason though. Her dislike of welfare comes from the way it controls her life, limits her choices, makes her most private decisions open to control by public policy.
>
> "Reagan's got the right idea about all of welfare, from what I've seen him say," the thin woman says. "It just don't help people to do nothing but get more welfare and get in your way when you're trying to get off."[2]

Such was the mood of the nation at the beginning of the 1980s, when the country was recovering from what Williams in his National Public Radio office in 2006 called the "malaise" from the Jimmy Carter administration.

"My sense was that going into the '80s, the country was disenchanted, not only with the Nixons of the world in terms of Watergate, but disenchanted with the whole power of Washington and the power of the presidency," he recalled. "We still see a little of this now with (then-Vice President Dick) Cheney, who was chief of staff under Ford and all that, and he thought that the presidency had been reduced in its power so now he's trying to reassert that power under the second President Bush. But when I think of that period I think of Americans moving more toward a belief in local power, local authority, that's when you start to see the shift away from the big cities, away from long-term corporate employment, you know the gold watch after forty years. People looking for new opportunities, new investments, it was a tremendous era of movement in the United States, people relocating, the birth of both the neocons (neoconservatives) and the fundamentalists as a major political and social phenomenon."

Williams himself was a part of another national phenomenon of movement and relocation, that of immigrants lured to the post-World War II

United States seeking economic and social betterment. Born in Colon, Panama on April 10, 1954, Williams moved with his family to Brooklyn, New York, in 1958. These were the days of McCarthyism and anticommunist fervor that would be a seed for the anticommunist, anti-socialist tendencies behind the Reagan era's activism against Marxist-inspired populist uprisings in Latin America and government-supported wealth redistribution at home.

Indeed, on the day of his birth, the headlines in the *New York Times,* the newspaper of what would become Williams' childhood city, detailed the communist scare and the fever of McCarthyism that was rampant in the nation during the 1950s. A front page story reported that President Dwight D. Eisenhower's attorney general, Herbert Brownell Jr., planned to work with Congress to use "'new and powerful constitutional weapons' to destroy the Communist party in this country." One measure the official reported to the nation in a radio and television address would be legislation introduced by Senator Homer Ferguson of Michigan designed to "take away the citizenship of any person found guilty of advocating the overthrow of the Government by force. This would mean the end of the Communist party, Senator Ferguson said in introducing the measure."[3]

Reported elsewhere on the front page, Wisconsin Republican Senator Joseph R. McCarthy had been granted a 24-hour delay in the beginning of the Army-McCarthy hearings to enable the senator to deliver "a controversial speech in Houston on April 21, 'Texas Independence Day.'"[4] The beginning of the decline of the demagogue's power would have to wait a day.

Inside the newspaper on the same day was the story out of Boston of Otis Archer Hood, "one-time Communist party candidate for Governor, [who] pleaded innocent today to the first two indictments brought under the Massachusetts anti-subversive law." He was charged with membership in the Communist Party, which the newspaper reported had been listed as a subversive organization in 1951 legislation.[5] In Washington, Toledo, Ohio publisher and broadcaster Edward Lamb criticized the Federal Communications Commission for questioning his loyalty based on charges that he had belonged to the Lucas County Communist Party from 1944 to 1948;[6] and a three-man special board of inquiry ruled unanimously to exclude a Hungarian-born carpenter from the nation based on government evidence that he had belonged to the Communist Party since 1924.[7]

Internationally, the battle against communism was being waged in Indo-China. French Premier Joseph Laniel outlined his country's policy in the French conflict in Southeast Asia. The three-pronged policy, he said, was to use any means to defend Dien Bien Phu from Vietnamese forces, to assure U.S. "material" assistance to the French military effort, and to enter negotiations in Geneva later that month "to seek to establish peace on a basis of respect for the rights of all the interested peoples."

In language foreshadowing the reasoning behind U.S. involvement in Vietnam following the French failure there, the premier told his National Assembly that avoiding communist domination of Southeast Asia was vital.

"M. Laniel told the Assembly 'American diplomacy holds that it is necessary to give repeated warnings and to leave no doubt on the part of communist China about the United States' determination not to allow the communists to dominate Southeast Asia.'"[8]

Elsewhere on the front page, the *Times* reported that Secretary of State John Foster Dulles was departing for Europe to meet with his counterparts in Britain and France to discuss winning the war in Indo-China. "In support of his proposal for collective action, Mr. Dulles will take with him the first pledge by an Asian nation—Thailand—to join a united front against Communist aggression in Southeast Asia."[9]

And the perpetual unrest in the Middle East also commanded front page space, as the *Times* reported that Arab representatives were planning to walk out of United Nations Security Council talks "on the Israeli frontier situation unless the Israeli attack on Nahhalin is treated as a separate item."

"The decision was made after an exchange of messages between the Arab delegates at United Nations headquarters in New York and the Arab capitals," the newspaper reported. "Jordan has refused to accept a Council review of the whole armistice line situation on the ground that such a comprehensive discussion would be used for bilateral peace talks between Jordan and Israel."[10]

At home, jazz artists including Mel Powell, Erroll Garner, Gerry Mulligan, Billie Holiday, and Gene Krupa had played a benefit concert at Carnegie Hall for The Lighthouse;[11] and the American Chamber Opera Society announced that four operas in concert form would be presented the following year at the Town Hall. One of these would be the American premiere of Vivaldi's *L'Olimpiade.*[12] Doris Day and Robert Cummings were starring in *Lucky Me* at the Paramount; Ann Blyth, Howard Keel, and Fernando Lamas were appearing in *Rose Marie* at Radio City Music Hall; and a cast of professional actors was offering a concert reading of *King John* at the Lexington Avenue Poetry Center.[13]

H.W. Perlman Corp. was selling new spinet pianos for $395 and rebuilt grands for $495,[14] and money-conscious parents could buy their sons flannel Easter suits with a "handsomely tailored single-breasted jacket with patch pockets" at Franklin Simon for $26.95.[15] Restaurants Lonchamps at Madison and 59th featured all-night service to the city that never sleeps, a "sandwich or supper—nightcap or daybreak breakfast,"[16] while Frank E. Campbell offered services "When Death Occurs," beginning with "Traditionally fine funerals from $250."[17]

As a child growing up in the streets of the city, Williams began to entertain the possibility of becoming a journalist as he read the stories and learned the power of the written word in the newspapers that his mother brought home.

"I'm an immigrant kid, sitting on the stoop waiting for my mom to get home from working in the garment district in lower Manhattan," he recalled. "The businessmen would leave newspapers on the subways, and my mom would bring the newspapers, like a gift, 'oh look what I got.' And I, being a young person, loved the sports sections, and I would compare the work of the different sports writers. I was a little tyke; this was like a dessert for me. I felt like my mother was just looking out for me. This was the late '50s, early '60s, the *New York Daily News, New York Times, Herald Tribune, Journal American, New York Post.* There were more than that. I would read these papers and think, 'I would love to be a reporter and be able to go to the game. I would love to be a reporter and be on the scene and talk to people.' And then as you get older and you start to look at everything from the funny pages to the arts section, it really just fascinated me. By the time I'm ten years old I'm just loving the front pages and how power works, and who has power, and who the players are. I'd gone from the sports page to the front page. I thought, 'newspaper reporting, man what a job, unbelievable. You mean they pay you to go and be there and talk to these people and understand the inner workings of power?'"

In elementary school, Williams won a city-wide essay contest about the city's fire department. "Suddenly," he said, "I knew the power of the word. It was a wonderful thing." He became the editor of his prep school paper at the Oakwood Friends School in Poughkeepsie, New York. While attending Haverford College, where he earned a degree in philosophy in 1976, Williams wrote for the local newspaper, which sometimes paid him with a check, other times with a byline. The byline is what he remembers.

"I just couldn't believe it, y'know, because of the way that I had grown up, reading other people with such care, and loving journalism, and loving newspapers. For me it was, oh my gosh, it was like your name in, what do they say about movie stars, your name in lights. For me, that was the equivalent. It was a thrill."

Other thrills awaited, including a summer job his freshman and sophomore years at the Philadelphia *Evening Bulletin,* followed by an internship at the *Providence Journal,* then back to Philadelphia and the *Bulletin* during his senior school year.

"All this time I'm getting paid professionally, and working at the big papers. But they (the *Bulletin*) wouldn't hire me because this was right after Watergate and everybody wanted to be Woodward and Bernstein, and they wanted more experienced people than just a college guy, even one with a lot of experience."

So he applied for internships and got offers at the *Philadelphia Inquirer* and the *Washington Post.*

"I figured if I'm going to be out of a job in a couple of months, I'll go to the *Washington Post.* But that's still an internship, and then I'm working on the metro desk, they had like twenty-some interns stay on to get what they called two-year internships. I felt so privileged, still. The difference was I worked all the time and I had so much experience coming in, other people were coming from Ivy League college newspapers, Harvard and Yale, but they hadn't worked in the way that I'd worked at a daily paper."

The internship turned into a full-time job that lasted 23 years, with Williams working in positions that included editorial writer, columnist, and White House correspondent.

American voters in 1976, when Williams officially became a full-time journalist, had delayed the Reagan revolution for another four years, as Republicans narrowly nominated President Gerald Ford as their presidential candidate over Reagan. Ford would lose to Jimmy Carter in the November general election. But many of the issues that would dominate the headlines of the '80s were in the news that year. Capital punishment was restored in July by a U.S. Supreme Court ruling that it is not unconstitutional; Canada the same month abolished the death penalty. West Germany legalized abortion that year; in September, the U.S. House of Representatives approved the Hyde Amendment prohibiting the use of federal funds for abortion except when the life of the mother is considered to be jeopardized. Women, meanwhile, that same month gained the right to hold the priesthood in the Episcopalian Church. In another major civil rights ruling, relating to sexual activities, the U.S. Supreme Court in March gave states the right to enforce laws banning homosexual activity.[18]

Concerns over depletion of the Earth's ozone layer were raised when the American Panel on Atmospheric Chemistry warned that chlorofluorocarbons from spray cans and refrigeration systems threatened the layer. A new, mystery ailment, to become known as Legionnaire's Disease, killed 29 people following a meeting of the American Legion in Philadelphia, and Indian-born U.S. chemist Har Gobind Khorana announced the creation of an artificial gene that functioned naturally in a bacterial cell.

In the arts and letters, Federico Fellini released *Casanova,* starring Donald Sutherland, in Italy, while in the United States Brian De Palma released the horror flick *Carrie,* based on a Stephen King novel and starring Sissy Spacek. Robert Redford and Dustin Hoffman starred in Alan J. Pakula's *All the President's Men,* based on the book chronicling Bob Woodward's and Carl Bernstein's Watergate scandal coverage for the *Washington Post.* Saul Bellow won the fiction Pulitzer Prize for *Humboldt's Gift,* and Alex Haley published *Roots,* which would become a television epic. Also published were the *Collected Poems of W.H. Auden,* Philip Roth's *The Professor of Desire* and Gore Vidal's *1876.* U.S. composer Philip Glass staged his opera *Einstein on the Beach.* Neil Simon's *California Suite* premiered at the Eugene O'Neill Theater in New York City, and Ntozake Shange's *For Colored Girls who have Considered Suicide when the Rainbow was Enuf* opened at New York's Booth Theater. Barbara Walters became the first female co-host of a national news program.

Four years later, when Reagan was elected president, Williams was well-established at the *Washington Post* as a full-time writer. Reagan came to town in January 1981, eager to reverse four decades of steady government growth and state welfarism. The actor-turned-president entered office on the tail of a Carter presidency that had experienced high inflation and interest rates; the new president brought an aggressive economic, anti-communist agenda that combined large tax cuts, an immense buildup in defense spending, and the promise of a balanced budget by 1984. A couple of *Washington Post* stories early in 1981 laid out a portion of the new president's domestic political agenda—cutbacks in welfare spending—along with an analysis of early difficulties accompanying Reagan's so-called supply-side economics that called for Americans and businesses to invest tax-cut savings into the economy and production. A November 1981 front-page story detailed plans for welfare and medical program cuts over the next two years.

"Proposals for massive new cuts in federal welfare, Medicaid, and Medicare benefits—totaling as much as $9.3 billion in fiscal 1983—have been outlined by Secretary of Health and Human Services Richards S. Schweiker in a confidential memo to the Office of Management and Budget," the newspaper reported.

> These cuts would be in addition to the more than $2 billion in fiscal 1982, Medicaid and Medicare cuts and more than $1 billion in welfare reductions already voted by Congress in last summer's budget bill at the request of President Reagan. Among the proposals for cutting cash welfare benefits (at an estimated savings of $635 million in fiscal 1983): forcing the states to adopt workfare programs for welfare clients and requiring at least one parent to participate if both parents are in the home; requiring all parents in the welfare program for mothers and children to search for a job regardless of the age of the child; reducing benefits if a welfare mother with a child lives in a larger household (with a grandmother, for example) and thus may be deemed to have savings on rent and electricity; paying benefits to aged blind and disabled welfare clients only from the date of application and not retroactive to the start of the month.[19]

Accompanying the story on the proposed welfare cuts was a front-age analysis of difficulties already facing Reagan's supply-side economic blueprint. Summarizing the president's election promise to fight inflation and foster economic growth at the same time, a scenario that "economists for years had said was impossible," the analysis detailed some of the plan's difficulties.

"Last week the president admitted to congressional leaders that he cannot meet all those goals, at least not by 1984," the piece reported. "Three weeks earlier he acknowledged that the United States has slid into a recession. Friday's report that unemployment jumped in September to 8 percent of the work force suggests the recession could be severe."

The analysis continued: "Has the supply-side bubble burst?

"Supply-siders say it has not. Inflation and interest rates are coming down, and supply-side theorists say that healthy noninflationary growth is just around the corner. They predict it will begin next year as more supply-side tax cuts come into effect."[20]

Indeed, the nation did experience a major recession and high unemployment during the Reagan administration. But this did not deter the president or his supporters, who looked beyond the economic woes to a larger conservative political picture that pleased them and fueled their optimism.

By 1983, Williams was reporting on the presidency, and a February front-page piece of a Sunday edition featured the president praising the accomplishments of what had come to be known as "Reaganomics"—an economic policy that not only relied on private-business investment and spending of income tax cuts, but also included a "trickle-down" formula whereby newly created wealth would seep down to the lower classes. The popular analogy of the time was that the rising economic tide would lift all boats.

"President Reagan, unabashedly flying the colors of his often criticized economic policies, said yesterday that 'Reaganomics' has reduced inflation, cut interest rates in half, started reviving the housing and auto industries, and is now beginning to bring down unemployment," Williams wrote.

The president, Williams reported, interpreted the statistics of high unemployment as a positive economic signal.

"On Friday, appearing buoyant over news that the unemployment rate had fallen from 10.8 percent in December to 10.4 percent in January, he said the economy and the country are 'on the move' and predicted that the nation will not again see unemployment as high as 10.8 percent," Williams wrote. "Departing from the bipartisan tone of his State of the Union message, Reagan last week stiffened his opposition to rolling back his income tax cuts, funding new job-creating programs or further scaling back his expensive defense buildup. Instead, apparently encouraged by recent rises in several economic indicators, the president began strongly defending his program."[21]

In fact, the economy was heading out of its 1982 recession, lending the president plenty of opportunity to boast of the success of Reaganomics. A Williams story early in 1983 featured the president citing decreasing world oil prices as contributing to the economic recovery at home and as a reason to avoid protectionist trade policies.

"President Reagan said yesterday that falling oil prices will aid a worldwide economic recovery, and he urged that western nations resist pressures for protectionist economic policies that would limit international trade," Williams wrote. "Secretary of State George P. Shultz said it will 'spur the free world's economic recovery' but warned that the lower prices could mean economic turmoil for Mexico and Venezuela, which rely on oil revenues to pay their foreign debts."

Reagan sounded an optimistic note near the end of the article: "'We in the West are on the threshold of a new economic era,' Reagan said. 'Our common problems have a common solution, economic growth.'"[22]

Later that year, sterling statistics offered the president another opportunity to take credit for strong economic growth and to call for a continuation of his policies.

"President Reagan yesterday hailed the government's announcement that U.S. economic output increased at a robust 8.7 percent annual rate last quarter, calling it a vindication of his economic policies," wrote Williams and John M. Berry. "The economy is 'growing with more vigor than most economists predicted,' he said."

Yet unemployment still hovered near 10 percent, and the president said the rate "is likely to remain high for many months, but . . . much of the pain from this is concentrated in a small part of the work force.

"And he endorsed the moderate new squeeze the Federal Reserve Board has put on the money supply to keep the recovery from getting out of hand and causing a revival of inflation. He also continued to urge Congress to reduce the impending deficit, but by spending cuts rather than by tax increases."[23]

That fall, during a speech to the National Federation of Republican Women in Louisville, Kentucky, the president argued that his policies helped all citizens, as would his proposed balanced budget amendment that would require outlays to equal government income.

"President Reagan yesterday unveiled his response to the growing female disapproval of his administration—the gender gap—by defending his economic policies and hard-line military buildup as crucial to a wealthier, more secure America for women as well as men," Williams reported. "The basis of the president's bid for female support is his argument that the economic recovery has benefited women. He strongly attacked Democrats who criticize his economic policies as being unfair to the poor and women."

The president offered the GOP women a line typical of his stance toward his Democratic critics: that their proposals would do more damage than his.

"'Our opponents preach to us like apostles of fairness,' Reagan said. 'Maybe they are fair in at least one way. Their policies don't discriminate: they bring misery to everybody.'

"Reagan responded to recent Democratic criticism of his record federal budget deficit by renewing his call for a balanced budget amendment."[24]

The apostles of fairness cited in Louisville by the president criticized his policies for benefiting the wealthy at the expense of the poor. In fact, the nation's underbelly of poverty detracted from the recovering economy, often prompting responses from the president that fueled the fire of the critics—such as his contention that homeless citizens chose their lifestyle.

"President Reagan, responding in a television interview and a political speech to charges that his administration has favored the rich over the poor, said today that people sleeping on outdoor grates in cities are homeless 'by choice,'" Williams reported early in 1984. "Asked on ABC's 'Good Morning America' in an interview from the White House why 'people across this country . . . say, "Yes, he is the nicest man and we like him but his policies are causing misery,"' Reagan responded that his administration is spending more on programs for the needy, health care and food stamps."

The story continued: "'What we have found in this country, and maybe we're more aware of it now,' Reagan added, 'is one problem that we've had, even in the best of times, and that is the people who are sleeping on the grates, the homeless who are homeless, you might say, by choice.'"

A presidential spokesman later cited studies supporting the president's claim, showing "that as much as 25 percent of the homeless refuse help from government agencies. Reagan added in the television interview that the problem has been 'aggravated' by new laws requiring some mental institutions to release disturbed persons when 'they have no place to go.'"[25]

But other statistics did not help the president's case, as economic recovery left some in its wake. The next year, Williams reported findings of a study that found black children more endangered than white children in terms of health and financial well being.

"Black children are twice as likely as white children to die in the first year of life, three times as likely to be poor, four times as likely not to live with either parent and five times as likely to be on welfare, according to a study released yesterday by the Children's Defense Fund," Williams wrote. "The study, drawn from a variety of government statistics, portrays a widening schism between black and white children in America. It concludes that during the past five years black children have been 'sliding backwards' and are increasingly suffering from 'inequality that denies opportunity to millions of black children.'"[26]

Another study the following year found equally dismal results for the nation's underprivileged children.

"One of three American children lives in a household that receives some form of government welfare, including food stamps, Medicaid or cash payments, the Census Bureau said yesterday," Williams and Spencer Rich reported early in 1986. "These benefits, based on a means test, are far more common among black and Hispanic children—under 18—than among white children. One of four white children in 1984 lived in households receiving one or more means-tested benefits, compared to 68 percent of black children and 52 percent of Hispanic children."[27]

Nor did it help the president that his director of the Office of Management and Budget early in Reagan's tenure faulted certain aspects of supply-side economics in a nationally circulated magazine piece. The incident prompted the president's young adviser, David Stockman, to offer his resignation, which Reagan declined after his chief of staff, James A. Baker III, and Vice President George H.W. Bush intervened on Stockman's behalf.

"Considered one of the best and certainly the brightest of the Reaganites in the heady spring of 1981, when he was highly visible in the media, Stockman fell from grace for the emperor-has-no-clothes disclosures he made to writer William Greider that appeared later in a celebrated *Atlantic Monthly* article in December, 1981," the *Post* reported in a 1983 article detailing Stockman's efforts to help the president understand "the intricate difficulties of shrinking the federal budget."[28]

Accompanying Reagan's domestic economic and social programs was a Latin American policy based on staunch anticommunism activism. The president carried out his policies through intervention in Central America with financial assistance and some military arms provided to dictatorships facing revolt from leftist insurgencies, such as in El Salvador, or to rebels fighting leftist governments brought to power with popular support, such as in Nicaragua.

Williams covered a presidential news conference in March 1983, at which Reagan defended his El Salvador aid request based on the perceived communist threat there.

"President Reagan said yesterday that there is no 'blackmail intended' in his telling Congress that it must approve $110 million in new military aid for El Salvador or the United States may have to send more military advisers to the civil war there," Williams reported. "In an 11-minute news conference with reporters in the White House briefing room the president dismissed criticism that his view of the communist threat to El Salvador is 'overblown.' He said fears that a large American role in El Salvador will lead to U.S. involvement approaching the scale of the Vietnam war are ill-founded because no combat troops will be sent to El Salvador."[29]

The president was again on the defense at the end of the next month, explaining at a fund-raising speech for Republican U.S. Senator John Tower of Texas that it sometimes is necessary to crawl under the covers with less-than-desirable bedfellows to promote the greater good of the nation.

"President Reagan defended his Latin American policies here today, arguing that support for governments with poor human rights records and paramilitary leaders is necessary if the United States is not to be 'paralyzed with indecision,'" Williams reported from Houston. "He said the security of the Western Hemisphere 'rests as much on (American) willpower as firepower.'"

The speech, presidential aides told Williams, "was intended to build public support and pressure on Congress for support of U.S. actions to aid friendly governments in Latin America. One said the president was seeking to bring America's policy 'out of the dark' by explaining why U.S. intervention in Latin America should not be perceived as an embarrassment and 'something to be done in covert operations.'"[30]

Late that summer, the Reagan administration, facing increasing criticism of its Latin American interventionism, linked the news media and

U.S. churches to the enemy, accusing them of skewing administration policy and lying to the public.

"A White House official trying to mobilize constituent support for President Reagan's Central America policy blames 'deliberate distortion' by the news media and major U.S. churches for continuing public ignorance of and opposition to the administration strategy in the region," the *Post's* Lou Cannon reported with Williams.

"'I think the media has tried to portray what we think are the bad guys, the communists, as Robin Hoods,' said Faith Ryan Whittlesey, the White House director of public liaison. 'And I think the confusion has been deliberate and that accounts for some of the ignorance.'"

The story continued: "Whittlesey, who is directing the White House campaign to line up conservative business, labor, ethnic and veterans groups behind Reagan's Central America policy, said she watched television every night and 'was appalled' by coverage she described as 'biased and one-sided.'"[31]

The president continued to play the communism card into the next year. In mid-April, in his weekly radio address to the American public, Reagan deftly tied his administration's support of the contra rebels in their battle against the Sandinista government of Nicaragua to the specter of Soviet Union involvement in that country and of communist designs on the Western hemisphere.

"President Reagan, explaining his decision Friday to bypass Congress in order to send more military aid to Central America, said yesterday that the Soviet Union, Cuba, elements of the Palestine Liberation Organization, East Germany and Libya had joined with the leftist Sandinista government in Nicaragua in an attempt to 'install communism by force throughout this hemisphere,'" Williams reported. "Reagan also noted that the Soviet Union and Cuba held joint naval combat exercises in Central America last week and that there were now 7,500 Soviet-bloc personnel in Nicaragua as well as 40 new military bases, built with Soviet aid at a cost of more than $300 million."[32]

The backing of the contra rebels was typical of the Reagan administration's foreign policy of working covertly, of usurping Congress, to resist what administration officials viewed as Soviet and Cuban intentions to install leftist governments in the Western hemisphere and elsewhere. But the covert activities backfired on the administration in 1986 in the Iran-Contra scandal that involved the sale of U.S. arms to Iran, with the proceeds used to help finance the contra rebels in Nicaragua.

The scandal began as a story of the United States sending arms to Iran in an attempt to free U.S. hostages being held in Lebanon by Islamic militants in retaliation for Israel's invasion of that country in 1982.

Sources told the *Post* early in November 1986 that the release of three U.S. hostages over the previous 14 months "followed a series of shipments of military cargo to Iran after secret discussions between top White House envoys and representative of the Tehran regime." According to U.S. intelligence sources, the talks involving former National Security Adviser Robert McFarlane and Lt. Col. Oliver North, a member of the National Security Council staff, had been taking place for more than a year and included "an Iranian need for 'defensive' military equipment, sources said, along with long-term financial stability that would occur with a rise in world oil prices."[33]

Reagan told congressional leaders later that month that the shipment of military gear to Iran was part of a "larger effort to support some dissident factions vying for power in Tehran," the *Post* reported. "The operation has provoked angry exchanges within the White House in recent days between chief of staff Donald T. Regan and national security adviser John M. Poindexter over how to explain the president's previously secret actions to Congress and the public, officials said."[34]

As public criticism of the Iran arms deal grew, the *Post* reported that the president had ordered CIA Director William J. Casey "not to inform congressional intelligence committees of a covert action involving the shipment of arms to Iran and release of American hostages in Lebanon, informed sources said yesterday."[35]

Meanwhile, the newspaper reported that Secretary of State George P. Shultz was distancing himself from the White House's Iran policy. "Shultz's spokesman, Charles E. Redman, said the secretary 'was not directly involved, although he was sporadically informed of some details' of the secret effort to deliver arms to Tehran to try to win friends there and get help in efforts to release U.S. hostages held by pro-Iranian Moslem fundamentalists in Lebanon."[36]

A week and a half later, the truth of the arms deal came out as the *Post* reported the full extent of the scandal, which now stretched from the Middle East and efforts to gain the freedom of hostages to meddling in the internal affairs of Nicaragua on behalf of the administration's anticommunist ideology. The lead story in the newspaper reported on the resignation of administration officials over the Iran-Contra scandal, while a second story revealed the details, including the amount of money involved.

"President Reagan yesterday announced the resignation of national security adviser Vice Adm. John M. Poindexter and the firing of a key deputy, Lt. Col. Oliver L. North, following the disclosure of a clandestine web of financial transactions in which profits from the sale of American weapons to Iran were diverted to help rebels fighting for the Nicaraguan government," the newspaper reported on November 26.

"A shaken and grim-faced Reagan, confronting the most serious crisis of his presidency, told reporters 'I was not fully informed' about 'one of the activities undertaken' in the secret weapons shipments to Iran. 'This action raises serious questions of propriety,' he said."[37]

The second story reported that between $10 million and $30 million paid by Iran for U.S. arms "was transferred to the contras through Swiss bank accounts with the 'precise knowledge' of Lt. Col. Oliver L. North, an NSC staff member who has been identified as the overseer of the White House contra aid program. Also aware of the contra cash transfer, according to [Attorney General Edwin] Meese, were North's two NSC bosses—the national security adviser, Vice Adm. John M. Poindexter, and his predecessor, Robert C. McFarlane."[38]

But the Reagan administration did opt for overt, direct military action in a couple of notable incidents, one in the Middle East, followed by another in the Caribbean. Following Israel's invasion of Lebanon in June 1982, in retaliation for the attempted murder of an Israeli ambassador in London and a Palestinian military escalation in South Lebanon, the United States committed U.S. military personnel to a peacekeeping force in Beirut. The following year, a suicide bomber drove an explosive-laden truck into Beirut National Airport and detonated it outside a Marine barracks in a gruesome slaughter that would have U.S. citizens clamoring for withdrawal of U.S. forces from Beirut.

"President Reagan vowed yesterday to maintain a U.S. military presence in Lebanon in the wake of the suicide bombing attack that killed 161 Marines and sailors in Beirut, but his advisers considered a plan to make the Marines less vulnerable by moving many of them to ships offshore," Williams and Lou Cannon reported the next day.

Defense Secretary Caspar W. Weinberger cited "circumstantial evidence" linking the attack to "Hezballah," a Muslim Shiite sect connected to Iranian leader Ayatollah Ruhollah Kohmeini, the newspaper reported.

"'We intend to respond to this criminal act when the perpetrators are identified,' White House spokesman Larry Speakes said last night.

"'We will not yield to international terrorism because we know that if we do the civilized world will suffer (and) our values will be fair game for all those who seek to destroy what we stand for,' Speakes said in a statement after a three-hour late afternoon meeting of the president and his top advisers."[39]

Early the next year, the *Post* was reporting administration plans to leave Lebanon.

"President Reagan yesterday ordered U.S. Marines to leave Lebanese soil for ships offshore in the face of a deteriorating situation in Beirut," said the story. "But in a statement following a day of high-level meetings behind a facade of normal activity, Reagan also announced that he has authorized U.S. naval gunfire and air strikes against Syrian-controlled positions in Lebanon under less restrictive rules of engagement that could alter the U.S. role in that country."[40]

Days after the 1983 Lebanese episode, U.S. troops were sent into action in the Caribbean when Reagan ordered an invasion of the island of Grenada, where a recent series of coups had instilled a sense of uncertainty about the small nation's political alignments and policy intentions. Administration officials said the invasion was intended to protect U.S. citizens and stop the spread of communism, but critics claimed it was an attempt to restore U.S. military prestige following the Beirut embarrassment.

"The Reagan administration justified its coordinated attack on Grenada yesterday as a preemptive strike to prevent about 1,100 Americans living there from being taken hostage and as a response to urgent requests from six Caribbean countries to restore order and stop the spread of Marxist revolution in the region," the newspaper reported.

Reagan and cabinet officials said an "'atmosphere of violent uncertainty' in the small island nation prompted a series of high-level meetings late last week and through the weekend, leading to a signed presidential invasion order at 6 P.M. Monday." The administration said the decision was supported by Jamaica, Barbados, and other eastern Caribbean countries.

"The concern of these nations, after the bloody coup last week in Grenada that pitted Marxists against Marxists, was summed up in a statement by Prime Minister Eugenia Charles of Dominica," the newspaper reported. "It is not a matter of an invasion," she said. "It is a matter of preventing this thing (Marxist revolution) from spreading to all the islands."[41]

In the main story reporting the invasion, Secretary of State George P. Schultz said the action was "not intended to 'send a message' to the Soviets or Cubans."[42] But the president diluted that claim later when he tossed the military operations in Beirut and Grenada into one ideological hat, defending both the Lebanese deployment and Grenada decisions as justified reactions to Soviet Union initiatives. The president claimed that U.S. troops found a Cuban base on Grenada, stocked with weapons, "enough to supply thousands of terrorists. . . . We got there just in time."[43]

"President Reagan, speaking to the nation in a week of foreign policy crises, last night defended the U.S. invasion of Grenada and the continuing deployment of U.S. Marines in Lebanon as a response to what he called Soviet encouragement of violence and terrorism in both countries," the *Post* reported in a companion story. "If the United States had not acted in Grenada or if the Marines were withdrawn from Lebanon, Reagan suggested strongly in his televised speech, the Soviet Union and its 'surrogates' would become the dominant force in those areas."[44]

Regardless of whether the invasion of Grenada was intended as a signal to Cuba and the Soviet Union, it nonetheless was a message received by nations friendly to the Soviet bloc in the region, judging by an interview Williams conducted with the president of Guyana the next month.

"President Forbes Burnham, saying Guyanese forces are on alert against a possible U.S. invasion, has bitterly assailed the Reagan administration for a 'failed policy' in the Caribbean and for seeking to 'crush independence' in the region," Williams reported from Belfield, Guyana. "'It is a question of the present administration feeling that the world is black and white,' Burnham said in an interview at his weekend home outside the capital of Georgetown. 'And if you don't slavishly accept their ideology, you are guilty of subverting the system. . . . You must obey the United States, (President Reagan) says, or be crushed.'"[45]

The neoconservative movement of the '80s was a force not only behind Reagan's economic and foreign policies; the neocons and Jerry Falwell's and other evangelicals' Moral Majority also played a major supporting role in the president's efforts to instill what they saw as a stronger Christian value system and morality in the nation—one supporting such proposals as prayer in the public schools, tuition tax credits for parochial schools, and banning abortion on demand.

Williams also was on this social agenda beat, reporting on the push by Reagan to grant the rising Christian Right's wishes. In January 1983, Williams reported on the president's intention to push its social agenda.

"President Reagan, promising not to lose interest in key conservative social issues as he fights the nation's economic problems, said yesterday that he will renew pressure on Congress to allow prayer in schools, ban abortion on demand and create tuition tax credits," Williams reported. "According to administration officials, Reagan will propose the tuition credits as part of his State of the Union message to Congress Tuesday night. But he announced his intentions in his weekly radio address yesterday even as he was completing work on Tuesday's speech, according to presidential aides."

The president told his listeners, wrote Williams, that he would discuss the nation's economic conditions in the speech, "but I also want you to know we'll not ignore the moral essentials in the coming months."

"Today," the president said in his radio chat, "5 million American kids attend private schools because of the emphasis on religious values and educational standards.

"And the overwhelming majority of these schools are church-supported—Catholic, Protestant and Jewish. And the majority of students are from families earning less than $25,000."

These families, most of whom lived in minority neighborhoods, the president argued, paid taxes to fund the public school system plus pay tuition for parochial schools.

"I think they're entitled to some relief since they're supporting two school systems and only using one."

School prayer: "The public expression through prayer of our faith in God is a fundamental part of our American heritage and a privilege which should not be excluded from our schools."

Abortion on demand: "Until someone can prove the unborn child is not a life, shouldn't we give it the benefit of the doubt and assume it is?"[46]

Later that year, the president urged the nation to dedicate itself to God, tying his call to an anticommunist theme.

"President Reagan, in an Easter message to the nation, called from the mountaintop on Americans today 'to live our lives and dedicate our country to truth, to love and to God,'" Williams reported from Santa Barbara,

California. "Reagan, speaking from his mountaintop ranch, said in his weekly radio broadcast that religious faith binds the people of the world despite attempts by some to make the state the omniscient power in human life."

"The brave Polish people, despite the oppression of a godless tyranny, still cling to their faith and their belief in freedom," Reagan continued.

"In Central America communist-inspired revolution still spreads terror and instability, but it's no match for the much greater force of faith that runs so deep among the people. We saw this during Pope John Paul II's recent visit there," he said.

" . . . If we live our lives and dedicate our country to truth, to love and to God, we will be a part of something much stronger and much more enduring than any negative power here on Earth," he said.[47]

But it was the armaments portion of the neocons' agenda that captured the bulk of Reagan's attention, as he used defense spending—led by development of a new multiple-warhead missile and a space-age antimissile defense system, dubbed "Star Wars"—to entice the Soviet Union to the bargaining table for arms reduction talks while forcing the Soviets to spend more on their own military arsenal. The name of the new MX missile—the Peacekeeper—symbolized the method of Reagan's approach, giving the most dangerous nuclear missile yet devised a moniker that was symbolic in its own right: a missile designed to, in effect, force peace upon the Soviets.

"President Reagan launched another effort to increase political support for development of the MX missile today, arguing that critics have failed to understand the 'dual approach' of seeking both to modernize U.S. nuclear weapons and to negotiate a reduction of superpower arsenals," reported the *Post* in the summer of 1983.

The story continued: "'There is no contradiction in this dual approach, despite what some of the critics in Washington might have you believe,' Reagan said. He added that the MX, as well as the effort to develop a new, small, single-warhead missile, will 'maintain state-of-the-art readiness' against the Soviets but also provide an 'essential incentive' for Moscow to negotiate seriously."[48]

The president introduced his Star Wars defense system in the same context, arguing that development of an antiballistic-missile system would help convince the Soviets that arms reduction talks were in their best interest.

"President Reagan last night called for a futuristic research and development effort aimed at providing a space or ground-based defense against Soviet intercontinental ballistic missiles by the end of the century," the *Post* reported in the spring of 1983.

An administration official told the newspaper that the proposal "was designed to dramatize the president's call for nuclear arms reductions."

"'We seek neither military superiority nor political advantage,' Reagan said in the speech, which drew criticism that the president was using red-scare tactics, announcing his proposal. 'Our only purpose—one all people share—is to search for ways to reduce the danger of nuclear war.'"[49]

Probably Reagan's most noted speech, though, was the one he made at the Berlin Wall in a Kennedy-esque moment near the end of his second term, in which he passionately urged the Soviet Union to knock down the structure that for so long had symbolized the Cold War and the division of East and West.

"President Reagan stood today before the Brandenburg Gate, the symbol of Europe's harsh division, and challenged Soviet leader Mikhail Gorbachev to create a new era of freedom by dismantling the Berlin Wall," the *Post* reported in June of 1987. "'Mr. Gorbachev, open this gate,' said Reagan in a forceful tone. 'Mr. Gorbachev, tear down this Wall.'"

The story continued: "The speech was intended as a dramatic capstone of Reagan's 10-day trip to Europe, and the setting was stark, with East German sentries watching through binoculars from atop the Brandenburg Gate."[50]

The Soviet Union's woes, dissent such as the Solidarity movement under Lech Walesa in Poland, the internal political strife led by Boris Yeltsin in Russia, the vehement anticommunist leadership of Pope John Paul II—all of these contributed to the fall of the Soviet Union. Indeed, two years after Reagan's speech at the wall, it did come down, figuratively. The *Post* reported in November 1989, that communist East Germany was allowing its citizens to travel freely to the West, a freedom they had not enjoyed since the wall was constructed.

"Communist East Germany today opened its borders to the West, including the Berlin Wall, announcing that its citizens could travel or emigrate freely, in the most stunning step since World War II toward ending the East-West division of Europe," the newspaper reported. "Confronted by a mounting political crisis that a top East German official said has placed the ruling Communist Party's very existence at stake, the government said authorities had been instructed to grant permission without delay for people to journey abroad or leave the country."[51]

So, the dissolution of the Soviet empire, which had stood for more than 40 years following the end of World War II, came officially on the watch of Reagan's successor and former vice president, President George H. W. Bush. But the origins of the fall were in the Reagan era, and his Berlin Wall speech remains a symbol of the wall's fall.

In retrospect, Williams said that speech, while dramatic, played a relatively minor role in the ultimate demise of the Soviet Union. Internal problems and other world events were the major contributors, he said.

"I believe in the power of words. I'm a journalist, so I don't want to diminish or dismiss President Reagan saying those words; I think it had quite an impact, maybe even more so in Germany than in the United

States, because it was in a sense daring language," Williams said. "But the real roots of the end of the Cold War and the crumbling of the Berlin Wall were economic problems that were worse in the Soviet Union than they were here. They weren't feeding their own people, they were having Chernobyl (the explosion at the nuclear plant near Pripyat, Ukraine and the resulting radioactive contamination in the region). They were having chaos. Their system wasn't working. We had been inefficient; they were on the door of depression. Technology was also banging at the door, they simply could not contain political dissent."

The decade that ended with the crumbling of the Soviet Union had begun with the people of the United States ready for change, Williams recalled.

"I think people wanted to feel good about themselves," he said. "We had been through Watergate, after Vietnam, and after the assassinations of the Kennedys and all that. The whole notion was that Reagan was sort of bright and sunny, and 'Morning in America, and we're going to make this happen and believe in me.' And he was not about apologies to Vietnam, apologies over race relations; he was about American triumphalism. So he was a very sort of enervating force in American life. I think people saw in him this sort of movie star looks and promise that everything is going to be OK. People would mock him, and journalists like me would say this guy reads from notes. People tell him what to do. But he had principles, and he had tremendous communications skills, which is what the presidency had become.

"Being devoutly anticommunist, free trade, he's selling a political package that's very appealing to the American people," Williams continued, "especially after the dour turn of Jimmy Carter and after the sadness of Nixon, here comes a guy who was unapologetic about America's strength and power and the possibility of a new America."

Despite the Stockman incident, Williams said, and the argument that trickle-down economics was ineffective, it nonetheless "was an effort to put in place tax policy that would benefit the rich on the premise that the rich then would have more reason to put it back into the United States," the journalist said. "That's not what turned around the economy, but it sold, and I think it had a tremendous impact. Jesse Jackson waged a campaign in '84 when Reagan was saying a rising tide raises all boats, and Jackson's retort was not if your boat has a hole in the bottom and is at the bottom of the river or lake or ocean to begin with, you just get left undercurrent.

"When the country starts to come out, when the economy starts to turn around," Williams continued, "it's largely a function of new engines, not the old one. The old one, the industrial base, was going away. The new ones that occur, things like Microsoft, by the mid- to late-'80s, this is a result of creativity, American genius, whatever you want, but it had nothing to do with trickle-down economics."

The recession of '82, Williams suggested, was largely "the aftermath of the '70s and I think you're also dealing with a huge shift in terms of the American economy. My goodness, cities like Detroit, Pittsburgh, Cleveland were at a low point in the early '80s, with a lack of confidence in our political leaders, and here's an economic theory to lift us. I guess there were some people who believed in trickle-down economics, but I don't think that the big boys believed in it. Remember, there was even a fear that we were losing advantage to people like the Japanese; their economy was bubbling along at that point, and there was 'oh gosh we can't compete with the Japanese in our educational system, our economic system,' all of that."

As for the Reagan administration's major scandal, Williams said that public revelation of the Iran-Contra fiasco dampened the Reagan administration's covert activity, which had become its preferred avenue of waging the anticommunist battle.

"Rather than taking express military action as the world's superpower," Williams recalled, "now we strive to act covertly; that was Reagan. And he could not—remember you've got the volunteer Army—he could not go to the Congress, much less the American people, and say 'we're going to engage in a military adventure.'"

The Reagan administration's covert and overt foreign activities were tied to a common theme, a post-Vietnam War sentiment of maintaining a U.S. presence in international affairs on behalf of democracy and freedom, Williams said.

"After Vietnam there was too much of a hangover still in place (for extended overt military activity), but with the neocons pushing from within, what you get is an effort to say 'we have to take steps, we can't simply build an American fortress here and continue to feel as if we're protected by these two great oceans," Williams said. "'We've got to be a player in the larger world. Latin America is right at our doorstep, we can't allow them to go communist, we can't allow the Middle East to fall into chaos, because of our failure to act.'

"I think the neocons were reacting to what they considered to be the excesses of the '60s," he continued, "and if you look back to the characters like Irving Kristol and the like, what they were doing and what they were writing had to do with America becoming more and more reluctant to exercise power on the global stage but also on the home front, concern that there is a willingness to tolerate excesses with regard to sexual behavior, to undermine the whole notion of merit and competition, especially with regard to racial set-asides, affirmative action. And the worry on their part that America was no longer willing to, given what happened in Vietnam, no longer willing to take a risk in the name of helping people, of standing up for its virtues, its values, at least that's the way they would have made the argument."

The God and guns agenda of the Reagan administration was, in part, a reaction to the 1960s peace movement, the sexual revolution, the secularization of the nation, and the heavy government investment in the welfare state, Williams suggested.

"You've got to look at people who said the '60s had been a mistake," Williams said of the reaction of the neoconservatives to what they viewed as the social and anti-military excesses of that period. "If Reagan was saying 'I have no problem with American military might, I have no problem in battling communists in Vietnam' and all that, there were people who were saying the left in this country has become myopic in the way it approaches foreign policy; it has become too much of a libertine with regards to everything from sexual politics, specifically abortion and gay rights, race relations, saying you're giving people something for nothing and all of that attitude."

It was a period, Williams recalled, marked by Reagan's principled conservatism of anticommunism, pro-tax cutting and union busting—a reference to the president's breaking of the federal air controllers' union.

"I think these are all the Reagan legacy, but to my mind he is the face of optimism, he's the face of American political optimism, unapologetic exercise of American willpower, that's Ronald Reagan," Williams said, adding that the mood of the nation at the end of the Reagan decade and the beginning of the first Bush presidency was "upbeat."

"But it's not to say that everything was fine and dandy," he said. "By the end of the '80s we go through that very difficult '88 election made famous by (former Massachusetts Governor and 1988 presidential candidate Michael) Dukakis and the tank, and Willie Horton, and you could still see the racial divide in the country. . . . There's this push back, and it's coming again from the South and the West, saying we're not playing second fiddle to the Northeast and the Midwest any longer, and we have this rising population and its rising economics. The new sports teams are all locating in that area of the country, in the Carolinas, Florida, Arizona, Texas, that's where the vibrancy was. You think of the '80s and you think of *Miami Vice*, you think of that kind of hip something's happening there. It wasn't 'Miami Cleveland' or 'Miami Detroit' or 'Chicago.'"

The nation ended the decade, Williams said, better off in terms of personal wealth but with questions politically. But it also had experienced large political and societal shifts and was entering an era of new science, economics, and social mores.

"People had higher incomes, we had come out of that economic trough at the start of the '80s," he said. But, "there were lots of questions about the exercise of power coming out of Iran-Contra, a lot of criticism attached to the politics of the period . . . there was a lot of fear-mongering, patronizing political appeals going on. So a lot of people may have been better off economically and had a sense of real possibilities, Microsoft, the whole high-tech industry emerging. There was a major economic shift, a major demographic change that took place, the emergence of new technologies, everything from genetic cloning to arguments over gays in the military. That stuff was going on big-time."

* * * *

It was theater, he put himself as the central actor in it. One legacy is just the power of his personality and his narrative and his storytelling and that everybody now tries to imitate that. When he told stories that were fact-based, and when he told stories that he thought were true but had been in the movies, it worked. His political theater, if you think about it, the telling of the individual story, the creation of an American narrative, he's the role model of the acting politician. And I mean that not because he literally was an actor, but people will roll tapes of Ronald Reagan to show how it can be done. He was the prime role model of how to spin a story and how to create a narrative that people would buy even if it was against maybe their economic interests, maybe their personal interest. So to me that's stunning. You can see that it's not exactly positive, but he knew how to do it. He really knew how to do it. And then, of course, we knew, probably toward the very end of his term, he was losing it. Right? And so, to what degree is one of the legacies that of the people behind the president, the figurehead president, too. That one I don't know.

—Ellen Goodman

The landscape around Fargo, North Dakota, was barren except for the remains of a farmer's crop. It was vast and leveled, as though swept clean

Ellen Goodman. © The Washington Post Writers Group. Used by permission.

by a huge brush. The big-city columnist observing the scene was witness not of the ruins of nuclear war, but of the plains of the Cold War and the dread of annihilation that hung over North Dakota and the nation like an imagined mushroom cloud for a period spanning half a century.

"The stubble from last year's wheat crop still stretches like an endless, awkward crew cut along the flat Red River Valley," *Boston Globe* columnist Ellen Goodman wrote in the spring of 1983, in the descriptive style that had won her the Pulitzer Prize for commentary three years before. "Any day now, the farmers who have sat through this wet spring of 1983 will begin seeding the prairie again."

Typical of a Goodman column, the lead was a deceptively literary depiction—what journalism students are taught is an anecdotal lead, as opposed to a straight news summary—that shows rather than tells the gist of the narrative.

"This is the breadbasket of America and the military zone," the columnist wrote, warming to the topic. "Less than a hundred miles north of here is another huge crop planted in the soil of The Peace Garden State: nuclear missiles."

The column continued: "Sooner or later, almost everyone I meet offers me the same odd tidbit from the state's identity. If North Dakota were to secede from the union, they say, it would be the third largest nuclear force in the world. I cannot figure out whether it is said with pride or irony."

The strength of the column, as in much of Goodman's writing, was its concentration on the scene and its people—including a comment from a North Dakota writer and grandmother who noted that she "lives in a state with the power to destroy the world, and 'nobody knows where we are'"—in the context of the federal nuclear arsenal housed in North Dakota.

It concluded: "But as another native mused, it's still hard to relate this global terror to a nuclear force that sits smack in the middle of wheat country. In the land of the third largest nuclear force in the world, she said, 'We keep an awful lot buried underground.'"[52]

Such is the Goodman technique—an eye for detail and character and description to not only tell a story but to starkly show her message: The Cold War, and the prospect of nuclear destruction at the hands of politicians who play a dangerous game of brinkmanship, is hell. And such is the journalistic territory that Goodman staked out for herself. While the rest of the nation's pundits analyzed politics and politicians and economic policies and military strategies, Goodman wrote about the people affected by these politics, policies, and strategies. She documented and created a national beat focusing on their cares, worries, and values.

Goodman defined her journalistic realm in the introduction to her 1989 collection of columns, *Making Sense.*

"Most of these columns began with a question: Why?" she wrote. "What's going on here? I write to figure that out for myself and others.

Why has character become the dominant political theme of the past four years? Why are we less concerned about public morality and more about private ethics? Why do we head into the 1990s still wrestling with the sixties?"

With the thawing of the Cold War, she wrote, the nation faced new struggles in rapidly changing "everyday lives." These changes included machinery intruding into life, transformed notions of marriage, divorce, health, diet—all shaped by science, technology, and altered American tastes, desires and attitudes about lifestyle topics ranging from gender and sex to life and death and how we think about them and deal with them. All in the context of public politics, policies, and strategies.

"Along with these ingredients are the personal observations that spice my attempts at making sense," she wrote. "I am not just an observer but a part of this work, these times. I know, firsthand and first person, about the one commodity in greatest demand and shortest supply: time. I also work, after all, from the perspective of writer, mother, daughter, wife, and now mid-life observer of generations."[53]

Goodman was a war baby, entering the world during World War II, growing up during the ensuing Cold War, coming of age during the Vietnam War, and chronicling the cultural wars during her newspaper career. Born April 11, 1941, in the Boston suburb of Newton, Massachusetts, Goodman is the daughter of Edith Weinstein Holtz and Boston lawyer and politician (two-time Democratic congressional candidate during the Eisenhower administration) Jackson Jacob Holtz. World War II dominated the headlines the day of her birth. United Press reported from Athens that British forces were engaged in a battle that could decide the fate of Greece.

"Britain's crack expeditionary forces went into action today against German panzer divisions, apparently on a 50-mile northern front, in a battle upon which the fate of Greece may hinge," reported the story on the front page of the *Boston Daily Globe.* "The British high command admitted that a German armored division had cracked the famous Monastir Gap, entrance to northwest Greece from southwest Yugoslavia, while another force has pushed west about 30 miles on the road from Salonika."[54]

The fighting was heavy throughout Europe; the front page of the *Globe* also reported that the Germans claimed to have "annihilated" south Serbian armies while Nazi forces were "racing toward Belgrade" to the north;[55] Britain's Royal Air Force bombers had destroyed factories in Dusseldorf and airdrome facilities near Bordeaux;[56] and President Franklin Delano Roosevelt had declared the Red Sea and Gulf of Aden open to American ships, "permitting United States commercial vessels to go up the east side of Africa to the Suez Canal."[57]

Elsewhere, Turkey was beginning to evacuate civilians from Istanbul,[58] the French were preparing to remove their nationals from the city,[59] and Roosevelt was reported to have signed a resolution, one day after including the island of Greenland in the U.S. defense system, "affirming a policy of nonrecognition of any transfer of Western Hemisphere land from one non-American power to another." The signature came, the story reported, "as word circulated that the Army and Navy would begin work immediately on construction of air bases on Denmark's big northern island without waiting for formal leases to sites."[60]

Sears was advertising a kitchen ensemble that included a 60-inch sink, two base cabinets, two wall cabinets, two shelf cabinets and two filler strips for $119.95 delivered—customers could make payments of $9 a month with a $10 down payment.[61] The price of top coats at a Boston department store ranged from $15.90 to $40, and a local grocer offered all the fixings for an in-home Sunday breakfast: a dozen Henfield eggs for a quarter, a pound of sliced, sugar-cured bacon for the same price, and a fifteen-ounce tin of Dole's pineapple juice for 23 cents.

Boston movie house fare included Ingrid Bergman starring in *Adam Had Four Sons* at the Paramount and Fenway theaters; Bob Hope, Bing Crosby, and Dorothy Lamour in *Road to Zanzibar* at the Metropolitan, and Ida Lupino starring opposite John Garfield in *Sea Wolf* at the Scollay and Modern theaters. And Paul Muni was in town starring in *Hudson's Bay.*[62]

Goodman didn't set out to be a journalist as she grew up in the Boston area or even later, as a 1963 graduate of Radcliffe College, where she majored in modern European history. The closest she'd come to journalism was selling subscriptions to the *New York Times* while in college.

"I'm not one of those people who wrote small newspapers and delivered them in my neighborhood and printed them in my garage," she said. "I did not work for my high school newspaper, I did not work for my college newspaper. In fact, when I was at Radcliffe you couldn't join the *Crimson* if you were a woman."

She fell into the field, as a researcher for *Newsweek* magazine, when she moved with her first husband, whom she married two weeks out of college, to New York City, where he was a medical school student.

"*Time* and *Newsweek* at that time were hiring overeducated young women to do the crappy jobs, to be researchers," she said. "You had to work your way up to being a researcher, believe it or not. You basically delivered copy and clipped wires; nobody knows what that means anymore because there are no wires, but at that time you ripped stories off of the telex machines, the AP wire and the UP wire, and delivered them around. If you were a woman, you then aspired to be a researcher for a reporter. The writers were all male, and the researchers were all female. That's the way it was in those days." Females for the most part didn't do any reporting at the magazine, she said, until after 46 women brought sex discrimination charges against the magazine in 1970.

The *Newsweek* job "sounded good at cocktail parties," she said. She needed a job in New York, and her sister was a journalist, "so that gave me an idea that I could do it. And so that did give me sort of an idea that this was fun, could be fun. But I was in a rather planning-free zone." The job was negative in some ways, she said, "because you were responsible for any of the mistakes without having any of the authority to get anything in it."

Once in the environment of the newsroom, she decided on journalism as a career. "Yes. Yes. Almost immediately, it was just a really good fit for me personally. And I started freelancing, since you couldn't write, I started doing some freelancing in New York for all kinds of little publications while I was working at *Newsweek.* It took me a year to get out of the training pool and into a researcher job. And when I was a researcher I worked for Peter Benchley (*Jaws*), who was the television critic at the time, and Peter and I had known each other in college; in fact we had both been in *Guys and Dolls* together. Peter was one or two classes ahead of me. He was immediately tracked in the boy direction, and I was tracked in the girl direction, and I worked with Peter very happily, he was a great guy."

She enjoyed interviewing people for her research, saying it seemed like a great way to earn a living. "You get to ask people the questions that you always wanted to ask but were maybe a little too polite to ask without the press pass." But she cautioned not to confuse polite with shy. "I was never shy, polite yes, but never shy."

Her husband's career played a role in moving Goodman more solidly into her own career when he graduated from medical school and they moved to Ann Arbor, Michigan. She interviewed with both Detroit newspapers, about an hour from Ann Arbor, joining the *Free Press* and its legendary future publisher, Neal Shine.

"Neal Shine was a fabulous city editor, he was just a joy. I had job offers at both papers and I sat down with Neal after having been interviewed by various people, and Neal was just like every Boston-Irish journalist, he was just like everybody I already knew except he was in Detroit."

The newspaper had just changed managing editors, and along with that shift came an altered attitude toward women journalists at the paper.

"A lot of my career is just at the cusp of women getting any of these chances," she said. "So I was maybe the second woman in the city room at the *Free Press.* The first woman was Jean Sharley Taylor, who a lot of people know because she later went on the L.A. *Times,* and Jean had just written page one features forever, and she's a fabulous feature writer, but her body had literally been kept out of the city room until this new managing editor came in and started welcoming women."

Goodman remembers the feeling of being a beginning reporter—"'Oh my God, do I actually know what I'm doing,' and going and covering a story, talking to people, writing it down, coming back and it got in the paper, and I was a little bit like 'well, they haven't found me out yet.' Because I'd never heard of the inverted pyramid, I'd never taken a journalism course, I'd never heard of the who, what, when, where, I had no idea. I learned it all on the job.

"Neal tells the story about when I wrote an obit, and I included in it the wrong day of either the funeral or the wake, and the family calls up, of course, irate, and Neal called me into his office, and he says that my response was 'well anybody who is really close to them will know the real day anyway.' He was sort of nonplussed. I remember, all my life to this day, being quite anxious about, you know occasionally waking up at 3 o'clock in the morning and saying 'oh my God did I say that it was 300 million or 300 billion?' You know, that kind of thing."

Reading the writing of Jean Sharley Taylor and other contemporaries helped her learn the craft, especially of feature writing. "At that time, it was also at the beginning of new journalism, and we were all reading the *New York Herald Tribune* and getting a sense of some creative freedom, what kind of writing you could do. Writing was always very important to me, the writing part, how you express yourself, how you engage people.

"Part of it was I had colleagues. People overestimate mentoring and underestimate colleagues, and when you're in a place like the *Free Press* was, which was very energetic and kind, you know, it was a very up and coming city room, and when you're in a place like that, there's a lot of kibitzing and collegiality and mutual admiration and people you would ask questions of 'how does this lead work?'"

The '60s were happening when Goodman officially began her newspaper career in Detroit; 1965 would see major advances and clashes as the nation struggled with civil rights. Martin Luther King Jr. in January led protest marchers in Selma, Alabama, as the Southern Christian Leadership Conference demanded that blacks be allowed to vote. The next month, Marion, Alabama police shot civil-rights activist Jimmie Lee Jackson as he participated on behalf of the rights of blacks to register to vote. One month later Selma police attacked protestors, and white civil rights activist Reverend James Reeb died of injuries on a day that became known as Bloody Sunday. Later that month, more than 3,000 marchers departed on a five-day civil rights march to Montgomery. On March 13, President Lyndon B. Johnson announced on national television that he would send the Voting Rights Bill to Congress, and it passed that summer, becoming law on August 6. Later that month, race riots broke out in the Los Angeles neighborhood of Watts following the arrest of a black driver for drunken driving. Thirty-five people died in the five days of violence that followed. That December, three Ku Klux Klansmen were convicted of the murder in March of a Michigan civil rights worker, Viola Gregg Liuzzo, in Selma, Alabama.[63]

Meanwhile. the Vietnam War roiled on the other side of the globe while antiwar protests raged at home. In February, the United States began the regular bombing of North Vietnam in an exercise dubbed Operation Rolling Thunder. That same month, U.S. agents arrested four suspected terrorists believed to be planning to blow up the Statue of Liberty, the Liberty Bell, and the Washington Monument. The next month, on the same day that the U.S. Supreme Court approved conscientious objector status for those with unconventional religious beliefs, "the first U.S. combat troops to enter the war" were two battalions of U.S. Marines, 3,500 of them ordered to defend Danang airbase in South Vietnam. In June, Congress authorized

U.S. forces to engage in offensive operations in South Vietnam. In October, Vietnam War protestors staged a series of demonstrations across the country. One demonstrator was arrested for burning a draft card, a violation of a new federal law. By December, 200,000 U.S. troops were stationed in Vietnam.

Also that year, Johnson sent U.S. Marines to the Dominican Republic following a military coup there that erupted into civil war. Civil rights demonstrators protested in Chicago against the city's desegregation policies; 350 of them were arrested over a period of five days. And in two key Supreme Court rulings, the justices deemed that the use of contraceptives was legal, and they struck down a federal law authorizing the seizure of communist propaganda by the U.S. Postal Service.

Domestic film audiences saw the U.S. release of *The Sound of Music,* which became the biggest box office hit of the decade, while Sean Connery starred in the latest James Bond film, *Thunderball.* Richard Lester's sequel to the Beatles' film *A Hard Day's Night,* titled *Help!,* was released in Britain. Rex Harrison won best actor for *My Fair Lady* and Julie Andrews snagged the best actress Oscar for *Mary Poppins.* The British rock music invasion was well under way; 9 of the top 10 places on U.S. charts were held by British bands. Leonard Bernstein completed his choral work, *Chicester Psalms.* John Updike published *Of the Farm,* Jerzy Kosinski published *The Painted Bird,* and Russian novelist Mikhail Sholokhov won the Nobel Prize for Literature. Neil Simon's *The Odd Couple* premiered at New York's Plymouth Theater, and Frank D. Gilroy won the Pulitzer Prize for Drama for *The Subject Was Roses.* Former Harvard lecturer Timothy Leary popularized the phrase "Tune in, turn on, drop out," describing the experiences of the hallucinogenic drug LSD, in *The Psychedelic Reader.* In San Francisco, the *Examiner* newspaper marked the rise of the hippie movement in a story on the Haight-Ashbury neighborhood of the city, which the newspaper noted had become a "hip hangout" for beatniks. Popular television programs included *I Dream of Jeannie, Hogan's Heroes, I Spy,* and *The Wild, Wild West.*

The issues and culture of the '60s excited Goodman at the *Free Press* and a couple of years later at the *Boston Globe,* where she landed after her husband's career took him to that city for his residency. She had grown up reading the *Globe.*

"When I got to the *Globe,* it was the moment: the *Boston Globe,* a writer's paper, and a reporter's paper, and all the energy around, the issues of the late '60s, civil rights, busing, and the women's movement," she recalled. "All of those issues really were talked out, laughed out, argued out. I'd had a lot of that collegiality at the *Free Press* too, there was a group of people, but at the *Globe,* really, it was really the place to be. This is my hometown, and I wanted to come back here."

It was at the *Globe* that Goodman would become a nationally-syndicated columnist, the journalist/observer writing a regular commentary that would win her newspaper's biggest prize in the '80s—a decade defined by Ronald Reagan, she said.

"He just dominated the '80s. When I think of the '80s I think of the emergence of the conservative backlash. I think of the re-emergence of, I mean the heightening of, Cold War anxieties, polarization of the country that began, really, during the '80s, the emergence of the religious right as a political force, not as a religious force. And underlying that, at the same time, the continuation of this social change in families, and more women going to work and into graduate schools and professional schools. So the '80s were kind of many different things going on."

The many things going on with women, families, changing lifestyles, and sexual attitudes all were Goodman territory as she steered her readers through this complex societal fabric by focusing on its people and their reactions to it all.

While the rank-and-file political columnists were writing pedantic analyses of President Reagan and his successor, George H. W. Bush, Goodman analyzed their first ladies—along with other women in the context of a beat Goodman staked out for herself: femininity and feminism.

The occasion was an August 1984 dinner at the National Federation of Republican Women's luncheon in Dallas, the conservative capital of the United States. Goodman took advantage of Nancy Reagan's speech to the gathering, at which she was campaigning for her husband's reelection, to compare the Nancy Reagan of three years before to this one.

"In the beginning, the changes were pretty tough ones. The wife of the president never had a honeymoon with the press. She barely got a one-night stand. If First Ladies bask in reflected glory, they also get singed by the spotlight. The early returns on this First Lady were perfectly dreadful."

The columnist described Nancy Reagan's early approach to her role as first lady as one that "looked a lot like a rich lady's decorating binge. We read about $200,000 of new china, $800,000 of renovations, free designer clothes, and not much else. Nancy took the reviews badly; in fact, she took them to the bathtub where she argued silently with the authors. As she says now, 'I wouldn't have wanted to know that person they were writing about.'"

Since then, Goodman observed, Nancy had changed.

> At some point, said a friend, "she stopped crying and started to cope." She began to show some humor. At the memorable Gridiron dinner, she came before the startled Washington press corps in tatters singing "Second Hand Rose."
>
> But the most important changes are substantive ones. Nancy Reagan has become less associated with Beverly Hills and more associated with an antidrug campaign. She has gone from donating her designer clothes to museums to donating her time in a campaign against addiction.[64]

Early in the George H. W. Bush presidency, Goodman greeted the new first lady, Barbara Bush, with a column that focused, as had her commentary on Nancy Reagan, on style and on impressions. In this case, the first lady won accolades from the beginning.

"The first impression of a nation was based, as these things often are, on appearances," Goodman wrote in January 1989, shortly after Bush's inauguration. "And Barbara Bush's 'hit' was in no small measure a by-product of the appearance of a woman on the center stage who dared to look her age.

"The official trend-watchers called it 'refreshing,' 'striking,' even, heaven help us, a true fashion statement. Worlds like *matron* and *grandmother,* banned from the vocabulary of East Wing reporters, suddenly began creeping back into the papers."

In her conclusion, the columnist expanded her commentary to take in a broader scope, that of the American woman and her expectations.

"But in this first week of intensive training, it was clear how much American women want from their elders," Goodman wrote. "We are eager to find a model who echoes in life the words May Sarton once wrote at seventy: 'Now I wear the inside person outside and am more comfortable with myself.' Barbara Bush sounds a lot like that person."[65]

Not only American women got the Goodman treatment. In her journalistic foray into international détente, she wrote a column in March 1985, profiling Soviet Union President Mikhail Gorbachev's wife. Again, impression and attitudes, typical subtopics of Goodman profiles, became the focus—mixed in with a bit of realpolitik.

"The stereotype of a Soviet leader is a man in a heavy overcoat, a fur hat, and no visible neck because he donated it to the war effort," she wrote. "The stereotype of a Soviet woman is one who poses for the socialist realism pinup calendar in basic black.

"But Mikhail's wife Raisa was dubiously dubbed, 'Bo Derek of the Steppes,' by the British press. She is said to be a fifty-one-year-old professor at Moscow University, a mother of two, and a grandmother of one. Her plumage was what won Western attention, especially during her December flight to Britain." British press accounts cited by Goodman used such adjectives as "chic" and one half of a "'Gucci Couple.' The implication was that as a duo they would charm détente back to life."

The irony, I suppose, is that many Americans think the ultimate attraction of this democracy isn't free speech or elections. It's style, it's shopping. There is the quintessential scene in *Moscow on the Hudson* when a Russian on tour in America impulsively defects in the middle of Bloomingdale's. He is converted by shopping. At some deep level, many Americans believe that the Soviets can also be converted by the lure of commercial goods.

There is a comforting subtext to all the stories on creeping Westernization. Americans presume that given time and the choice, the citizens of the socialist world will inevitably become just like us: a people with a supermarket. This is probably as true and as false as the communist belief that if people keep sleeping on grates, class warfare is inevitable.[66]

But women of power comprised only one hue on Goodman's feminism palette. She also celebrated women of science, of intellect, of achievement, painting them with a broader stroke of exemplars of the potentials, possibilities and triumphs of women who take advantage of opportunity and who persevere.

Hailed by Goodman as another "First Woman," NASA astronaut Sally Ride became the first American woman to rocket into space in 1983, aboard the Challenger shuttle. What the nation witnessed in Ride, Goodman wrote in June 1983, "is a classic case of First Womanitis, a social disease that comes with prolonged exposure to the spotlight. Sally Ride, First American Woman in Space, is taking this trip right into history while her male companions are destined for the trivia shows. ('For ten thousand dollars and a complete dinette set, name one of the four astronauts who flew with Sally Ride.')"

The columnist attached extra significance and responsibility to Ride's accomplishment and to Ride because of her gender. "Being a full-fledged First Woman means taking every step for womankind. It's not easy, but the company is fine."[67]

Three years later, another first woman—Christa McAuliffe, the first participant in the Teacher in Space Project—died along with astronauts Judith Resnik, Michael J. Smith, Dick Scobee, Ellison Onizuka, Gregory Jarvis, and Ronald McNair when the shuttle Challenger burst as it soared toward space. The nation and the world mourned a tragedy that grounded the shuttle program for two-and-a-half years.

Goodman, vacationing in the Caribbean at the time, heard the news on the radio. She returned to Boston to write a February 1986, column about the deaths.

"Our heads were home or at least in Cape Canaveral. We felt as inappropriately dressed in our bathing suits as a garish visitor to a funeral," she wrote. "We sat in this odd mourning garb and listened, feeling simply out of place."

Searching for some kind of meaning in the tragedy, she took up the theme of a conflicted world that, viewed from space, appears unified.

"I remembered then how every astronaut who has circled the planet comes home to report that he or she has seen no borders, no frontiers, no fences. There are no neatly colored countries from the perspective of outer space. The Earth is one."

She merged that theme into one of the tragedy of a planet rent by human differences: "We live today with both the lofty possibility of one world without boundaries and the deadly image of a whole Earth wasteland." Yet, she wrote, our leaders "are neither hopeful enough nor frightened enough. They are stuck in the 17th century, making maps as if we hadn't already transcended them."[68]

A woman who transcended the traditional maps of womanly behavior was former First Lady Eleanor Roosevelt, whom Goodman eulogized in an October, 1984, column honoring the 100th anniversary of Roosevelt's birth. The columnist remembered Roosevelt's pioneering feminist spirit. "As the most public woman of her era, Eleanor Roosevelt was mercilessly reviled and admired for breaking female traditions. The woman who once opposed suffrage became the most visible model of what women could do in public life." She was, Goodman wrote, a woman "who did not begin her work outside the home until she was nearly forty" and who "transformed the job of First Lady into one of advocate, taking up the cause of one beleaguered group after another. . . . This is a moment to remember not the disappointments, not the sadness, but the power of an idealist."[69]

These themes of tradition-breaking, of transforming roles and expectations, echoed throughout Goodman's columns on womanhood, gender, and relationships. The roles of gender sometimes changed in small ways, such as who decides where to go for dinner. A July 1982 column, early in the Reagan years, told a tale of a couple trying to decide where to eat.

"'I'll go anyplace you like tonight,' he repeats. 'Where do you want to go?' There is an edge of impatience now lining his voice."

The woman ponders, wondering what he is hungry for, about their choices.

"His question is simple; hers is complex to the point of absurdity.

"It happens even with her women friends," the column continues. "They are not, individually, uncertain. One makes editorial decisions about national policy with confidence; another makes plans for natural conservation with aplomb; a third makes a career of challenging conventional wisdom."

This "dance of indecision," the columnist wrote, takes in other steps: "an arabesque of martyrdom, a plie of self-sacrifice. Sometimes, under the guise of pleasing others, the women she knows waltz away from conflict and responsibility. If the movie is lousy, if it rains at the seaside, if the pizza is cold, it won't be their fault."

So she considers all of this, but, as Goodman concluded in the column, the country was changing.

"One dinner. No one will arrest her for selfishness if she chooses the restaurant. In fact, the consensus is that it's her turn to make the decision."[70]

The next year, Goodman found herself fantasizing in a February piece about the possibility of the nation's first female president. It was sparked by the upcoming presidential campaign in which Reagan would run for a second term against Walter Mondale and Geraldine Ferraro, a Democratic member of the U.S. House who would be the first female vice-presidential candidate in U.S. history. But Goodman did not know this when she wrote her column, in which she borrowed from feminist intellectual Elizabeth Janeway, who had predicted in a conference speech the previous December that the nation's first woman president would rise from the vice-presidency.

"Our First Woman," wrote Goodman, picking up on Janeway's suggestion that the "Number One Woman would emerge in the next generation," "will also have stamina, an impressive political background, and, because she's had to break stereotypes about female docility, she may be a touch pigheaded.

"This candidate," Goodman's column concluded, "is just a composite, a species of first woman president, and not a first choice in my catalog of candidates. But even her existence, in this saga of long-term change, says something about a climate that is slowly, yet perceptibly, warming."[71]

This candidate also might wear a Maidenform bra. As women marched into the workplace in the '80s, Goodman noted that the advertising industry was preparing to help them succeed fashionably.

"We are plunging into the 'successful woman as sex object' syndrome," she wrote in an October 1982 column. "The more real women break out of the mold, the more advertisers force them back in. We are now told that, for all the talk, the New Woman is just the Total Woman in updated gear."

Borrowing from an ad for bras in which a female medical doctor posed "exposing her lacy magenta bra and panties" as she was making her hospital rounds, Goodman wrote that the

> advertisers are betting that these women want, as the Maidenform ad puts it, "just what the doctor ordered." So the doctor is ordered to strip, literally, her professional cover. She is revealed in the flesh, to be—yes indeed—just another woman insecure about her femininity, just another woman in search of sex appeal, just another woman who needs "silky satin tricot with antique lace scalloping."
>
> Pretty soon, I suppose, she will need it in the Senate, in the Supreme Court, even in the Oval Office. The Maidenform Woman. You never know where she'll turn up.[72]

When Ferraro did turn up in 1984 as the running mate for Mondale, Goodman observed in a July column filed from the Democratic convention in San Francisco that the candidate from Queens had generated "more genuine enthusiasm" than did Mondale.

"The most common sentiment on the floor is seen in the green-and-white sticker that reads WOMAN VP NOW. The fastest-selling button on the street carries a portrait of Ferraro. The largest cheers at the rallies greet Ferraro. At one Mondale press conference the questions were directed to the man but the eyes were on the woman."

But, Goodman concluded, in the coming campaign, Ferraro would need to remember, as women had been admonished throughout history, her place.

"The test for Ferraro will be to keep the current of excitement high, but also to transfer that wattage back to Mondale. After all, running mates aren't trained to win alone."[73]

Ferraro and Mondale lost the race, but women continued their foray into the male-dominated workplace during this decade of change, as Goodman noted in a January 1989 column that focused on the themes of two films centering on women in the workplace: *Nine to Five* and *Working Girl.* The difference in the second film, she wrote, was that it featured "women playing the games that mother never taught them. Both the villain *and* the heroine, boss *and* secretary, insider *and* outsider, are females, sisters under the silk." And it touched on a down side of the changing gender power relationships—that women can be just as doltish as men.

"*Nine to Five* predicted that after the revolution it would be all day-care centers and solidarity," she wrote. "The premise of *Working Girl* is that, during the evolution, the daughters and sisters of the establishment look a lot like their fathers and brothers.

"This subtle and disappointed idealism," she continued, "can be seen on or off the screen. It infuses a strain between women who manage and the women they manage—whether it's doctors and nurses, account managers and typists, management trainees and clerical workers."[74]

The decade saw major advances in the cause of working and professional women, and some big setbacks. One of the major victories was the nomination by Reagan in July 1981 of Sandra Day O'Connor to be the first woman on the U.S. Supreme Court. The news sparked a celebratory commentary from Goodman in which she almost grudgingly lauded Reagan, "a man notoriously myopic toward women," for selecting O'Connor to honor his campaign pledge of nominating a woman to the court.

The nomination sparked controversy among moderate and conservative Republicans, what Goodman termed the "extreme right and the merely right." The Moral Majority crowd disapproved, complaining that her "voting record as majority leader in the Arizona Senate was not pure enough to pass the test of the Republican Party Platform."

"In any case," Goodman wrote, "it was quite a stroke for Reagan, in the midst of all the budget cuts, to find an appointment criticized as too 'liberal.'" Nonetheless, she concluded, "So what we have here on the way to confirmation hearings is this person, Sandra Day O'Connor, as much of a conservative as you can find in a qualified woman, and as much of a feminist as you can find in a conservative.

"By gum and by grudge, Reagan's done it again."[75]

O'Connor and the court came through. Another victory was the court's 1987 ruling that upheld a California county's voluntary plan that included gender in hiring and promotion policies—a ruling that Goodman saw as clearing up "the fuzzy legal status of plans such as the Santa Clara County one" but that "can also be used to clarify the whole peculiar matter of 'qualifications.'" The county's affirmative action plan, she argued, "did just what it was intended to do, added weight to her side, to open up the door for women."[76]

The official death of the Equal Rights Amendment, aimed at ensuring legal equal rights in the nation regardless of sex, early in the decade was a political development that slammed a door on women. The failure of the amendment to gain ratification by the necessary three-quarters of the state legislatures by 1982 meant defeat for the decade-long constitutional amendment process on its behalf.

"We can make optimistic comparisons," Goodman wrote in June 1982, evoking the constitutional amendment that gave women the right to vote. "In 1920, when the Nineteenth Amendment was passed, those who believed in women's rights went home with the illusion of victory. As the Twenty-seventh Amendment goes down (1982), those who believe in women's rights are fresh out of illusions. Women who have stood in the chambers watching their rights treated callously will take that memory to the ballot box."

The amendment, she concluded, was "no guarantee of Utopia, but it promised something: progress. For the moment, the bad guys have won. It's a moment worth mourning."[77]

Another setback for the women's movement came when the U.S. Supreme Court decided in the case of *Rostker versus Goldberg* that the rules of the military draft applied only to men.

"The court has ruled that it is constitutional for the government to pass over the houses where our daughters dwell and pluck our sons off to war," Goodman wrote in a June 1981 column lamenting the court's ruling, which upheld the congressional exemption of women from the draft. Goodman cast her opinion in the context of women not only as potential soldiers but as potential voices for peace as well. "They continue to perpetuate the myth that we have no stake," Goodman quoted Eleanor Smeal of the National Organization for Women. "Now they have taken away our voice of protest. We can't even say, 'Hell, no, we won't go.'"

"If there is a war, women may not be equal soldiers. But they will be equal victims," Goodman wrote. She concluded that in the era of "so much anxiety about the new militarism, the spread of nuclear bombs," one thing was clear. In the courtroom, "women lost one vigorous voice for peace, the sound of a might-be soldier. Now it is more crucial than ever to increase the decibel level of the might-be victim."[78]

That might-be victim was a crucial character in the Goodman journalistic fabric as she added her voice to those caught up in the angst of the Reagan administration's policy of increased defense spending coupled with cuts in welfare programs. She worried over such proposals as the space-based antimissile system, known popularly among its critics as "Star Wars," and other military spending and development proposals that Goodman and others saw as provocatively fueling the threat of nuclear war. On this subject, she called on an arsenal of satire and sarcasm along with a sense of the ridiculous.

For example, writing in February 1982, about the possibility of nuclear war, she made reference to the civil-defense booklet provided by the federal government's Emergency Management Agency, FEMA, in satirizing the Reagan administration's nuclear war contingency plan of folks cooly driving to a designated host community to avoid the worst of the atomic holocaust.

In case of nuclear war, she wrote, citing her "handy" booklet, "I am to calmly pack my car with a list of essential items, including extra socks, a plastic drop cloth, shaving articles and my credit card.

"Thus supplied against the worst, I am to drive in a leisurely way to my designated 'host community,' Laconia, Hew Hampshire, where the people will be eagerly awaiting my arrival along with the rest of the fleeing urban hordes."

She quoted Yale psychiatry professor Robert J. Lifton in discussing the absurdity of the government's civil defense plan: "As Lifton, the author of *Broken Connection,* puts it most articulately, 'Civil defense tends to coincide with belligerence and preparation for nuclear war. In itself, it seems like a natural and appropriate thing to do. But it increases the possibility of nuclear war by making it more acceptable. That's why it's immoral.'"

Her wry conclusion: "Laconia, New Hampshire, is a nice place to visit. But frankly, I don't want to evacuate there."[79]

Still on the theme of the notion that nuclear war is not only survivable but winnable, she took aim at the Star Wars missile defense proposal, shooting it down with rhetorical irony.

"If there is a favorite fantasy for those of us who share the four-o'clock-in-the-morning fears of nuclear war, I suppose it is the fantasy of some ultimate safety, some impenetrable self-defense," she wrote in February 1984. "It must be the same fantasy that fueled the imagination of those who once built castles, moats, city walls, even the Great Wall of China."

Concluding that the idea of citizen safety in a nuclear holocaust is a delusion, she wrote: "The reality is that we are stuck here on earth with the most human problem: how to save ourselves. Our only weapon is that familiar and flawed software called the human mind."[80]

It also was dangerous for the president to romanticize or idealize war, she wrote in a column published in the winter of 1983. Goodman cited a Reagan speech in which he made reference to the days of the "good old wars," in which rules of warfare were followed to ensure "'that soldiers fought soldiers, but they did not victimize civilians. That was civilized. Today we've lost something of civilization in that the very (nuclear) weapons we're talking about are designed to destroy civilians by the millions. And let us, at least, get back to where we once were.'"

Pay close attention to the president's message, she wrote, citing the brief war against Grenada to drive her point home, "and you can comprehend the president's pleasure, and even the national support for the war in Grenada. Grenada made war fun again. Here we are, restrained from a big confrontation by the mutual suicide pact of the two superpowers. What a relief it was to discover that we can still whack someone small, still win one for the Gipper."

She concluded: "The president of the United States went beyond explaining why war may be right. He told us that it may be civilized. What a long way we've come from the days when war was hell."[81]

Besides the anticommunist war being waged by the Reagan administration, cultural warfare was under way domestically. The nation's social agenda included not only a growing army of women entering the work force, but also a lot of behavioral and social debris, including some rather irrational activity, stemming from the sexual liberation of the 1960s and '70s. Some of the fallout from the evolving attitudes and liberations surrounding sexual relations included divorce, abortion, sexually transmitted diseases such as AIDS and herpes, and attempts by the conservative Religious Right and Moral Majority to instill and regulate family and so-called moral values.

Goodman, in an October 1982 column, entered into a public debate with one of those would-be regulators of public morals, Phyllis Schlafly of the right-wing Eagle Forum, who had published a pamphlet about the dangers of genital herpes. Accusing Schlafly of blaming the herpes epidemic on "the four Ps: *Playboy, Penthouse,* and *Planned Parenthood*" and citing Schlafly's prescription of abstinence and faithfulness to partners, Goodman suggested that something else was at work in Schlafly's crusade.

"Frankly, I don't know a soul who is in favor of herpes, a disease which has been on more magazine covers lately than Jacqueline Onassis," Goodman wrote. "But I have an uneasy feeling that the Schlaflys of the world regard this virus as a godsend. At least, a modern punishment for sex, a warning from the heavens above that human beings must mend their ways or suffer the sores of sex."

Goodman suggested that if the disease did not exist, Schlafly would have invented it as a deterrent to sex without the benefit of marriage. In her last paragraph, she made reference to a foreign treatment. Schlafly's pamphlet, she wrote, suggested "how disappointed some will be if the new Finnish remedy, something called gossypol, actually works against herpes. What would the Schlaflys do with a cure? Ban it?"[82]

An even greater deterrent to random sex, though, was the scourge of acquired immunodeficiency syndrome, or AIDS, which was first reported, by the U.S. Centers for Disease Control and Prevention, in June 1981. The deadly disease, contacted primarily through the exchange of bodily fluids such as during sexual intercourse, or through needle exchanges or blood transfusions, spread like the Great Plague worldwide, including in the United States, during the decade. It also carried a stigma, as the disease initially was heavily associated with homosexual relations.

Goodman wrote of this stigma in a July 1983 column, when she suggested that the word "leper" would sooner or later enter any conversation about AIDS. Noting that contamination was rare among health professionals and others who knew how to protect themselves against the disease, she wrote that the "epidemic of fear in the straight community" that accompanied the disease was "frustrating."

"The notion of a fatal disease spreading sexually through the homosexual community is rife with meaning among those who believe that homosexuals are 'sick,'" she wrote. "The idea that it is catching, that it could spread to the straight world, is explosive politically and psychologically."

The best treatment for that paranoia, she prescribed in her conclusion, was finding a cure. Meanwhile, she wrote, "a customer sitting in a gay bar watches to see if I order a drink in a bottle or a glass. . . . In the meantime, a man with AIDS wonders whether he is society's new leper."[83]

By the end of the decade, when AIDS had attained greater recognition as a disease that did not discriminate among races, classes, religions, or sexual preferences, Goodman wrote that the condom had returned to popularity—this time not so much as protection against pregnancy but as a barrier to HIV transmission.

"At this moment, when AIDS has turned the sexual revolution upside down, one of the tricks of social policy is to get men to take the initiative again," Goodman wrote of the sexual ploys of the liberated woman seeking safe sex. "The much-heralded 'Return of the Condom' must also be a return to mutual responsibility."[84]

Goodman also loosed her rhetorical darts on the Religious Right. When Jimmy Swaggart, a leader of the movement, committed hypocrisy and resigned his Assemblies of God ministry in 1988 in the heat of rivalry with a competing televangelist, Goodman was there, computer keyboard ready. As his flock wondered why Swaggart had regularly cruised a motel strip and hired prostitutes, Goodman wrote in March 1988 that she saw two answers to the question that were evidence of the cultural divide the nation was experiencing.

"They reveal a split in American society that runs deeper even than the split in Swaggart's life," she wrote. "A split between those who analyze human failings in the terms of psychology and those who analyze them in terms of scripture."

The gap in American culture, she observed, invoking the names of three leaders of the Religious Right, Swaggart, Marvin Gorman, and Jimmy Bakker, "is particularly great in regard to sex, the centerpiece for the Bakker-Gorman-Swaggart trilogy." Swaggart, she noted, "said more than once, 'Victory over flesh does not come easily.' But no child of the Freudian era would speak of victory over flesh as if Eros were the enemy of Psyche. Indeed Freud believed that trouble came when sexuality was in conflict with the spirit."

Thus, the columnist concluded, the Swaggart saga was the "essence of a larger melodrama, played before two American cultures. One that thinks the preacher had been led astray and another that thinks he's a neurotic mess. One thinks he can be saved and the other thinks he could use a good shrink. And it isn't just one congregation in Louisiana that speaks in tongues that sound strange to outsiders."[85]

The agenda of the Religious Right entered the public education arena as the debate over the teaching, or nonteaching, of scripture and religious beliefs took a seat in the classroom. The president had responded to the push by the neocons and the Religious Right by calling for prayer in schools, and Goodman in a November 1986 column summarized the difficulty that textbook publishers were having with the religion issue.

"They must avoid alienating either atheist or fundamentalist," she wrote. "And still these books have become centerpieces, controversial sources of evidence in courtrooms."

She referenced a Tennessee judge who had allowed students to "opt out" of a class because the texts "violated their religious beliefs. Their parents had managed to read religious subtexts, even witchcraft, into such tales as 'Goldilocks,' 'Cinderella,' and 'The Three Little Pigs.' Nothing was safe enough or bland enough to please them."

In Alabama, parents sued a school district, accusing its textbooks of "teaching a state religion masquerading as 'secular humanism.' Not to teach about God is to teach about no God. The attempt to keep religion out of the textbooks was no guarantee against controversy either."

"The common ground of values, neutral turf in the religious strife, threatens to shrink to the size of a postage stamp," she concluded.

> If textbook publishers keep retreating to a shrinking patch of safe ground, they will end up editing chunks out of "The Three Little Pigs." The task is not to shy away from our diversity, but to teach it to our children, and proudly. The strength of our system, what's worth telling the young, is not that Americans deny their differences or always resolve them, but that we have managed, until now, to live with them.[86]

The abortionist, though, was the biggest bogeyman of the Religious Right, ever since the U.S. Supreme Court's 1973 *Roe versus Wade* ruling legalizing abortion. It was the subject of many Goodman columns, a legal touchstone that symbolized more than any other issue the cultural, religious-secular divide in the nation.

As antiwar protestors had become routine street décor in U.S. cities during the 1960s and early '70s, antiabortion pickets took up their posts at the women's health clinics during the 1980s.

"In my town," Goodman wrote in November 1988, "there is a women's health clinic. To go there, whether you need a pap smear or pregnancy counseling, you have to run a gauntlet of anti-abortion picketers."

Establishing a bond of commonality with the protestors, Goodman wrote that she too would like to close down the abortion business, but in her fantasy, "the abortions would be phased out because every pregnancy was a welcome one. But in the real world of imperfect and sometimes desperate human experience, I put my hopes on a new pill to replace the surgery. The pill called RU-486.

"There are two distinct ways to close an abortion clinic," she continued. "Make it illegal or make it unnecessary. And right now they are in a conflict that is generating extraordinary heat." The big debate in the abortion arena, the columnist surmised, quoting Planned Parenthood President Faye Wattleton on the abortion pill, was "'whether it will come unsupervised and unsafe or supervised and safe.' And that's what the debate has been about all along."[87] And that is where the abortion debate left off in the 1980s, to be continued into the next two decades, at least.

Besides changes in traditional marriage, such as an increasing number of wives entering the work force and contraceptives helping couples delay or avoid creating families, old-fashioned divorce also was changing during the decade. Once upon a time, the storyteller begins, people fell out of love and they went to court to divide up their money and their children. In the 1980s, they went to court to fight over custody of frozen fertilized human eggs at the *in-vitro* fertilization (IVF) clinic.

In a March 1989 column, Goodman told the tale of a Tennessee couple who had gone to an *in vitro* fertilization clinic "where doctors fertilized eggs in a petri dish and tried unsuccessfully twice to implant them" in the woman's uterus. "When the marriage disintegrated, the remaining seven pre-embryos became its most dramatic leftovers." A judge restrained the man and woman from accessing the fertilized eggs, but it remained for the court to decide the eggs' fate.

"This is more than a bioethics freak case," she wrote. "There have been well over 4,000 children born from IVF. Only this once have pre-embryos been part of a property claim in a divorce settlement. But the questions it raises are at the center, not the periphery, of this still new technology."

Technology crosses into the realm of religion. It allows us, Goodman wrote, "to imitate the act of creation in a laboratory petri dish. But it has devised no biogenetic way to resolve everyday human conflicts."[88]

In these everyday human conflicts that Goodman considered her beat, her focus most frequently was on the human aspect of the conflict. After the Iran-Contra scandal involving the use of funds from the sale of American weapons to Iran to help rebels fighting the leftist Nicaraguan government came to light, she didn't so much follow the money and the political skullduggery. She departed that routine route of her brethren political commentators and followed instead the human trail, writing about the characters in the drama. In a July 1987 column, she profiled Lt. Col. Oliver North, a key player in the scandal.

"For pure entertainment, you couldn't beat the guy. His daytime ratings outdid the soaps," she wrote of North, who would be convicted on three of sixteen federal counts brought against him in connection with the scandal. "He was producer, director and star all wrapped up in one. He even titled his own show: *The Good, the Bad and the Ugly.* And if you ever wondered who was going to play him in the movie, he left only one conceivable choice: Oliver North."

> Here was a man for all seasons. A guy who would go one-on-one with terrorist Abu Nidal and still buy leotards for the kids. A man who hated communism and never "hanky-panked" with his secretary despite her "God-given beauty." A man who packed a poison pill on his mission to Iran and worried about a security fence to protect his "best friend" Betsy and the kids.
>
> Oliver North's squared-off shoulders and take-charge glare (he blinked so rarely that if he had contact lenses, they would have dried out) began by mesmerizing the committee members and the country. North presented not just a masterful self-defense but, more importantly, a fascinating dramatic profile.[89]

With physical descriptions done, Goodman summarized the ugly portion of the drama, concluding with a swipe at the Reagan administration's lapse in morality.

"These hearings are not just about whether Ollie North is a great character actor, a swell husband, a loving dad and all-around honorable fellow by his own code," she wrote. "They're about illegally trading those arms, weapons of murder. What counts in this drama is the public morality. The plot. The good, the bad and the very, very ugly."

Of that beautiful secretary who helped North shred incriminating government documents in that scandal, Goodman wrote in June 1987:

"It will be ironic if Fawn Hall, the secretary who 'can type,' goes down in history for a $10 million typo. It will be equally ironic if the leading female role in the Iran-Contra scandal is cut to a bit part, one night of shredding bliss and a transposed number on a Swiss bank account."

The secretary was 23 when she came to the National Security Council, Goodman wrote, "and twenty-seven when she left, stuffing documents into her clothes. It's heady stuff to be that close to power, to action, to the colonels and generals of the world. Heady to type words that may change history."[90]

After John Hinckley, Jr. shot President Reagan on March 30, 1981, to impress actress Jody Foster, Goodman wrote not of the political implications of the assassination attempt or the possible effects on international relations. She went to the courtroom during the trial and filed a piece about Hinckley's parents, about their anguish, about what might have gone wrong with the upbringing of the troubled defendant.

The lawyers would argue the legal definition of sanity and would depict Hinckley as a "spoiled brat" or as a delusional, troubled man, she wrote, "But in a larger world, we know that something went wrong with John Hinckley, Jr. We want to know what it was, how it happened. What goes wrong with people? What distorts the thing we call the human personality?"

Goodman displayed in this column the method that came to identify her style, an ability to find the everyman in the news, to pull the reader into the world of her subject for the purpose of driving home a larger, moral question. She concluded the piece by putting the reader in the shoes of Hinckley's mother, who had testified that she wanted nothing more for her son than any mother wants for any son.

"In the courtroom finally there will be a decision about guilt and innocence. But in real life there is only the pathetic echo of JoAnn Hinckley's simple wish: 'We wanted John to be self-supporting, to be a happy child, to stand on his own feet.'"[91]

The emotion of a mother grieving for a son accused of attempted murder, the tale of a secretary caught up in a national scandal standing by her boss—this was Goodman's journalistic territory in a decade that saw her write not only of scandal and nuclear war angst and abortion debate and AIDS anxiety, but also of the emerging national resentment toward big tobacco, of people selling their vital organs to those seeking transplants, of presidential candidate Gary Hart daring reporters to catch him womanizing and then getting caught womanizing, of negative political campaigning that did in presidential candidate Michael Dukakis, of an Iranian imam forcing novelist Salman Rushdie into hiding to avoid a death order against him because of something negative he wrote about Islam.

It was quite a decade, but its central character for Goodman, in the end, was Reagan, whom she dubbed the nation's supreme teller of stories. In retrospect, peering back at the decade from her kitchen table, she dismissed his successor, George H.W. Bush, as a man that "history seems to have just passed over, like a wave, because he was in the shadow of Reagan the storyteller."

She recalled one of Reagan's favorite stories, about the Cadillac-driving welfare mother.

"The welfare argument, I'd say, which began with the Reagan era, was very much imbued with the social change for women going back to work, so increasingly you had more and more low-income working women. If you look at welfare and see that it was established in the '30s in order to actually keep women at home as well as to help women at home, and then you fast-forward, and there are fewer and fewer women at home and those who are struggling to work and take care of their children now join a constituency of people who are hostile to taking care, to giving money to 'stay home and eat bon-bons,' that was when the last constituency to support welfare started bumbling away as more and more women went into the work force."

What of trickle-down economics, the theory of the Reagan administration that economic policies favoring businesses and development would create jobs and help the lower classes—did wealth indeed seep down to these citizens?

"It was in that era that the gap between rich and poor started to widen," she said. "If anything was trickling down, it didn't trickle very far. It seems to me that the long-term trend was in the gap direction."

The storyteller also was the ultimate politician/performer, she recalled of the former Hollywood actor who moved to the presidential stage. One of his strongest performances was at the Berlin Wall, when he chided the Soviet Union's president to tear down the wall.

"It was pretty powerful," she recalled. "It was theater, he put himself as the central actor in it. One legacy is just the power of his personality and his narrative and his storytelling and that everybody now tries to imitate that. When he told stories that were fact-based, and when he told stories that he thought were true but had been in the movies, it worked. His political theater, if you think about it, the telling of the individual story, the creation of an American narrative, he's the role model of the acting politician. And I mean that not because he literally was an actor, but people will roll tapes of Ronald Reagan to show how it can be done. He was the prime role model of how to spin a story and how to create a narrative that people would buy even if it was against maybe their economic interests, maybe their personal interest. So to me that's stunning. You can see that it's not exactly positive, but he knew how to do it. He really knew how to do it. And then, of course, we knew, probably toward the very end of his term, he was losing it. Right? And so, to what degree is one of the legacies that of the people behind the president, the figurehead president, too. That one I don't know."

Goodman recalled the ability of Reagan to weave a story on behalf of the notion of outspending the Soviets on defense, of ending the Cold War by sheer will.

"Reagan cast the story of the Cold War as, basically, we have to break the Soviets," she said. "And that's been around to this day, people think that he ended the Cold War, not Gorbachev. In the '80s, the best storyteller around, maybe the best storyteller in the half century, the best storyteller since FDR, was Ronald Reagan. And that was very powerful. Star Wars is complete craziness. That, I think, was the storyteller. My grandmother used to have an expression about somebody who talked himself into something, and Reagan talked himself into something. He talked himself into a belief that people play Pac-Man, you can shoot them out of the sky. It's just a nut case, and it's still going on."

The massive military spending did not square with another portion of the Reagan's conservative philosophy, that of tax cuts, she said.

"They grew—somehow or other 'grew' became an active verb in my lifetime—they grew the deficit until Clinton came in," she said, adding that the president managed to frame increased defense spending along with cuts in social spending and taxes in one big, tidily wrapped conservative package.

"It wasn't like everybody sat around the kitchen table and said, 'y'know, it's probably a good idea to spend more on the military, increase the deficit, and let our kids pay for it. I think it's good, let's vote for that.' It's not on a ballot. It just kind of happens in this low-key mysterious way, and people don't pay attention because their lives are busy and they've given someone the chit of their trust, and the rest of us, the journalists, are going around saying, 'hello, Earth to public,' you know what I mean. But it isn't like it was a rational decision on the part of the American public."

The rise of the neocons, Goodman recalled, actually was an uncomfortable social/religious pact that she sees as coming apart today.

"It was a combination of people's economic interests, and their social conservatism. It was an uneasy alliance at that time, and it's an uneasier alliance at this moment. I think the Republicans are struggling to hold it together, even as we speak. I mean the Republicans, they were always—Barry Goldwater, his wife was the founder of Planned Parenthood in Arizona, all those Republicans were Planned Parenthood Republicans. You still see vestiges of them when you go places."

The cultural gap in the nation, she suggested, is not so simple as right and left, blue state and red state, right and wrong. The shift from the Jimmy Carter years to the conservatism of the Reagan years was a murky phenomenon.

"My sense is that people are far more ambivalent about almost everything than we give them credit for, that we tend to see things as polarized when in fact it's ambivalent," she said. "Take for example the gay marriage movement; we tend to see people as hostile to gay marriage or pro gay marriage or whatever, and we forget how such a change takes place so that what was once the radical position of civil unions becomes the conservative position, or the moderate position, so that attitudes change without our acknowledging the way in which they change, and people are in fact more ambivalent than we tend to acknowledge. Leaders succeed or fail because they crystallize and make some of that ambivalence more powerful. In other words, they create a story, or a storyline, and Reagan did that."

But more than storytelling and spin was going on. There was an agenda, a conservative one, coupled with the belief that the Reagan path was the true path to American salvation and to legitimizing the nation as the beacon on the hill of right. The Iran-Contra scandal, she said, was the result of the arrogance of the Reagan administration—"just the exercise of unchecked power. It's what Eisenhower warned against. It can happen. And it often happens by people who have had the least experience with war."

The nation ended the decade with some citizens better off, others not so, she said.

"Was it better for those women and minorities who were able to get into the mainstream, get jobs open, filling graduate schools? Was it better for new immigrants to this country? How do you define it, what do you look for? Everybody's lives are so specific, or communities' lives. In terms of whether it was better for the way Americans thought about the government? No. Was it better in terms of dealing with real issues of the class divide? No. I can't give you a blanket 'we were a better people at the end, or we were a worse people.' Were we a more divided people? I think so. I think it was the beginning of this. And don't forget, it was also the beginning, if my memory serves me, of the whole sort of media divide, the divisiveness of spin, the divisiveness of talk radio, the deliberate creation of wedge issues. So, to the degree that you want Americans to feel that they have a lot in common with each other and that they're invested in civic life, the answer has to be that it was worse. But, for a million different people, things were better."

NOTES

1. Juan Williams, "Nation's Poverty Increasingly Wears a Child's Face," *Washington Post,* June 9, 1985, A1.
2. Juan Williams, "A Reagan Welfare Mother," *Washington Post,* November 9, 1981, A15.
3. Luther A. Huston, "Bronell Seeks New Laws To End Communist Party," *New York Times,* April 10, 1954, 1.
4. W.H. Lawrence, "M'Carthy Gains Delay In Inquiry," *New York Times,* April 10, 1954, 1.
5. UP, "Ex-Red Pleads Innocent," *New York Times,* April 10, 1954, 9.
6. UP, "F.C.C. Scored On Charge," *New York Times,* April 10, 1054, 22.
7. "Hungarian Who Jumped His Ship in '23 to Enter U.S. Is Declared Security Risk," *New York Times,* April 10, 1954, 9.
8. Lansing Warren, "Laniel Lists Aims In Asian Conflict," *New York Times,* April 10, 1954, 1.
9. Walter H. Waggoner, "Dulles Off Today For London, Paris On Indo-China War," *New York Times,* April 10, 1054, 1.
10. Kennett Love, "Arabs Threaten to boycott U.N. On Frontier Feud With Israel," *New York Times,* April 10, 1954, 1.
11. "Jazz Concert Aids Lighthouse," *New York Times,* April 10, 1954, 11.
12. "Operas In Concert Form," *New York Times,* April 10, 1954, 11.
13. "Lucky Me," "Radio City Music Hall," and "Tonight at 8," *New York Times,* April 10, 1954, 11.
14. "Buy With Confidence At H.W. Perlman Corp.," *New York Times,* April 10, 1954, 16.
15. "Franklin Simon," *New York Times,* April 10, 1954, 7.
16. "Follow the Crowd to Where the Lights are Bright All Night!" *New York Times,* April 10, 1954, 2.
17. "When Death Occurs," *New York Times,* April 10, 1954, 15.
18. Milestone listings for 1976 for this paragraph and those that follow taken from Neville Williams, *Chronology of World History Volume IV: 1901–1998/The Modern World* (Santa Barbara, CA: ABC-CLIO, 1999), 666–76.
19. Spencer Rich, "Schweiker Targets Welfare, Medical Plans for '83 Cuts," *Washington Post,* November 9, 1981, A1.

20. Caroline Atkinson, "Supply Side: Is the Bubble Bursting?" *Washington Post,* November 9, 1981, A1.

21. Juan Williams, "President Extols Accomplishments Of 'Reaganomics'," *Washington Post,* February 8, 1983, A1.

22. Juan Williams, "Falling Oil Prices Will Aid Recovery, Says Reagan, Opposing Protectionism," *Washington Post,* February 25, 1983, A3.

23. Juan Williams and John M. Berry, "President Hails Economic Growth, Backs Fed Policy," *Washington Post,* July 22, 1983, A1.

24. Juan Williams, "Economic Policies Aid All, Reagan Tells GOP Women," *Washington Post,* October 8, 1983, A1.

25. Juan Williams, "Homeless Choose to Be, Reagan Says," *Washington Post,* February 1, 1984, A1.

26. Juan Williams, "Black Children Sliding Backward, Report Finds," *Washington Post,* June 4, 1985, A1.

27. Juan Williams and Spencer Rich, "1 in 3 U.S. Children Found to Live In Households Receiving Welfare," *Washington Post,* January 31, 1986, A4.

28. David Hoffman and Lou Cannon, "Stockman on the Mend, Reeducates Reagan," *Washington Post,* February 6, 1983, A1.

29. Juan Williams, "El Salvador Aid Request Defended," *Washington Post,* March 12, 1983, A27.

30. Juan Williams, "President Defends Latin Policies At Texas Fund-Raiser for Tower," *Washington Post,* April 30, 1983, A6.

31. Lou Cannon and Juan Williams, "'Distortion' on Latin Policy Decried," *Washington Post,* August 10, 1983, A1.

32. Juan Williams, "Defending Latin Aid, Reagan Decries Soviet Role," *Washington Post,* April 15, 1984, A27.

33. Walter Pincus, "Secret Talks With Iran Described," *Washington Post,* November 6, 1986, A1.

34. David Hoffman and Walter Pincus, "Meant to Aid Iran Factions, Reagan Says," *Washington Post,* November 13, 1986, A1.

35. Bob Woodward, "Reagan Ordered Casey to Keep Iran Mission From Congress/Written Notice Conflicted With CIA Chief's Pledge," *Washington Post,* November 15, 1986, A1.

36. Walter Pincus, "White House Fails To Calm Concerns On Secret Deals," *Washington Post,* November 15, 1986, A1.

37. David Hoffman, "Iran Arms Profits Were Diverted to Contras; Poindexter Resigns, NSC Aide North Is Fired," *Washington Post,* November 26, 1986, A1.

38. Walter Pincus and David B. Ottaway, "Up to $30 Million Transferred," *Washington Post,* November 26, 1986, A1.

39. Lou Cannon and Juan Williams, "161 Marines Killed in Beirut," *Washington Post,* October 24, 1983, A1.

40. Don Oberdorfer and Fred Hiatt, "U.S. Marines to Leave Lebanese Soil; Strikes on Syrian-Held Posts Appoved/ Reagan Says Troops to Relocate Offshore," *Washington Post,* February 8, 1984, A1.

41. Patrick E. Tyler and David Hoffman, "U.S. Says Aim Is To Restore Order," *Washington Post,* October 26, 1983, A1.

42. Jim Hoagland, "U.S. Invades Grenada, Fights Cubans; Reagan Cites Protection of Americans," *Washington Post,* October 26, 1983, A1.

43. David Hoffman and Fred Hiatt, "President Defends Invasion, Marines in Beirut/Cuban Arms Cache Found, Reagan Says," *Washington Post,* October 28, 1983, A1.

44. Lou Cannon, "In Speech, Reagan Offers No Deadlines," *Washington Post,* October 28, 1983, A1.

45. Juan Williams, "Guyana's President Burnham Assails U.S. Move Into Grenada," *Washington Post,* November 8, 1983, A6.

46. Juan Williams, "Reagan Vows to Push Prayer, Abortion, Tuition Tax Credit Plans," *Washington Post,* January 23, 1983, A3.

47. Juan Williams, "Reagan Calls for Dedication to God," *Washington Post,* April 3, 1983, A3.

48. David Hoffman, "Reagan Urges Arms Buildup, Talks as a 'Dual Approach,'" *Washington Post,* August 24, 1983, A1.

49. Lou Cannon, "President Seeks Futuristic Defense Against Missiles," *Washington Post,* March 24, 1983, A1.

50. Lou Cannon, "Reagan Challenges Soviets To Dismantle Berlin Wall," *Washington Post,* June 13, 1987, A1.

51. Robert J. McCartney, "East Germany Opens Berlin Wall and Borders, Allowing Citizens to Travel Freely to the West," *Washington Post,* November 10, 1989, A1.

52. Ellen Goodman, "In the Heartland Of Missiles," in *Keeping in Touch* (New York: Summit Books, 1985), 182.

53. Ellen Goodman, *Making Sense,* (New York: The Atlantic Monthly Press, 1989), xix–xx.

54. UP, "British Fighting: Clash With Nazi Blitz Troops Trying to Flank Defense," *Boston Daily Globe,* April 11, 1941, 1.

55. UP, "Serbs in South 'Annihilated,' Germans Claim," *Boston Daily Globe,* April 11, 1941, 1.

56. AP, "R.A.F. Bombs Battleships and German Cities," *Boston Daily Globe,* April 11, 1941, 1.

57. UP, "Red Sea Opened to American Ships," *Boston Daily Globe,* April 11, 1941, 1.

58. UP, "Turks Begin Evacuation of Istanbul," *Boston Daily Globe,* April 11, 1941, 3.

59. UP, "French Prepare to Quit Istanbul, *Boston Daily Globe,* April 11, 1941, 3.

60. AP, "F.D. Signs Pact Barring Sovereignty Transfers," *Boston Daily Globe,* April 11, 1941, 4.

61. "Sears Modern 1941 Kitchen Ensemble," *Boston Daily Globe,* April 11, 1941, 2.

62. "Amusements," *Boston Daily Globe,* April 11, 1941, 19.

63. Milestone listings for 1965 for this paragraph and those that follow taken from Neville Williams, *Chronology of World History Volume IV: 1901–1998/The Modern World* (Santa Barbara, CA: ABC-CLIO, 1999), 546–54.

64. Ellen Goodman, "The New Nancy Reagan," in *Keeping in Touch,* 62–63.

65. Ellen Goodman, "Barbara Bush: The Silver Fox," in *Making Sense,* 31–33.

66. Ellen Goodman, "Raisa Gorbachev: First Wife of the Soviet Union," in *Keeping in Touch,* 78–79.

67. Ellen Goodman, "Sally Ride: Another First Woman," in *Keeping in Touch,* 72–73.

68. Ellen Goodman, "The Shuttle: For Us A Return to Reality," *Washington Post*, February 8, 1986, A21.

69. Ellen Goodman, "A Battered Little Girl Named Eleanor Roosevelt," in *Keeping in Touch*, 60–61.

70. Ellen Goodman, "Where Do You Want To Eat?" in *Keeping in Touch*, 134–35.

71. Ellen Goodman, "Fantasy of the First Female President," in *Keeping in Touch*, 222–23.

72. Ellen Goodman, "I Dreamed I Was Liberated In My Maidenform Bra," in *Keeping in Touch*, 204–05.

73. Ellen Goodman, "Role of the First Female Vice President," in *Keeping in Touch*, 224–25.

74. Ellen Goodman, "Working Girls," in *Making Sense*, 109–10.

75. Ellen Goodman, "He's Done It Again," *Washington Post*, July 14, 1981, A13.

76. Ellen Goodman, "Was The Woman Really Less Qualified?" in *Making Sense*, 128–29.

77. Ellen Goodman, "Eulogy for an Amendment," in *Keeping in Touch*, 210–11.

78. Ellen Goodman, "Mothers, Daughters, and the Draft," in *Keeping in Touch*, 214–15.

79. Ellen Goodman, "Nuclear Follies: I," in *Keeping in Touch*, 86–87.

80. Ellen Goodman, "High-Tech War," in *Keeping in Touch*, 98–99.

81. Ellen Goodman, "The Good Old Wars," in *Keeping in Touch*, 92–93.

82. Ellen Goodman, "Crime and Punishment and Herpes," in *Keeping in Touch*, 30–31.

83. Ellen Goodman, "AIDS II: The New Lepers," in *Keeping in Touch*, 164–65.

84. Ellen Goodman, "The Return of the Condom," in *Making Sense*, 373–74.

85. Ellen Goodman, "Sin, Salvation and a Good Shrink," in *Making Sense*, 18–19.

86. Ellen Goodman, "Religion in the Textbooks," in *Making Sense*, 228–29.

87. Ellen Goodman, "How to Close a Clinic," in *Making Sense*, 115–17.

88. Ellen Goodman, "A Custody Fight for an Egg," in *Making Sense*, 72–74.

89. Ellen Goodman, "Oliver North: The Good, the Bad, and the Boffo," in *Making Sense*, 41–42.

90. Ellen Goodman, "Fawn Hall: The Fantasy Secretary," in *Making Sense*, 53–54.

91. Ellen Goodman, "Where Did The Hinkleys Go Wrong?" in *Keeping in Touch*, 274–75.

CHAPTER 6

The '90s of David Broder and Judy Woodruff: Clinton and Monica and Political Divide

> Clinton's strengths were stunning. I mean, he is very smart and has an extraordinarily retentive mind, once he learns something he keeps it always, he grasps the connections probably better than anybody else that I know in the public policy world, sees how this relates to that, and that relates to a third thing. He is extraordinarily skillful at human relations, he can give people a sense that he is terribly interested in them as individuals and in what they're thinking. And he is a very smart politician. He has all of those talents, and he had displayed them so early in life that people were always there so that when he misstepped, they were ready to pick him up, dust him off, and say, "keep going kid, we've got a lot of confidence in you."
>
> —David Broder

Tracer fire from anti-aircraft guns filled the night sky over Baghdad. Much of the city experienced power blackouts about an hour after the bombing raids had begun. "A smoky pallor had settled over the city," wrote *Washington Post* correspondents David S. Broder and Rick Atkinson. Yet, despite the scenes of war, the operation had been pulled off with relative ease. Operation Desert Storm, the first war against Iraq undertaken by the first President George Bush, was under way.

Government sources expressed "surprise and relief at the lack of any effective Iraqi military response in the early hours of hostilities," the reporters wrote of the war's initial forays. "Despite U.S. anxieties that Israel would be drawn into the war by an Iraqi strike, Baghdad launched no attack on the Jewish state, officials said."

Secretary of Defense Dick Cheney said in a briefing that early reports from the gulf "'were very, very encouraging. The operation appears to

David Broder. © The Washington Post Writers Group. Used by permission.

have gone very well. . . . We achieved a fairly high degree of tactical surprise.' The combat, Cheney added, is 'likely to run a long period of time.' Casualty reports were sketchy, but officials said that few if any allied planes had been lost in the raids."

General Colin L. Powell, chairman of the Joint Chiefs of Staff, would not reveal specific details of the battle to reporters but said that "'so far there has been no resistance' from the Iraqi air force. U.S. fighters returned from their missions with air-to-air missiles still slung beneath their wings, having found no enemy planes to engage in dogfights."

Thus began, on January 16, 1991, the military operation by U.S. and allied forces to liberate Kuwait from the occupying troops of Saddam Hussein's Iraq. It was an undertaking, launched by President George H.W. Bush, designed solely to oust the Iraqis from Kuwait and to reestablish Kuwait's sovereignty. Some of the administration players were the same as those involved in the invasion of Iraq undertaken by Bush's son, George W., during his presidency 12 years later.

In a broadcast on the state-run Baghdad radio station five hours after the onset of the air strikes, "a voice identified as Saddam's responded defiantly, calling Bush a 'hypocritical criminal' and vowing to crush 'the satanic intentions of the White House.' Declaring that 'the great duel, the mother of all battles has begun,' the speaker said, 'the dawn of victory nears as this great showdown begins.'"

At home, members of Congress and the public voiced support of the president's decision.

"An overnight Washington Post-ABC News Poll showed three of four persons interviewed approved of Bush's action," Broder and Atkinson reported. "But several hundred demonstrators gathered in front of the White House before midnight, shouting 'Shame, shame, shame.' More than a dozen were arrested amid rock and bottle throwing.

"'The world could wait no longer,' Bush said. Congress, which had agonized for months over backing Bush's hard-line stance, appeared substantially united behind the president's decision in the first few hours of the war. Republicans rallied quickly to his support, and so did some of his prominent Democratic critics."

The voices of Democratic support included those of Senate Armed Services Committee Chairman Sam Nunn of Georgia and Senate Intelligence Committee Chairman David L. Boren of Oklahoma, who said "there would be 'unanimous support for our troops. . . . You'll see Congress play the role of supporting player.'"

The most striking similarity of the first Gulf War to the second, though, was the ease with which coalition forces carried out the attack.

"We don't quite understand it," White House spokesman Marlin Fitzwater told reporters. "We are surprised that there was so little response this first night. But we are keeping in mind that this is only the beginning, and a guy with a million-man army is bound to respond."[1]

But there were some dissimilarities. One was the diplomatic channels that the first Bush administration employed, including working closely with the United Nations to try to force a peaceful solution to the problem of Saddam's occupation of Kuwait. Also, some of the nations on the list of participating coalition forces would be noticeably different than in 2003. They included Egypt, France, Germany, and Syria. And the size of the U.S. force involved, nearly 500,000 troops and six aircraft carriers, was noticeably larger.

"The order to launch attacks marked the end of 5½ months of diplomatic and economic efforts by the United States to force Saddam to roll back the forces he sent into oil-rich Kuwait on Aug. 1," Broder and Atkinson reported. "It came less than 17 hours after the expiration Tuesday midnight of the United Nations deadline for Iraq to withdraw from Kuwait."

The correspondents wrote that Secretary of State James A. Baker III had "logged thousands of miles in assembling the anti-Iraq coalition and futilely seeking a diplomatic solution." Before the attack, Baker "spent yesterday notifying allies of the decision to go to war." The notification included that of King Fahd of Saudi Arabia, by secret code, who "assented to the attack with another code word."[2]

Another difference was Saddam's decision to broaden the war. Broder and Atkinson reported the next day that Iraq had launched missiles into Israel and Saudi Arabia. But the war continued to go well for the allies otherwise.

"The sobering news of the attack against Israel came at the end of a day that had been filled with encouraging news from the battlefront," they reported. "Wave after wave of allied bombing runs encountered little Iraqi resistance."

Also, Iran was reportedly considering joining the fighting against Iraq, and "the Turkish National Assembly voted overwhelmingly yesterday to allow the United States to use Turkey military bases for direct attacks on Iraq, rather than simply as a refueling way station."

The article reported losses by one of the coalition countries. "Four of the French Jaguar bombers that participated in the allied assault were hit with antiaircraft fire and one pilot was slightly wounded, Defense Minister Jean-Pierre Chevenement said yesterday. The French targets included airplane and helicopter shelters, ammunition depots and SAM batteries."[3]

The major difference between the two conflicts, however, was the decision by the first President Bush not to invade Iraq with ground forces, but to declare mission accomplished with the ouster of Saddam's troops from Kuwait, whereas the second Bush invaded Iraq. The successful completion of Operation Desert Storm less than a month and a half after it began popularized the first President Bush despite the feeling by some that coalition forces should have entered Iraq and finished the job against Saddam.

"The military success in the Persian Gulf War has triggered an unprecedented surge in national optimism, a new Washington Post poll shows," Broder and Richard Morin reported on February 28. "Several private pollsters and opinion analysts cautioned that the euphoria bred by the victory over Iraq could prove to be fleeting. But they also said that if the optimism is sustained, it could have major beneficial effects for the economy, President Bush and the Republicans."

A Democratic pollster agreed: "My gut tells me this war has been a good thing for the American psyche," William Hamilton told the reporters. "People feel good that something we did worked. In time, I suspect some of the cynicism will come back."[4]

The first Bush made the right decision to end the war after Kuwait was liberated, Broder would assert 15 years later.

"I think he did exactly what he set out to do in Iraq, which was to throw back the invasion of Kuwait," the columnist said in his *Washington Post* cafeteria. The president decided, "I believe correctly, that since this was a coalition strategy that they should do the things the coalition agreed to do and not go off unilaterally on a venture of our own, which meant stopping essentially at the border. I do think he got it right."

The columnist's recollection of the first Gulf War came as he was in his 53rd year as a print journalist, a career in which he rose from a general assignment reporter at a small newspaper in Illinois to reporter and then columnist at the *New York Times* and the *Washington Post*. Politics became the defining *métier* of Broder's career, which included winning the 1973

Pulitzer Prize for commentary—an honor Broder likely did not foresee as a young man in Chicago Heights.

Born to Albert I. and Nina M. Broder on September 11, 1929, David Salzer Broder was a child of the Great Depression. But the stock market crash that precipitated the economic crisis was still more than a month away when Broder entered the world; the *Chicago Daily Tribune* headlines on the day of his birth were of politics, scandal, technology, the seemingly ever-present American theme of red scare, and a Chinese-Russian military skirmish at the Manchurian border.

In a story somewhat foreshadowing the Republican-Democratic battles that Broder would grow up to cover as a newspaper correspondent, the big political item of the day was a piece on the front page reporting that some wealthy U.S. industrialists would be required to reveal certain earnings.

"Republican regulars were routed overwhelmingly today in the first test of strength in the senate tariff fight," reported *Tribune* reporter Arthur Crawford in a story datelined Washington, D.C. "By a vote of 51 to 27 the senate adopted the Simmons resolution directing the finance committee to obtain from the treasury department information contained in the income tax returns of tariff beneficiaries.

"The Democrats, 30 in number, stood solidly for the resolution and were joined by 21 Republicans, including several not ordinarily identified with the Democratic-radical coalition," the story continued. "All of the 27 negative votes were cast by Republicans."[5]

Elsewhere on the front page, the Herbert Hoover administration and the Senate were reported to be investigating the dealings of a shipbuilding representative.

"President Hoover today called for the most searching investigation of the activities of William B. Shearer, naval expert, and his connections with the three big shipbuilding corporations he represented as an observer during the sessions of the 1927 three power naval limitation conference called by former President Coolidge," the newspaper reported.

"Simultaneously the senate naval affairs committee voted to investigate Shearer's activities at Geneva and arranged for another meeting Thursday when the course of its investigation will be determined," the story continued. "Senator William E. Borah (Rep., Idaho) introduced the necessary investigating resolution in the senate this afternoon and favorable action is expected tomorrow."[6]

On the newspaper's inside pages, a United Press story reported that fighting continued between Chinese and Russian troops in a conflict over the Chinese seizure of the Manchurian Chinese Eastern Railway. "Chinese sources estimated their casualties in a five hour clash last night at more than 100."[7]

In North Carolina, the newspaper reported that the state had begun an investigation of the previous evening's raids "upon Red strongholds in which three national textile workers' union members were kidnapped and one of them severely beaten."

"Public sentiment as expressed on the streets of Gastonia and in Charlotte, where the trial of 16 Red workers charged with the murder of Chief of Police O. F. Aderholdt was declared a mistrial yesterday when a juror became insane, made it plain that the mob spirit is growing and that trouble may flare up at any time."[8]

At the movies, William Haines was starring in *Speedway* at the Chicago; the Orpheum featured *The Hottentot,* and Betty Compson starred in the "All-Melody, All-Talking" *Street Girl* at the State and Lake theaters. The Marx Brothers were all over town, starring in *The Cocoanuts* at the Paradise, Uptown, and Tivoli theaters for 35 cents a seat during matinee hours.[9]

Chicagoans wanting to look their best for the movies could find a good price on shirts—Oxfords, broadcloths, chambrays, madrases, all in "smart patterns, in white and the newly popular pastel colors," starting at $2 at the College Men's Store,[10] and before the show they could grab dinner at the Stevens Building Restaurant—featuring entrees and sides that included shrimp cardinale, broiled black sea bass, vegetable dumpling, broiled tenderloin, potato salad or mashed potatoes, and cauliflower in cream *au gratin.*[11]

Broder grew up reading both the *Tribune* and the *Chicago Sun,* along with his local paper, the *Chicago Heights Star.* He particularly enjoyed reading Bill Kent, "a great political reporter." Broder majored in, naturally, political science at the University of Chicago, earning his bachelor's degree in 1947 and a master's, also in political science, in 1951. He followed this with a two-year stint in the Army, where he worked as a reporter for the Army newspaper in Austria.

But as a boy, journalism was more of a sideline to his interest in sports. "I don't know that I ever actually made a formal decision (to be a journalist)," he said. "I mean, as a kid I was like all kids interested in sports. But I was a terrible athlete. I was the slow white guy on our track team in high school, so the closest I could get to sports was to write about it for the school paper. And I knew that was fun, but I had no idea whether you could make a living as a reporter or not.

"When I got out of the Army, obviously I was looking for work," he continued. "The only thing I'd ever done up to that point was work on newspapers, so I sent out a whole blizzard of letters to papers, mostly in the Midwest, on the coasts, and asked anybody who would interview if I could come interview." He and his wife, the former Ann Creighton Collar, were both hired by the Bloomington, Illinois, *Pantagraph.* There, Broder honed his newspaper reporting skills under the guidance of a team of editors and colleagues.

"The *Pantagraph* was a great place to break in," he recalled. "I was so lucky that I ended up there because it was a high-quality newspaper with a cadre of local people who had a career, a lifetime commitment to it. And they were the core of the staff, particularly the editing staff. It was a very companionable place, and people paid attention to you, you got feedback on your work and criticism when you needed it. I didn't know anything when I went to work there; I had worked on a weekly paper, but I didn't have much supervision on a weekly paper."

McCarthyism and the budding civil rights movement were two of the major political and social issues receiving newspaper play the year that Broder began his career at the *Pantagraph.* Two years before the Montgomery, Alabama, bus boycott sparked by the Rosa Parks episode, a bus boycott in Baton Rouge, Louisiana, in June 1953 led to an amendment to rules requiring blacks to sit at the rear of city buses.[12]

As the Korean War was winding down, with United Nations forces and their communist counterparts in April agreeing to a prisoner exchange and an armistice being signed in July, anti-communist fever continued to ravage the nation domestically. In January, a federal judge in New York convicted 13 leaders of the U.S. Communist Party of conspiring to overthrow the government; three months later the Justice Department ordered the party to register as an organization controlled and directed by foreigners. In May, the government fired 3,002 employees considered security risks because of alleged communist ties, and the next month, Ethel and Julius Rosenberg were executed at Sing Sing Prison in New York after their 1951 conviction on spying charges for passing nuclear weapons secrets to the Soviet Union. Following the federal government's lead, the General Electric corporation in December announced plans to fire all communist employees, and that same month, the former head of the Manhattan Project that developed the atomic bomb during World War II, J. Robert Oppenheimer, was accused by the government of having communist sympathies. His security clearance was revoked in 1954 despite his being cleared of disloyalty charges.

The post-World-War-II economic recovery continued apace, as the federal government lifted salary and wage controls in February, and the next month the government ended all price controls. In April, Congress established the Department of Health, Education, and Welfare, and President Dwight D. Eisenhower in August proposed extending Social Security benefits to 10.5 million American citizens who had not enjoyed the program's protections. At the end of the year, Eisenhower proposed his Atoms for Peace program calling for the establishment of an International Atomic Energy Agency to monitor the development of atomic technology for peaceful uses. Fueling the fears of nuclear war, though, the Soviet Union in August exploded its first hydrogen bomb (though not a true hydrogen bomb but a hybrid fission-fusion device; the Soviets' first true H-bomb would be detonated two years later), and the U.S. Navy announced in March the development of a jet-propelled guided missile system.

In the arts and letters, French artist Henri Matisse created a collage, *The Snail,* and U.S. artist Jackson Pollock painted *Blue Poles.* English writer

C.S. Lewis published the fourth volume in his *The Chronicles of Narnia*, titled *The Silver Chair;* German author Heinrich Boll published *Acquainted with the Night;* and U.S. author James Baldwin published his first novel, the autobiographical *Go Tell It on the Mountain*, while science-fiction writer Ray Bradbury published *Fahrenheit 451*. On the stage, Samuel Beckett's absurdist *Waiting for Godot* made its premier in Paris, while in the United States Arthur Miller's *The Crucible* premiered in New York and Welsh writer Dylan Thomas' *Under Milk Wood* was first performed at Harvard University. William Inge won the Pulitzer Prize for drama for *Picnic*. U.S. film audiences, meanwhile, attended Fred Zinnemann's *From Here to Eternity* starring Burt Lancaster, Frank Sinatra, and Deborah Kerr; and Gregory Peck and Audrey Hepburn costarred in *Roman Holiday*.

The year marked the first of a two-year stint that Broder put in at the *Pantagraph*. In 1955, he joined the reporting staff of the *Congressional Quarterly*, where he worked for five years before joining the *Washington Star* for five years, followed by a year at the *New York Times* after which he moved to the *Washington Post*. There, he established a national reputation for his political and governmental reportage. By the time Bill Clinton came to Washington in 1992, Broder enjoyed the title of dean of the nation's political reporters.

The decade of the '90s was marked by the rise and fall of Clinton. But first came the fall of the first President Bush, George H.W., who inherited the Ronald Reagan presidential cloak in 1989 and who oversaw the collapse of the Soviet Union.

The first spring of the decade would see a U.S.-Soviet summit meeting in June 1990. Bush and Soviet President Mikhail Gorbachev sat down in the waning days of the Russian leader's presidency as the forces of democracy gathered steam in the Soviet bloc. Using a frequent method of gauging citizen reaction to public policy in his political reporting, Broder told the story of the summit meeting through the eyes of a group of American voters who watched the postsummit news conference.

One summit viewer saw the conciliatory Bush policy toward Gorbachev and his nation as the correct course. '"He's trying to modernize his society,' a 39-year-old man of Ukrainian descent said of Gorbachev. 'And in order to do that, he needs time. He needs stability outside his borders. I look at everything going on here as getting him that stability.'"

As one observer told Broder, the intention of Bush during the summit was to lend visible support to the Russian leader in his effort to stabilize his nation.

"To 19-year-old Trinity College student Patricia Pierson, the Bush-Gorbachev summit was 'just like the shampoo ad,'" Broder wrote, "with the American president in effect letting his Soviet counterpart know, 'If you don't look good, we don't look good.'"

A key to the meeting, claimed one observer, would be whether the much-anticipated peace dividend—a U.S. economy and society invigorated by an end to the decades-long Cold War—would materialize in an agreement between the United States and Russia on the unification of Germany, which was one of the subjects of the summit meeting.

"'I think what we really need to work on is getting the agreement so we can cut back on military spending,'" another viewer told Broder, "'and using that money for education, training, for increased technology. . . .'"

"But the peace dividend," Broder wrote, "seemed ephemeral to many of these voters. 'The savings and loans and the budget deficit will soak it up,' said truck driver David L. Dowd, 38, and [Republican real-estate agent Mary Lou] Blauvelt agreed. 'Not only is there not going to be a peace dividend,' [tool-and-die company executive Roger J.] Kern argued, 'there's going to be a peace cost, because East Germany, the Baltic States, Panama, all of them are going to require an infusion of U.S. dollars to survive. They're expecting it.'"

In the end, one participant in the forum voiced an optimistic note to the summit.

> Just when the group began to be depressed about the emerging shape of the post-Cold War world, Earl Shepherd offered a more hopeful consensus:
>
> "I think it presents really an opportunity for us to get our house in order . . . to decide where we want to go, who we are, how we're going to do it in the next century. If we maintain that kind of focus, that we need to begin to look at ourselves and really form the new directions for the future, then I think we might be okay. If we begin saying, 'Well, we're one up on them, or we're two up on them,' I think we're missing the boat. I think it's an opportunity. It's not a solution."[13]

Broder visited Moscow the next month to assess the mood of Russian citizens toward the changes in their nation and the crumbling of their communist empire. A dominant theme was hope for a steadying force in the nation. When Broder asked one woman, a doctor and member of the Communist Party, of her hopes for the convening 28th Congress of the Soviet Communist Party, "she shrugged. 'I would just like the situation to stabilize. There has been so much turmoil,' she said, referring to the infighting between Gorbachev and his critics and also to the breakaway movements that comprised the Soviet Union. 'I feel we have reached a dead end,' she said. 'The relationship between the party leadership and the people has no place to go. People no longer believe the leadership.'"

Broder found that some citizens wondered why U.S. leaders and citizens "put Soviet President Mikhail Gorbachev 'on such a pedestal,' as one man put it.

"The Soviets living under Gorbachev see his faults and shortcomings in a way most Americans from President Bush on down have chosen to ignore. To them, his fabled charm has worn thin. Even his diplomatic successes shrink in comparison to his domestic failures."

The citizens on Moscow's streets felt the nation had lost its rudder.

"My favorite comment came from 85-year-old Oksana Meshko, a Helsinki Watch human-rights activist who was arrested early in her life by Stalin and again, at age 75, by Brezhnev," Broder wrote. "Asked about Gorbachev, she said: 'Despite the enthusiasm everyone felt for his words, there have been no visible results of his decisions. This great statesmanship leaves many of us cool to him. But we see no one to replace him—at the moment.'"[14]

Later in the same year as his Moscow visit, Broder cast an ominous Bush political line in musing whether the U.S. president could escape the restless political mood that he saw in Russia and the United Kingdom.

"The impatience with status-quo politics is breaking down the barriers to change from Moscow and Warsaw to London and points west," he wrote of the emerging international political tides. "It would be foolish to suppose that the United States will be immune for long from this worldwide trend."

Citing the "sudden downfall" of British Prime Minister Margaret Thatcher, who had been a close political ally of President Reagan, Broder speculated that other leaders were feeling similar pressure.

"Canadian Prime Minister Brian Mulroney, another personal favorite of the last two American presidents, holds deeply diminished authority because of his low standing at the polls," Broder wrote. "The common factor that has derailed the former heroes is economic frustration. Britain, after recovering handsomely under Thatcher's leadership and scoring significant economic gains during most of the '80s, has slumped back into a high-inflation/low-growth pattern."

He wondered: "Could George Bush be next? . . . He may be spared by the Democrats' persistent inability to offer the nation a plausible alternative. But if they break their pattern of nominating weak candidates, Bush will be lucky to avoid the worldwide trend."[15]

Broder detected weakness in the president's foreign policy, which the columnist viewed as long on pragmatism but short on democratic idealism.

"Bush was swift to lift economic sanctions against South Africa—a nation in which we have significant strategic, economic and resources interests—even though the struggle for freedom there is far from complete," Broder offered in a July 1991 column. "He is adamant in opposing measures to restrict credits and trade with China, even though a clear majority in Congress regards that government's treatment of its own citizens as unacceptable. Bush argues that his way will increase our influence with Beijing's current rulers. He appears willing to ignore the effect of our actions on those who are struggling for democracy in China."

Broder cited comments by the conservative Hoover Institution senior research fellow Larry Diamond as evidence of a sentiment in the American right that Bush's policies were flawed. As U.S. citizens had observed in their remarks regarding the Bush-Gorbachev summit the year before, the hoped-for post-Cold War peace dividend was not materializing—and this was one of the reasons behind the demise of the Bush presidency.

"Diamond argues that Bush needs to expand his vision in order to seize the 'once-in-a-generation' opportunity provided by the end of the Cold War," the columnist wrote. "So far, he observes, Bush's 'New World Order . . . has seemed more concerned with order than with freedom, more committed to the stability of borders than to the pursuit of democracy, self-determination or justice.'"

In a prescient observation foreshadowing the pro-democracy policy that would become a cornerstone of the second President Bush's foreign policy, Broder observed: "Diamond proposes that 'a long-term strategy of promoting democracy . . . should be the central focus, the defining feature, of our foreign policy,' carried forward by economic assistance to fledgling democracies and the cultivation of pluralistic institutions through the National Endowment for Democracy."[16]

In the end, though, as the future President Bill Clinton would observe in his campaign for the presidency, it was the economy that brought down George H. W. Bush. Following a series of interviews with voters in San Bernardino, California—an informal polling method perfected by Broder in his political reporting that helped him project a sense of the nation's mood to his readers—Broder found the president in trouble because of domestic economic woes.

"His international achievements count for little in their reckoning," he wrote of the president, citing the successful foreign policy initiatives of Bush and Reagan.

> The fall of the Berlin Wall, the peaceful liberation of Eastern Europe, the end of the Cold War, the renunciation of communism in the Soviet Union and even the lightning victory by a U.S.-led international coalition over Iraqi aggressors in Kuwait might as well not have happened, so rarely are they raised spontaneously by voters. In four days of door-knocking hereabouts, I did not hear one person mention Bush's achievement of finally getting the antagonists in the Arab-Israeli struggle into the same conference hall.
>
> All that is buried under a rising tide of economic apprehension.

Broder cited the headlines he spotted at local newsstands, which "sounded a drum-roll of deepening concern: 'Construction Decline Heightens Fears.' 'Home Sales Faltering Locally, Nationwide.' 'State Home Sales Fall for Fourth Month.' 'Office Boom Goes Bust.' 'Economy Absolutely Stalled.' 'Factory Orders Tumble; Unemployment Claims Up.' 'Budget Shortfall of $3 Billion Faced by States.' All this in five days.

"Bush has reason to be nervous," Broder wrote, citing the president's famous campaign read-my-lips promise not to raise taxes. "A year ago, when he swallowed his 'no new taxes' campaign pledge and agreed to a budget deal with Congress, his economic advisers told him that was the way to ensure that the then-starting recession would be over well before his reelection year. And that was vital, for, as Bush well remembered, the 1982 recession dragged President Reagan's approval ratings down to a scary 41 percent, before recovery set the stage for his landslide reelection."[17]

No landslide reelection awaited Bush, as the economy continued to falter—to the advantage of the Democrat who would challenge Bush's bid for reelection, Clinton. Broder had begun chronicling the rising political waters of Clinton, the "plausible alternative" the Democrats had been seeking to stop Bush in his bid for a second term, in 1991. His coverage of the "New Democrat" Clinton and the opposing Republican forces offers textbook political journalism that Broder, the mentor and instructor of this form of reportage, refined during the 1990s. It was a form of journalism that combined reporting from the political front with analysis from the political rear and took in a sweeping view not only of hard numbers and political tally sheets but also public sentiment and policy analysis.

In May 1991, Clinton was staking out his centrist platform in the Democratic Party, as noted in a Broder column on the upcoming Cleveland meeting of the then-six-year-old Democratic Leadership Council, "the self-styled 'mainstream voice of the Democratic Party.'" The council, Broder wrote, was preparing for battle "for control of the party's agenda and future." Its chairman was Clinton, and its mission in the meeting was to "dispel what the DLC says in draft resolutions is a widespread belief that Democrats support 'government programs that don't work,' put 'special interests before the interests of ordinary people' and exhibit 'a reluctance to assert American values at home and abroad.'"

Broder observed that controversy "surrounds the meeting" and that organized labor "has discouraged union officials from attending." Also, there was a worry among traditional Democrats that two-time presidential candidate Jesse Jackson had not been invited to speak at the gathering. Jackson planned to go to Cleveland anyway, "to support striking bus workers and draw coverage away from the DLC convention." The council, Broder reported, had renewed a dispute with Jackson that had marked its 1989 meeting in New Orleans by issuing a draft resolution that "endorses affirmative action but asserts, 'Government cannot mandate equal outcomes; therefore we oppose quotas and public policies that enshrine racial, gender or ethnic preference.'"[18]

A few days later, Clinton set the theme for the conference, and for the emerging centrist Democratic Party leadership, in the conference's keynote speech.

"'Too many of the people who used to vote for us, the very burdened middle class we're talking about, have not trusted us in national elections to defend our national interest abroad, to put their values in our social policy at home or to take their tax money and spend it with discipline,' Clinton told the delegates. 'We've got to turn these perceptions around or we can't continue as a national party.'"[19]

By early the next year, the allegations of womanizing that would dog Clinton during much of his career on the national political stage had surfaced as the Arkansas governor, now a presidential candidate in the Democratic primaries, campaigned in New Hampshire.

The candidate still was strong in state polls, but "many Democratic politicians say Arkansas Gov. Bill Clinton faces a critical period before knowing whether his presidential campaign has been damaged by the controversy over his past marital problems," Broder and *Post* staff writer Dan Balz reported. "Even as Clinton advisers said yesterday they believed the campaign had 'stopped the hemorrhaging' caused by allegations of a 12-year love affair with Gennifer Flowers, the Arkansas governor found himself attacked by an angry New York Gov. Mario M. Cuomo (D), who accused Clinton of an ethnic slur in one of the telephone conversations contained on tapes Flowers says she made of conversations with Clinton."[20]

Clinton had lost his New Hampshire advantage by the second week of February, with former Massachusetts Senator Paul E. Tsongas claiming the polling lead. But he demonstrated dogged determination on the campaign trail.

"'I'm electable,' he told a panel of 10 highly sympathetic questioners assembled by his campaign staff," Broder and *Post* reporter Thomas B. Edsall reported on February 14. "'I've always been able to come out of it (negative attacks) and work it through, and I will if there is enough time. . . . If you say I'm electable, by definition, I'm electable.'"[21]

His feisty stumping along with an appearance with his wife, Hillary, on *60 Minutes* helped Clinton regain some momentum and take second place in New Hampshire, a showing that prompted him to declare himself the "comeback kid." He followed this up with victories in Southern state primaries, but another ghost from his past stepped into the campaign that spring, reports of his "manipulation of the Vietnam-era draft laws" to avoid military service.[22] Following a meltdown by Tsongas, former California Governor Jerry Brown claimed a primary victory in Connecticut and emerged as the strongest challenger to Clinton in the large primary states of New York and California. But the "comeback kid" overcame the reports of sexual dalliance and draft evasion to win those states and claim the Democratic nomination.

The general election race against the incumbent Bush included the independent campaign of Texas billionaire H. Ross Perot, whose candidacy Broder termed "startling."

"For two months—without even announcing his bid for the White House—the Dallas billionaire has dominated the contest, topping President Bush and Democratic challenger Bill Clinton in many polls and preempting a giant share of this political news coverage," Broder wrote in June 1992. "Yet at the center of it all is a man with a strange mixture of naïve, idealistic, cynical and conspiratorial ideas in his head—and a handful of aides who are groping their way toward a strategy for the campaign."

The upstart candidate, Broder wrote, was confident "of the purity of his own motives" and hung out conspiracy theories "for you to see."

"The manipulator-in-chief is 'the president, backed by the Republican Party opposition research team,' whose leader—a person Perot would not name—was rewarded with an invitation to the White House dinner for [Russian President] Boris Yeltsin. The goal at the moment, Perot says, is the destruction of Ross Perot."[23]

The main event of the campaign, though, was the incumbent versus the young Southerner. Broder characterized the contest as an "uphill fight" for Bush, who played the Iraq card among other successes of his administration to try to overcome domestic woes that included a weak economy. Iraq leader Saddam Hussein obliged Bush with his attacks on his own citizens. The incumbent used the foreign events to his advantage, but the challenger scored points in his comeback to the president's gambit.

"Bush gave another hostage to fortune last week when he joined U.S. allies in ordering patrols of Iraqi air space to stop Iraq military attacks on Shiite Muslims in the southern part of that country," Broder reported in August. "Although Iraqi President Saddam Hussein chose not to challenge the air patrols, administration officials were warning by week's end that other steps may be necessary to protect the Shiites—an escalation that could carry more risks to U.S. lives."

This foreign affairs development helped Bush politically, Broder opined, as it "pushed Clinton out of the news and underlined the stature difference that Bush aides said had also been obvious when Bush and Clinton made back-to-back appearances Monday at the American Legion convention in Chicago." Still, Clinton played the military experience card deftly.

> Bush spoke there as a fellow veteran and commander in chief, taking the legionnaires into the Oval Office for a vivid description of the final moments of the Persian Gulf War. Clinton, who avoided military service during the Vietnam War, tried to bond with the vets by recalling his youthful experiences as a budding politician at American Legion boys State and Boys Nation gatherings, then made a political pitch by promising improved veterans' benefits.
>
> Clinton's defense of his Vietnam draft record took the news play away from Bush's speech, and many of the commentaries gave Clinton credit for raising the issue before a potentially hostile audience.[24]

As the campaign moved into late summer and early fall, Bush was conceding economic problems while differing with Clinton on how to fix them. Clinton, in a network television interview with NBC's Tom Brokaw, called for a "'jobs program,' which he would finance from defense savings and a cut in the costs—but not the benefits—of government medical programs."

Bush meanwhile, also interviewed by Brokaw, "said he would rely on tax cuts of the kind he urged last January to stimulate home-building and business expansion."[25]

Two days later, on September 9, Broder and Kent Jenkins Jr. reported the candidates "virtually in a dead heat" as Clinton borrowed a theme from his former Democratic rival, Tsongas, in promoting what the reporters termed a "pro-business" message of tax incentives and federal spending as part of an "overall 'investment strategy' he previously outlined . . . financed, aides said, by further reductions in the Pentagon budget."[26]

Tipping the scales in the virtual dead heat would be the candidacy of Perot, who claimed nearly 19 percent of the popular vote, though no electoral votes, tossing the win to Clinton much as the previous most popular third-party candidate, Theodore Roosevelt, had done to the benefit of Woodrow Wilson in 1912.

Just days after Clinton's election, Broder, ever the political journalistic animal, was busy laying out the future of the Republican Party.

"Within hours of the polls closing Tuesday, the two faces of the Republican future became clear," Broder wrote in an article published on November 8. "Senate Minority Leader Bob Dole, just reelected to a fifth term in Kansas, proclaimed himself the de facto leader of the Republican opposition inside the Beltway, adding that he would be happy to speak for the Ross Perot voters as well. And columnist Robert Novak, semi-official court chronicler of the non-loony right, declared Jack Kemp the 'clear Republican heir apparent' across the country."[27]

But before the next presidential election, which would see Dole rise to the top of the Republican ticket, the new Democratic president had some challenges awaiting him from other GOP faces—including a number of them in the Republican takeover of Congress in 1994, and in the rise of one Republican, Georgian Newt Gingrich, who led the Republican revolt in the House of Representatives.

Broder in the spring of 1994 was observing that while a Republican takeover of the House was unlikely, a number of Democratic retirements "combined with the normal off-year trend against the party in power and the continuing public hostility toward incumbents could jeopardize working control of the House by the predominantly pro-Clinton party leadership." A revival of a conservative coalition, he wrote, "could make the final two years of Clinton's term a lot more uncomfortable than anything he has seen so far."[28]

By that summer, thanks largely to the president's difficulties in enacting universal health care as proposed during his campaign for office, the administration's hold on Congress had become a struggle.

"The midterm elections in November are likely to bring more Republicans to both the House and the Senate, reducing the president's leverage and influence on any controversial issue, including reform of the health care system." That issue, the columnist wrote, "is the biggest single piece" of Clinton's "vision of the domestic policy change that he thinks is needed . . ."[29]

By September, the battle for Congress had become an epic political war, a metaphor that Broder evoked in his description of the political landscape, one that took in the personality of the Democratic president as its focus.

"To visualize the 1994 campaign, think of a battlefield. On one side is a Republican army moving forward in mass formation, flying banners proclaiming 'No More Clintonism. We're Reviving Reaganism.' On the other side, defensive Democrats are dug into their scattered, individual foxholes, saying, 'We'll fight for the home folks,' but secretly hoping that the advancing Republicans just pass them by."

Even more interesting than the number of seats involved in the looming Republican power grab, Broder wrote, were the strategies used by the two sides. "Republicans clearly want to run this as a national referendum on Bill Clinton and his policies. Democrats, just as obviously, hope to prove that [Democratic House Speaker] Tip O'Neill was right when he said that 'all politics is local.'"[30]

One month before the election, Broder in a front-page analysis summed up the phenomenon of the surging Republican trend as a Democratic dream turning into nightmare.

In the autumn of 1992, Bill Clinton was hailed as the savior of the Democratic Party, the man who had brought it back to the White House after 12 years in exile. He had reversed the Republican advantage among young voters and first-time voters. He had beaten George Bush and Ross Perot in the suburbs in every part of the country, while building Democratic turnouts in the minority communities and center cities. He and his running mate, Al Gore, had become symbols of the coming to power of a new generation of baby boomers, who might hold sway for decades. Their redefinition of what it meant to be a "New Democrat" had helped make the Democratic Party the vehicle most voters trusted to handle the economy, crime, welfare, the budget and a host of other issues on which the GOP had held sway.

"Today," Broder succinctly opined two paragraphs later, "those dreams seem like fantasies."[31]

The Republican victory that November was decisive. The GOP claimed its first majority in the Senate in 8 years, its first majority in the House in 40 years, and its first majority of state governors in 24 years. The Republicans also made significant gains in state offices and legislatures, "often regarded as the training camps for future congressional and gubernatorial candidates." The Republicans claimed not only their traditional turf of the Midwest, "but they may have put the finishing touches on the 30-year-old effort to make the South their new foundation." It was a Republican trend of groundswell proportions.

Broder cast the election in epic terms, writing that the victory, "as deep as it was wide, could be one of those rare events that reshapes the landscape of American politics. Digging through the returns yesterday, analysts in both parties and neutral observers found evidence that the GOP may be in a position to reclaim a dominant role in American government that it has not had since the 1920s."

The primary reasoning behind the voters' decision, he concluded, "was the voters' identification of Clinton and the Democratic Party with big government and higher taxes. Try as he might to convince voters that he represented a different kind of approach, the upper-bracket tax hike in his 1993 budget plan and the scope of his failed health reform convinced people that Clinton was not the 'New Democrat' he had sketched in his 1992 campaign speeches."[32]

In a year-end column, Broder laid out the task the Democrats and Clinton faced.

"As Ohio Gov. George Voinovich (R) remarked last week, the Republicans are ushering the country into a serious debate on two bedrock questions: What should government do and what level of government should do it? They have staked out their side of the argument. They want to end scores of federal programs or turn them back to the states. That is where they are going."[33]

The main-aisle usher in this new Republican theater was the Georgia representative and incoming Speaker of the House Gingrich, a politician Broder described in 1994 as "one of the most vexing politicians I've ever tried to figure out. His strengths—both intellectual and political—are so large and his weaknesses so glaring that they are difficult to reconcile. The good Gingrich is a man possessed by arresting, powerful ideas, the bad Gingrich a man possessed by demons he seemingly cannot control."[34]

The name Gingrich became a common one on Capitol Hill as the House speaker parlayed the Republican election victory into policy and power. Broder in a summer 1995 piece observed that Gingrich "has set the agenda and dominated the news far more than President Bill Clinton,"[35] and that fall, while chronicling voter discontent over political leaders of both parties, Broder noted that though voters "have a negative view of House Speaker Newt Gingrich (R-Ga.), they sense that the 'revolution' he is leading in Washington could bring at least some of the changes they want."[36]

That revolution, Broder wrote in a 1995 year-end analysis, was a movement that Gingrich "had been plotting even before he became a member of the House. . . . From the moment he arrived in 1979, Gingrich made it clear that his purpose was to overthrow what he always called 'the corrupt liberal welfare state.'"

By the 1994 Republican takeover of Congress, "the Gingrich machine was a juggernaut, encompassing a think tank, a political action committee, a communications network and virtual control of the leadership structure and campaign apparatus of House Republicans." Clinton's response to the juggernaut was a political ad-lib.

Meanwhile, down at the White House, Clinton was "triangulating" around, responding to cues from his once-banished but now restored political guru, Richard Morris. As Clinton sought to carve out a middle ground between the Gephardt liberals and the Gingrich revolutionaries, he zigged and zagged so often that his frantic maneuvers drew more attention than any of his specific policy stands. One moment he was defending traditional Democratic policy on affirmative action; the next, he was signing a defense bill that included billions of dollars beyond what he had said was sensible.

The bobbing and weaving came to center on the budget—with Clinton changing his position quarterly, monthly and, in the end, almost daily. The battle was still raging as Christmas neared, and the White House was making at least short-term political gains. But in the end, the Constitution virtually dictated that if there were to be a settlement, the president would have to make substantial concessions to the Republican Congress, which holds the power of the purse.[37]

Those concessions were by and large made to Gingrich, who had begun his tenure as House speaker by refusing to take a telephone call from the president during a talk-show appearance. Over the years, he jousted with the president, and compromised with him, on domestic policies primarily over issues that Republican House members had included in their election campaign Contract With America. The contract proposed limitations on government through reduced revenue from tax cuts, congressional term limits, and a constitutional amendment requiring a balanced budget. The political gamesmanship also included battles over the line-item veto and agreement on welfare to deal with the federal budget deficit. On that last issue, the president donned the hat of conciliation and of co-option—a ploy that critics within his party viewed as a sellout.

"The decision to move off his standpat budget and join the opposition-party majority on Capitol Hill in seeking to eliminate the deficit within a decade has left Clinton with a virtual rebellion among many congressional Democrats and traditional Democratic constituencies," Broder wrote in June 1995.

But administration defenders said Clinton feared being seen as "the guilty party if budget gridlock leads to the necessity of shutting down the government when current appropriations expire Oct. 1—the 'train wreck' that House Speaker Newt Gingrich (R-Ga.) has warned is imminent."[38]

Clinton employed the three Cs of politics—concession, conciliation, and compromise—to forge a centrist Democratic Party and to bring about achievements, some with the cooperation of Gingrich, that included a balanced budget (without a constitutional amendment), a tax reduction, a new telecommunications act, and welfare reform. But by March 1996, thanks to "two government shutdowns, the Republican Congress and the leader of the Revolution of 1994, Speaker Newt Gingrich (R-Ga.), are taking a shellacking in the polls."[39]

Indeed, as the Republican Revolution of Gingrich and his Republican allies wound down, replaced in 1996 by the "New America" with its families-first agenda,[40] Gingrich was heading toward political disgrace and to subsequent resignation over allegations of ethics violations.

The Contract With America had expired, along with the downfall of its leader, at the same time that the president was facing political difficulties over ethical questions of his own. Broder summarized the contrast of these two leaders in an October 2, 1996 column that highlighted their coming together in the end and in the wake of the government's recent failures. These shortcomings included "problems of a public school system that is failing for too many students, an urban underclass that turns to drugs and crime in the absence of jobs, and a health care system that squanders huge sums while leaving almost one-sixth of the people uninsured—all of these remain substantially unaddressed.

"But if you focus on what was done—rather than what was left undone," Broder continued, "a rather striking pattern appears. It is the story of two men who overreached, were brought down and then found ways to recover. Put differently, it is the story of two parties that set out to enact ideological agendas, were punished and then found their way back to the center of the political road.

"In the end," Broder added, "despite all the rhetoric and the recriminations, they have become more partners than antagonists. And that is why the past four years on Capitol Hill became something more than an exercise in futility."[41]

So, in Broder's view, it was all about the center; that was where political and policy achievements took place. Not the least of these achievements—or errors, in the minds of some, but a product of centrist and conciliatory politics nonetheless—was the enactment of the North American Free Trade Agreement (NAFTA). This pact, signed by the United States, Mexico, and Canada in December 1992, and awaiting approval by the U.S. Congress, provided for more open trade among the three nations. The NAFTA debate preceded the Republican takeover of Congress but was evidence early in the Clinton administration of his style of political tradeoff, in this case pitting those supporting protectionism favored largely by the trade unions against those who believed in *laissez-faire* trade operations devoid of governmental interference.

Clinton's campaign for NAFTA accompanied his "ambitious overhaul of the health care system . . . along with controversial legislation on crime, immigration, welfare reform and Vice President [Al] Gore's 'reinventing government' initiative," Broder and colleague Balz wrote in August 1993. The bipartisan political tradeoff pattern that marked the president's second term showed its roots in the NAFTA campaign, as Broder and Balz reported that Republicans appeared ready "to abandon their tough partisanship and become full partners of the president on NAFTA and active participants in what will undoubtedly be a long debate on health care."[42]

The Republicans weren't Clinton's problem when it came to NAFTA; his fellow Democrats were the roadblock. Likening the debate over NAFTA to the divisions that tore apart the Democratic Party in 1968 because of the Vietnam War, Broder wrote later that August:

> President Clinton's attempt to secure congressional approval of a free trade agreement with Mexico confronts the Democrats with the same kind of divisive issue

that wrecked them in 1968. On the surface, the emotions generated by the North American Free Trade Agreement with Mexico and Canada are mild compared with those that tore apart the Democratic National Convention in Chicago 25 years ago last week. But party insiders are belatedly recognizing that the potential damage could be as great.

The problem, Broder surmised, not only was fear that NAFTA would pose environmental problems but primarily that it would destroy American jobs. He wrote that the agreement created a "sense of betrayal. Listen to Lynn Williams, the head of the steelworkers, talk about millworkers whose bosses give them a choice of cutting their wages from $10.50 an hour to $4.50 or seeing their jobs moved to Mexico, and you can measure the anger and frustration that fuel the fight against NAFTA."

Nonetheless, Broder in the same column found a strong argument on behalf of the pact, writing that economists "can persuade disinterested observers like me that, on balance, the pact is likely over time to expand the economies of both Mexico and the United States. But their economic models do little to counter the powerful emotional appeals of those denouncing the White House policy."[43]

Unlike his failed effort over health care reform, Clinton succeeded in stitching together a bipartisan cloth of support for NAFTA, which Congress ratified in November 1993. The ratification prompted an appraisal from Broder that took note of the odd political bedfellows—Republican support for the Democratic president's initiative—behind the congressional action.

The columnist, in a November 19 piece assessing the ratification, noted the sense of betrayal felt by hard-line Democrats over an agreement that would at last partially redefine the party and its traditional constituencies.

"As they saw a Democratic president line up the votes to pass a free trade agreement envisioned and negotiated by his Republican predecessors Ronald Reagan and George Bush, civil rights leaders like Rep. John Lewis (D-Ga.) and union loyalists like Rep. David Bonier (D-Mich.) called on their fellow Democrats not to 'betray' those 'unfortunate' low-wage workers who they said would be 'losers' if NAFTA passed," Broder wrote of the opposition.

"These NAFTA opponents were dramatizing a decade-long struggle to determine whether the Democratic Party will speak for losers or winners in the rapidly changing American economy and society."

But political victory was more important to Clinton than was Democratic tradition. Clinton, Broder wrote, "does not want the Democrats to be the party of losers. He and his baby-boomer, high-tech partner, Vice President Gore, cast the NAFTA fight as a battle between 'hope and fear,' telling their party it should ally itself with economic change. By winning that fight, Clinton may have taken a major step toward proving himself a 'different kind of Democrat.' But his party did not follow him."

The columnist concluded that Clinton, in the long run, "cannot govern with votes from Bush's constituents, and he has not converted his party from what it was. The Democratic Party may move to his position by 1996—or it may welcome someone who will challenge Clinton and his views. Either way, this NAFTA vote will be seen as a landmark in the Democrats' struggle to choose whether to be the party of losers or of winners."[44]

By the 1996 presidential campaign, the question of whether it would be Dole or Kemp who carried the new Republican torch into the next century had been answered: it would be both, as Dole claimed the GOP nomination and brought Kemp into the fold as his running mate in the last major test of Clinton's political career. But the outcome of the campaign would be "relatively unimportant," Broder suggested in an August 11, 1996, column, because the possibility of a third-party candidacy in 2000 loomed. Nonetheless, he noted, "it is customary for politicians to proclaim each presidential election the most important in decades if not in history. Both Clinton and Dole are applying that superlative to their contest."

"It is easy to argue the uniqueness—and therefore the importance—of the November choice," the columnist continued. "If President Clinton wins, as current polls suggest, he would be the first Democrat elected to a second term since Franklin D. Roosevelt 60 years ago. And it was Roosevelt's second election, even more than the first, that cemented the New Deal coalition that was dominant for so long."[45]

The second election of Bill Clinton along with the retention of a Republican majority in Congress did not so much cement Clinton's brand of New Democrat as it produced evidence of a torn electorate and nation, as summarized by Broder in a postelection column.

"The most expensive campaign in American history has ended with the American voters hedging their bets," he wrote. "By reelecting President Clinton while giving Republicans a dominant voice on Capitol Hill, the electorate said in effect yesterday it was not willing to entrust the transition to a new century exclusively to either party."

The voters selected Clinton, he wrote, "with their fingers crossed and reducing the risks by giving Republicans a renewed lease on their power base in Congress." To underscore the unique nature of the voters' decision, he pointed out that "Clinton is also the first Democrat in history to be elected with an opposition Congress."

Based on the exit polls of voters, the ingredients that brought about this division of power, Broder suggested, included a healthy economy—a factor that propelled Clinton to a second term but that also "served to cushion congressional Republicans—including the 70 GOP freshmen on the ballot yesterday.

"Even before the final returns," Broder summarized, "several observers said the election would push both parties toward centrist policies—and a pattern of conciliation and compromise."

"For now," he concluded, "the voters are watching both sides warily—and telling them to shape up."[46]

The looming ethics scandals that would topple Gingrich from power and lead to the House's impeachment of Clinton stemming primarily from his sexual dalliance with White House intern Monica Lewinsky would shove many of the normal political dealings to the inside pages for much of Clinton's second term. But he and Congress had, as Broder suggested, set the nation on a centrist course, trending politically toward polarization entering the new century and millennium.

Almost as a sidebar to the dynamic political battles and compromises of the decade was the ominous rise of terrorism on U.S. soil from within and without—the 1993 federal government raid and ensuing siege at the Branch Davidian compound in Waco, Texas, that left an estimated 80 dead; the terrorist bombing of the World Trade Center that same year that killed six people and injured more than a thousand; the bombing of the federal building in Oklahoma City two years later that killed 168 and injured more than 800.

Writing about Senate hearings following the Oklahoma City bombing, Broder chronicled sentiments and worries, including poor intelligence gathering and government snooping on citizens, which today seem eerily familiar and prescient.

"At the Senate hearings following the Oklahoma City bombing, [FBI Director Louis] Freeh said two things that sound contradictory. First, he said that 'for two decades, the FBI has been at an extreme disadvantage with regard to domestic groups which advocate violence. We have no intelligence or background information on them until their violent talk becomes deadly action.'

"But he also said that his agency did not need any broader authority than it now has in order to do the required job. It's all a matter of interpreting the existing law and regulations."

In the wake of the bombing, Broder continued:

> President Clinton and members of both parties in Congress are pressing for broader anti-terrorism authority. Some of the measures—like setting up a domestic counter-terrorism center to coordinate the federal response to this threat and enlisting the armed forces' expertise on nuclear, chemical and biological weapons—clearly make sense.
>
> When it comes to surveillance of domestic political groups, however, it would be wise to figure out how much authority the Justice Department already has before giving it more. . . .
>
> If current guidelines, properly interpreted, are adequate to the situation, as Freeh, [Deputy Attorney General Jamie] Gorelick and [Attorney General Janet] Reno all say, then Congress should not enlarge the FBI's surveillance authority. The political abuse of wiretaps and other investigative tools is too recent and too flagrant to court that danger again. Oklahoma City should not usher in a return to Big Brother government.[47]

But despite the nascent terrorist threat, the political scandals and battles, the failed universal health care movement, and foreign entanglements, Broder said the nation ended the decade better off than it had been 10 years before.

"We had a period of sustained, non-inflationary growth, we had made some headway on some of the social programs, not dramatic, but I think that most of the trends were moving in a positive direction," including a decreased number of abortions and improvements in the public schools, he recalled. "We were beginning to make some headway."

The nation had entered the decade, he said, with a sense of relief over the end of the Cold War.

"There was beginning to be some urgency about attending to those matters, that was the underlying theme of the 1992 campaign—that we needed to get on with it. But I think the country was in a hopeful frame of mind at that point." This, he said, was despite the "growth of a new threat in the form of Islamic radicalism that would challenge the nation."

The Bush presidency, Broder recalled, was marked primarily by the end of the Cold War and collapse of the Soviet Union, "the unification of Germany, all of those things where we could have, by misplaying or overplaying our hand, made it much more difficult for Central and Eastern Europe to make the transition. I think he did it exactly right, leaving the room to make that adjustment without (Russia) feeling that they were having their nose rubbed in it by a United States coalition."

Recalling his trip to Moscow during that period, Broder said he was "astonished to meet people, small-d democrats there, who would tell you stories about how small groups of them had been meeting all during that dark period when Communists were running the most brutal kind of police state. But they never entirely suppressed that movement for freedom and democracy within the old Soviet Union, and I have to think that there is a kind of latent, unquenchable thirst among people for political freedom and freedom of expression that, when the regime began to show some cracks, rose to the surface."

Did the breaking of his read-my-lips pledge not to raise taxes bring about the Bush loss in the 1992 election to Clinton?

"It was partly that," Broder said. "And it was partly a sense that he was, in effect, I always thought, a victim of his own success. When the Cold War ended, people began to refocus on some of the problems here at home and decided, I think correctly, that this was not a president who was very engaged" in domestic issues. "He didn't care much about the educational system in the country or the health care system in the country, so when the public agenda shifted, his agenda did not shift with it. And as a result people decided 'well, we don't know a hell of a lot about this young guy from Arkansas, but he seems interested in the same things that we're interested in, so we'll give him a shot at it.'

"Clinton's strengths were stunning," the columnist continued. "I mean, he is very smart and has an extraordinarily retentive mind, once he learns something he keeps it always, he grasps the connections probably better than anybody else that I know in the public policy world, sees how this relates to that, and that relates to a third thing. He is extraordinarily skillful at human relations, he can give people a sense that he is terribly interested in them as individuals and in what they're thinking. And he is a very smart politician. He has all of those talents, and he had displayed them so early in life that people were always there so that when he misstepped, they were ready to pick him up, dust him off, and say 'keep going kid, we've got a lot of confidence in you.'"

Did this young guy from Arkansas betray the Democrats to achieve political success? Was Clinton a Republican in Democratic clothing?

No, said Broder, in retrospect. Clinton was a Democrat.

"He fundamentally believes in using government to intervene to achieve certain social policy goals, and that's a very different mindset from what most Republican thought. He adopted a markedly conservative fiscal policy, but other than that I don't think there was much Republican in his approach to public policy."

Broder singled out Clinton's treasury secretary for the fiscal and political policies that helped bring about a balanced budget and then a budget surplus by the end of the Clinton presidency.

"I think what Clinton did—and I give Bob Rubin a good deal of credit for moving him in this direction, because it was not a posture that he had taken during the campaign—was essentially recognizing that to make the kind of long-term investments that we needed to make in education and health care in particular in this country, we had to somehow start paying the bills of the government. And he opted for a degree of fiscal discipline that had not been seen in recent years that I think has had all kinds of beneficial effects."

Lost in the political fallout of the decade was the much-ballyhooed peace dividend many had predicted following the end of the Cold War.

"I think the so-called peace dividend was very hard to find in reality," Broder recalled. "We did reduce our military budgets for a few years, but not significantly, and this was more important for a variety of reasons, some of which had to do with just pure accident, but failing to make use of that sort of respite to deal with some of the serious structural problems. I'm thinking of things like Social Security and Medicare, which could have been addressed in the '90s and were not because of Monica Lewinsky and a whole lot of other reasons."

Near the end of the Clinton presidency, Broder said, the voters were somewhat satisfied with the status quo, not looking for big change.

"The 2000 election, I think, many people felt it really didn't make that much of a difference who won. You had one fellow who was a little bit more conservative to the center and another a little bit more liberal than the center, but they were both pretty competent, and neither of them was going to shake things up very much, and they weren't looking for things to be shaken up at that point."

As for the Clinton legacy, Broder said, "his economic record is there to stand. That's clear, what he did. There were several pieces of social legislation that stand, the Family and Medical Leave Act, for example. In international affairs, I don't think his mark is large one way or the other, and in some respects he left the Democratic Party weaker than it was when he was first elected. So politically, it was a very mixed legacy, I would say."

* * * *

The Clinton presidency just angered and frustrated and caused resentment in many Republicans who felt that the White House was theirs, and it had been taken by someone who didn't deserve to be in the White House. That was how it came across as a reporter to me. You talk to Republicans then, they weren't just disappointed in the '92 loss, they were furious, and they were resentful, and they didn't feel that Clinton deserved to be president. They felt they were going to do everything they could to win back the presidency. They tried in '96, and it didn't work, but it did in 2000.

—Judy Woodruff

Judy Woodruff. © Don Perdue. Used by permission.

Christmas was a week away on that December day in 1998. The U.S. military was half a world away, engaged in battle in Iraq. Outside in Washington, D.C., thunder rumbled and lightning flared as, inside, members of the House of Representatives were preparing to take a historic vote of impeachment against President Bill Clinton. Hours earlier, U.S. Representative Bob Livingston, a Louisiana Republican scheduled to become speaker of the House following the resignation of Georgia Republican Newt Gingrich over alleged ethics violations, had announced he would not take the speakership and would resign from office in about half a year.

Livingston had become caught up in his own ethics scandal, involving an extramarital tryst. It was the same sort of allegation, of conducting an affair with White House intern Monica Lewinsky and then lying to a federal grand jury about it, that had brought Clinton to the brink of losing his presidency. Republican House members were now urging the president to follow the example of Livingston and resign his office rather than force the country to undergo grueling, divisive impeachment proceedings.

Cable News Network coanchors Judy Woodruff, Frank Sesno, and Bernard Shaw were reporting the proceedings live.

"Let us very quickly bring you up to date on what has happened on this momentous day," Sesno told the viewers. "Bob Livingston, who is going to be the next speaker of the House, says he will not take that position and will quit the House altogether in about six months following revelations and admissions of extramarital affairs. In so doing, he's called on the—he's called on the president to resign.[48]

"I'm going to be handing things over to my colleagues Judy Woodruff and Bernard Shaw," Sesno continued. "As that happens, here is [Democratic Michigan Representative] David Bonior."

The camera switched to the House floor, where Bonior was making an appeal against the impeachment proceedings.

"The politics of personal smear is degrading the dignity of public office and we must not let it continue," Bonior argued. "We must put an end to it. And the only way we will stop this vicious cycle is if we stand up and refuse to give in to it, whether it's Bill Clinton or Bob Livingston.

"To the speaker-elect, I would say: This is your decision, the decision of your family, the decision of your conference. But for my own part, I would say you should not allow a campaign of cynicism and smear to force you to resign from office, and you should not have called on the president to resign."

Bonior cited the will of the American voters, who had reelected Clinton to office two years before; he cited popular support of the Clinton administration's policies; and he invoked history and precedent.

"A vote for impeachment today will only feed the corrosive and destructive politics of personal attack. It will prolong and escalate this whole sorry episode," he said. "Mr. Speaker, in this building are the marble halls where Daniel Webster and Henry Clay and Abraham Lincoln debated the fate of the union. Have we sunk so low that in these same halls we would allow the likes of Ken Starr and Monica Lewinsky and Linda Tripp to ignite the constitutional crisis of our age? Does such a spectacle really strengthen our nation? Does it dignify our democracy? Does it honor our Constitution?"

He continued: "Six days before Christmas, our troops are in battle, and a lame-duck Congress is rushing to overthrow the commander-in-chief. This is surreal. The scenario reads like the plot of a cheap paperback novel, not the deliberations of history's greatest democracy."[49]

Following Bonior's speech, Shaw confirmed for viewers that CNN reporter Christiane Amanpour had "confirmed in her reporting just a short while ago that another air strike indeed is under way, and that is confirmed by the Pentagon."[50]

The president had ordered the military operation against Iraq four days before, announcing it to the American people in a live broadcast. The president's words were eerily similar to the language that would be used by his successor five years later to justify invading Iraq.

"Saddam Hussein must not be allowed to threaten his neighbors or the world with nuclear arms, poison gas or biological weapons," the president said in announcing Operation Desert Fox, a series of attacks to be carried out over several days by U.S. and British forces.

The CNN report continued: "'Their mission is to attack Iraq's nuclear, chemical and biological weapons programs and its military capacity to threaten its neighbors,' said Clinton.

"Clinton also stated that, while other countries also had weapons of mass destruction, Hussein is in a different category because he has used such weapons against his own people and against his neighbors," the report summarized.

Arguing that Iraq had failed to cooperate with United Nations weapons inspectors, despite previous air attacks against Iraq ordered by the president, Clinton cited an intelligence report by Richard Butler, head of the U.N.'s special commission in charge of finding and destroying Iraqi weapons, which he termed "stark, sobering."

The president then called for a regime change in Iraq to end Saddam's threat to his own people and to world security.

"'The best way to end that threat once and for all is with a new Iraqi government—a government ready to live in peace with its neighbors, a government that respects the rights of its people,' Clinton said."[51]

As the bombs thundered in Iraq, the political tempest continued in Washington beneath the clouds of an actual storm.

"As if there weren't enough political thunder in Washington, that thunder you may be hearing in the background as [correspondent] Bob Franken speaks outside the Capitol is actually the weather," Woodruff told her viewers. "It is real thunder and lightning happening over the capital city in the event you're wondering."

Woodruff then turned to Senior White House Correspondent Wolf Blitzer.

"Judy, the thunder and lightning has not yet reached over here at the White House, but presumably if it's over there, it'll get over here fairly soon. The mood here at the White House is obviously one of deep depression. A lot of officials are very cognizant of the history of this very day: the almost certainty that the president of the United States will be impeached."[52]

The gravity of the debate was no light matter. Clinton would be the first U.S. president to be impeached since Andrew Johnson 130 years before; he would be the second U.S. president and the first elected U.S. president to be impeached. Johnson had assumed office following the assassination of Abraham Lincoln.

House Democrats, led by Richard Gephardt of Missouri, tried to head off the impeachment vote, seeking censure instead. Gephardt appealed for an end to the political bickering that had marked much of the Clinton presidency since its beginning, when the young president from Hope, Arkansas, with help from populist third-party candidate H. Ross Perot, wrested the presidency from George H. W. Bush.

"Mr. Speaker and members of the House," Gephardt, the House minority leader, intoned, "I stood on this floor yesterday and implored all of us to say that the politics of slash-and-burn must end. I implored all of you that we must turn away from the politics of personal destruction and return to the politics of values."

Gephardt tried to reverse the Republicans' use of Livingston as an example that Clinton should emulate in resignation; instead, he urged that Livingston reconsider.

"It is with that same passion that I say to all of you today that the gentleman from Louisiana, Bob Livingston, is a worthy and good and honorable man," Gephardt said, evoking applause from the House floor. "I believe his decision to retire is a terrible capitulation to the negative forces that are consuming our political system and our country." More applause. "And I pray with all of my heart that he will reconsider this decision." Again, applause, followed by Gephardt's claim that sin is shared by all men. "Our Founding Fathers created a system of government of men, not of angels. No one standing in this House today can pass a puritanical test of purity that some are demanding that our elected leaders take." Applause. "If we demand that mere mortals live up to this standard, we will see our seats of government lay empty, and we will see the best, most able people unfairly cast out of public service. We need to stop destroying imperfect people at the altar of an unobtainable morality."[53]

Representative Charles Canady, Republican of Florida, responded for his party and, as it turned out, for a few, minority, Democrats who also would vote for impeachment. The case against the president, Canady argued, was not based on his morality so much as on his crimes; and the proposal for censure did not pass constitutional muster.

"We do not sit in judgment on the president for his frailties, or his human failings," the representative said. "That is not our responsibility. But today in this house we do sit in judgment on the president of the United States for his crimes.

"And it is because of his crimes that this motion [for censure] must be rejected. It must be rejected first, because the proposal for censure is outside the framework established by our Constitution. As the chairman of the Judiciary Committee so eloquently explained, the Constitution establishes a single method for this Congress to sit in judgment on the misconduct of the president."

And that method, Canady argued, is impeachment.

"We must reject censure because the president's defense rests squarely, we must sadly conclude, on the denial of the obvious and the assertion of pure nonsense," Canady said. "To this day, the president's defense rests on the claim that he told the truth in his deposition when he denied that he had any specific recollection of ever being alone with Ms. Lewinsky. Who in this House believes that?"

He continued: "Who in this country believes that? To this day, the president's defense rests on the argument that Ms. Lewinsky had sex with him, but he did not have sex with her. How sad it is that the president of the United States is reduced to making such nonsensical arguments. What rational person can accept such a defense? Such a defense is an insult to our intelligence, an insult to judgment and to common sense."[54]

On and on the representatives argued for forgiveness and against judging their fellow man, or for punishment deserved for crimes committed. The Democrats' push for censure failed and the vote to impeach was put to the floor, prompting a massive walkout by the Democrats—a political theater of protest that did not change the outcome: the House voted for impeachment, as reported by coanchor Shaw.

"The vote stands at 291 for, and on the no side, five Republicans sided with the Democrats. Looking closer at the Democratic column 199 Democrats voting against impeachment, of course, but five Democrats crossing over to the Republicans."

"There it is," announced Woodruff when the impeachment vote passed. "President William Jefferson Clinton is now the second president in the history of the United States to be impeached by the House of Representatives. The members having voted on the first article declaring that the president committed perjury before a grand jury."[55]

"As a reporter, I thought it was a remarkable moment in American history," Woodruff would remember nearly eight years later. "Of course, it went to the Senate and he wasn't convicted." The impeachment was pure politics, she recalled, "clearly driven by partisan considerations." It quickly became clear, she said, that the Republicans "were reaching and reaching for impeachment, that they had overreached and the American people, through the worst of Bill Clinton's darkest times, after the Lewinsky scandal his approval rating, if I'm not mistaken, went below 40 percent. Bill Clinton had this reservoir of support among the American people, many Democrats, and many Republicans, who felt that the Republicans were coming after him on the wrong thing, that it was something he didn't deserve to be drummed out of office for."

The live broadcast represented television at its journalistic strongest: cameras on scene to record the speeches followed by an historic vote, reported by a team of broadcast reporters that included a veteran journalist who had already covered the White House for a national broadcast outlet.

Woodruff had attained the coanchor chair at CNN that day a woman born 52 years earlier in the heart of Republican country, Tulsa, Oklahoma, where her father was stationed in the Army at Fort Sill. He had joined the service as a teenager to "escape from an almost certain career in the local cotton mill" in North Carolina. In Oklahoma, William Henry Woodruff met Anna Lee Payne, who was working as an elevator operator to help support three siblings following the death of their father.[56]

"I was an Army brat," Woodruff said, explaining that she lived in Tulsa for only the first five years of her life before moving with her mother and father to Germany, than back to various bases in the United States, then to Taiwan for a couple of years. There, she attended a Navy school for children of military families. She also lived with her grandparents for a time and finished high school at the Academy of Richmond County in Augusta, Georgia.

Labor unrest was the big news in the *Tulsa Daily World* the day Woodruff was born, November 20, 1946. An Associated Press dispatch on the front page that day reported that the U.S. Army was prepared to intervene in a coal mining dispute.

United Mine Workers leader John L. Lewis maintained an "impenetrable silence on a federal court order designed to head off a full-scale bituminous strike," the story reported. "Lewis, United Mine Workers chief, gave no slightest hint of his attitude toward the order, under which he risks jail unless he cancels his notice that his contract with the government is terminated Wednesday night."

Figures provided by the government's Solid Fuels Administration revealed that 288 mines operated by the government had been idled, involving 89,000 workers.

"The miners, to whom the words 'no contract' are traditionally a signal to fling down their tools, were jumping the gun," the story reported, adding that the day's loss of production had been estimated at 468,707 tons.

"Even should he promptly withdraw his notice to the government that his working contract with it is terminated tomorrow, as the court directed him to do" the dispatch reported of Lewis, "much coal production is sure to have been lost. Government officials talked of possible electricity 'brown outs.'"[57]

Meanwhile, another strike, in the housing industry, had been averted, as the newspaper revealed in a neighboring front-page report that the National Apartment Owners Association had endorsed a recommendation that landlords would be allowed to increase rents by 15 percent above established rent ceilings.

A Texas delegation of landlords had been urging a strike "to withhold rental units vacated by tenants from the market until OPA controls are removed," the story reported. "The plan would not have involved eviction of tenants."

An association spokesman said the association's resolution committee "was faced with a strong demand for a resolution asking immediate decontrol of rent ceilings, but it was decided instead to ask for the 15 per cent increase, similar to the advisory committee's recommendation, because it was believed it would ease the housing situation to the point where controls would not be needed."[58]

Government controls and rent ceilings also had local political repercussions, as Tulsa Mayor Lee Price's emergency housing committee "attacked the housing shortage Tuesday in a verbal bombardment at rent ceilings, construction, material shortages and government controls and when the conference came to an end, the housing situation was just as acute as ever."

The mayor, though, "said he felt the meeting had accomplished one definite objective as everyone had aired opinions, most of them constructive."[59]

Regionally and locally, though, the postwar economy was booming, thanks to the oil industry and real estate sales. The *World* reported on Page 1 that preliminary crude oil price gains of the previous week had become industry-wide.

"The 10-cent-a-barrel advance posted for East Texas field on Nov. 15, was followed by a general price raise for all wells in Oklahoma, Kansas and the panhandle field," the newspaper reported.[60]

And in Tulsa, property deals totaling nearly half-a-million dollars primed the local economy.

"Real estate transactions in Tulsa struck a rapid pace for the fall season Tuesday with sales aggregating nearly $500,000 as three business properties changed hands," the newspaper reported.

"Largest single negotiation was the sale of Engineering Laboratories, Inc., property at 602–24 E. 4th St., to a New York investor at a price in excess of $300,000. . . . The Scott-Rice Co., 617 S. Main St., announced purchase of a two-story building at 610–12 S. Main St., for a consideration in excess of $150,000, and H.R. Boyd, former hotel operator, purchased the Elgin hotel, a two-story brick structure at the northwest corner of E. 3rd St., and Elgin Ave., for $35,000."[61]

Economic news also dominated the inside pages, as the Associated Press reported that school teachers in Warren County, Tennessee, had gone on strike "to enforce their demands for bigger salaries to cover the cost of living,"[62] and in Washington, the chairman of the House Ways and Means Committee, North Carolina Democrat Robert Doughton, had came out against a tax decrease "until the federal budget is balanced and some payment is made on the public debt."

"The veteran legislator made this statement to newsmen who asked him to comment on a Republican proposal to cut individual income taxes by 20 percent in 1947, and to reduce excise levies sharply beginning next July.

"Representative [Harold] Knutson (Rep., Minn.), who succeeds Doughton as Ways and Means chairman, has set tax reduction as the first committee business when the new congress convenes."[63]

Roosevelt-era government work projects also gained headlines, as the local U.S. engineer announced to the Tulsa community that construction of a planned $57 million flood control project calling for five dams on the Arkansas River "will continue without any contract cancellation or violation of agreements with contractors."[64]

Early holiday season movie-goers had a choice of fare that included John Ford's "new thrill epic" *My Darling Clementine* at the Orpheum; a double-feature, James Cagney and Sylvia Sidney starring in *Blood On The Sun,* with Robert Stanton and Lynn Merrick in *Blonde From Brooklyn,* all for 25 cents at the Gem; or Robert Benchley starring in *Snafu* at the Will Rogers.

For Tulsans' dining and dancing pleasure, Tommy Flynn and his orchestra were appearing from six o'clock to midnight in the After 5 Room at the Hotel Tulsa. Those seeking a livelier night out could take in Tolly Weeden and the Night Hawks at the Club Flamingo; while the Orchid Club offered dancing until 2 A.M. for no cover charge for dinner guests.[65]

To help set the mood in those Tulsa nightclubs, large text just below the Listerine ad promised flavor that was "Clean," "Fresh," and "Pure"; and another ad offered "America's FINEST Cigarette!" Phillip Morris. The tobacco company included this added inducement to try its product: "No other cigarette can make this statement! Of all the leading cigarettes, Phillip Morris is the *only* cigarette with an *exclusive difference* in manufacture—recognized by eminent medical authorities *as being to the advantage of those who smoke!*"[66]

Ten pounds of red potatoes were selling for 49 cents and a half pound of pea salad for 19 cents at Wolferman's;[67] and Santa Fe Trailways appealed to economic-minded travelers with trips to Dallas for $5.25, to Muskogee for $1.05, or to a cooling dip at Hot Springs for $5.55.[68]

Woodruff didn't have much idea where she wanted to go or what she wanted to do with her life growing up in the postwar years.

"I am not one of those people who started out early in life knowing exactly what I wanted to be," she wrote in her autobiography.

> Instead, I wanted to be everything: all-American girl, straight-A student, class president, and college thespian, career woman and wife and mother. Growing up as an only child until I was eight and being the center of my parents' attention provided me with a healthy dose of self-confidence. There was never any doubt that I would go to college, even though no one else in my family had. I grew up believing that people can accomplish whatever they want, if they set their minds to it."[69]

Such was the mood of the 1950s, despite the Cold War: that the nation was a land of opportunity, and of freedom. That was what the allies had fought for in World War II. Indeed, Woodruff did become an all-American girl, winning a beauty pageant when she was crowned Young Miss Augusta at the age of 17; and she did go on to college, attending Duke, where she earned a degree in political science.

Entering her last year of college, she was not sure about a career. She had worked during summers as an intern for her home district congressman, Democratic Representative Robert Stephens, an experience that she wrote was "revelatory—my first glimpse of a world filled with exciting, interesting people whose ambitions seemed to have more to do with making their mark than with merely making a living."[70]

But the experience also presented obstacles. Other women she met on the Hill in Washington, D.C., were discouraging about opportunities for women there, she said, "and basically sent me this loud message: 'You don't want to come back to Washington right after college; even with a graduate degree women are not being given great opportunities.' And so I went back to Duke my senior year sort of shaken by that message, and I thought, 'What am I going to do?' I happened to be taking a class in mass communication. I had taken another course like that, the media and something, but in any event I got the idea that maybe I could cover politics, and then that way get back to working in government and politics."

Journalism, she wrote, "was a field that attracted some of the best and the brightest in Washington. More important, journalism seemed to offer an opportunity to touch the lives of others, and, being an idealist, I wanted to 'do good.'"

But she had never worked for a newspaper, not even in high school. So she considered television, a field that she thought offered

> better opportunities for an aspiring young reporter than did newspapers, particularly for one who hadn't been trained as a writer. Even the most casual viewer during the sixties could see that TV was a news medium that was growing in size as well as influence. It was television to which the country turned for the stories of political assassinations, civil rights marches, urban riots, student demonstrations, and the battlefield of the Vietnam War. Television news was at the center of these explosive, turbulent times.[71]

She wrote to three television news directors in Atlanta, she recalled nearly four decades later, "and said I'll do anything to get my foot in the door, I'll clean the film, I'll answer the phone, and interviewed essentially for a position as an assistant or a secretary. I was hired by the ABC affiliate news director to be a secretary for the newsroom."

She interviewed with Bill Conover of WQXI-TV, she wrote, and was hired after 10 minutes.

"'Besides,' he added, grinning, 'How could I turn down somebody with legs like yours?'"

"As it turned out, good legs were the best qualifications for the job, since I spent most of my day running for coffee and for the telephone."[72]

"Two weeks after graduation," she would recall, "I went to work answering the phone, writing letters for him, cleaning the film, organizing the news room, and just proceeded to fall in love with journalism in that little stand of time. I fell in love with it, kept bugging the news director to let me go out on a story and his answer was 'we already have a woman reporter.' So I found out very quickly that whatever I'd heard about Washington politics, the same thing was true everywhere; it was the 1960s, end of the '60s."

After the departure of her news director, her new boss urged her to audition for weekend weather girl. "I said I was not interested, I wanted to do serious news, I had a political science degree from Duke, and he said, 'look if you ever want to get on the air you're going to have to get your feet in it, get some experience, you're going to have to do something or nobody's going to hire you.'"

He was right. She took the weather girl job, and the local CBS affiliate hired her "after two years of being the secretary and six months of being the Sunday night weather girl. So in other words, two years out of college, I was hired by the CBS affiliate news director to cover the Georgia state legislature. I had no training in legislative experience, but they put me to work with a cameraman who was a very smart guy, and he introduced me to the chairman of the House Appropriations Committee and people like that, and I quickly learned how to do it, thanks to a lot of drive and determination."

So in 1970, the all-American Duke political science graduate and former beauty queen became a broadcast reporter. She entered the field during a period of turbulent change in the nation's society, culture, and politics, of widespread protests against the Vietnam War and on behalf of civil rights, of altering sexual mores, and of emerging feminism, of which she and her career were a part. Indeed, 1970 was the year that Germaine Greer published *The Female Eunoch,* a book-length argument for women's independence, urging women to "take responsibility for their lives rather than blaming men"; and the state of New York enacted legislation allowing abortion on demand, while the state Supreme Court in California struck down a state law prohibiting abortion. And the Gay

Liberation Front later that year would stage its first public demonstration in Britain.[73]

The U.S. Supreme Court in January 1970, set a February 1 deadline for six southern states—Alabama, Florida, Georgia, Louisiana, Mississippi, and Tennessee—to desegregate their public schools. Five months later in Ohio, four Kent State University students died after National Guardsmen opened fire during an antiwar demonstration, one of several such demonstrations at universities throughout the nation to protest U.S. military intervention in Cambodia; also, in May city and state police shot at demonstrators at Jackson State College in Mississippi; two students died. Anti-Vietnam War rallies drew hundreds of thousands of protestors that same month in numerous U.S. cities, including 100,000 participants at an event in Washington, D.C. In Manhattan, construction workers attacked demonstrators, leading to violence on Wall Street. President Richard Nixon the previous month had announced the withdrawal of 150,000 troops from Vietnam as representatives of his administration and the Soviet Union began a second set of Strategic Arms Limitation Talks in Vienna. In July, thousands turned out in a pro-war demonstration for Honor America Day. In August, four people died during a courthouse jail break in San Raphael, California, and two months later militant dissident Angela Davis was arrested in New York in connection with that incident. In December the president announced an end to the use of chemical defoliants in the Vietnam War.

The war and its protests brought other activity in the legal realm. In February, the U.S. Army promised to stop surveillance of political activists and anti-war protestors, while seven of eight political activists accused of inciting violence at the 1968 Democratic National convention in Chicago were acquitted of conspiracy charges; but five were convicted of a charge of crossing a state line intending to incite riot and were given five years in jail. The U.S. Supreme Court in June allowed conscientious objectors to base their status on moral grounds as well as religious; two months later, the FBI captured escaped convict Reverend Daniel J. Berrigan, a Jesuit priest convicted of destroying draft records in 1968. In November, FBI Director J. Edgar Hoover would tell Congress that Berrigan and his brother, Philip, also a Jesuit priest, were suspected of plotting to kidnap National Security Adviser Henry Kissinger and to bomb federal buildings in Washington, D.C. That same month, Lieutenant William L. Calley went on trial in Georgia for his involvement in the March 16, 1968, My Lai massacre in which hundreds of Vietnamese civilians were shot by U.S. troops overseen by him. Despite the revelation of secret peace talks in Paris between Kissinger and Le Duc Tho of North Vietnam, the year ended with no progress being reported on peace talks to end the war.

The year saw continued fighting in the Mideast, including Israeli and Syrian troops battling in the Golan Heights, civil war involving Palestinians in Jordan, and an Israeli air raid on factories near Cairo, killing

70 civilians. Also, the terrorism bogeyman arose: Palestinian militants hijacked four aircraft in just one month, September; and in Canada, Quebec separatists in October kidnapped British trade commissioner Jasper Cross and labor minister Pierre Laporte, whose body was found later. In 1970, the *New York Times* index listed the word "terrorism" for the first time.

The U.S. Environmental Protection Agency was established in December, the same month that saw President Nixon sign the Clean Air Act, requiring domestic carmakers to cut emissions of nitrogen dioxide, carbon monoxide and hydrocarbons by 90 percent by the mid-1970s.

The antiwar film *M*A*S*H* won the Cannes Film Festival's Palme d'Or, and Mike Nichols' war farce *Catch 22* was released in the United States. Jack Nicholson starred in the new film *Five Easy Pieces,* and Michael Wadleigh's documentary based on the 1969 Woodstock concert was released in the United States. John Schlesinger won the best director academy award for his dark study of human sexuality, *Midnight Cowboy.* Gwendolyn Brooks published her collection of poetry, *Family Pictures,* while Maya Angelou published volume I of her autobiographical *I Know Why the Caged Bird Sings.* Erich Segal and Richard Bach had literary hits with *Love Story* and *Jonathan Livingston Seagull.* Saul Bellow published *Mr. Sammler's Planet,* which would earn him the National Book Award.

This was the state of the national culture as Woodruff began her career covering state news for the local Atlanta CBS affiliate in an era that saw advertising playing an ever-increasing role of dominance in television journalism, helping to set the agenda for the nation's media. The name of this particular media game had by 1970 clearly become ratings.

"By the late 1960s and early 1970s," she wrote in her autobiography,

> local television news had become an asset rather than a liability for many stations. What pushed the local evening newscast into the asset column of the ledger was the crucial role it played in building up evening audiences early, which surveys had shown was the key to assembling blocs of viewers for prime time, when advertising rates were highest.
>
> At the forefront of this turnaround stood the market researchers and the "show doctors." The marketing people told station managers the size of their audience (their "audience ratings") and who their viewers were in terms of such demographics as age, sex, race, education, and income level. This was valuable information with which to approach advertisers, if your station was lucky enough to have the highest ratings among the most coveted purchasing bloc, the eighteen to forty-nine age group. And if your station wasn't number one, you went out and hired a television news consultant, or show doctor, to tell you how to package your newscast to attract a greater share of that prized group. [74]

By the time Woodruff sat on the CNN anchor desk covering the President Clinton House impeachment vote, she had jumped from that local Atlanta affiliate to NBC, which transferred her to the White House beat during the Carter presidency and the early Reagan years, then to public broadcasting as the first Washington correspondent of the MacNeil/ Lehrer NewsHour, followed by a move to the cable CNN network in 1993. In that time, she experienced first-hand the changing dynamics of the American television industry in its evolution from domination by the big-three networks of CBS, NBC, and ABC, to the fringe but valuable programming alternative of public television, to the expansion of television into cable and its many and varied niche viewing offerings. It was a transformation of production, ownership, and oversight of media companies that would be accelerated, to the detriment or benefit of the nation and its media, depending on the economic and political interpretation, by the 1996 Telecommunications Act signed into law by the president whose impeachment proceedings she was covering at the opening of this chapter.

Two controversies led to the impeachment proceedings: allegations of ethical violations known as the Whitewater scandal, and accusations of womanizing highlighted by the reports of sexual misconduct by the president with White House intern Monica Lewinsky.

Whitewater took its name from a real estate investment undertaken in the 1970s by the Whitewater Development Corporation. Clinton, then governor of Arkansas, and his wife, Hillary Rodham Clinton, were partners in the undertaking, with the financial backing of the Madison Guaranty Savings and Loan, which was to go bankrupt at the end of the 1980s. James and Susan McDougal were controlling partners of the financial institution and the land deal. Hillary Clinton's Little Rock law partner, Vincent Foster, who would join the Clinton administration in the early 1990s, represented the Clintons when they sold their shares of Whitewater.

Accusations of misuse of campaign funds, of favors relating to financial and political ties and tax benefits swirled around the Whitewater affair; but tragedy of a more personal nature—Foster's suicide in 1993—ignited the controversy nationally. Woodruff was hosting CNN's political analysis program, *Inside Politics,* following the suicide.

"At the White House it is a day of grief, reflection, and unanswered questions," she told her viewers on July 21. "President Clinton canceled public appearances today except to share his sorrow over the apparent suicide of his deputy-legal counsel and old friend, Vincent Foster. Even in the pressure-cooker of the White House, the news is hitting hard."

The coverage featured comments from Clinton, including a stammered response to the question of if he had any idea why Foster "apparently had taken his life":

"No, I really don't—and none of—frankly none of us did. You know, we—his closest friends sat around discussing it last night at some length. None of us do. For more years than most of us would like to admit, in times of difficulty, he was normally the Rock of Gibraltar while other people were having trouble."[75]

At the end of the year, Woodruff would report on her program about the mounting political turmoil of Whitewater. It had become the target of an investigation by the Justice Department, which had seized Foster's files relating to the land development project two days after his suicide. Spicing the controversy were the accusations and investigations into womanizing that dogged Clinton during his administration.

"There has been a spate of media attention over the past several days over allegations about President Clinton's personal life," Woodruff reported in reference to the president's alleged womanizing, accusations that had been with him from his campaign for the presidency. "But some political observers believe another burgeoning controversy could ultimately cause greater problems for the president. Today there were new comments on the matter of the so called Whitewater files."

Senior White House Correspondent Wolf Blitzer reported that the White House was trying to douse "a political fire storm involving the first family's relationship with an old business partner and political fundraiser, the owner of a failed Arkansas savings and loan. A senior administration official says it's virtually inconceivable president Clinton and first lady Hillary Rodham Clinton would not hand over to the Justice Department the files on their investment in an all-fated land development project."

Blitzer reported that Attorney General Janet Reno, who had said on camera that she had not been contacted by the White House regarding the Whitewater file, "opposes naming a special prosecutor."[76]

Woodruff summarized the history and context of the "political fire storm" in a January 3 *Inside Politics* report:

> The story is a tangled one, involving Mr. and Mrs. Clinton. Their 1979 investment in the Whitewater real estate venture with their then close friend, James McDougal and McDougal's operation of the failed Madison Savings and Loan, which eventually cost $50 million in taxpayer money. Questions have been raised about the Clintons' financial and personal involvement with McDougal.
>
> The questions include whether Mr. Clinton received fraudulent loans or campaign contributions from the Madison S&L; whether Mr. Clinton used his influence as governor to keep Madison in business, even after it was deemed insolvent by federal regulators; whether Hillary Rodham Clinton, who became Madison's lawyer for a time, intervened with state banking regulators on Madison's behalf; whether files on Whitewater, the real estate development, that had long been deemed lost were actually removed from the office of deputy White House counsel Vince Foster shortly after his July suicide; and finally, whether Foster took his life, in part, out of fear that the Whitewater affair might implicate the Clintons in civil or criminal wrongdoing.[77]

As Mark Twain might suggest, reports of no Whitewater special counsel proved exaggerated as Reno that same month appointed Wall Street lawyer Robert Fiske as a special prosecutor to investigate the Whitewater affair. Fiske promised, reported Woodruff, a "complete, thorough and impartial" inquiry.[78]

Public and political attention to Whitewater escalated in March 1994, with Republican senators calling for Senate Banking Committee hearings into the affair[79] and the resignation of White House legal counsel Bernard Nussbaum. The resignation came after White House Chief of Staff Thomas McLarty released a memo taking away Nussbaum's authorization over White House contacts with agencies investigating Whitewater and criticism over his handling of administration appointments.[80] Ten days later, Associate Attorney General Webster Hubbell resigned "amid a growing dispute with the law firm where he and the first lady once were partners," Woodruff reported;[81] a few days later the U.S. Senate voted 98–0 for hearings on Whitewater.[82]

The Whitewater chronology continued through the summer of 1994, as Congressional hearings did indeed take place, investigating the death of Foster and White House interference with the Whitewater probe.[83] The hearings included testimony from administration officials, the president, and the first lady. As the Watergate hearings had done two decades before, these proceedings demonstrated the power and capability of the medium of television to air, openly, government proceedings affecting the nation's democracy.

"Welcome to day five of our coverage—live coverage—of the Senate Whitewater hearings," Woodruff, anchoring the August 4, 9 A.M. news report, told viewers. The hearings before the Senate Banking Committee, she said, involved

> a series of incidents that covered over the last several years. And after a few days of testimony from high level Treasury Department officials, this morning, members of the Senate Banking Committee will be taking testimony from former White House Chief of Staff Thomas "Mack" McLarty and from the first lady's chief of staff, Margaret Williams, also known as Maggie. Ms. Williams and Mr. McLarty are also—also hold the positions of assistant to the president. And we might add that Mack McLarty is a long-time friend of President Clinton's, going back, I think, to kindergarten days even.[84]

The investigation would take a new course, into the president's sexual conduct, in August when Fiske resigned amid Republican criticism.[85] He was replaced by Kenneth Starr,[86] who eventually would take the investigation to a federal grand jury. During Starr's tenure, the scandal that would lead to Clinton's impeachment and the Senate trial of the president, arose: Monica Lewinsky.

The Lewinsky case followed another Clinton sexual scandal involving former Arkansas state employee Paula Jones, who accused Clinton of violating her federal civil rights in 1991 when he was governor of that state. Jones claimed Clinton invited her to his motel room and tried to have sexual relations with her, which she claimed in a lawsuit to have rejected. The Jones case, filed in 1994 in U.S. District Court, included potential witnesses involving accusations of sexual advances by Clinton to other women. Judge Susan Webber Wright granted a summary judgment favoring the president and dismissing the suit in April, 1998, and following an appeal by Jones, the accuser and Clinton settled. But one of the names listed as a potential witness in the Jones case was Lewinsky, who had joined the White House staff in 1995 as an intern. During depositions in the Jones case, Clinton denied having "sexual relations" with Lewinsky and testified that he could not remember ever having been alone with Lewinsky.[87]

Lewinsky's name was given to the attorneys by former White House employee Linda Tripp, who had befriended Lewinsky. In January 1998, Tripp gave tapes she had secretly made of her conversations with Lewinsky, which included details of Lewinsky's involvement with the president, to Starr during his investigation of Whitewater. Starr expanded his Whitewater investigation to include the Lewinsky matter. On January 21, the *Washington Post, Los Angeles Times* and ABC News broke the story of the allegations nationally. Woodruff and fellow anchor Shaw reported the story, including the accusation that Clinton had urged Lewinsky to lie about their relationship, in a special edition of *Inside Politics*.

"The new allegations against President Clinton, if proven, could be the biggest scandal to hit the White House since Watergate," Shaw reported. "They go far beyond old questions about Mr. Clinton's alleged sexual conduct in Arkansas to what he did or did not do while serving in the Oval Office, and whether the nation's chief executive tried to obstruct justice. On top of it, there are tapes of telephone conversations, which purportedly detail the alleged tryst and cover-up."

The president denied the allegations on-air in videotape provided to CNN by Woodruff's former news organization, *The News Hour with Jim Lehrer*.

"There is not a sexual relationship," the president was quoted. "That is accurate. I did not ask anyone to tell anything other than the truth."

Woodruff interrupted the CNN coverage of the breaking news to take the readers to a live interview being conducted of the president by National Public Radio's Mara Liasson and Robert Siegel.

ROBERT SIEGEL, HOST, NPR, *ALL THINGS CONSIDERED*: . . . is investigating allegations that you or you and [Clinton friend and confidante] Vernon Jordan encouraged a young woman to lie to lawyers in the Paula Jones civil suit. Is there any truth to that allegation?

CLINTON: No sir, there's not. It's just not true.

SIEGEL: Is there any truth to the allegation of an affair between you and the young woman?

CLINTON: No. That's not true either. And I have told the people that I would cooperate in the investigation, and I expect to cooperate with it. I—I don't know anymore about it than I have told you, and anymore about it, really than you do. But I will cooperate. The charges aren't true and I haven't asked anybody to lie."[88]

The president repeated his denial during a January 26 meeting with the national press corps, in which he issued his famous statement about never having sex with "that woman." CNN was there and reported it on *Inside Politics* hosted by Woodruff and Shaw.

"I want to say one thing to the America people," Clinton said in a videotape aired on the news program. "I want you to listen to me. I'm going to say this again. I did not have sexual relations with that woman, Ms. Lewinsky. I never told anybody to lie, not a single time, ever. These allegations are false and I need to go back to work for the American people. Thank you."

Woodruff called it "the president's most forceful denial to date, made at the end of a White House pitch for new after-school child-care programs. As he spoke, First Lady Hillary Rodham Clinton was close by his side. The first lady then took time out from her reported role as lead damage control strategist to visit a school in New York City."[89]

Starr that summer granted immunity to Lewinsky, who had joined Clinton in denying the sexual allegations, and she admitted to having sexual relations with Clinton that did not include intercourse. She continued to deny that she had been asked to lie about her involvement with the president. In August, Clinton testified via closed-circuit television from the White House before the Grand Jury. He admitted a relationship with Lewinsky while denying that he had lied during the Paula Jones deposition, explaining that he did not consider his relationship with Lewinsky as including sexual relations.[90]

Following his testimony, the president confessed to the public. CNN broadcast the event. The president admitted to having a relationship with Lewinsky "that was not appropriate. In fact, it was wrong. It constituted a critical lapse in judgment and a personal failure on my part for which I am solely and completely responsible."

He did not ask anyone to lie, he said, "to hide or destroy evidence or to take any other unlawful action. I know that my public comments and my silence about this matter gave a false impression. I misled people, including even my wife. I deeply regret that."[91]

The Starr investigation continued on to the end of summer when, early in September, the prosecutor gave Congress a report that concluded finding "substantial and credible information that President William Jefferson Clinton committed acts that may constitute grounds for impeachment" on at least two counts: perjury in his testimony in the Paula Jones case and obstructing justice by urging Lewinsky to lie. The House approved two articles of impeachment accusing the president of perjury in the Paula Jones case and in his relationship with Lewinsky and of obstructing justice. The Senate impeachment trial began on January 7, 1999, and in their vote nearly a month later senators failed to provide the required 67 votes, or two-thirds majority, for conviction. Despite additional legal difficulties related to Whitewater in Arkansas[92] the Whitewater matter and the Lewinsky scandal, which together had consumed much of Clinton's second term, had come to an end.

Shaw reported on May 15, 1997, that the Whitewater grand jury had gone home.

"The 2-year-old federal grand jury here in Washington looking into Whitewater is now history," reported correspondent Wolf Blitzer. "It's gone on for so long that independent counsel Kenneth Starr was barred from asking for yet another extension of its mandate. It's been dismissed without any known indictments."[93]

And on February 12, 1999, Woodruff told CNN viewers that the Senate impeachment trial was over.

"After more than a year of scandal and divisiveness, there may be something approaching a sense of national unity tonight on at least one point—a widespread relief that the impeachment trial is over," she reported. She added that publicly, the president "was careful not to show any joy in his acquittal on both articles of impeachment or in the fact that Republican prosecutors failed to get a majority vote for conviction on either count."[94]

One other major setback of the Clinton presidency would be his health care initiative. This was an issue Clinton had targeted in his bid for the presidency; it became a high priority early. He partnered with his wife to push for national health care, which would become a defining—though largely disastrous—issue of the early Clinton presidency. The president made the opening gambit in September 1993, in a speech to the nation, eight months into his first term. Woodruff introduced the speech as a theme-setting oration of the young presidency.

"I think, as Wolf [Blitzer] just said, most people would agree that this is—may well be the most important speech coming up of this, what, eight-month-old presidency," she said. "And I think a lot of people would agree that other . . . other than the shape of the economy, the fate of this health care plan could well decide what's going to happen to this presidency."

Woodruff explained that the administration had signaled its willingness to make changes to the plan—an ominous foreshadowing to the give-and-take political bartering to come involving not only Democratic and Republican lawmakers but also Hillary Clinton and the health care and insurance industries. It was a plan, she reported, citing comments from Health and Human Services Secretary Donna Shalala, that "has been ready since practically before the president was elected, and it was just a lot of window dressing, frankly, all the talk we've been hearing about task forces and so forth."

In his speech, covered live by CNN, the president introduced his topic as a coming together "to write a new chapter in the American story." Clinton showcased his oratorical prowess as he invoked history and the American dream to sell his health care proposal.

> Our forbears enshrined the American dream—life, liberty, the pursuit of happiness. Every generation of Americans has worked to strengthen that legacy, to

make our country a place of freedom and opportunity. A place where people who work hard can rise to their full potential. A place where their children can have a better future. From the settling of the frontier to the landing on the moon, ours has been a continuous story of challenges defined, obstacles overcome, hew horizons secured. That is what makes America what it is and Americans what we are. Now we are in a time of profound change and opportunity. The end of the Cold War, the information age, the global economy have brought us both opportunity and hope, and strife and uncertainty. Our purpose in this dynamic age must be to make change with discipline, whether we're reducing the deficit, creating tomorrow's jobs and training our people to fill them, converting from a high-tech defense to a high-tech domestic economy, expanding trade, re-inventing government, making our street safer or rewarding work over idleness. All these challenges require us to change. If Americans are to have the courage to change in a difficult time, we must first be secure in our most basic needs. Tonight I want to talk to you about the most critical thing we can do to build that security. This health care system of ours is badly broken and it is time to fix it.

The president identified his wife as the "navigator" of the proposal, explaining that she had already been at work the previous eight months, meeting with "literally thousands of Americans to understand the strengths and the frailties of this system of ours." Those meetings, he said, included sessions with health care organizations, doctors, pharmacists, drug company representatives, hospital administrators and insurance company executives. Her efforts were aimed at meeting six principles, he said: security, simplicity, savings, choice, quality, and responsibility in delivering health care to all Americans regardless of economic class.[95]

The speech was an immediate success among the citizens. Two days later, *Washington Post* columnist and political analyst David S. Broder appeared as a guest on Woodruff's *Inside Politics* and pronounced the president's address as a strong beginning, "a good launch. There was passion and some conviction in this. I think what came across to people, at least to me, was that this is something that the president really has his heart in. It's quite different from the battle over the budget." What the citizens were waiting for, Broder said, were the details "of how we're going to get to this kind of wonderful world that the president described."[96]

But reaction on Capitol Hill was mixed, with Democrats speaking in support of the president and Republicans expressing doubts.

"We need health care reform now," said Representative Rosa DeLauro, a Connecticut Democrat. "Rising health care costs are devastating to our economy, our families, our senior citizens and our small business."

But Oklahoma Republican Senator Don Nickles asked: "Where's the money coming from? I'm very concerned about political leaders, if we come out and say here's a multitude of benefits that we're gonna give everybody and not really be straightforward in where the costs are going to come from."

Kansas Republican Senator Bob Dole, who would oppose Clinton in the president's reelection campaign, offered a more conciliatory tone: "The more plans the better, the more ideas on how to deal with this big, big issue, the better."[97]

Thus was the mold of the coming debate cast, with Clinton supporters and those on the left urging change as radical as modeling American health care after the Canadian single-payer system to those on the right urging a system of care managed by existing insurance and health care organizations and paid for by companies and workers. But at first, all seemed to agree that change was needed. Even that consensus, though, would unravel.

By the spring of 1994, administration officials were scrambling to maintain, or actually to restore, the initial public support that had greeted Clinton's plan. Numerous other plans had emerged to compete with the president's initial proposal.

"Cabinet members on the president's health care task force are mobilizing to sell the Clinton health care plan," Woodruff reported at the end of March. "A CNN/USA Today Gallup poll out today shows that support has slipped to the lowest point since the plan was unveiled last September. Forty-four percent of Americans support it. Forty-seven percent oppose it. The number of people who think the Clinton plan should be amended before it passes remains fairly steady. Nearly half of those questioned say that Congress should pass the Clinton plan with major changes. Nineteen percent say it should pass with no changes, while 26 percent say it should be rejected. The Clinton plan was the only health care proposal the public was asked about."

As for the other proposals, correspondent Charles Bierbauer told Woodruff in response to her questioning that Congress and the White House were on

> separate paths. They're each doing their own thing—the White House corps out doing the sell, sell, sell, and Congress actually still building the product that the White House is selling. One congressional source compares this process to the NCAA basketball playoffs. There were 64 teams at one point and now there are four, and soon there will be one, and in health care, there'll be five bills in Congress with lots of differences—three in the House, two in the Senate. Eventually they'll merge into two bills, one in the House and one in the Senate, and then one coming from Congress. Those White House officials say that what they're really interested in is the end game, not micromanaging the bill-writing process itself.[98]

By summer, a national health care plan actually seemed on track, as Woodruff reported on her *Inside Politics* program. The issue, she said, "has been through many stages in the U.S. Congress so far. Members' attitudes about it have variously ranged from enthusiasm, to denial, to belligerence, to hints of compromise. This week, the subject finally seems to be picking up some legislative pace."

The plan, though, seemed headed toward a compromise involving individual and employer responsibility, with Bierbauer reporting that under a plan in the Senate Finance Committee, "95 percent of Americans will have to have it by the year 2002 or Congress would pull the trigger requiring them to buy it themselves. That is the compromise emerging from the Senate Finance committee, where Republicans and Democrats are fashioning a moderate bill."[99]

Opposition, though, also picked up steam. Opponents' reasoning ranged from the conservative viewpoint that rejected government involvement in health care, to special interest groups protecting their turf, to religious groups urging rejection of any plan that would cover abortion, which, CNN reported, "is exactly what all five bills that have been approved by congressional committees now do."[100]

Other political factors also played a role in deflecting the president's, and Congress', attention from health care. An August presidential news conference, at which the president planned to discuss the health care plan as one of several topics on his agenda, became engulfed by questions concerning the Whitewater affair. In his opening remarks, Clinton told reporters that his administration was "fighting for health care reform not just for those who don't have health insurance but for those who do have it and who could use it—lose it because they have to change jobs, because someone in their family gets sick, because they simply have to pay too much for it. They deserve better and we're fighting to see that they get it."

By this time, however, the plan had taken on a new face. The president explained:

> We want to guarantee private, not government, insurance for every American. The plan I originally proposed has been changed and much of it for the better. The proposals before Congress are less bureaucratic. They're more flexible. They provide more protection and support for small business. They contain a reasonable phase-in time, over a period of years, to make sure we get it right. No bureaucrat will pick your doctor. You can keep you own plan or pick a better one. This approach controls government spending but relies on competitive forces in the free market to restrain the growth of private health insurance premiums. Much of it has changed for the better. But one rock-solid principle remains—private insurance, guaranteed, for everyone.[101]

The news conference then veered to prospects of an invasion of Haiti, to North Korea's work on developing nuclear weapons-grade plutonium, and then to Whitewater. By the end of summer, the president's health care reform proposal had suffered a slow political death, done in by special interests and by the administration's own handling of the issue—including the president's wife and other advisers handling much of the negotiations and plan development in secretive, closed deliberations.

"Senate Majority Leader George Mitchell has pulled the plug on the Clinton Administration's top domestic priority declaring health care reform is dead for this legislative year," Woodruff reported on September 26.

And the prospects of a resurrection were dim, reported correspondent Bob Franken, who summarized Mitchell's sentiment for Woodruff.

"Well, he brought it up himself, he said that health care will be an issue in some campaigns and won't be an issue in others," Franken said in response to Woodruff's comment that Mitchell was trying to blame the Republicans for the demise of the health care proposal. "Which really, is a commentary on the state of this. At one time, it was the burning domestic issue in the United States, but by now it has been sidetracked to the point that it probably won't be an issue in great many parts of the country."[102]

By year's end, the Republican takeover of Congress buried the universal health care initiative deep in a political coffin as the Newt Gingrich-led Republicans, Whitewater, and the Lewinsky scandal took the nation into a new political direction far away from the notion of providing health care coverage for the estimated 43 million Americans who did not have it.

As the president and Congress grappled with the domestic issues, such as the economy, health care, and welfare reform, the president faced foreign crises that included military encounters—from keeping Iraq's Saddam Hussein in line, to armed intervention in Somalia that led to international humiliation of the United States military when a slain soldier was dragged and his body abused by a mob of Somalis, and Clinton's largest military undertaking, the war in Kosovo.

The Battle of Mogadishu in October 1993, marked a decision by Clinton early in his administration to use U.S. military forces to intervene in a civil war in Somalia, where the humanitarian relief efforts begun during the previous administration of George H.W. Bush had given way to international efforts to stop the bloodshed and to oust one of the faction leaders, Mohamed Farrah Aidid. But early in Operation Gothic Serpent, Pentagon sources refused to acknowledge that Aidid was the target while confirming that a military operation was under way.

"A military operation involving U.S. troops is reportedly ongoing in Mogadishu, Somalia, at this hour," CNN's Jeanne Meserve reported on October 3. Correspondent Jamie McIntyre told Meserve that it had been "a bloody day and night for U.S. peacekeepers in Somalia, in an operation that is still going on. Two U.S. Blackhawk helicopters were shot down during the operation." The Pentagon acknowledged that 20 Somalis connected to Aidid had been taken into custody, and McIntyre reported that five U.S. soldiers had died, with another two dozen wounded.[103]

The next day, CNN reported that 12 U.S. soldiers had died, and this dispatch included a report by *Toronto Star* correspondent Paul Watson that he had witnessed a mob of "about 200 Somalis cheering as they dragged a U.S. soldier, who was naked except for his underwear. They were pulling him by ropes, and pausing every few minutes to stomp on the body and to cheer the name of their hero, the fugitive warlord General Mohamed Farah Aidid." McIntyre closed his report surmising that the operation, rather than a victory for the United Nations forces, was a "huge psychological victory for Mohamed Farah Aidid because of the large number of U.S. casualties and the large number of dead. As you can see already, it's increasing the pressure on the United States to give up and pull out."[104] U.S. forces were subsequently evacuated.

The president found greater military success in another military humanitarian mission, this one in war-torn Kosovo. The operation began in the spring of 1999 in an effort to stop the ethnic cleansing of Albanians in the Yugoslavian province by Serbian dictator Slobodan Milosevic. The military action came after failed diplomatic endeavors. The president framed his looming decision to intervene in terms of humanitarian assistance during a news conference in March a month after his impeachment trial in the Senate ended in acquittal. During the news conference he issued a direct warning to the Serbian president.

"I will say again to Mr. Milosevic, as I did in Bosnia, I do not want to put a single American pilot into the air," the president said. "I do not want anyone else to die in the Balkans. I do not want a conflict. Make no mistake: if we and our allies do not have the will to act there will be more massacres. In dealing with aggressors in the Balkans hesitation is a license to kill. But action and resolve can stop armies and save lives."[105]

The threatened U.S. and NATO intervention came later that month. Woodruff announced the decision for air strikes during a live report, noting the historic significance of the NATO operation.

"For the first time in its 50-year history, the Western security alliance NATO is attacking a sovereign country," she told her viewers. "The bombs began falling in Yugoslavia when a diplomatic solution to end the crisis in Kosovo failed. U.S. President Clinton says now is the time to use military force."

Again, the president couched his explanation for the military involvement in humanitarian language.

"We act to protect thousands of innocent people in Kosovo from a mounting military offensive," he explained in a CNN video clip. "We act to prevent a wider war, to defuse a powder keg at the heart of Europe that has exploded twice before in this century with catastrophic results. We act to stand united with our allies for peace."[106]

The military operation would last about two and a half months before the installment of NATO international peacekeeping forces, and it would cost the lives of Yugoslavian civilians and the taking of American soldiers as hostages before its end.

On April 1, Clinton issued another warning to Milosevic, this one intended to protect the lives of American soldiers abducted by Serbian forces while on patrol near the Macedonian border.

"On the eastern coast of the United States, darkness," Woodruff told viewers, "but in Yugoslavia, a new day is about to begin, a day in which Serbs are promising a military court martial for three captured American soldiers—cavalry scouts, part of the United Nations peacekeeping force in Macedonia. For their families, a day filled with anxiety and relief, mixed emotions as they viewed these pictures of the three on Serbian television. Each bruised and battered, but alive, and standing upright."

As broadcast outlets had done during the Vietnam War, CNN's cameras delivered the war images into the living rooms of Americans as Clinton warned that "President Milosevic should make no mistake: the United States takes care of its own. . . . We will hold him and his government responsible for their safety and their well-being."[107] The soldiers were released early in May with the assistance of a group of American religious leaders, led by Jesse Jackson, who negotiated their freedom.

Meanwhile, the deaths of Yugoslavian civilians, victims of the new age of so-called smart bombs developed in the new era of high-tech military, brought criticism of the war effort. Coupled with these reports were allegations of atrocities committed against Kosovar refugees by Serb military and police forces—evidence that would be turned over to prosecutors of the international war crimes tribunal convened in response to Milosevic's 10-year reign of terror.[108]

In mid-May, Woodruff reported the deaths of "at least 100 civilians, many of them ethnic Albanians," as a result of NATO air strikes. In the same report, she told viewers that CNN had obtained videotape "of the aftermath of the alleged mass killing of ethnic Albanians by Serb forces."

Correspondent Brent Sadler, in a voice-over during footage of the aftermath of the bombing of the village of Korisa, reported that the NATO air strike killed primarily ethnic Albanian refugees, according to Belgrade authorities. "There was much destruction—blazing tractors and trailers, the most common form of refugee transport, and gruesome images of death amid the carnage."

Later in the news segment, correspondent Amanda Kibel described footage by a Kosovo television journalist showing

> the aftermath of the massacre of ethnic Albanians by Serb soldiers inside Kosovo. The journalist, Loshi, and three eyewitnesses say 127 men from the village of Isbeesa (ph) in the Drenesa (ph) valley, were executed by Serb soldiers on March 28. These pictures were taken three days later. This is the first time these pictures have been shown publicly.
>
> The journalist, Loshi, says he was fleeing from the Serbs himself. He says his house had been burned, and he was hiding in the mountains. There he met some women from Isbeesa who had fled the village. They told him of the massacre. He decided to go to the village to see what had happened.[109]

World pressure against Milosevic grew; in late May, the United Nations War Crimes Tribunal indicted Milosevic, "the first-ever sitting head of state on charges of war crimes."[110] Early in June, NATO forces were preparing to enter Kosovo upon completion of a peace agreement, reached by NATO and Russia.[111] Two days later, CNN announced that NATO had suspended its 79-day Yugoslavian bombing campaign and that "Serb forces have begun to withdraw while peacekeeping forces have begun the task of ensuring a safe homecoming for more than 800,000 refugees."[112]

The winding down of the Yugoslavian campaign enabled Clinton to sound one of his rare high notes during the second term of his presidency.

"My fellow Americans, tonight for the first time in 79 days, the skies over Yugoslavia are silent," he told the nation. "The Serb army and police are withdrawing from Kosovo. The one million men, women and children driven from their land are preparing to return home. The demands of an outraged and united international community have been met."[113]

The mop-up and trial of Milosevic, including the discovery of mass graves that would put the proof to allegations of his atrocities against his own people, were yet to come; but for the most part, this successful post-World War II foreign intervention involving U.S. stoops had ended.

"The war in Kosovo was one of the first manifestations of the twentieth century post Cold-War world order," Woodruff would recall seven years later of the Yugoslavian military operation. "In the aftermath of the collapse of the Soviet Union, former Soviet arc nations, including Yugoslavia, experienced an upsurge in ethnic divisions. The war ensued, pulling NATO and the United States in, and was a test of how the United States defined its own national interest, and the interests of its allies in Europe.[114]

"America was seeking, in the wake of the fall of the Soviet empire, to find a way to fit into the new world and in some ways to impose its will on the world without doing it in a blatant territorial world," she recalled. "As I think back on that period, I don't think of the United States being sort of a hegemonistic force on the planet in the '90s; I think of the United States in the '90s as trying to figure out what its role was."

She continued: "Clearly there was a sense that we were left as the one super power, that with the Soviet Union gone, the U.S. was it. But what does that mean? I mean, how are we going to impose, or were we going to impose our will on others, and how?"

Despite Yugoslavia, Somalia, and some success in Middle East diplomacy and Haiti, the strength of the Clinton presidency was domestic policy and issues, she said. His election signaled the willingness by the nation to move to a different kind of chief executive.

"We were in a new era," she said. "We were comfortable electing a president who didn't have a distinct military background. Ronald Reagan had served, but not necessarily served in combat. But Clinton, born after the war, World War II, not only had not served in the military, had taken distinct steps not to serve in the military, to stay away from service."

His election, she added, "said that we're moving into another era, we're not quite sure where we're headed, but we're comfortable with a president who's not steeped in international affairs, as Clinton was not. He was clearly a domestic figure, had been governor of a small state. His strength was in his knowledge of domestic issues and his political skills. And I think the nation was saying we need somebody who's paying attention to what's going on in this country."

Despite his compromises with Republicans on domestic issues that included the budget and NAFTA, Woodruff said he was a "real Democrat."

"But is he an ideological Democrat? No. To me he's much more of a practical Democrat who wants solutions, he's a Democrat who was willing to work with Republicans to get solutions to problems. Welfare reform was an example of that, where he made a lot of Democrats very unhappy because he moved in the direction of getting people off the welfare rolls. It was a triangulation, where he was able to work with Democrats and Republicans, and the funny thing is that many Republicans don't give him any credit for doing that. They just say he was a liberal Democrat, but the fact is it's much more complicated than that."

The impeachment trial, she said, marked the climax of a political battle and era that had seen a strengthening of religious conservatives' morality agenda, of a Republican Party power grab that had swung the congressional majority to the GOP, and of the political bickering that had marked much of the Clinton presidency.

Clinton's defeat of President George H. W. Bush in 1992 triggered much of this partisanship and resentment, Woodruff said.

"I think if George H. W. Bush had been reelected in 1992, I don't think you would have had nearly the impetus. The Clinton presidency just angered and frustrated and caused resentment in many Republicans who felt that the White House was theirs, and it had been taken by someone who didn't deserve to be in the White House. That was how it came across as a reporter to me. You talk to Republicans then, they weren't just disappointed in the '92 loss, they were furious, and they were resentful, and they didn't feel that Clinton deserved to be president. They felt they were going to do everything they could to win back the presidency. They tried in '96, and it didn't work, but it did in 2000."

The GOP takeover of Congress in 1994 was a result of the same sentiment, she said.

"There was almost a sense, I think, on the part of many Republicans, of entitlement, that the White House had been theirs for eight years under Reagan and four years of Bush, and they resented that a governor from the small state of Arkansas had defeated George H. W. Bush, who had been vice president for eight years and president for four years."

The Republicans saw Clinton as smart, she said, "but they didn't think he belonged in the White House. They also felt that he had some personal issues that disqualified him from being the sort of president who they thought the country should have, and I think that motivated a lot of them to go out and work like crazy to get Republicans into Congress. Newt Gingrich was able to articulate that and lead the effort in the '94 elections."

Asked why and how Clinton got into so much political trouble for an extra-marital affair when a Democrat he had come of age admiring, President John F. Kennedy, escaped political wrath for his sexual dalliances, she said times and circumstances had changed.

"For one thing, it was early 1960s versus thirty years later, and the news media, we had a cultural shift in the news media. Watergate, I think, and Vietnam were principal reasons that the media were no longer willing to just sit back and be complacent and be spoon-fed by the government, not that the media were entirely spoon-fed."

The press, she said, was less willing to accept the idea that politicians were "perfect people." It was becoming a different institution during the 1960s and 1970s.

"You had news reporters coming into the media after Watergate, and Woodward and Bernstein and Vietnam, the Pentagon Papers. They came in thinking 'my gosh, there's stuff going on here that we need to uncover for the good of the public, and we need to ask questions,' and that just washed over the media's attitude toward everything. Do I think it's enough? No, I still think there are plenty of areas the media don't cover very well. I think we do a better job of covering business, I think we do a better job of covering religion, there are just so many places we could do a better job. But I do think that explains the differences between the '60s and the '90s."

The failure of the health care initiative was a missed opportunity, Woodruff said.

"I think that what went wrong was that the Clinton administration at the very highest levels did not adequately reach out to all of the different groups with an interest in the outcome of that shift, or what would have been a shift in health care reform," she said. "They had a fairly closed approach, one that had some people represented but not others, and I think it was doomed to fail from the beginning for that reason. And I do think it was an enormous opportunity, the consequences of which we still are suffering from today."

Clinton came into the presidency, she said, during a time of economic uncertainty. "The recession was defined as having started in '90, '91, and we had done well definitely in the '80s, but there was some sense of overreach. There was the Gordon Gekko (Michael Douglas' protagonist in the film *Wall Street*) sense, people made so much money off the markets in the '80s, there was a sense that money was more important than anything under Reagan. Whether he was responsible for it or not, there was still this notion of greed, I think, that was kind of rampant. To me, that was kind of where we were coming into the '90s. We didn't feel quite the sense of compassion in the country."

By the end of the decade, she said, "there was a sense that we were suddenly into a new era in the world, and that the United States was preeminent, because we survived, we prevailed over Soviet communism;

the United States was still standing triumphant at the top of the hill and yet having uncertainty about what was going to replace it, some uncertainty about who the enemy was, what was our reason for being, how far should American values be imposed, how hard should we work on imposing American values. What was our role in the world? Was it to be the world's policemen?"

Or, she wondered, were we supposed to ensure human rights?

"I think that we had seen enough of what it was like to be ascendant, so that in my mind there was a question about what our role was going into the new millennium."

NOTES

1. Rick Atkinson and David S. Broder, "U.S., Allies Launch Massive Air War Against Targets in Iraq and Kuwait," *Washington Post,* January 17, 1991, A1.
2. Ibid.
3. Rick Atkinson and David S. Broder, "Iraq Retaliates With Missile Attacks Against Israeli Cities, Saudi Air Base," *Washington Post,* January 18, 1991, A1.
4. David S. Broder and Richard Morin, "National Optimism Surges On War Success; Poll Shows Unprecedented Rise in Opinion That U.S. Is Headed in Right Direction," *Washington Post,* February 28, 1991, A33.
5. Arthur Crawford, "Beneficiaries Of Duties Must Reveal Income," *Chicago Daily Tribune,"* September 11, 1929, 1.
6. "Senators Move To Investigate Navy Lobbying," *Chicago Daily Tribune,* September 11, 1929, 1.
7. UP, "2 Chinese Cities Under Fire; War Front Spreads," *Chicago Daily Tribune,* September 11, 1929, 3.
8. Tom Pettey, "Carolina Mob flogs 1 Red; 2 Other Kidnapped," *Chicago Daily Tribune,* September 11, 1929, 7.
9. "MOTION PICTURES DOWNTOWN," *Chicago Daily Tribune,* September 11, 1929, 38.
10. "College Men's Store Suggests," *Chicago Daily Tribune,* September 11, 1929, 9.
11. "Stevens Building Restaurant," *Chicago Daily Tribune,* September 11, 1929, 13.
12. Milestone listings for 1953 for this paragraph and those that follow taken from Neville Williams, *Chronology of World History Volume IV: 1901–1998/The Modern World* (Santa Barbara, CA: ABC-CLIO, 1999), 427–35.
13. David S. Broder, "Selected Viewers' Consensus: Superpower Opportunity Is at Hand," *Washington Post,* June 5, 1990, A17.
14. David S. Broder, "The View of Gorbachev on the Arbat," *Washington Post,* July 5, 1990, A19.
15. David S. Broder, "Headaches for Heroes," *Washington Post,* November 28, 1990, A23.
16. David S. Broder, "A Penchant For Dealing With Elites" *Washington Post,* July 31, 1991, A21.
17. David S. Broder, "Recession Obsession," *Washington Post,* October 30, 1991, A23.
18. Davis S. Broder, "'Mainstream' Democratic Group Stakes Claim on Party's Future," *Washington Post,* May 3, 1991, A15.

19. Dan Balz and David S. Broder, "Democrats Argue Over Quota Clause; Meeting to Reshape Party Image Opens," *Washington Post,* May 7, 1991, A8.

20. Dan Balz and David S. Broder, "Clinton Support Holds Steady in N.H. Polls; Critical Period Ahead on Infidelity Controversy, Many Democratic Politicians Indicate," *Washington Post,* January 29, 1992, A9.

21. Thomas B. Edsall and David S. Broder, "Clinton Tells Voters He Is 'Electable'; 11th-Hour TV Spots, Testimonials Seek to Counter Attacks," *Washington Post,* February 14, 1992, A1.

22. David S. Broder,". . . As Tsongas Stumbled With Message," *Washington Post,* March 18, 1992, A23.

23. David S. Broder, "The Washington In Perot's Mind," *Washington Post,* June 28, 1992, C7.

24. Davis S. Broder, "Perils of the Candidate-President; Past Week Demonstrated Both the Benefits and Pitfalls of Incumbency," *Washington Post,* August 30, 1992, A6.

25. David S. Broder, "Clinton, Bush Spar Over Jobs; Candidates Set Forth Contrasting Proposals for Reviving Economy," *Washington Post,* September 7, 1992, A1.

26. David S. Broder and Kent Jenkins Jr., "Clinton Capitalizes On a Tsongas Theme," *Washington Post,* September 9, 1992, A12.

27. David S. Broder, "What Future for the GOP?" *Washington Post,* November 8, 1992, C7.

28. David S. Broder, "The GOP's Midterm Leverage," *Washington Post,* April 20, 1994, A21.

29. David S. Broder, "The Lame Veto," *Washington Post,* June 26, 1994, C7.

30. David S. Broder, "Anti-Clinton Platform," *Washington Post,* September 18, 1994, C9.

31. David S. Broder, "Disillusioned Public Puts Social Issues at Top of Fall Campaigns; 2 Years in Office Have Washed Away Clear Image of 'New Democrat' Clinton," *Washington Post,* October 2, 1994, A1.

32. David S. Broder, "Vote May Signal GOP Return as Dominant Party; Victors Push Beyond Solid Southern Base," *Washington Post,* November 10, 1994.

33. David S. Broder, "Clinton Can't Just Play Catch-Up With the GOP," *Washington Post,* December 21, 1994, A25.

34. David S. Broder, "The Good Gingrich and the Bad," *Washington Post,* November 16, 1994, A25.

35. David S. Broder, "No Imperial Presidency," *Washington Post,* August 9, 1995, A19.

36. David S. Broder, "Looking for Leadership; Voter Rage Cools, Worries Remain," *Washington Post,* November 6, 1995, A1.

37. David S. Broder, "Rebels Without a Pause; As they seized power in the House, Republican newcomers discovered that revolution demands as much stamina as fervor," *Washington Post,* December 31, 1995, W8.

38. David S. Broder, "Choosing Conciliation Over Confrontation," *Washington Post,* June 14, 1995, A1.

39. David S. Broder, "When Unity Becomes Division; Party's 'Contract With America' Is Now a Footnote," *Washington Post,* March 1, 1996, A1.

40. David S. Broder, "Two Manifestos," *Washington Post,* June 30, 1996, C7.

41. David S. Broder, "Stumbling Out of Gridlock," *Washington Post,* October 2, 1996, A17.

42. Dan Balz and David Broder, "Budget Rift Aside, Future Clinton Successes Will Demand Coalition," *Washington Post*, August 8, 1993, A15.

43. David S. Broder, "For Democrats, This Means Civil War," *Washington Post*, August 31, 1993, A19.

44. David S. Broder, "NAFTAmath; The fight has shown that Clinton does not want the Democrats to be seen as the party of losers," *Washington Post*, November 19, 1993, A29.

45. David S. Broder, "The Party's Over; By 2000 the GOP or the Democrats Could Fade in Favor of a Third Party," *Washington Post*, August 11, 1996, C1.

46. David S. Broder, "Parceling Out Power to Both Parties; Voters Unwilling to Trust Either One in Transition to New Century," *Washington Post*, November 6, 1996, A1.

47. David S. Broder, "Does the FBI Have the Tools to Fight Domestic Terrorism?" *Washington Post*, May 3, 1995, A21.

48. "House Prepares for Historic Impeachment Vote," Cable News Network, CNN Live Event/Special 10:59 A.M. Eastern Time, December 19, 1998, transcript 98121905V54.

49. Ibid.

50. Ibid.

51. "Clinton: Iraq has abused its last chance," Showdown with Iraq, CNN.com, December 16, 1998, http://www.cnn.com/US/9812/16/clinton.iraq.speech/ (accessed June 25, 2007).

52. "House Prepares for Historic Impeachment Vote," Cable News Network, CNN Live Event/Special 10:59 A.M. Eastern Time, December 19, 1998.

53. Ibid.

54. Ibid.

55. Ibid.

56. Judy Woodruff and Kathleen Maxa, *This is Judy Woodruff at the White House*, (Reading, Mass: Addison-Wesley Publishing Company, 1982), 77.

57. AP, "Army Is Ready for Mine Call: Lewis Silent," *Tulsa Daily World*, November 20, 1946, 1.

58. AP, "Rent 'Strike' Sidetracked By Landlords," *Tulsa Daily World*, November 20, 1946, 1.

59. "Parley Fails to Discover Housing Key," *Tulsa Daily World*, November 20, 1946, 11.

60. Paul S. Hedrick, "Crude Prices Are Advanced," *Tulsa Daily World*, November 20, 1946, 1.

61. "Trio Of Tulsa Realty Sales Near $500,000,"*Tulsa Daily World*, November 20, 1946, 1.

62. AP, "Tennessee Teachers Strike for Living Cost Pay Raise," *Tulsa Daily World*, November 20, 1946, 3.

63. AP, "Tax Slashes Are Opposed," *Tulsa Daily World*, November 20, 1946, 3.

64. "U.S. Engineers To Keep Dams On Schedule," *Tulsa Daily World*, November 20, 1946, 11.

65. Entertainment listings, *Tulsa Daily World*, November 20, 1946, 17.

66. "The Flavor's *All* Yours . . ." *Tulsa Daily World*, November 20, 1946, 13.

67. "Wolferman's Have the Quality Meats!" *Tulsa Daily World*, November 20, 1946, 2.

68. "The Economy of Santa Fe Trailways Buses Means More Today!" *Tulsa Daily World*, November 20, 1946, 5.

69. Judy Woodruff and Kathleen Maxa, *This is Judy Woodruff at the White House*, 77.

70. Ibid., 81.

71. Ibid.

72. Ibid., 82.

73. Milestone listings for 1970 for this paragraph and those that follow taken from Neville Williams, *Chronology of World History Volume IV: 1901–1998/The Modern World* (Santa Barbara, CA: ABC-CLIO, 1999), 598–607.

74. Judy Woodruff and Kathleen Maxa, *This is Judy Woodruff at the White House*, 85–86.

75. "White House Expresses Grief Over Loss of Vincent Foster," CNN *Inside Politics*, July 21, 1993.

76. "Reno Says Special Prosecutor Not Needed for Whitewater," CNN *Inside Politics*, December 23, 1993.

77. "Guests Discuss Potential Direction of Whitewater Affair," CNN *Inside Politics*, January 3, 1994.

78. "Robert Fiske Selected as Whitewater Special Counsel," CNN *Inside Politics*, January 20, 1994.

79. "Clinton Changes Tack on Dealing With Whitewater," CNN *Inside Politics*, March 3, 1994.

80. "Clinton Regretfully Accepts Nussbaum's Resignation," CNN *Inside Politics*, March 4, 1994.

81. "Hubbell Resignation Means More Trouble for Clinton," CNN News, March 14, 1994.

82. "Arkansas Ties to Clinton Questioned," CNN *Inside Politics*, March 18, 1994.

83. "Senate Begins Hearings on Vincent Foster's Suicide," CNN News, July 29, 1994.

84. "Senate Whitewater Hearings, Day 5, Part 1, August 4, 1994.

85. Ibid.

86. "Fiske Replaced as Whitewater Special Counsel," CNN *Inside Politics*, August 5, 1994.

87. "Clinton Impeachment," Eagleton Institute of Politics, Rutgers, The State University of New Jersey web site, http://www.eagleton.rutgers.edu/e-gov/e-politicalarchive-Clintonimpeach.htm (accessed June 30, 2007).

88. "Special Edition: Clinton Called On the Carpet For Alleged Affair," CNN *Inside Politics*, January 21, 1998.

89. "Clinton Adamantly Denies Sexual Allegations," CNN *Inside Politics*, January 26, 1998.

90. "Clinton Impeachment," Eagleton Institute of Politics, Rutgers, The State University of New Jersey web site, http://www.eagleton.rutgers.edu/e-gov/e-politicalarchive-Clintonimpeach.htm (accessed June 30, 2007).

91. "Investigating the President: The President Speaks," CNN Live Event/Special, August 18, 1998.

92. Jim Guy Tucker, who succeeded Clinton as governor of Arkansas, and the McDougals were found guilty in a 1996 state trial of fraud in the Whitewater case. Based on this and other political scandals in Arkansas, Republicans in Washington accused Hillary Clinton of trying to suppress information that could be damaging politically and administration officials of lying under oath (see "Whitewater," Answers.com, http://www.answers.com/topic/whitewater-scandal, accessed May 25, 2007).

93. "Washington-Based Whitewater Grand Jury Goes Home; Still No Movement On Balanced Budget Agreement; Gore and Bush Have A Lot In Common; Does Gore Have A Real Political Future; Politicians Play Culture Wars Again To Score With Constituents," CNN *Inside Politics,* May 15, 1997.

94. "Trial of the President: The Finale," CNN Live Event/Special, February 12, 1999.

95. "Health Care: A Presidential Address—Clinton's Speech," CNN Specials, September 22, 1993.

96. "David Broder Analyzes Clinton Health Care Beginnings," CNN *Inside Politics,* September 24, 1993.

97. "Clinton Health Care Plan to Put Partisanship to Test," CNN *Inside Politics,* September 23, 1993.

98. "White House Working to Sell Health Care Reform Plan," CNN News, March 31, 1994.

99. "Health Care Compromises Mean Real Progress," CNN *Inside Politics,* June 23, 1994.

100. "Health Plans Face Opposition Over Abortion Stance," CNN *Inside Politics,* July 15, 1994.

101. "Text of President Bill Clinton's News Conference," CNN News, August 3, 1994.

102. "Health Care Reform Bill Dies in the Senate," CNN *Inside Politics,* September 26, 1994.

103. "More U.S. Troops Die in Clashes in Somalia," CNN News, October 3, 1993.

104. "United States Troops Suffer Losses in Somalia," CNN News, October 4, 1993.

105. "President Makes Strong Statement About Kosovo," CNN Worldview, March 19, 1999.

106. "Strike Against Yugoslavia: NATO Launches Airstrikes Against Yugoslavia," CNN Live Event/Special, March 24, 1999.

107. "Strike Against Yugoslavia: President Clinton Warns Slobodan Milosevic Not to Harm Abducted U.S. Soldiers," CNN Live Event/Special, April 1, 1999.

108. "Strike Against Yugoslavia: Pentagon and State Department Claim Evidence of Atrocities," CNN Worldview, April 16, 1999.

109. "Strike Against Yugoslavia: Exclusive Videotape of Alleged Mass Killings of Ethnic Albanians; Yugoslavs say NATO Airstrikes Kill 100 Civilians," CNN Worldview, May 14, 1999.

110. "Strike Against Yugoslavia: U.N. War Crimes Tribunal Indicts Milosevic," CNN Worldview, May 27, 1999.

111. "Nato Prepares Troops to Enter Kosovo Once Deal is Finalized," CNN Worldview, June 8, 1999, and "Nato and Russia Reach Agreement on Kosovo Peace Plan; Speaker of the House Warns GOP Caucus to Stop Squabbling, CNN *Inside Politics,* June 8, 1999.

112. "Kosovo After the Strikes," CNN Live Event/Special, June 10, 1999.

113. Ibid.

114. June 7, 2007 e-mail to the author.

CHAPTER 7

Like the Times, the Industry Is a-Changin'

Former *New York Times* columnist Anthony Lewis never could break his typewriter habit, which he developed as a young reporter. He keeps a manual on reserve even today, just in case.

"I'm a technological Luddite," he said. "I went right through to the end writing columns on a typewriter and reading them on a telephone to New York. I still write on a typewriter, when I write something for the *New York Review* or for the *New York Times*. I fax it to them, and they have to have somebody put it into the computer. I use a computer, and it's wonderful, but I don't write on it."

He proudly showed off the manual he keeps in his apartment office. It is a Royal.

"I've got four," he said. "One in the office, one here, one in the country, and one in reserve."

Former United Press International correspondent Helen Thomas, now a nationally syndicated columnist, remembers sometimes having to run two blocks to find a telephone to report breaking news. Or she and other reporters would pay some kid to hold a telephone open for them when they knew that news would be breaking.

"We ran across a broken field or anything else, we knocked on the doors of homes to try to get to a phone. Today, you carry a cell phone, you have laptops, the instancy of communications, the whole technology, electronic journalism came into being. Television and so forth, people could see with their own eyes, and it's phenomenal, now you can have your telephone, you can take a picture."

But cell phones have a different meaning for former *New York Times* reporter Earl Caldwell. To him, they represent a leash.

"I could see the cell phone as a marvelous thing, but geez, would you want to be a reporter out on assignments where your editor could grab you on a moment's notice all of the time?" he said. "I think that would be very difficult, because a lot of the time your editors want to give you too much direction. On the other hand, if people have some good advice, they can get it right to you. The cell phone to me is a humongous thing, the little computers. We used to go out on these stories and you had to phone in to an answering machine, somebody's got to transcribe that, and then send your copy along to the desk. Stories used to go through three, four, five editors, different people would be reading it before it got to the paper. So journalism is hugely different."

As American society and its culture changed, from the postwar euphoria and the red scare of the '50s to the culture wars in which religion and morality became a dominant force in domestic politics, and the polarization of the nation between conservatives and centrist so-called liberals, the media reported, interpreted, and in some cases (Pentagon Papers, Watergate, Vietnam War coverage) helped set the national agenda.

The peace protests and civil rights marches; the Yardbirds, Byrds, Guess Who and Who; dogs orbiting the planet and men walking on the moon; hearts, lungs, and kidneys transplanted from one human being to take root inside the breathing body of another; polio conquered and AIDS and cancer researched but still uncured—the U.S. media attended them all, changing with the times, from clacking typewriters, hot lead presses, hand-held tape recorders, and bulky video cameras, to laptop computers, instantaneous on-scene broadcast or cable reporting of calamity and twenty-four-seven Web site news reports. It is important to remember that as the methods and equipment of newsgathering have veered into new gadgets and communication platforms, people still run the machines, be they the typewriters and dial telephones of the '50s or the hand-held computers delivering news to the home-base server as it occurs today. As in the old song about time going by, the fundamental things still apply: the human elements of curiosity, analysis and critical thinking remain in play. Human reporters have continued to probe the issues, to dig out the facts, to ask the questions—the time-honored who, what, when, where, why, and how.

But as they apply these same questions to their own business—the business of informing the public, of trading in a lively marketplace of ideas that helps preserve and promote the American democracy, of participating in the vital role of political and societal watchdog—they see an altered media landscape that worries them, that threatens the purpose and ideals of journalism. News industry economic patterns of the last half of the 20th century have brought conglomeration, increased demands for profit, and decreased investment in newsgathering, all affecting competition and information content. Agendas have shifted, along with reader demands and interests. It is an industrial evolution that has altered not only how journalists do their business, but the business itself—in ways that are not necessarily beneficial to the media and the public they serve and that often are detrimental to both.

TECHNOLOGY

The most striking and apparent change is the technology. Even the small differences, like the transition from lead-filled wooden pencils with erasers on the end to disposable plastic ink pens, are what strike some news veterans as they contemplate the technological alterations to the journalistic fabric.

Former *Washington Post* editor Ben Bradlee notices the missing ink.

"There's no ink in this building anymore, there's no presses," he said from behind his clean, polished wooden desk at the *Post* building in Washington, D.C. "There's a production facility that is one half of one floor, if it's that, when it used to be four floors. It's just totally different. We could print this paper in Timbuktu as easily as we print it here."

Syndicated columnist Georgie Anne Geyer fondly remembers the layout and camaraderie of the newsroom where she started out in Chicago, the *Daily News*. And she notices the lack of old newsroom noises.

"I think the greatest thing about it was our desks all abutted one another," she recalled. "We were all together, jammed together in our desks, with typewriters, a very cozy city room. You can see the structural differences, they're all in private alcoves with the computers, and very little talking going on. It's so quiet. We used to chatter all the time. Our place was hysterical; people would get up and dance around."

Washington Post syndicated columnist David Broder also notices the quiet of today's newsroom, and the loss of the old newsroom accoutrements such as glue pots, the pneumatic tubes that would carry rolled-up reporters' copy to the composing room, and the old flash-bulb cameras.

He recalled with a laugh that when he began at the *Pantagraph* in Bloomington, Illinois, the newspaper did not have a separate photography staff.

"We used to lug those big, heavy Speed Graphics with us on assignments. We typed up our stories and had to put carbon paper in between copies and all of those slow, manual things. Now everything is swift, and most of it is automated. Everything is electronic. There's no type, there is no tubes, there's no copies of anything, it's all in the computer. The noise, we've got carpeting on the damn floors, nothing, nothing, no noise emerges."

And no cigarette smoke, a staple of the old newsroom that Broder shared with his wife, also a reporter at the time. "My wife, who smokes, used to be furious at the *Pantagraph* because male reporters could smoke, women reporters could not." Now, of course, newsrooms are smoke-free.

Syndicated columnist Ellen Goodman has tracked the emerging technological and news delivery changes through the national political conventions at which the Democratic and Republican parties select their presidential candidates every four years. One of the symbols of the evolving media coverage of the conventions was the reporter's name tag.

"The first convention I went to was in '72, and at that point I had a 'press' tag. And then, somewhere in '76 or '80, I had a 'media' tag. And at one point almost all of the journalists were print, and then television as well as print, television and radio, and then you get to cable, and then you get to blogging. If you wanted to track the profession through these giant professional conventions called political conventions—but they're also giant media conventions—that would be another way to track it."

National Public Radio senior correspondent Juan Williams, who also is a commentator for television's Fox News Channel as this book is written, likewise referenced the era when print journalists dominated the reporting industry before technology altered the media's course.

"When I came in, journalism meant newspapers," he said from behind his desk in his Washington NPR office, adding that in the early days of broadcasting, the newspaper model was adapted to the airwaves. "Watergate was a newspaper story, the TV networks were slow to come around and uncertain about how to do investigative work. The big shift was the emergence of things like CNN. All of a sudden, twenty-four hour cable news, and an endless news cycle emerged."

Another phenomenon he noted was the development of talk radio during the '90s, "which becomes a huge phenomenon and the whole notion of news as infotainment, which I believe is more of a '90s model. So we move away from newspapers, more clearly to TV and to people who were never newspaper people in terms of journalistic training, prompter readers, beautiful faces, TV personalities. If (Dan) Rather was better than (Walter) Cronkite, he was also more dramatic, and more on the scent, the intrepid journalist. But it was never about the kind of gritty reporting that had an impact coming out of World War II, Korea, and Vietnam that had been done by newspapers. We had become during the latter part of the twentieth century an information-based society largely based on the power of TV as the primary news source."

Judy Woodruff, who has worked in all three television venues—national and local broadcast, cable, and public (her milieu during the research and writing of this book)—noted how technology has altered delivery of television news.

"When I first went into television we used film cameras, and we had thirty-five millimeter, sixteen millimeter film. I learned how to use a sound camera and how to edit film. I was never very good at it, but that wasn't my prime function," she said at her office on the perimeter of Washington. "Today, everything is digital, the cameras are digitized, everything is much smaller and faster. You had to process film in those days. We'd bring a story back from the state capital and have to wait forty minutes, thirty-nine and a half or whatever before we could rip it off the processors, and as soon as it was off get it on the air. Now it's instant."

Thus deadlines have changed. Once, reporters and editors faced time restraints for the midday newscast, the prime-time reports and the morning news; now the deadlines are constant.

"It's instantaneous. As soon as you get the information you've got to get it on the air, especially with cable television."

CBS News' *60 Minutes* correspondent Morley Safer also spoke about the immediacy of the news, but in a different light.

"There's nothing you can't cover live now, there's virtually nothing you can't cover live" he said in his book and gadget-cluttered CBS office. "You can cover it with a device as big as this tape recorder (referring to a palm-size digital recording device used for this interview). So that's a fundamental change. Has it made the reporting better? I don't know."

His comments, he said, spoke to the reporting of a story, not to the images accompanying the reporting.

"I think there was a certain advantage to the delay. When we covered a story in Vietnam of any kind, there was a serious time lag. The obvious time lag that you had to put it on an airplane to fly to a place to transmit it from, which generally was in the United States, it was only fairly late in the war that you could transmit from Bangkok, for a while, or Tokyo. Which meant that as a reporter you had anywhere from a half a day down to an hour or two to actually sit down and think about what you wanted to say."

This applied especially to war coverage, he said, arguing that more than mere images and immediacy in reporting is needed to provide necessary context for a report.

"If you're simply describing it as it's happening, generally the information that you're giving people is really lousy because you have no time to think," he said. "The scene you are describing, however articulate you may be and however perceptive you may be, you're only describing what you see. That's it. And I think if you're covering it and can sit back and have the leisure of an hour to sit down and write something, to think about it, that's more thoughtful, more balanced, more whatever, rather than describing something that you don't know."

He continued: "I'm waiting for somebody to cover a story live, and when they ask him a question, 'well, what's happening out there?' and the guy says 'how the fuck do I know? I know as much as you know, I can see a guy with a gun, I can see this, I can see that.' I'm just waiting for a reporter to do that; I think it's the most honest response you can give. So I don't know that the technology has improved the quality of the reporting, that's what I'm saying."

Woodruff, noting that the new technologies have broadened and hastened a reporter's access to information, shared Safer's frustration over context and depth because of the demands for immediate presentation.

"Reporters don't have as much time to do background research and get on the phone and get information," she said. "The more you're expected to show up on camera and talk about something, the less time you have to work the phones, or read, read the background. And so, there's this fine balance."

TIME, MONEY

"Reporting," Woodruff said, "takes work. You don't just suddenly understand everything, you have to work at it, and so I worry a lot about whether reporters have the time to do the reporting they need, and whether we have enough reporters, because the industry, hand-in-hand with all these technological changes, the industry has gotten larger, and more companies are publicly traded. The expectations are that they will return a profit, bigger profit bigger margin every quarter, and when you've got Wall Street analysts looking over your shoulder, you're going to cut back, you're going to lay people off, you're going to shut down newspapers and trim costs, and that doesn't lead to better reporting."

Staff cutbacks, especially the closing of foreign bureaus, concerned some of the journalists. Safer said that when he joined CBS, the network had a bureau in London, Paris, Tokyo, Rome, and Moscow. He opened the Saigon bureau during the Vietnam War.

"We now have one in London, Moscow, I guess in Baghdad, and Tokyo," he said. "Four. Maybe at the most."

Geyer has watched news organizations steadily thin the ranks of her colleagues in foreign affairs reporting.

"I don't know that a lot of people would know what was going on in Iraq, or Afghanistan, or Iran, without the handful of foreign correspondents who are out there," she said. "The numbers, the way they've been cut back in the last twenty years, has just been horrendous."

The old foreign correspondents "who really roamed around and got the unusual story, you hardly find them anymore," she said. "Why were we surprised by 9–11? 9–11 was horrendous, but it was no surprise to me whatsoever."

This was because she had been in Beirut, where bomb explosions were the norm, and she had covered airliner hijackings in the Middle East.

"The Trade Center had been attacked in 1993, anyone who knows anything about the criminal mind knows that they would try to do it again," she said. "We had virtually no foreign correspondents in Afghanistan in the 1990s, we could get no information whatsoever."

News organizations have replaced foreign bureaus with a system of rotating reporters among hot spots, she said, "what we call the parachutists, the young girls who would parachute into a country one day, be there two days, and then parachute to the next crisis center. And all they could do in that kind of coverage was bang-bang stuff, because they didn't know enough to do the good in-depth political analysis or anything."

Bradlee, though, defended the closing of some foreign bureaus on cost-efficiency grounds and said that today he likely would use the parachute system decried by Geyer.

"Foreign affairs is an economic decision. It costs a hundred and fifty thousand dollars per bureau to start a bureau somewhere, and if you were a publisher, where do you want to spend that hundred and fifty thousand dollars to make the paper better?" he said. "I think if I had a hundred thousand dollars to improve the paper, I wouldn't open another bureau overseas, I can't see where the bureau is what we need to have. If I had a hundred thousand dollars to spend, I'd probably add it to the travel budget so I could send somebody to Cuba when I wanted to rather than open a bureau."

So much of news today is about the money—but not always in such simplistic terms as budget requirements, as discussed by Bradlee, or balancing advertising revenues with supporting the news function. News now is about "product," the word of choice here, denoting that information has become more of a commodity than a responsibility for some in the industry. Just as campaign donations and lobbyist largesse has corrupted politics, so has the concern for profits, the pressure for greater and greater profit margins, affected the journalism industry. The news business has become more business and less news, many of the journalists said, and this has played a role in everything from how the news is gathered and presented to the overall agenda of journalism.

Time was, Safer said, that the news division of CBS was a money loser, a sort of loss-leader, which was a source of pride for the network's executives.

"Bill Paley (chief executive) loved the newsroom," he said. "Frank Stanton (president) loved the news division. They really thought that's what gave them the license to do the crap, and I'm overstating, the license to do other things, was this place. That's no longer the case. This place (the news division) is now a profit center, it's got to show a profit the way every other division shows profit. When Frank Stanton was still at this company, and it was not that long ago, we used to get notes from him, we used to hear from him about stories, specific stories, generally positive notes. I don't think I ever got any notes from any of these guys or from anybody else around here. I think their priorities are different, their interests are different. They're in the entertainment business and they want news to really be part of the entertainment. I mean, they'll issue all these pious things that come so trippingly off the tongue about the importance of the news division, the right to know, all of that." But, he said, there is no doubt that entertainment drives the newsroom today.

Caldwell has observed the same phenomenon in print news.

"Now we see news as a profit center, product, profit," he said. "If it doesn't produce profits, we don't want it."

Caldwell remembers the day when his newspaper would choose a story over an ad—a day he laments as long gone.

"One of the things that made me proudest, and I used to argue, not just me but everybody, all of the reporters, 'hey, this is the *New York Times*. At our paper we're different, if it's between a big ad and an important story, we throw the ad out.' I've had editors tell me, 'we're clearing out a page for you today,'" he said. "Now they create whole sections for the ads and put these little bullshit stories around the ads. It breaks my heart sometimes to read the Style section in the *Washington Post,* a paper I dearly love. But they don't have the caliber of stories they used to have in the 1960s."

And as the drive for advertising revenue increases, so does the cost-cutting.

"I just read it the other day," Caldwell said, "the *Washington Post* said 'we're going to get rid of seventy people,' based on what? Based on they're over fifty years old and we want to get them out because we want to make more money." The result, he argued, is lowered quality control. "You can't take all of your senior people out of the newsroom. These are the people who can sit there and read a story and say, 'something about that story doesn't look right, I don't know what it is, check this boy's story, something's not right about it.' And they'll pull the plug on it, they will know, and now, because of the money, they want to get rid of all the senior people."

Lewis said the economic reality of producing journalism is a factor that cannot be ignored and that business-versus-product concerns sometimes require trade-offs that allow the news business to be about news.

"If you're the gatekeeper at CBS News and you see that your evening show is running behind the other networks, what are you supposed to do, say 'the public needs more hard news, they don't like it but we're going to give it to them anyway?' And your ratings continue to decline? You can't do that. The answer is there has to be a niche, but in a very large sense, niche, serious conveyers of news. The *New York Times* is one. It has made its peace. It does do things to attract readers, it does have sections about food and home, and I think that's fine, let them do it, I don't care. It makes money and keeps the paper going. But it provides a service for those readers in the United States who want to have serious news, and they can read it, and the *New York Times* doesn't have to compete with the *New York Post,* but you have to find an economically sustainable basis for this niche. The *Times* has more than a million circulation, so it's a large niche."

The question for companies that desire to continue producing good journalism becomes a decision of what must be done to do that, said Goodman.

"A lot of what they're doing is not journalism," including investing in nonjournalism enterprises, she said. "I love the home section, so I have no problem with that if it brings in revenue and keeps a Baghdad reporter."

The question concerning this issue for reporters, Broder said, is not so much a question as it is a decision.

"The trends in terms of Wall Street and its investment philosophy when it comes to the media are, I think, almost beyond the capacity of an individual journalist to do much about," he said. "So we keep trying to put out the best product we can and hope there is a market for that product."

Much of the bottom-line concerns regarding journalism and the media have to do with ownership—chains, conglomerates, and monopolies in an industry increasingly dominated by multi-media ownership concentrated in fewer and fewer hands, as opposed to the old model of family ownership. Many of the business decisions concerning journalism and its content are made by boards of directors responding to shareholder demands for profits rather than by single-owner publishers with a journalism heritage that includes a responsibility to fully inform the public as equally important, if not more important, than large profit margins.

"Alex Jones wrote a tremendous book called *The Trust* (coauthored by Susan E. Tifft) about the *New York Times'* early days and how this family would agonize over whether eight percent, seven percent profit was too much, where was the line for the trust," Caldwell said. "Now, twenty-five percent is not enough, you've got to have thirty. It's all about the money. And this, to me, is impacting negatively on everything."

COMPETITION, OWNERSHIP, AND DEMOCRACY

The higher profit margins cited by Caldwell are partly the result of the fundamental transition of the media from the era of lively competition involving a mix of voices in markets that offered not only more than one newspaper but also radio and television reporters. Broadcast journalists vied with print reporters for the attention of an audience and for the advertising revenues that large and demographically diverse readerships and audiences would bring. As the number of newspapers declined, along with the decrease in the number of cities offering daily newspaper competition; as broadcast outlets lost viewers and audience share to niche-rich cable channels; as newspapers and broadcast companies have been gobbled up so that the bulk of media content today is controlled by a few media giants, competition has waned dramatically—despite the appearance of a glut of media outlets that on the surface seem to offer a wealthy marketplace of ideas. Trouble is, when the marketplace is monopolized, when a handful of companies such as Disney or Rupert Murdoch's News Corporation or Gannett control a disproportionate share of media outlets, there is less room for competing philosophies and ideologies. Homogeneity thrives.

So, the impact cited by Caldwell goes beyond the profit opportunism of a few newspaper owners; it goes to the heart of the democracy because of the need by voting participants in the republic for information about their government and society. It goes to the vital watchdog role of newspapers, which, through an informed electorate, have played primary roles in stemming corruption and wrongdoing—from the abolitionist press of the 1800s to newspaper reporting of the Teapot Dome and Watergate scandals of the last century.

"We had four papers in Chicago when I was there," said Geyer, who said she worries about the diminishing media competition, particularly in the newspaper industry. "The more serious it becomes, it's much easier to keep stories covered, or uncovered, by the paper. Something in the city hall of Chicago, if that one paper doesn't want to cover it then it doesn't get covered. There are lots of one-paper cities now, most of them. These guys are the real bottom-line crowd."

Like Caldwell, she cited the demand for profit margins of 25 to 35 percent, "but that's still not going to be enough for them. You just don't have enough competition of reporters and cartoonists and people thinking."

The danger to democracy of this diminished competition of newspaper voices, she said, is that agendas and gatekeeping become the responsibility of a limited number: "very few people can make all the decisions, and you don't have the competition between the reporters, you don't have the competition between the editors. None of the editors."

She added: "When I came in, my first paper, the *Daily News*, was owned by John S. Knight, and he was a giant in his field. I don't see any John S. Knights around. I see Rupert Murdochs. And that is a very different thing. When you're not covering foreign news very seriously, how are Americans supposed to know what's going on in the world at the same time they're being fed a diet of fear about the rest of the world, which is unhealthy?"

Lewis, arguing that newspaper conglomeration leads to diminished quality of reporting and writing, cited the example of the *Louisville Courier-Journal,* a prominent Kentucky family-owned newspaper that was bought by Gannett in the mid-1980s. The *Courier-Journal,* Lewis said, "was a distinctive newspaper with community values, cared about the community deeply, and was rooted in that community but had very good news coverage in general. Gannett took it over, now it's bland, like other Gannett papers. Gannett papers are not completely worthless, I'm not going to condemn them out of hand; when I read *USA Today,* which is when I'm traveling, I always find something to read in it, good things, but it's a bland, stamped-out-of-machine product on the whole."

Lewis sees conglomeration of media and the monopolization of news voices by a small number of owners bringing about a homogeneity of media reporting that is the antithesis of the purpose of the First Amendment. This poses an increasing danger of censorship, not from government, but from businesses that place bottom-line interests above those of informing the public.

"It's exactly against the Madison theory of the First Amendment, which was you're not allowed to censor what any voice says in the press because there will be lots of voices," he said. "This guy says something wrong, the other guy will correct it and so on and so on. That doesn't work if one person owns all the voices."

Bradlee, though, did not share the concerns of Lewis and others over the decline in the number and variety of newspaper voices.

"Listen, this is heretic, but I don't spend much time worrying about that," he said in response to a question regarding the dangers of monopoly media voices. "I mean, if there is a need for a second voice, there will be a second voice, it's just as simple as that. If somebody is getting a monopoly and totally dominating the news in a certain area, sources of news will pop up. Why does there have to be four daily newspapers in every city? There really doesn't, because there's so many ways now you get news. Much more than say a city that had four daily newspapers like Washington. There are many more ways of getting news now than there were then, and there are only two—we like to say one and a half. I think the newspapers that exist, the quality of the journalism, the quality of the reporters, education of the reporters, is so much higher than it was when you had four newspapers in this town. It's just a provable fact."

But Bradlee did share Lewis' low regard for news done Gannett-style, and he took advantage of the topic of news company mergers and conglomeration to take a shot at his old competition on the national stage, the *New York Times* and its purchase in the early 1990s of the *Boston Globe*. Such mergers, or purchases, can lower the morale of news company employees, he suggested.

"I don't see why it's good for society that Gannett owns a hundred newspapers, but I don't think it's wrecking society the way they run them," he said, adding that if Gannett imposed a one-size-fits-all news content and delivery edict, "that would be a disaster. But I don't see much signs of that. I don't read a whole lot of Gannett newspapers. And I don't think, for instance, the purchase of the *Boston Globe* by the *New York Times*, I don't think that's done the *Boston Globe* any good at all. I think it took some of the snap out of the *Boston Globe;* they think they work for somebody else, and they do."

Goodman, who can speak first-hand about the experience of working for the *Boston Globe,* did not share Bradlee's concern about morale or about diminished quality. It is important, she said, that as chain ownership and conglomeration thrive, the business owners remember the importance of the newspaper franchise and its responsibility.

"I don't think it's like the intrinsic evil," she said of chain ownership. "But what happens in a lot of these companies is that they think that the profit margin has to be what the profit margin is in some other businesses. There's nothing wrong with McClatchy owning a lot of papers, not intrinsically wrong. There's nothing wrong with Newhouse owning a lot of papers, there's nothing wrong with the *New York Times* owning a lot of newspapers. It's only if they start thinking that news has to have the same profit margin that something else does and treating it that way, then we run into the problem. We run into the problem also if it's Disney that owns you and wants you to do long features on Disney world."

Caldwell, though, sees a possible benefit to chain ownership—distance, which brings the advantage of neutrality when it comes to parochial, outdated values.

While an argument can be made for the benefits of local, nongroup ownership, such as owners who are involved in and care about their communities, sometimes this local involvement can be detrimental, he argued.

"Almost every day, you have these anniversaries of various events back in the '50s, early days of the civil rights movement, and the papers didn't cover certain things, or they covered certain things in the one kind of way, and papers are apologizing now for their coverage," he said. "I'm down there in Virginia, and the papers are apologizing for not really covering all of the issues around the closing of schools down there. But maybe if they had national ownership instead of local ownership they would have told the truth. This thing that you're seeing now, maybe it's better."

Conglomerate ownership of different platforms, as opposed to group ownership of one platform particularly, raises another problem, cited by NPR's Williams: synergy, in which multi-media organizations use their various subsidiaries to promote their own products. Citing the example raised by Goodman, Disney, he said this is one of his primary worries concerning media mergers and conglomeration.

"When I'm watching ABC and I realize they're owned by Disney, and Disney also owns ESPN, and you see all this kind of . . . where programming is sort of mutual, and they trade on each other's programs, or they use reporters interchangeably and reporters become content providers as opposed to journalists, or they become personalities," he said. "It's almost like Mickey Mouse can appear on ESPN and on ABC. He can be at the theme park, he can be in the movie department that's owned by Disney, and it's all cross-promotion. When it comes to the news department, I have not seen lines broken in terms of people told do this, don't do that, report this, don't report that. I think that would be a sin, I think we'd hear about that. But what you see is an attitude prevail, we are the news division, we have to make money, and we don't see a large appetite for foreign news, so we're not going to deliver foreign news. Well, that has a real impact on the American mindset."

Woodruff spoke to the same problem—from the perspective of a journalist who has been on the inside of all platforms of broadcasting: network, cable, and public. The increasing drive for profits, she said, has brought decreased emphasis on reporting resources.

"I worry a lot about the democracy," she said. "To me, the democracy depends on a free and healthy press that is free to ask questions and to challenge authority when necessary, and to explain what's going on to the American public. With fewer reporters, and more deadlines, constant deadlines in some cases, and fewer resources, I worry about where that's headed. I see newspapers closing down, reporters being laid off; I've already watched television networks lose bureaus overseas and in this country. Overall, the trend is toward less reporting. Why? Because it's expensive. And these news companies are being held to a higher business standard in order to satisfy the needs of the corporate entities that own them, the big companies that answer to Wall Street every quarter, and they have to answer to this division and that division. They're under pressure to cut costs."

ALTERED CONTENT, AUDIENCE

Related to the media conglomeration and monopolization phenomena are the changing nature of media, and newspaper, competition and the new directions in news and information focus that the evolving ownership structures bring about.

Broder argued that journalism has become more competitive with the new technologies and ownership patterns, but it is a different kind of competition—a theme echoed by many of the journalists.

"For years we didn't worry much about what the competition was here in Washington, and we were putting out one product, which was one newspaper once a day," he said of the *Washington Post.* "Now we are competing not just in this market, we are competing with the world on the web, we are in radio as of a month ago (April, 2006), and it's very different. You have to worry about a lot more, think about a lot more dimensions to your job than simply the old job."

Along with these new dimensions, he said, have come new directions and processes in news delivery, such as less depth and more focus on political and governmental outcomes rather than process.

"In Washington, there's much less attention to the steps in the process. We used to cover hearings on bills with some detail. People are not interested, editors are not interested in that anymore. You get to the bill when it reaches final stages of floor debate, and not much before. There is, I think, increased concentration on the White House, less concentration on the departments and agencies. In many respects, we're less thorough in our coverage of government overall than we were."

Plus, he added, the changing audiences have brought different coverage demands.

"There's clearly concern about whether we are holding an audience or not, particularly a young audience," he said. "There are a lot of people grasping a lot of straws trying to figure out what we can put in the paper that would be of interest to folks other than a diet of official news. Whether any of those tactics work or not I don't know, but obviously you can't just sit there and say we're going to keep doing exactly the same thing we've done last year, because there are fewer people reading us now than last year. I said that wrong. There are fewer people reading us in the old format. There are more people reading us overall than ever before, but that's because of the shift to the Internet, and the questions about how you capture revenue off the Internet side of the business. There are a lot of concerns about what you can do in terms of content to hold readership."

In the broadcast realm, Woodruff similarly cited an intense atmosphere of competition, but with a similar shift in the subject—away from hard news about government and politics, toward celebrity and a journalistic herd mentality.

"We have this pack mentality, where if one network goes off to cover the courthouse in California when Michael Jackson is arriving," she said in reference to a court appearance tied to allegations of sexual misconduct involving the pop singer. "One day I was anchoring the noon news on CNN and Michael Jackson was late, and he finally arrived in his pajamas, and we stayed on that site, on that picture, for an hour and a half or something while we waited to figure out what they were going to do about that, what the judge was going to say. I'm sure in that instance all three cable channels went immediately to that scene, but if, say, CNN went first, then I'm sure Fox and MSNBC, because there's competition."

Williams cited the focus on a 24-hour news cycle as the dominant, technology-driven shift in media competition, a move that has taken the emphasis away from scoops and in-depth reporting and toward providing constant updates to breaking news.

"Who had it first used to be important," he said, citing as an example the assassination of President Kennedy. "People grabbing for the phone, UPI and AP and all that, and special editions of the afternoon paper, it's always been important to get the story first. But in the cable era, every little thing became this huge, the primary, *the* story. Even when you had an AP wire service story for the afternoon paper before, the idea was that you could come back the next morning and be more in depth to the news that would be done by a local correspondent or someone in the Washington bureau or traveling to the scene. Now it was a matter of the latest being what did you hear in the last half hour if not the last ten minutes kind of story, and the ability to do in-depth reporting, to compete for the investigative piece, totally went out of fashion. It was all about the kind of values that dominate cable news."

Those values, Williams argued, have come to be driven by technology, with a focus on celebrity and entertainment—with profit, rather than news value, the primary aim.

"The best example I guess would be CBS' *60 Minutes*. Hey look, *60 Minutes* makes money, it's the number one rated show on TV. If this makes money, why can't the nightly news make money? Or why can't we do a cheaper version of *60 Minutes* with another kind of magazine, and you had all kinds of imitations, *20–20* and all of that, and you say this is cheaper than the dramatic programming out of Hollywood. We can make money, so all of a sudden news became a profit thing rather than a place where people say, 'listen, we have been given the gift of the airwaves by the American people and we are going to do everything possible to maintain the traditions of Edward R. Murrow, holding high the flag of virtuous, principled journalism, journalism for journalism's sake, we believe in the light that comes from public disclosure, working on stories that take time, we're going to hire people who may not look like movie stars but have a dogged respect of good journalism.'"

Why is this kind of journalism important?

"Well, you know, you just don't understand how this society works if you are simply a captive of the public relations firms and the lobbyists and the political speechmakers and the political strategists," Williams said. "At the moment, the media is the captive of those camps. It's just a matter of whose endowment is at the moment."

What the nation gets much of the time instead, particularly on the airwaves and cable, Williams argued, is opinion and anger without the solid support of research and context.

"Where do you have to go to get the news? I think people are frustrated, and I think you see it when you have people like (CNN's) Lou Dobbs who say, 'I speak for the little guy on immigration, and I'll tell you what's really going on with immigration, and I'll tell you why the business community and the politicians are wrong.' But he is a demagogue in his own right, driving up his own ratings, and off on a bent, as opposed to someone saying 'well, here is insightful journalism where we have spent time and money, and we have a sense of exactly who's coming over this border and what impact they're having on America,' and you can go to a place you can trust, that they are truly trying to tell you a story without regard to the politics of it or trying to sell you something, that it was an important story well told. An important story well told is rare in American journalism."

Similarly, Goodman cited demagoguery and opinion-mongering substituting for hard, research-supported reporting that she said is now found primarily in serious newspapers, in magazines, in documentary films, and in books.

"Politics is now, on talk radio and talk television, a food fight," she said. "You talk about political life being polarized, well political coverage has become incredibly polarized. You have on the one hand these newspaper people, the good newspapers, who abide by very traditional standards, getting points of view and not telling you what they think, and then you go to the round tables and the food fights and whatever, and the only thing they do is hurl opinions at each other."

The definition and meaning of journalism has become vague, she said.

"Do you have to have a certain number of journalistic standards that newspapers have? Have you ever heard a cable television show running a correction? Is there anybody on (Bill) O'Reilly, any editor, who says, 'excuse me, yesterday we made a mistake, we'll be running a small correction in a box or in the crawl even,'? No. What is journalism? Is it a journalist sitting in his, you know the classic statement, sitting in his house in his pajamas? You just sort of give everyone a pass and call them journalists, which is fine, but that doesn't mean that they're all doing what we grew up thinking was journalism."

She joined the chorus of other journalists blaming the drive for profits, such as the bottom-line motivation of corporate-board operated chain newspapers, for the decline in journalistic standards and in-depth, contextual reporting.

"Look what happened to the *Philadelphia Inquirer.* I mean, Knight-Ridder took one of the best newspapers in America and wrecked it, I mean it was the deliberate murder of a great newspaper. That's a wrecking ball. That wasn't a danger of voice, that was just a danger of 'we don't care what you put out, we're just going to wreck it because we want the money. Show me the money.'"

Goodman invoked what she called the "golden age of print, print way back when it was yellow journalism" to lodge her complaint about cable television news and information programming.

"Cable is yellow journalism, I mean the cable talk shows where people yell at each other, the food fight," she said. "I mean the yellow journalism was a little different, but the totally opinionated, unabashedly opinionated, the political brief kind of journalism, or made-up facts, or whatever. It's still highly competitive, across the board, and at the same time the nature of the competition has changed. I think it's both simultaneously. People are competitive not so much to get the story first, to get the on-the-spot story, you know, the white SUV going down the Los Angeles freeway; that's sort of been ceded to television, you know, the get-there-first-get-the-pictures sort of nonstory of the month. And the Internet gets the story out so instantly now that the newspaper is no longer competitive really for the news story, the immediate, the fire, the break-in. Everybody who reads the newspaper already knows what happened, and so that sort of competition has really been ceded to the faster media from print. Competition to do deeper stories that you don't need videotape for, competition to know 'hey, what's really going on,' that now has gone for those who even care to newspapers, to magazines, to documentaries, to books. And in a way you could argue that newspapers are what magazines once were because everything is speeded up so fast."

And the faster, more immediate journalism produced by a larger number and volume of information sources does not equate to better journalism or journalistic content, she added.

"A lot of these new voices are just redundant," she said. "They're all imitating each other, they're all searching for an audience, and they're all saying the same thing. It's a kind of dumbing down. It doesn't all mean that you have better journalism."

Lewis also took notice of the increased rush by news organizations to get information into the public realm—but in a positive light—and of the increased number of voices, including one that he singled out worthy of greater attention: individual bloggers who put news and opinions on the Internet without benefit of an established news organization behind them.

The emerging sort of journalistic competition, Lewis said, is "beneficial to the reader." The benefit, he said, includes quicker access to the news.

"Even putting apart the instant computerized thing," he said, "when something happens, anybody who cares can know it right away. The deadlines at the *New York Times,* for example, because of computerized typesetting, printing and everything, the paper closes about 10 o'clock now. You get late sports results and late events which you never did. In terms of ease of acquiring information, it's phenomenal."

The increased number of voices from all sources is part of this phenomenon, Lewis said, a phenomenon different from the sort of competition he faced as a young reporter, when newspapers were trying to respond to the challenges of television.

"The *New York Times* in my day was struggling to learn to compete with broadcast, Murrow and CBS News. What can we do, people find out what's happened on CBS News, what can we do that will take them farther and make then want to read the paper? That was the sort of theme at the moment, what can we do that broadcast doesn't do? There was a great editor at the *New York Times,* Lester Markel, who was the Sunday editor. I first worked for him as a copy boy, that was his shtick, 'we have to broaden it, give people the background.' He hated opinion, he didn't want it called opinion, he called it news analysis, that was his way of avoiding the word opinion. But it was a framework, it was the very thing that was lacking with (Senator Joe) McCarthy, give people some setting in which to make sense of the isolated event or the statement or the declaration.

"Now it's competition with unnumbered sources of news," Lewis continued, "uncountable bloggers. We have to care about the bloggers, because they occasionally say things that matter. We have to care about broadcast and nonbroadcast, Fox news."

THE INTERNET AND BLOGGING: A NEW JOURNALISTIC PLATFORM

The Internet and the blogging phenomenon, which has spread into traditional journalism with newspapers posting web pages and maintaining blog sites operated by staff reporters, has taken on a greater role in the mix of information platforms. It is a trend that some of the traditional journalists interviewed here see as beneficial, but with some drawbacks, such as lack of reporting resources, editing support, and some basic journalistic principles such as fact-checking.

For Thomas, the problem of blogging and Internet journalism, which she sees as beneficial because of the added informational voice they bring to journalism, is the reliability of the reporting—a drawback cited not only by journalists but also by academics and researchers who face a growing glut of often unverified and unverifiable information on the Internet.

"They don't follow our rules of journalism, and accuracy and checking and so forth," Thomas said. "Anybody with a laptop thinks they're a journalist. They're all getting into the act."

Broder likewise cited blogging and the Internet, along with cable broadcasting, as beneficial by bringing more voices and information to the public. But, he was asked, is democracy being better served, or is it not being served as well as it should be by these additional sources of information?

"I think both," he said. "I think it is better served, I mean the one great advantage the Internet provides is it allows people to have a voice and an audience they would not have had otherwise. This newspaper before e-mails used to get something on the average of one-thousand-two-hundred to fifteen-hundred letters to the editor a week, of which we published eighty to a hundred, which meant that we were frustrating more than a thousand people every week who took the time and effort to tell us what they thought. Now those folks have lots of places they can go, or they can create their own blog site and become in effect their own newspaper. And I think that's got to be healthy to the society, they can vent some of that frustration. But whether it's healthy for journalism is a different question, because there are obviously no standards that apply to a lot of what happens on the Internet, and as a result a great deal of what goes out is unverified, unverifiable and, I think, more clutter than value."

Goodman encountered first-hand the verifiability problem as she was researching information for a column she had written on celebrity heiress Paris Hilton. Noting that many newspapers now require their staff writers to also blog, she pointed out the same problem already cited by others, the lack of an editor to help ensure accuracy.

"You know, I had an interesting example yesterday," she said. "I was doing this story on Paris Hilton and the estate tax, so I got to the end of this, and I was looking for, OK, so what is her inheritance, and how much is she due to inherit, what's the dollar figure? I found many different answers to that question. Finally, I spoke to my editor, because we were on deadline, and I said, 'so what do wc usc? I mean there's nothing reliable here whatsoever, you know." And we finally went with, I think it was Forbes finally, it was some reliable source. Do I know that they know, or that they figured it out? You know what I mean. It's like, 'who's checking what here? Where's the information coming from? Now who cares?' In that case, it's no big deal if she's going to inherit fifty million dollars or sixty million dollars, you know, but who's out there? It's all out there, unedited. Well, I care, right; but it's not a matter of life and death."

To Woodruff, as to Broder, some of the blog phenomenon is beneficial—primarily in the role of bloggers as watchdog over the mainstream media. And some of it is not beneficial, such as when bloggers obsess on single subjects.

"It's a mixed picture," she said. "Some of it's healthy because it's passionate, and it's an effort. I think the blogs have held the journalists' feet to the fire. A lot of journalists get lazy, because it's got to be a little comfortable. You get the story, you get it on the news, and nobody's really looking over your shoulder. The blogs started paying attention, and I think what kicked it off was the 2000 election, and the networks were so wrong in calling the election in 2000. And so, I think that really gave impetus to the blogs, and they've been out there as a kind of mainstream media nudge saying, 'wait a minute, you got that wrong, you got that wrong.' And I don't think that should be their only function. I think the mainstream media still perform an enormous service to the American people, no question, but I also think that it's healthy to have a watchdog. I think the blogs can also be unhealthy, because I think that sometimes they go off on a tangent and they, you know, they get all riled up about something that you know probably doesn't deserve as much attention as they give it."

One other problem with Internet journalism, said Geyer, is its narrow scope. The Internet cannot provide the overall view of a newspaper; and for that reason the trend of newspapers closing troubles her. The Internet, she said, offers "one story here and one story there," while with newspapers, the readers have not only the information they seek out but also other stories they might not find, even while surfing the Internet.

"Everything is disconnected, and newspapers were the primary thing that held them together," she said. "If this trend continues, and I think it will, then a very different, another administration can get us into another war, can get us into anything, because there's nobody there caring enough, or knowing enough. And this is what really, really worries me; the newspaper is a view of the world, and you can disagree with its editorial opinions, but you get a view of the world, and the young people today are not getting that view of the world."

Williams discussed blogging, and the Internet, as one more voice in a large mix of information outlets that offer a new and unique format for gathering and presenting information, but one limited in terms of depth and investigation.

"If I am interested in black ties with square dots," he said, "I can go online, I can write in 'tie sales,' or 'tie manufacturers,' and I will get a list, you wouldn't believe it."

The offerings of news on the Internet are similar, he said.

"If I type in things, I can find blogs, I can find Web sites. You can get news not only through the radio, you can go to the NPR Web site. You can get NPR goodies, you can to a certain extent go to NPR archives, you can download NPR stories onto your iPod and travel around with your stories more. That's a different experience of news. So, there's more of the news than ever."

Unfortunately, he continued, there is less investigative reporting presented on the Internet, at least by the independent Internet news sources. "There's less reporting based in foreign countries that give you a global perspective, there's less of reporting that has no political agenda. And I think we're worse off for that. So the good of it is there's more of it, but I think it's all about niche journalism, which is part of that corporate structure that feeds a specific audience that is willing to pay to have a perspective on the news, not willing to hold by the old adage that was true when I came along, that journalists are here to comfort the afflicted and afflict the comfortable. Now we're here to comfort the comfortable, especially if they have some money, and we can give them, you know, what I consider a sleeping pill. We can tell you everything you want to know about your favorite sports team or your famous rock and roll star or your famous movie star, or who had a baby, or Britney Spears. We can give you pornography on line. There's no end to the kind of pacifier that we can make modern media into."

Caldwell, though, sees blogging as a potential to be a "great equalizer" in a journalism industry that often is viewed as part of the nation's power elite structure rather than as watchdog and a check on that power structure.

But, he asked, "how do we know they're telling the truth? Hey, how do you know the *New York Times* is telling the truth? Or how do you know what truth they're telling? They're not giving their sources. It's 'trust me.' And you find out who these sources are, and you say, 'oh my God, if I would have known that.' So we're in the shakeout period, and maybe out of this will come something that is better than we ever could have imagined, and I do see this Internet as being, already you can see it's not whether everybody can get it, they're trying to get it in everybody's hands. The stuff is there, and think of the potential. It's a reading tool largely; a lot of kids don't read, but I believe it is possible that we might be looking at the beginning of exciting new ways that's not only going to make us examine how we deliver news, but education and all kinds of things because of the promise of the technology."

CREDIBILITY

Reliability of information, then, seems to be the primary objection the journalists have to Internet reporting and blogging. But this problem is not unique to bloggers. The problem of inaccurate reporting, from reporters such as the *Washington Post*'s Janet Cooke and the *New York Times'* Jayson Blair fabricating and plagiarizing information, to the epidemic of anonymous sources that haunt most reporting out of Washington and other government centers, existed and exists with traditional journalistic platforms.

The increasing use of anonymous sources, as referenced by Caldwell in his rhetorical question involving truthful reporting at such prestigious papers as his own *New York Times,* troubles many journalists today. The two *New York Times* reporters interviewed here in particular spoke at some length on the use of anonymous sources—how it clashes with privacy rights and the legal system, and how it affects journalistic integrity and credibility.

Lewis cited the case of former *New York Times* reporter Judith Miller, who was jailed in 2005 for refusing to divulge her source for her 2003 research involving the leak to the press from government sources of the name of a CIA operative, and the case of freelance journalist Vanessa Leggett who spent 168 days behind bars after she refused to testify before a federal grand jury and to turn over her research data in a murder case.

Lewis, who said he is skeptical about claims that the First Amendment provides immunity to journalists for refusing to divulge their sources, also cited the federal government's prosecution of an American of Taiwanese descent who was accused of spying in 1999 for the People's Republic of China while employed at the Los Alamos National Laboratory. After the government dropped the charges and Wen Ho Lee pleaded guilty to wrongful handling of restricted information in a plea bargain, the *New York Times,* the *Washington Post,* the *Los Angeles Times,* and the Associated Press joined with the federal government in 2006 in announcing they would pay $1.6 million to Lee to settle his claim that government leaks regarding his case had violated his privacy.

"I'm always at odds with my friends, the lawyers for the press, press law groups," said Lewis, who has been an instructor on the First Amendment and the press at the Columbia University Graduate School of Journalism for more than two decades, "because I don't believe in it, and I don't believe in it for reasons that are evident in the Wen Ho Lee case. The press played it up, especially the *New York Times,* 'Nuclear Spy,' big, big. They convicted the guy in print, horribly, and he was held in solitary confinement for nine months, and then the government admitted that it had nothing on him, and he pleaded guilty to one count. Fifty counts, or charges, forty-nine dropped, one count for mislaying secret documents because he couldn't remember where he'd put something. No conviction, nothing about conveying . . . saying the only reason we agreed to pay this money to help settle the case was because we always must protect our reporters' sources and this was the best way to do it blah blah blah.

"The truth of the matter," he continued, "is they knew they had performed rotten journalism and they didn't want to be exposed for having told lies about Wen Ho Lee on the basis of a corrupt and lying and awful source who was out to get Wen Ho Lee for personal reasons. That's the truth, and we didn't even have the decency to say it."

Protecting sources is valuable, Lewis said, "I don't deny that, but the press must understand I think that there are other values. Reputation is one of them. You shouldn't be allowed to destroy Wen Ho Lee on the basis of confidential sources. That's bad journalism."

Lewis said he tells journalism students in his classes that, rather than relying on shield laws where they exist or may be enacted, they should be prepared to spend time in jail.

"That is part of the price for good journalism. That's what I've been saying for years. Mostly it doesn't happen. But every once in awhile, like with Judy Miller, it happens. Somebody goes to jail. Her case didn't turn out to be as noble as advertised, but you know, some of them have been noble."

One such noble case, he said, was that of Leggett.

"A wonderful woman; I met her. Not a journalist, a woman who had never published anything, was not a journalist, but got interested in a murder case and decided to write a book about it. She interviewed the suspect; the police interviewed him for months, then they dropped it, said 'forget it, he's not guilty,' so they just dropped the case. She went on interviewing him and wrote a book. Then the police subpoenaed her and wanted to see all her notes. And she declined to produce the notes, and she stayed in prison for five months.

"So my question for journalists is, are we privileged and she is not because she happened to have not worked for a newspaper? Why not? So, I was on this program with her in New York about the Judy Miller case. I thought she was wonderful because she said 'I think it depends on the circumstances and the balance of interests. I wouldn't give an absolute rule of privilege to everybody who writes something.' And this was a woman who spent time in jail. I thought that was very honorable.

"Part of the irritation of the press elitism is that we're better than everybody else."

Caldwell also cited grand jury testimony, in a case involving the government's investigation of the use of steroids by professional athletes and the leaking of damaging information concerning former San Francisco Giants slugger Barry Bonds to two *San Francisco Chronicle* reporters—it was later learned that the information had been provided by an attorney involved in the case.

Anonymous sources, Caldwell said, have become the biggest source in the newspapers today, to the detriment of credibility.

"You say people don't believe you. I don't believe you either. Right today I'm agonizing over writing a letter to the *San Francisco Chronicle.* They ran a story in the paper where everybody from the University of California School of Journalism signed this letter and sent it to the paper supporting these reporters who are covering this Barry Bonds thing. Their primary source is somebody (who) was stealing the grand jury testimony, which is supposed to be secret, unchallenged, and giving it to the paper."

Caldwell said such leaking of information raises the question of motive; and it raises the question of whether anonymous sources are using the press to further their own agendas.

"I want to know what is the motivation," he said. "The letter to the paper says these reporters did this outstanding journalism, investigative reporting. Where is the investigative reporting? They've got his girl friend who, they've had a flap, she's saying stuff, they've got the grand jury testimony, and they've got the rumors. I don't see where they're doing this reporting. I don't even know what to call it. I don't know whether to call it jive journalism. I'm not saying they're making it up, but to me, I don't see what gives the reporter the right, or the paper the right."

CONSUMER DEMANDS VERSUS CONSUMER NEEDS

Coverage of the Bonds trial, of the Michael Jackson trial, of the O.J. Simpson trial—all of these fit into a growing pattern of journalistic agendas centered more on celebrity and entertainment than on journalism's more traditional subject matter of government and politics. The changing agendas of journalism raise questions of audience and reader demand and of journalistic responsibility.

Journalism has evolved from the printing press owners of the revolutionary era and the political party mechanisms of the 1800s to a bottom-line-driven enterprise supported by advertising revenues. In this context, audience desires and ratings become more important and must be taken into account in the modern journalistic platforms. But audience needs and wants, measured by circulation and ratings, and their role in shaping journalistic agendas raise some important questions. Do readers, listeners, and viewers care about what is in their newspapers and magazines or what is on the air, and if so, what subjects are important to them? Has it come to the point that journalistic agendas are set more by what audiences claim or seem to want than by what journalistic gatekeepers perceive the audiences and the democracy and society need?

Williams said that as technology and lifestyles changed, so did reader and audience demands; thus, journalism had to change.

When people get home now, he said, they turn on the news. "They hear it on the radio going home, they can turn on the TV when they get home, that's their major source of news. And newspapers, of course, couldn't compete because the afternoon paper you're reading at four o'clock was printed at noon and now you turn on the cable for your nightly news and this is fresh, the latest, right there.

"We had to change," he continued. "Journalism had to change, and that we have more sources of information and a larger amount of information available to more people than ever in the history of man, that's good stuff. That's all positive."

But there is a difference, he said, between catering to audiences and pandering to them, "and I think that's the line that's been crossed. We pander now to people, so that if you are of a political stripe, we'll say we'll give you exactly what you want to confirm your pre-existing views, and we will diminish, we will make devils out of your political opponents for you, we'll make fun of them, we'll mock them. All for your entertainment. It becomes political pornography."

And this, Williams said, puts journalism on a "downward spiral, just down, down, down, down. So once you start giving people a sugary diet, people want more sugar and more fun, and they think news should be all infotainment and 'why do I have to pay attention to any serious news and why do I have to invest any attention into what's going on, why can't I just vote my emotions and my guts rather than my head?' And that's what journalism today is, and it's very profitable, but it's not good journalism. The standard I would hold up for good journalism is journalism that allowed people to be better informed so that they make better decisions about their leadership and the future of their country, their community, better decisions for their families."

Williams shared with Geyer and others dismay over the decrease in foreign news, a trend driven more by finances than by the traditional news organization mentality that placed a high responsibility on the delivery of information that citizens need to help them make decisions about their government.

The prevailing attitude, he said, particularly in broadcast, is "'we are the news division, we have to make money, and we don't see a large appetite for foreign news, so we're not going to deliver foreign news.' Well, that has a real impact on the American mindset. 'We're having trouble attracting female readers, female viewers, we're going to soften the news or make the news more celebrity driven, more like the *National Enquirer* in order to try to attract this imaginary female viewer.'

"I don't mean to pick on TV," he continued. "Newspapers during the '80s and '90s came up with home sections and garden sections and science sections and health sections and weekend out sections, all, again, to try to capture this market. But on TV they put that in at the expense of the delivery of news. So whereas you used to complain that there was only twenty-two minutes of news to be delivered in any half-hour news—that was (Walter) Cronkite's complaint back in the '60s, we only have twenty-two minutes, that's why you have to keep these things short—now they do the news basically in these little bites at the top, you don't have correspondents overseas basically unless the correspondent is at the war zone. So they might give you foreign news; they do very little in terms of in-depth political coverage, they're just simply covering the controversy of the moment, large trend stories whether it's the aging of the population, immigration demographic shifts, the growth of the Hispanic population. That's what is viewed as boring, tired, and so they're off to the latest on Britney Spears, or they love an O. J. Simpson or a Duke lacrosse incident or a Clarence Thomas hearing; those are what drive the numbers.

"Do these stories actually tell you much about our time, who we are as an American people? Do they suggest a direction, do they inspire, do they give you a sense of a New Frontier and the way people felt so positive about America like under Jack Kennedy or even Ronald Reagan and a sense of possibility? No."

Journalists are better educated, but they have lost track of the audiences they are supposed to serve, said Caldwell, adding that he worries about the modern journalists' "sense of mission."

"When I was a reporter, newspaperman, we used to say, 'I represent the little guy,' and that was our thing. I'm not sure that's at all true anymore, that the reporters identify with and see themselves as representing the little guy. I don't think anybody gives a shit that much about the little guy in that same kind of way. We're in the period where there's a lot of celebrity. Even the journalists, the leaders, are considered celebrities themselves."

Consequently, he said, journalists and news organizations are less likely to deliver information that is crucial to the lives of readers and listeners—celebrity journalists who have become part of the system instead of its independent watchdog have disconnected from their audience.

"There is something else that's happened, and maybe this is something that runs through all of these things that we've been talking about. The '50s, I was talking about the radio, listening to the conventions on the radio. Now, it's not only that you're right there, the reporters are like players in the convention, and then they decide, 'well, this is too boring, it's not going to get the ratings, so we're not going to cover it,' and they're not going to even cover and let you see and understand. 'We'll wrap it up on a one-hour special at night.'

"What is news has changed, too," he continued. "And our attitudes about news, all that's changed. Television has become such a huge player in our lives that, what fascinates me now, and I think this is an element of things, it's like Jon Stewart with *The Daily Show*, we get one group of the people that this is where they get their news. It's like it's a different world, a different universe. Are we better? Is it better? People obviously have more education, but on the other hand, I'm from the old school, so I say, it's a craft. This is something you can teach people."

Journalism, Caldwell said, is in transition, "and whatever's going to come out the other end, we're not there yet, I can see that it's possible that these big companies like the *New York Times*, I've noticed they're diversifying, they're getting so many other things. But that thing they were built on, I can see that that's over. You couldn't have a Woodward-Bernstein (Watergate scandal) story, it would be impossible for them to do that today. I doubt the paper would have the courage to do it, but I don't think the papers have the credibility. People don't believe us. And I'll tell you, when I read the paper, there's a lot of stuff I don't believe, a lot of stuff I can't understand."

He cited coverage of the Middle East and U.S.-Israel relations and that alliance's role in the debate about Iran's development of nuclear technology.

"To me, one of the big pieces of that story is Israel," he said, "because we're saying, wait a minute, the Israelis are our allies and we've got to protect them, but then there's this little silent thing. You don't even see a sentence in the story that says Israel already has these weapons. That should be a discussed part of the story, but for some reason is not a discussed part of the story. My point is that we're in charge, there needs to be a closer look at what we're doing."

Geyer also spoke of a journalistic emphasis on infotainment, and of a disconnect between journalists and their audience, with news providers, particularly in television, offering a plethora of information about celebrities and entertainers along with an increasing focus on individual tragedy, "the baby in the well, the girl beaten up and cut into teeny pieces. These are all horrible stories, and they're important stories, but they're not the only thing, and that's what we're getting now, on television. Of course, another bomb went off in Iraq. But you get very little in-depth, anticipatory coverage."

This lack of depth, she warned, will hurt the nation.

"The cost we'll pay will be Americans won't know what's going on in the world," she said, arguing that the lack of information can lead to poor decisions by leaders without the public having the necessary knowledge, or the interest, to understand the decisions made by leaders. "And that can only happen when you have a disconnected country and people who are not watching."

The audience, she said, also is to blame for the disconnect. Young people are not reading newspapers, she said, and people are relying more and more on television and the Internet for information.

"There's no comprehensive view of the world. It's a society that wants to be amused all of the time," she said. Though the nation has numerous outlets of information, including cable broadcasting, the Internet and specialty magazines along with traditional sources of newspapers, broadcast and magazines, this variety of sources actually contributes to the disconnect, she said.

"Each one of those communications, while valuable in itself, goes to a very specific readership and divides the country more," she said. "Each one of those divides and does not bring together. People are reading more and more, they're reading the magazines that have their political viewpoints, whereas the newspaper is the one thing where you see a coherent view of the world, you get a little bit of everything. The newspaper intertwines; we're connected. Cable TV is all kinds of things; each one is good, the History Channel is good, the Discovery Channel is good, but you still don't get the big picture. I watch CNN a lot, but you don't get the coherent picture, the comprehensive picture, about society. You're not getting the community. Community news. More and more Americans don't know anything about the community they're living in. And newspapers are the only one who can do that."

Broadcaster Safer cited the same disconnect—from a television perspective rather than a newspaper one. Half a century ago, he said, three networks dominated the broadcast television spectrum, and that, along with newspapers, was where the nation got the bulk of its news. Ironically, though there were fewer sources of information during the 1950s and '60s, broadcast news offered more serious, in-depth reporting then, he said.

"If you go back, say you just looked at the number of special reports, documentaries, on Vietnam, whether they were stories out of Washington or out of Saigon, say in the period of 1965 to 1968, just look at any three years, and then look at the same number of special reports, documentaries, on the Iraq war in the three years of the Iraq war, it will be the most brilliant study you've ever made," he said. "I'm not just talking about CBS, the others as well, NBC particularly. This (Iraq) war doesn't even make the news every night. It may make the news only twice a week, I don't know. There is a lot of feel-good news, much more feel-good news, than we ever used to broadcast. There's endless medical reporting, which I really am uneasy about because it's once over lightly, y'know. I don't want to have medicine for idiots. I want to have a doctor tell me what's wrong with me."

While noting along with the other journalists the vastly larger number of news sources available today, Safer argued that the nation's political leadership shares some of the blame for the disconnect.

"What's interesting to me is why there are so many sources of information, but people generally feel more disengaged from, for example, politics in the country. I don't know what causes it, but that could be, one effect of that could be the utter mediocrity, utter, utter mediocrity, of political leaders in this country. Beyond mediocrity. You could even say criminal mediocrity. So what has that got to do with news? With broadcasting? I don't know. We hold the mirror up."

Woodruff framed the issue of audience needs and demands in a marketing perspective, discussing journalism as a product. News, she said, has become "much more of a commodity. But it's not a simple picture, because hand-in-hand with that, you have part of this whole effort to keep your head above water and keep the number of viewers." This has resulted, she said, in more sensationalism and, as other journalists noted, a focus on infotainment.

"Some news has gotten more personal, more celebrity driven," she said, "more sort of covering the Michael Jackson trial, for example, rather than health care reform. Health care is a crisis in this country, but we almost never hear about it."

She said she had recently read that the ratio of Michael Jackson stories to stories about the genocide and starving in Darfur is fifty-five or sixty-five to one, based on total numbers of minutes devoted to the coverage.

"Well, which one is more important?" she asked. "Or you could say, 'well, Michael Jackson's a star and we all want to know what he's up to, and what happened to him and so forth,' but Darfur's pretty important too. So, maybe if it was one-to-one, OK I could live with that, but fifty-five times more minutes devoted?"

Woodruff suggested that public demand, or lack of demand, for hard and serious news is a factor that must be considered. For reasons ranging from busy schedules to lack of interest in the larger issues, many citizens simply are tuning out.

"I think people are human and they get lazy and they've gotten busy, plus they have busy lives, they have children to raise and drive to and from school and soccer practice, and they have their jobs, and women are now working outside the home as well as raising children. Everybody's life seems to be busier than ever now, so it's harder to keep up," she said. "And I also think that sometimes people, you know, they'd rather watch *American Idol* than watch a documentary about Darfur or about health care in America. And one way to get them to watch it is to make it a little sensational, to do a story about somebody who died because of a medical mistake, you know, some tragic story. It's easier to do that than to do a dry documentary treatment of health care issues. Those in the commercial media have to think of ways to make it interesting. I think that's why the *News Hour with Jim Lehrer* is so terrific. People know they're going to treat it seriously. Not boring, but seriously, and they don't have the need to make it scintillating and sensational so that people will watch."

That, she said, is the advantage of public television—its seriousness—while the strength of cable is its around-the-clock immediacy and that of the big networks is their audience size (reach) and financial resources.

Broder, while noting that the industry debate about consumer wants versus consumer needs is an old one, also gave the issue a market perspective. Journalism is a business, so ways must be found to pay for the production of the information.

"I think there's always been that balance," he said. "As long as I've been in the business, people have argued in the newsrooms about what do we want to do with this newspaper, what's our job, what's our mission, and that's healthy. I think the anxiety level is higher now because of the changes in the economics of the business. I suspect it is a stage we're going through. At some point, my guess is we'll have to find a way to capture revenue from the Internet more systematically than we're doing now or we're not going to be able to sustain the expense of journalism. And if that's where the audience is going, and that does seem to be the trend, we're going to have to find ways to get that audience to pay for the journalism."

Audiences today have a short attention span, and they face numerous informational diversions when they do seek out news, said Lewis, though he believes fewer citizens care about the news today.

"You know, the average audience member now, in fairness, is beset by entertainment—distraction would be a more general term—distractions that didn't exist," Lewis said. "When William Jennings Bryan spoke through his bullhorn for four hours, people went to listen to him because they had nothing else to entertain them, there was no radio, there was no nothing. Nowadays there's a million things that can distract anybody, television eight hours a day, so newspapers have to fight a lot of distractions."

People care less about the news today, Lewis contended, partly because of what is in the news.

"When there's a really big news event, 9–11 to take a horrible example, people want to read the newspaper, they want to know everything they can about something like that. But day-in, day-out, the news, hard news, isn't very exciting. People have tuned out. I mean, after all, fifty percent of the people or more don't bother to vote, so you shouldn't be surprised if they don't bother to read the newspaper."

This lack of public interest in the news exists despite what Lewis said is journalism that for the most part is well-done, if "more cautious. We don't have the gung-ho type of journalism, but I think reporters do a wonderful job on the whole. I'm constantly impressed by them, you know, like in Iraq. I can't imagine the risks, you know quite a few have been killed. It's not funny, and they take terrible risks. I really do have a lot of respect for today's journalists. People make mistakes, there are bad people, there's a Jayson Blair and so forth, but on the whole they do a good job."

Along with the informational distractions Lewis cited, he blamed the money-driven political system for much of the public's disconnect, "the sense that what you do doesn't affect the outcome, that the power of money is so great, and the modern style of gerrymandering, and, you know, all the things that make politics unresponsive to the individual voter just discourages participation."

A couple of the journalists, though, disagree on the issue of public interest in the news, including hard news. Like Lewis, Thomas cited 9–11 as an example; but in this case, she saw it, and the shifting of the war on terrorism to the war in Iraq by the George W. Bush administration, as spurring citizen interest in public affairs.

"I think they care more and more now," she said. "They're beginning to realize what has happened and they've been had. I think there was a vast silent wasteland after 9–11 where the fear card was really there and people were afraid, and there were different alerts and so forth. But now I think they're coming out of that and realizing they have to know more. And I think they also realize they've been told untruths."

Goodman likewise believes that people care about public issues, and not only the war in Iraq. But, as discussed by others, she said they feel a loss of power, or disconnect, from public policy and those who decide it.

"They care about their kids going to school, they care about the future. They care about these things, it's just a question of whose voice, who they trust is immediately up for grabs, whether it's media or politicians. And whether they feel they have the power to change anything is really up for grabs. I think that people feel pretty powerless right now, and so fragmented. This is not a time of collective action. People are feeling extremely fragmented, and the media is so fragmented, by which I don't mean journalism. I mean all of it is so fragmented, and narrowcasting to various parts; and politicians are narrowcasting, they're trimming their speeches to putting together various voters. So I think that people rather don't quite know whom to trust and whether anything, but do they have any power?"

The fragmentation, she said, shows up in audience choices of media messages. For example, some might choose to listen to, and obtain their news from, talk show host Rush Limbaugh, while others might tune their radios to National Public Radio.

"It's not like, 'I think I'll listen to Rush Limbaugh now and NPR later,'" she said. "they segment, so there's a whole group that believes Rush Limbaugh, you know, and there's a whole group—I'm not equating, like NPR is the left wing to Rush Limbaugh at all. I mean there are people who go to what the president called the reality-based community, and there are people who are looking for just a dramatic rendition, a narrative rendition of the story that gels with what they already believe."

Newspapers, Goodman said, are "in the state of, it's great uncertainty about the future and how to cope with it. So there's lots of floundering. It's not like they say, 'we know that if we put more Britney Spears and more about Brad and Angelina in the paper, it will sell, so let's go there.' It's more like they don't know, and it may be nothing to do with the content, it may be the form that people want."

AN UNCERTAIN FUTURE

That uncertainty extends to practitioners of all media. Asked whether they are optimistic or pessimistic about journalism's future, the journalists gave mixed answers and explanations about what they see coming from newspapers, broadcasters and hi-tech purveyors of news and information.

On the positive side, they cite the good work being done by journalists and a continuing need for that kind of information gathering and reporting. On the down side, though, is the increasing emphasis on profits, particularly in the newspaper industry, at the expense of solid reporting that they see as vital to the society and its culture.

At one end of the spectrum was Safer, who offered a blunt appraisal of the future of journalism: "I find nothing to make me optimistic. I'm not going to say I'm pessimistic, but I find nothing to make me optimistic."

At the other end was Bradlee, who sees a continued citizen demand for information no matter what the venue.

"I can't imagine a society where a newspaper does not answer basic, urgent priority needs," he said. "If you want to know more than a hundred words about a single subject, you're going to have to read it in a newspaper." Specialty publications, such as those geared to a business readership, will not be enough, he said. "You've got to have a general source of news, some. If you sat by a television set you could probably get it, if you listen to CNN, although you'd go crazy after a few hours."

Thomas offered a similar assessment, seeing journalism, the public's need for information, as a continuum.

"I'm always optimistic about journalism because I think that it's an absolute necessity," she said. "As long as there are people on this planet there will be news and it will be reported. I do think that we ought to forget the greed, and the corporations should understand when they take over the newspaper or the media that if they're going to make money, make it somewhere else and let's have some real good products. Spend some money, man the barricades, cover the story."

Lewis, who agreed that journalism will continue to be important to society, believes that a growing public fascination with journalism will help keep it alive.

"I guess I'm optimistic," he said. "I know everybody is pessimistic, or many people are, but I think it's too important, and also I think the public is fascinated with journalism. Journalism has become a consuming subject for theater, television; people are interested in journalists, and I don't think it'll go away."

Geyer, citing the good work being done by reporters, described her attitude as "in the Murray Kempton middle, turning toward pessimism" because of the changing economics of journalism.

"I'm optimistic because I see so many really, really good journalists working on so many levels," she said. "I see so many of my colleagues overseas taking so many chances to cover places like Iraq. I predicted exactly a year before the war what would happen in Iraq, because it couldn't happen any other way, it was cultural, completely, and I see people standing there and reporting day after day, and have great respect for them.

"On the other hand," she continued, "I see the business side of newspapering killing it because they want to make so much money, and they're making so much money, but it's not enough for them, and they're not putting back into the papers in quality. They're taking out of the papers, and I don't know how to stop that."

Similarly, Woodruff described herself as both optimistic and pessimistic. She expressed enthusiasm about the technological gains of journalism and the voice the Internet provides to citizens, allowing them to participate in an electronic community of journalism. As with the other journalists, though, she saw the financial aspect as the down side of the modern journalistic coin.

"I'm optimistic because I think the technology is very exciting, and the fact that more people have a way to report the news themselves and participate in a blog, if they've done some research or they know something, they can get it on the Internet. They can share it with a news organization or they can get it on a blog and get it out there. And it's a much more democratic, small 'd,' kind of journalism that there's a possibility for that now that you really didn't have before. More people can participate in journalism, in reporting. Not that they've been trained; I'm not saying we don't need editors, we do. We need editors and we need people to vet the information and so forth. But I love that idea that people feel more ownership of the news, and they feel they can participate, and I think that's what you see with the blogs and these other sorts of interactive sites where people can react to what's going on."

Cutbacks in resources and on reporting make her pessimistic about journalism's future, she said.

"I think I am very sad, I'm concerned, very concerned, about the direction that we're going in in terms of resources for reporting. I think you must have reporters who take time to report a story; you can't just turn it around in thirty minutes. You must give the reporter time, pay him a salary; they have to spend some time on the phone, they have to spend some time reading documents to do a good job. And if there are fewer of them and the salaries don't keep pace with everything else, then how do we maintain our democracy, how do we support, how do we say we are informing the American people when we are spending less money to cover what's going on? We're not. I think democracy depends on that kind of information, and I worry about it."

Broder pointed to the evolving technology, arguing that journalism is in a dynamic period of change but that people continue to care about the issues of the day.

"We do a lot of talking with voters," he said, citing the sort of street reporting that has long been his trademark brand of journalism. "They care about things that are important in their lives, and they know that those things, or some of them, are at the local level, and some of them involved places like Iraq, which are a long ways away.

"There are many, many, many people who now read the *Washington Post* online rather than read it in the old format," he continued. "You can't regard that as a loss if there's interest in the subject matter. They just find it more convenient or less expensive to read it in that respect. I don't think we've lost the audience for news overall."

He added: "I do think that we are going through, obviously, a huge transition now. But it is a transition, and I think that, as I said earlier, I think at some point there will be ways found to capture more revenue from the Internet side of the business to sustain quality journalism."

The young journalists coming up, along with the new technological possibilities at their disposal, excited some of the journalists, lending them hope for the future of news and information gathering and reporting.

Caldwell told the story of a student doing journalism at Hampton University, where he was the Scripps Howard endowed professor of journalism. The student decided to do a documentary on racial language using a small camera as his primary tool, Caldwell said. Specifically, the student wanted explore the meaning of the word "nigger" and how it has changed.

"I'm thinking, 'how are you going to do anything with that?'" Caldwell said of the camera and recorder, which the student set up on a tripod to interview his subjects. The student invited Caldwell to a showing of his documentary.

"And I go over to the student union, and there must have been a thousand kids in there," he said. "You could see it wasn't as grand, but in some ways you'd look at it and it was just like looking at a movie. And I'm thinking, like, 'wow, my God.' I went back to the kid and said 'how much that little camera cost?' I think he told me it cost like fifteen hundred dollars or something. So what gives me hope about stuff is this technology and these young people. They're not tied down, they see it a different way. I'm thinking of the money I have to have to do this. No, you don't have to have that money. There's a new thing happening. Look at this we can do.

"It tells me that just like in our generation, we said we're going to professionalize these newsrooms, and we're going to eliminate what we used to call yellow journalism, and we were going uphill, and we got to the point that the public had so much support for us that when they saw us coming they would applaud because they believed in us," he continued. "The bottom line is what we're trying to do is give the people the solid information they need to make decisions that they have to make in their lives and be able to set their priorities, and maybe there is another better, more effective way to do this, and maybe that's what the people whose names we don't know, maybe that's what they're down there in the valley dealing with."

Despite the downward-trending newspaper industry and the polarization she sees on cable programming, Goodman gets a dose of the vigor of the emerging journalistic generation every year when she participates in the Livingston Awards for young journalists.

"Here we all sit around amid the moaning and groaning, 'what's the state of journalism, what's the state of reading, does anybody, will anybody advertise,' and so forth, and then you do the Livingston Awards for young journalists and you see what these young reporters and writers do at the beginning of their career in great enterprise, and that really does—I don't mean to sound, you know, like Frank Capra—but it makes you feel good again.

"This year we gave our prize to a kid working for a newspaper in South Dakota or Idaho who took on a Boy Scout pedophile scandal in a small town paper in a Mormon town where the Boy Scouts are all run by the Mormons," she said. "You know, I wouldn't still be doing it myself if I didn't feel that you had the chance to make people see through an issue and look at it differently and spend five or ten minutes in the morning thinking about something that's important. And I still feel myself, when I'm working, just what a great gig it is to be able to spend the day thinking about something you're curious about, your opinion, and having somebody actually care.

"That doesn't mean I'm optimistic about newspapers, about the fate of the newspaper; it doesn't mean that I'm optimistic about the current phase of polarized cable shows," she continued, "but about the enterprise of people reporting on and communicating what's going on in the world and that that communication matters. That I'm optimistic about."

Williams was looking forward to the annual influx of reporting interns at NPR and the enthusiasm they bring to the newsroom—but with a qualification: the motivation seems to be changing toward financial concerns and away from idealism.

"This is summertime as we're talking, or late spring, and we have the interns coming," he said. "And man, I tell you they just, they love this profession, they want to do it. Now a lot of them, they think that you can make a million bucks and that you can become the next Katie Couric and you'll be paid ten million dollars and that's why they're into it. OK. But there are still some young people who come in who actually are like idealists, and for me, it's a kick in the ass. I just love it. They show up and they really want to do hard stories, and they think they can try to get those stories on the air and in print; they don't know how to do it, but that's where they're starting. Just God bless them, and I think it's great. That's a positive sign, that these people keep coming. They give me hope.

"But I must say," he continued, "that by the time they're in their late twenties, early thirties, they tend to be on the treadmill. They tend to have given up. They see that, you know, it's really hard to do that, it's hard to hold up those ideals, especially if you're going out to the smaller papers. It used to be that newspapering was a profession of people who were high school grads, or had some college. And now, if you go to the *New York Times* or *Wall Street Journal* or *Washington Post* or NPR, these are all highly educated people. Oh my gosh."

Williams said that when he was coming up, the thrill was in the byline, in the ability to tell a good story. The question was, "Can I do it? I want to tell a good story that makes a difference in people's lives, that allows them to be better informed. And I think the kids today tend to be much more self-absorbed, self-involved, with their friends and their interests. They don't have that kind of global attitude that I had."

Would he do it again, knowing what he knows now about the business of journalism, the changes in journalism that he has witnessed?

"I think I would do it. It's almost for me like going into the seminary to become a priest. I feel that way about journalism, that you get a calling, that you have a sense of being on the road where you can do something really important to contribute to society. I know that this might sound a bit Pollyannaish, or sugary, but that's the best of me, that's my highest aspiration for myself, for who I am, for what I can do. I want to be a journalist."

But, he said, the altered agendas of modern journalism would trouble him.

"I think that the pressures, the culture that surrounds young people today is all about, you know, like *Seinfeld,* hanging out with your friends, very little political consciousness, very little awareness of those who are in need whether it be people suffering from AIDS," he said, "or people in poverty or in bad schools, or any of those issues, immigration. Those things fascinate me, those are the things that interest me much more than personalities that dominate *People* magazine and now, unfortunately, even *Time* magazine."

Only Caldwell said he would not enter the field again, given the conditions of journalism today—primarily, in his case, what it has lost.

"One of the things, and it's true with anything you're doing, you want to be able to have fun, enjoy it, you want to have respect for people and respect for your work," he said. "So many things that attracted me to journalism, that were exciting for me in journalism, they're not there."

Caldwell said he worked in newspapers during a period that he called "the last great time to be a journalist, a newspaperman, in America. It's gone, it has just, it's changed. I used to love to read these Red Smith columns, and Red Smith used to say one of the great things about being a sports writer is the game starts at one, it's over at three, you can tell people the whole story. But now, it's not the game anymore. It's everything but the game. The game's almost secondary, and that's because the game's on TV. And then the reporters on TV, they are out on the court like they are part of the official game thing, instead of up in the press box."

The public fears journalism, he said, adding that journalism has lost its purpose, its high calling.

"So much of what we used to do, for example, the name, the age, and the address, nobody's going to give you the name, age, and address to put in the newspaper. People won't do it. People are afraid to do it, afraid for all kinds of reasons and maybe rightfully so. America's changing. I don't want to be a part of that. The sense of mission, the things that I was really excited about writing about, they just don't put those kind of stories in the paper anymore."

Gone, he said, are the storytellers, writers such as Mike Royko in Chicago, Jimmy Breslin, and Murray Kempton in New York.

"Now, it might be that maybe we're coming up with a new kind of storytelling that we'll one day wake up and say 'oh my God.' But right now, I don't see it. But why I say I'm excited and have hope for the future is because it's like the mimeograph sheet, what it's possible to do, even while this money's taking this big thing and dominating, it's possible for the little guy to come in with his own idea and no money. I believe it's true that these people at the top, they're so obsessed with getting the money, they're so obsessed with—it's like we're trying to please everybody and nobody, but I believe that it's possible if you've got a good idea to fly in under the radar and do things that could be very effective, and that's what I like, that's what excites me, is that possibility."

Broder diverted the question from himself and spoke optimistically, as, like Caldwell, he touched upon what might come.

"A lot of young people are doing it," he said. "I teach a seminar out at the University of Maryland journalism school one afternoon a week, and we get lots of good young people coming into the business. So I don't see any lack of interest there."

These students are mostly seniors or graduate students, he said, and have already made the decision to enter journalism. "But talking about the field and so on, I certainly don't discourage them from going into it. I do think there is a future for this business."

Goodman said she would enter journalism again "in a heartbeat. I'm curious, and I like writing, and I have found a great way to go through the world."

It is gratifying, she said, when a reader approaches her and tells her that something she wrote has helped the reader understand or think about an issue. Like that reader, Goodman said, she hears about something, "and I figure out what it means, or I try to, or I try to explain it, and that is fun. It's interesting. It's not fun like, you know, like playing golf or playing with my grandchild or something, but it's fun, it's interesting."

Lewis' response was a succinct yes.

"Wonderful life," he said. "Wonderful business. I avoided the word 'profession.' I think it is professional to a large degree, but it doesn't have licensing requirements, and mustn't, I should say. Yes, I think it's a great, great job."

Lewis then invoked an attitude toward journalism that other journalists cited: the notion of a higher calling. It is a job he would recommend to youngsters pondering a career, he said, "within limits." They "have to have a calling, they have to have a sense that they want to do this, because you don't go into it for the money, although the money's better than it used to be. There are a lot of risks."

Geyer, in responding that she would enter the field again "because this is what I want to do," cited a similar commitment to purpose, or mission.

"We need people who want to do it, and they'll make changes in it. You can still do an awful lot of stuff on your own, if you're determined. I'm an independent contractor, and I've found ways to do exactly what I want, nobody tells me what to write or anything. And to make enough money, to travel, it can be done, it's just getting harder."

Woodruff said the murky future of journalism might enter into her consideration. Her decision, if she were to face it again today, would depend on "how ready I am to face a rocky, uncertain road for the next few decades. I don't think we know where journalism is headed. We could end up with a journalism that's stronger in some ways, maybe the current trend toward competition and cutting corners is going to tail off and someone will see the light of day and we will have great newspapers and great television for years to come and on the Internet.

"On the other hand," she countered, "we could be facing a very dark and difficult time with sharply reduced resources, sharply dramatically fewer reporters and reporting, and I think that would be tough. What I say to young journalists is, you've got to be prepared to go in any one of many directions, you have to be ready to report for the Internet as well as for newspapers or television, and I think more and more of them know that. And you also have to be prepared for an uncertain business model; you don't know where it's headed."

If she comes across a young journalist who she believes writes well "and has a great interest and passion for reporting," she said, "I would by all means encourage them to go into journalism."

Safer, while citing the numerous benefits that have offered him a fulfilling career, questioned whether he would be able to endure in broadcast journalism in its modern form.

"Given the greater breadth of opportunities in journalism, I probably would find it attractive," he wrote in an e-mail response to this question. "Nevertheless, given the narrow demand for interest in foreign news, the likelihood is that I probably would not have lasted very long—at least in broadcast journalism. Which is not to say that if the opportunity to be part of '60 Minutes' had presented itself, as it did, thirty-seven years ago, I would of course have seized it and would find myself precisely where I am today. The broadcast remains pretty true to its beginnings with, I admit, a few lapses that I will not go into."

It would be hard to imagine any other career, he said.

"From my very first day on the job on a small daily newspaper in western Ontario more than five decades ago, this work has consumed me, amused me, frightened me, fed my ego, my pride and my passion for history," he wrote. "In short, I guess, I cannot imagine doing anything else and at seventy-five have no intention of quitting."

Thomas didn't hesitate to offer that she would do it again, "absolutely."

"I think I'm the luckiest girl in the world for having picked a profession that's just an education every day. You have to keep learning, it's one field where it's a necessity. You do keep learning, and what other jobs give you that kind of excitement? And also, to be there, you can feel you are keeping the American people informed. You can't have a democracy without an informed people. It's a public service; it's a way of life."

Afterword

When I was in elementary school in suburban west Denver, Jefferson County school district officials decided to stage a practice mass student evacuation in preparation for the outbreak of nuclear war with the Soviet Union. Our teachers sent flyers home, informing our parents of the evacuation drill. Students would be loaded on school buses and driven west, into the Rocky Mountains, which were considered a natural shield from the devastating effects of an atomic bomb blast—the concussive wave of the explosion and the searing heat.

School leaders also thoroughly taught us about those potential effects. I remember one film in particular, which showed an atomic bomb being detonated on a plain somewhere. The fiery explosion flashed, followed by the formation of the rising mushroom cloud. The scene then switched to a set of wax dummies, figures of children sitting in a classroom. The camera recorded their faces beginning to melt, followed by the force of the explosion blowing them apart. If ever you are caught in such an explosion, we were taught, get on the floor, away from and below the windows.

The threat of nuclear war became more real for me during the Cuban Missile Crisis, 13 years after I was born. I remember sitting on my front porch steps after school, folding and rubber-banding my 101 *Denver Posts* for my paper route. Except that instead of folding and rubber-banding, I was reading the front page stories about the escalating crisis. As the Soviet ships steamed toward Cuba, carrying supplies, possibly more armaments for all anybody knew, toward Fidel Castro's island nation, an airplane flew overhead. I glanced up, wondering if it might be the one carrying a hydrogen bomb—even more horrific than the atomic bomb—to drop on Denver and obliterate me.

No time to get on my bicycle and pedal to the mountains 10 miles away, should the bomb drop. School was out for the day, so the evacuation would not be in effect—if such an evacuation by then even was still part of the school district plan. I would not have participated, if it were. When I had brought the flyer home to my mother that day when the mountain evacuation plan was first announced, she dismissed the project out of hand.

"If we're going to die in a nuclear war, we're going to die together," she said. "I'll leave work and come pick you up at school if it happens." Barring that possibility, we drew up an alternate plan. Should the war come and we become separated, we decided, we would meet on the western shore of Sloan's Lake, right across the street from the small law office where she worked as a legal secretary, easy running distance from my school, four blocks from the lake, or our home, five blocks away.

Not only is the past a prologue for the present—an adage driven home to me by the research and interviews of this book and its findings of the roots of modern-day terrorism; Middle Eastern strife and bloodshed; Latin American animosity toward the United States and its territorial, often imperialistic, policies; the merging of culture and politics and religion; the cultural and political divide tearing apart the fabric of this nation today. Much of history also is personal. Most often, its effects are felt by each of us far away and after the fact—policies and customs fashioned in reply to events of yesterday or years ago: Social Security payroll deductions in response to the insecurities brought about by the Great Depression, for example, or government assistance for military veterans seeking houses or college educations, spurred by the sacrifices of soldiers during World War II. But for those of my generation, tagged the baby boomers by the sociologists who study us, many of the historical events of the last half of the 20th century that are the subject of this book were experienced first-hand by us. We are that history. Because I lived through these events, observing them as a young man or covering them or at last some of their effects in my communities as a journalist for three of these five decades, I feel compelled here to offer my answers to and interpretations of the events and categories I offered to my interview subjects for this book. Here, then, is my discussion of the major events and trends of the era, divided into the same categories offered to my interview participants: military, crime, foreign affairs, politics, legal, science, technology, sports, business, arts/entertainment, and the major cultural or societal shift of the era. This will be followed by my thoughts on the journalism-related questions I posed to my interviewees, ranging from the changing technologies and economics of the news industry and how these changes affected news coverage to the altered audience demand and expectations of the industry and my expectations of its future.

The Cold War involved the sort of personal history and experience discussed earlier—a history of fear and angst felt not only by me but obviously, from the remarks of those I interviewed for this book such as Helen Thomas and Ellen Goodman, on many U.S. citizens. Because of the personal emotions it evoked along with the phenomenal impact it had on U.S. politics and policies, from tax expenditures for weapons research and development, to formulation of foreign policy, to the creation of community bomb shelters and evacuation plans, the Cold War is my selection as the most important military story of that period. It was a time in which two Asian wars—indeed, the Vietnam War was a large military story of the era; but it was part of the larger Cold War—provided a testing ground for United States and Soviet weaponry and ideology. It, the Korean War, and other military skirmishes were fought by nations acting as proxy for the East and West superpowers separated by an ocean but with an arsenal of nuclear missiles armed and aimed at each other. It was a period spent largely in preparing for and striving to avoid the use of those weapons. And it was marked, remarkably, by the fact that the nuclear bombs hovering over the national psyches of both nations did not drop on United States or Soviet Union soil.

Another event remarked upon by the journalists interviewed for this book was one felt personally by this author. As CBS News correspondent Morley Safer recalled exactly where he was and what he was doing when President John F. Kennedy was assassinated, so do I. My classmates and I were in Norman Michaels' English class at Jefferson County's Belmont Junior High School, just a few blocks west of the city limits of Denver on Colfax Avenue, when the principal's voice interrupted our discussion of U.S. literature. Horace Hix informed his teaching staff and students via intercom first of the attempt on the president's life, then of the president's death. We spent the remainder of the day, as we shuffled from English and then to Physical Science and then to our other classes of the afternoon, in stunned silence. A few years later, assassins killed Bobby Kennedy and Martin Luther King, Jr.

Political assassination is my selection for the major crime story of the 50 years leading up to the 21st century—again, because of the far-reaching effects and devastation of the killings. These include not only the despair of citizens in the United States, the sense of shattered dreams, that these killings produced in the nation, but also the profound sadness and sense of smashed hopes that reverberated through Latin America, Europe, and Africa. Citizens of all these continents had looked to the Kennedys and King as idealistic symbols of a better, fairer, and yes, a younger and newer world.

Years later, as I worked at my first metropolitan newspaper covering county government for the *El Paso Times,* I and an investigative reporter colleague drank beer and shot pool in a downtown tavern while discussing, and envying, the exploits of similarly young journalists who were in the process of uncovering the dirty tricks of the Watergate scandal that brought down President Richard M. Nixon. This story was one of crime; but more than that, it was the most important political story of the half century. My reasoning once again has to do with long-term effects. Watergate played a role in the electoral loss of Nixon's successor, Gerald Ford; in the election of President Jimmy Carter, who campaigned on behalf of political decency and honesty; in the rise of President Ronald Reagan in reaction to Carter's failed presidency and that represented, as Juan Williams and others have noted, the restoration of Republican and conservative legitimacy. The Nixon saga also played a role in the development of political and campaign ethics movements, and of greater press scrutiny of not only the politics of presidents and congressmen and governors, but also of their character.

I agree with those in this book, including Georgie Anne Geyer, who saw the collapse of the Soviet Union as a major foreign affairs event, but I go one step further to include not only the fall of the Soviet empire, but also its rise. While the Bolshevik revolution and the communist nation it spawned played a major role in the red paranoia that swept through the United States early in the 20th century, the emergence of the Soviet Union and its client states, such as Poland, Yugoslavia, and Czechoslovakia, at the end of World War II largely shaped United States and European foreign policy from 1950 to 1990. Yes, the failure of the United States to capitalize on the peace dividend following the dissolution of the Soviet Union was lamentable; but consider the opportunities lost and political and financial capital spent on behalf of the anti-communist struggle during these four decades. It was an effort that included not only massive defense budgets but that also affected scientific research, political strategy and even educational priorities and programs. The effects of this foreign policy story were widespread and enduring, transferring with some ease from the ideologies and ideologues of anti-communism to those of anti-terrorism.

Likely influenced by my career as a journalist, I depart from the sentiments of Anthony Lewis and others on behalf of the *Brown versus Board of Education* Supreme Court ruling, which I believe fits better into another topic category to be discussed later, as the major legal story of the era. The Supreme Court still is the driving force behind my selection, which is court rulings affecting the freedom of the press and the First Amendment, in positive and negative ways. The court's 1971 decision upholding the right of the *New York Times* and the *Washington Post* to publish the classified Pentagon Papers dealing with the policies and decisions pertaining to the Vietnam War was a significant victory for press freedom over government censure and censorship. But it also meant so much more, and not only because of the representative role the press plays on behalf of the citizenry and democracy. The ruling validated in the legal domain the right of the public to know how and why the United States became involved in the war—any war—and of the press and public not only to have access to this information but to use it in their debate and criticism of not only war policy, but other material that might be deemed secret by the government for reasons of national security. Thus, the ruling was important not only for its effects on the immediate case at hand, but also for its larger statement on behalf of the Constitutional guarantee of free speech and redress that was deemed so valuable by the nation's founders.

The court also reached a significant ruling protecting press and speech freedom in its 1964 decision in the *New York Times versus Sullivan* case. The significance of this decision, which grew out of a libel action brought against the *Times* because of an advertisement that criticized police and a commissioner in Montgomery, Alabama, in connection with civil rights protests in that city, is its strengthening of press freedoms hindered by the threat of legal action. While some of the information in the ad, which was placed to help raise funds to defend Martin Luther King., Jr. in a tax evasion case, was false, the court ruled that plaintiffs in libel cases must prove actual malice to win a libel case. In defining malice as willful and reckless disregard for the truth and requiring plaintiffs to prove such disregard, the court erected a strong barrier to the use of the court system to intimidate the press, particularly in cases involving criticism of government officials in civil rights and other issues of political gravity. The result has been a press more likely to foster the marketplace of ideas and public debate that are vital to a vibrant democracy.

That sort of public discourse took a hit, though, in the court's 1972 decision in *Branzburg versus Hayes.* The court combined three cases, all of which focused on reporters who had witnessed unlawful activity and had been subpoenaed to testify before a grand jury. One of these cases involved Earl Caldwell, which he alluded to in interviews with this author, and the federal government's attempts to force him to testify and to reveal his sources in connection with his reporting of the activities of the Black Panthers. Though Caldwell won in a lower court, the Supreme Court ruled that the First Amendment guarantee of freedom of the press and speech does not give reporters the right to refuse to testify and answer questions put to them in grand jury proceedings. One small victory that emerged from this ruling, however, was the establishment of press shield laws in the majority of states that protect journalists from revealing their sources; but in federal cases and some states, such protections still do not exist. Overall, though, the press' free speech rights—and by extension, those of the public the press serves—came out of the half century significantly strengthened.

The major business/finance story of the era came late in the half century: the North American Free Trade Agreement (NAFTA). This agreement was significant not only for its official recognition of the U.S. role and participation in a hemispheric, if not global, economy, but also for its bipartisan flavor. The agreement took root during the Reagan presidency and was implemented during the Bush and Clinton presidencies, with the support of both of these Republican and Democratic administrations. The agreement, along with other initiatives aimed at economic and trade cooperation at the international level, has political and economic ramifications that continue today, including debate over the export of American jobs overseas, over concerns that environmental issues take a back seat to economic development, over U.S. trade deficits, and even over immigration policy and politics.

While I recall with Ben Bradlee and others the scourges of polio—I remember a girl in my grade school who lugged her useless legs through my grade school hallways with the assistance of crutches, and my first girlfriend in junior high school who danced with a limp during our after-school socials because of her bout with polio—the marvelous breakthroughs in transplant technology get my nod as the top medical story of the half century. I read with awe the news story of the transfer of a beating heart from one human being to another in 1967 by South African surgeon Christiaan Barnard. Though the patient died a couple of weeks later from pneumonia, the story was a phenomenal example of the possibilities of intense medical research and technological innovation. Today, the issues and problems related to organ transplants, be they hearts, lungs, livers, or kidneys, are economic and political, having to do with supply and demand, rather than technological or medical. The operations have become routine to the point that transplants no longer are front-page, or even inside-page, news—and the relegation of these stories from major news to practically non-news is stark testimony to the possibilities of medicine and science if only the research and development funding can be found.

Another testimonial to the potential of scientific research and development efforts when removed from political considerations and placed on national agenda priority lists was the successful landing of men on the moon. American Neil Armstrong became the first resident of Earth to walk on the moon in 1969, just 66 years after the Wright Brothers flew their first planes at Kitty Hawk. Besides the remarkable science involved in the project—development of a missile capable of carrying living beings into space, of technology to keep them breathing and functioning in an environment without oxygen or gravity, of returning them safely to Earth after they walked on the surface of the moon—this mission demonstrated for the first time since World War II what can be achieved when a nation sets its collective sights on a goal. It also was a journalistic coup; televisions in living rooms all over the United States and throughout the world broadcast images of Armstrong treading on the moon in clear pictures that used to be the stuff of science fiction movies and Hollywood film sets. The moon landing took place just eight years after President John F. Kennedy, citing the success of the Soviet Union in launching Sputnik and taking a significant scientific and technological lead over the United States in missile development, had challenged the nation to put a man on the moon by the end of the decade. The goal was achieved with better than five months to spare.

Television provided images of news events that included war protests, Vietnam War campaigns, presidential speeches, and scientific moon walks; it also, as a communicator of artistic creations and performances, brought into the living room live drama, sports and music—including a moon walk of a different kind, that of the pop music phenomenon Michael Jackson. Television to my mind was the single most significant artistic achievement, not in terms of the medium as a work of art, but rather in its ability to transmit works of art into the homes of those not likely or unable to attend such events. Along with this ability and incredible promise, though, came the most significant artistic letdown—the dumbing down of the arts, from theater, dance and even Vaudevillian comedy, to a baser appeal of violence- and sex-laden productions that were more profane than profound. From *Playhouse 90* came *American Idol*. From Rod Serling's *Twilight Zone* came *Bay Watch*. From nights at the Boston Pops came profanity-laced rap concerts in drunken night clubs. Television offered soaring artistic, dramatic and comedic achievements, from live ballet—usually found on public broadcasting spectrums—and musical performances to innovative programming that offered useful and interesting commentary on U.S. society, such as *M*A*S*H, Taxi, The Smothers Brothers, The Honeymooners, The Ed Sullivan Show,* and *The Wonderful World of Disney*. Programs of this quality become rarer as cable and network stations divvy up their share of the vast television audience, though occasional pearls are found in the murky depths of the medium, usually on PBS or in programming offered by cable outlets that include A&E, the History Channel, and Discovery. The journalistic triumphs, possibilities, and failures of television will be taken up later.

Television also offered, and continues to offer, a vast array of programming on sports, ranging from live broadcasts of major sporting events from pro football, golf, and bowling to the Olympics and even high school and little league contests. Thus, television has covered extensively, just by its mere presence during the last half of the 20th century, what I consider the most significant sports story of the era—the desegregation of professional and amateur sports. From the breaking of baseball's color barrier by Jackie Robinson to the phenomenal impact on the game by Central and South Americans, from the claiming of a national basketball championship by Don Haskins' Texas Western College (later University of Texas at El Paso) team of African Americans to the first Super Bowl victory by an African American quarterback when Doug Williams and the Washington Redskins beat John Elway's Denver Broncos in Superbowl XXII in 1988, the slow and for the most part successful desegregation of sports has mirrored the gradual diversification of American society at large. My selection of the integration of sports, then, really speaks more to the phenomenon's representation of the difficult, but steady, process the overall culture has achieved in overcoming its problems of race.

And that, the methodic march toward civil liberties, is what I view as the most important cultural and societal shift in the United States during the last half of the 20th century.

This category is where I place the *Brown versus Board of Education* ruling intended to desegregate the nation's public schools. I agree with the journalists in this book who view this ruling as a major legal story of the half century—culminating in 2008 with the election of Barack Obama as the nation's first African American president in a trend that has seen African Americans move to leadership roles on several political, intellectual, artistic, and athletic fronts.

But this is only part of a larger whole of what Earl Caldwell called the race story, one that is still being written and that continues to reveal problems not only in black-white racial relations that remain strained and backward in some communities, but in other manifestations. These include Hispanics or Asians or Muslims replacing African Americans as the object of racial or ethnic prejudice, or gays and lesbians becoming the objects of fear and scorn. They also take in legislation and social action on behalf of the handicapped and the frail; the ascent of women into corporate boardrooms; the flutter of antiwar protests across the nation in response to a prolonged war in Iraq.

The civil rights movement of the 1950s and '60s was much more than *Brown.* The race story by itself involved more than the judicial branch of the U.S. government interpreting the Constitution. It also included the legislative branch, with Congress enacting laws designed to ensure education, voting, and access for minorities, and the executive branch, with presidential administrations from Eisenhower (begrudgingly) and Kennedy (actively) using the armed forces and the bully pulpit to enforce these laws and court rulings. And it included activist involvement by African Americans and their Anglo supporters who took politics into the avenues and sidewalks of U.S. cities and small towns to protest the injustices, who offered their bodies up to police batons in a Gandhian show of civil disobedience. And it finally included riots in black ghettos where angry mobs disrupted their own neighborhoods to say: Enough. No more.

But the civil rights movement of this era expanded to take on much more than racial issues: the free speech movement on the West Coast, in Ann Arbor, and other college communities were spearheaded by students and intellectuals seeking to uphold the constitutional guarantee of free speech, assembly, and petition; the beatnik and hippie cultures celebrated religious, artistic, and even hedonistic freedoms on behalf of individual rights congruent with free speech and the pursuit of happiness. The antiwar movement merged with the racial civil rights storm to produce a powerful alliance of educated and angry citizens intent on ending an unpopular war and creating a color-blind society.

This shift took on dimensions of an altered cultural paradigm, and its effects linger today in the music, art, sexual mores, and lifestyles of this nation's society. The national fiber has become more colorful, at the least. At the same time, though, the protest and civil rights explosion of the '50s, '60s, and early '70s almost seems to have been a last hurrah; the youthful rage that filled the streets with chants of black and flower power and no more war seems to be more of an occasional and polite interruption to today's war and social policies. The response to the '60s question, 'where have the flowers gone?'—the flowers have gone to seed.

The chant at the turn of the century seemed less We Shall Overcome and more We Shall See.

THE CHANGING JOURNALISM

The *El Paso Times* was my second newspaper job less than a year out of college and following a six-month stint as a sports and county government reporter at a tiny daily newspaper in Wyoming. I sat next to the veteran police reporter at a metal desk with a manual typewriter. This cops reporter bellowed on the telephone, which he cradled between his left ear and shoulder, as he chomped on his fuming cigar and typed his notes onto a sheet of copy paper. He was a big man, especially in the waist, which he cinched with a broad belt. He wore a sport shirt open at the collar with a half-tied necktie dangling below his red throat. A pair of goggle-like plastic frames were always perched on the end of his bulbous nose. His hair was gray, with spots of black, and combed back in waves that curled down to his neck and to the top of his big ears.

He kept an open bottle of whisky in his right-hand bottom drawer and a pistol in his lower left-hand drawer. It was loaded. I often prayed that the contents of the right drawer never mixed with the contents of the left drawer.

To my left, at a desk in the center of the room, sat our federal courts reporter. He always wore a crisp, white shirt and neatly worn necktie, and a pair of black framed glasses over a set of small, black-button eyes beneath a shiny bald dome that sprouted a tuft of hair just at its peak. He looked like a Mongol warrior. With a single index finger from each hand, he typed up the rulings and procedures of our local federal judge, dubbed the "hanging judge" by the local attorneys. As he typed, he muttered aloud: "God damn bastards." Sometimes it was loud and agitated enough to bring me and the others to a shuddering halt in our typing of the day's stories. "Out to get me! Christ! To do us! No!" After turning in his stories, he crept silently out, and the newsroom let out a collective sigh of relief at having survived another day without a dangerous explosion from the federal reporter—an explosion that never came.

In front of him sat the executive editor who by 5 P.M., when the early throes of deadline were under way, was either gone to dinner and drinks with friends, or nodding off at his desk while the newsroom bustled around him. As we worked, pneumatic tubes carried our copy, edited with thick black pencil, to the linotype machines and then to the composing room down one flight of stairs from the newsroom.

After we filed our stories, more often than not we climbed into one or two cars and drove across the border, where we drank cheap Mexican beers and told our war stories of the day and boasted of novels in progress. We on the night shift of this metropolitan daily newspaper were mostly young, and our workday didn't start until 11 A.M. or noon. We usually had our breakfast when others had lunch.

In my last newsroom, an afternoon daily where I was editor, my staff of mostly young reporters typed their stories on quiet computers, working from interviews to which they listened on earphones. They punched a key on their computers that sent the stories to me, usually a half hour or so before the 11 A.M. deadline, and I called the stories up to the screen for editing. The staffers had already placed their own bylines at the top of the stories—bylines had evolved from their occasional use in my El Paso newsroom, where the editor would scrawl my name at the top of an enterprise piece as my reward for a story well done, to standard usage serving to inform the reader of the identity of a story's author in an ongoing effort at transparency. After editing, I tapped the "send" key to transmit the story to a page designer, formerly known as a copy editor, for placement. Once completed, an entire page then was sent to the composing department in the next room where it was processed and prepared for filming and placement on the offset press.

Most of the reporters at my last paper drank fruit juice or water instead of coffee; cigarettes, let alone cigars, had long been banned from newsrooms. At the end of the day, if they had no night meetings to attend or interviews to conduct, they were likely to head to the gym to work off the day's stress. Oh, and most of them were women—graduates of journalism schools or university English programs with live-in boyfriends who pursued other careers, such as computer technology or managing a business or in law or government and who earned the primary money in the household.

So yes, as the other journalists have observed for this book, technology has changed the newsroom and how journalists gather and present the news—but so have the demographics and cultures of the newsroom changed. War stories today more frequently lean toward celebrities interviewed, what they said, and how they said it, than toward politicians skewered by their own words or deeds and hypocrisy. The front pages and leading broadcast stories more often are lifestyle or trends pieces dealing with personal finances or with coping in a stressful world or with overcoming medical ailments or bureaucratic snags. Breaking news? Yes, it's still in there—the occasional gunman gone amok, government official caught in an ethical lapse, along with the other big stories of the day: rock stars coming to town, football teams winning, local businesses opening or closing. And there might be an occasional investigative piece featuring in-depth interviews with unnamed sources revealing the possibility that a local company just might be leaking a carcinogen into a fishing stream; details to be revealed later, by which time the company's public relations firm has spun the problem away. Meanwhile, a war rages in Iraq or Afghanistan—for depth, turn to your local public radio station, if you're lucky enough to live near a university that has one, but forget about the stories from the local big-city paper's foreign bureau. It no longer has one.

That, then, is my long answer to the first question I asked these ten journalists about the state of journalism today: how has it changed since you began?

Other changes emerge in our responses to the rest of the questions—all designed to focus on how journalism has evolved in the United States not just since World War II, but since its infancy, when the owners of the printing presses and the pamphleteers were the nation's first journalists, through the days of the presses sponsored by political parties, the rise of advertising-supported journalism and the concepts of objectivity and impartiality, on through New Journalism, chain ownership, to the more recent journalistic environment of merger, conglomeration, downsizing, and convergence.

Is journalism now more competitive than it used to be? Part of the answer lies in the changing agendas and ownership structures. Newspapers, broadcast, cable, and Internet media are highly competitive in covering stories involving pop singers, steroid-abusive baseball sluggers, the frequent tragedy-of-the-week exposes such as school teachers falling in love with their middle school and high school students and mothers killing children, the natural calamity *du jour* such as floods and fires, singers or actors falling in and out of love and having babies, and loves and spouses who slay their current or ex-mates. Along with this phenomenon of changed news agendas is the synergy that has come to dominate much of the news programming of the day, in which huge media conglomerates report heavily on their broadcast or print subsidiaries about the latest film, product or book that has been produced by their entertainment subsidiaries.

But journalism has become less competitive in the vital and historical role it—primarily newspapers—has played as a watchdog of government and business and as a purveyor of the marketplace of ideas. The number of cities with competing daily newspapers that are not foreign-language or university-sponsored newspapers is fewer than 30 today, compared to the hundreds that thrived early in the 20th century; and a number of those monopoly newspapers no longer are the organs owned by families that had a personal stake in their communities. They are overseen by absentee stockholders or corporations that take the bulk of the profits out the community, that encourage homogeneity if not of opinion at least of reporting methods and operations, that place profit margins and business efficiencies above the investigative and foreign reporting and other traditional functions performed by journalistic companies. Hence, reporting and editing staffs are smaller, and citizens in most U.S. communities have no alternative available if their hometown newspaper or cable and broadcast outlets fail to adequately report on the governmental, educational, social, and cultural issues of the community. Small-market television and radio stations do indeed compete—not with newspapers in political and hard-news coverage, as they used to when they had one or two investigative or consumer reporters on their staffs. Rather, they compete with each other in reporting automobile fatalities, weather calamities, personal finance, health and gardening tips, and features on community festivals.

The Internet offers a plethora of voices, including some well-meaning and sometimes well-researched blogs, that often serve as a watchdog at the national and occasionally at the state level—including keeping tabs on the establishment media and picking up stories that the major news outlets overlook or misplay. But blogs and garage and basement Internet reporters do not have the staff, the editors, and the fact-checkers to produce thorough, comprehensive, and accurate reporting. And, as Georgie Anne Geyer noted, the Internet and other outlets don't provide the sense of shared community, or the public opinion, imagined or real, that newspapers offered in their own roles as replacements for the old town-hall meetings of New England or *agoras* of Greece.

So while we may have a greater variety of voices, from the Internet to the myriad and specialized offerings of cable television and niche magazines, the traditional notion of competition in the context of a marketplace of ideas from which truth will emerge has disappeared except in a few instances at the national level—the *New York Times*, the *Wall Street Journal* and *The Washington Post* competing with books and with magazines such as *The Atlantic Monthly*, *Harper's*, *The New Yorker* and *Vanity Fair* to produce investigative pieces on national issues. It has been replaced by voices, as Ellen Goodman observed, shouting on the screen; by opinion tailored to the particular audience of the talk-show or broadcast or cable outlet; and by sport, celebrity, and entertainment rather than the substantive, issues-oriented reporting the democracy needs.

While much of this agenda is in reaction to audience wishes in terms of classical capitalist economic supply-and-demand theory, research nonetheless has shown that the agenda-setting role of the media is powerful. Yes, readers are busier today, many of their information demands have changed—but this does not remove the responsibility of journalism companies to provide the information that is vital to those who do care about politics, ethics, and scandal to provide a public and historic record of the local and national community—or, in the case of broadcasters, to carry out the public information function that once was required of them in return for the use of the limited, publicly-owned airwaves.

My answer, then, to the question of whether journalism is giving the public what it needs or what it wants is: what it wants—as measured by the advertising buys and market ratings rather than by the broader gauge of journalistic responsibility that comes with membership in the Fourth Estate and the political and societal and agenda implications that term implies. Polls ought not drive all political decisions, especially because they measure little more than a momentary preference rather than an enduring or long-term need—and because political and social conscience (principle) ought to play at least an equal role in the process. Similarly, market analysis and weekly ratings ought not be the sole driving force behind content and coverage decisions of journalism companies. Journalistic enterprises are, or ought to be, unique from other kinds of corporations, such as producers of entertainment or widgets, in that their product is different and carries important social- and cultural-driven responsibilities. These responsibilities would be more akin to those of the medical, educational, psychological, or legal fields, all of which provide services pertaining to the social good. Health, education, and law are not commodities; neither should news—defined in this context as thorough journalism about policy and public service—be.

Is there hope? Sure. As Thomas said, so long as people populate the Earth, they will be interested in other folks, in their institutions and cultures, and in how they cope with events, catastrophes, and life. The economic forces that threaten journalism, including ownership patterns, advertising-driven content and agendas, and bottom-line-centered management, might also contribute to their salvation as owners come to realize that news is part of the journalism brand. Also, savvy owners already are showing evidence as this new century unfolds of learning to use the Internet as a complement to their printed pages; they are figuring out how to, as David Broder suggested, transfer the advertising component, along with the accompanying wealth, to etherjournalism—which comprises not only newspaper Web sites but also independent Web-based journalistic enterprises. The dynamics of conglomeration and the cross-disciplines that come with the new technologies of journalism are spurring innovations, as referenced by Earl Caldwell, that include inexpensive cameras and means of delivery that are hip and thus appealing to young journalists who, like their print predecessors, have stories to tell and wrongs to right. The new journalism of Breslin and Thompson and McPhee is transferring electronically to independent documentaries and storytelling, including a rising band of journalistically inclined filmmakers. Alternative ownership patterns have emerged that are rare but that offer an opportunity for journalism independent from profit-margin pressures. These include foundation journalism—newspaper ownership by content-focused groups such as the Poynter Institute, or investigative and in-depth journalism produced by independent organizations such as the Pulitzer Center on Crisis Reporting. They also take in public-sector journalism—university-sponsored independent presses such as those at the University of Missouri, Southern Illinois University, Colorado University, and Ohio University, all of which routinely out-perform the independent commercial presses of their communities or regions—and government/listener broadcast partnerships such as NPR, PRI, and PBS (though the English model is preferable because of revenue streams relatively independent from political whim). They also include cable and satellite broadcasting, which allow audiences with the financial means—and they don't necessarily have to be wealthy, only committed to specialized programming that includes news—to support noncommercial, independent programming. Outlets such as Pacifica Radio offer alternative news outlets that mainstream press adherents might call radical but that are viable sources of news nonetheless—as are other so-called alt-news endeavors that use the Internet, broadcast (including low-power FM bands made available by the FCC early in the 2000s) and even print to deliver nonmainstream news reports concentrating on traditional watchdog and investigative reporting. Some commercial news outlets, such as Bloomberg News, are reshaping and moving away from the traditional advertising-based models. And while corporate newspaper owners continue to moan about declining advertising revenue, we should remember that newspaper profit margins remain equal to or better than those of other major industries such as automobiles and airlines. They simply are not as high as previously, or as stockholders demand.

And finally, the Internet offers great promise similar in scope to the changes in communication wrought by the printing press and broadcast and specialized tools that include typewriters and cameras—media that, in their infancy, promised a democratization and broadening of voice that they continue, albeit in limited scope, to deliver. Much as the owners of printing presses in this nation's youth discovered, this communications technology offers a means of widespread information dissemination limited only by imagination. I remember a student in a mass media ethics course I taught at Southern Illinois University who showed promise as a photographer who told me a couple of months before he graduated that he was considering putting together an Internet journalism venture with friends.

There are hopeful signs on the media landscape of Internet reporting enterprises that might help fill the investigative reporting void, similar to the role of ProPublica or Politico, at the local level. Sites offering such reporting include MinnPost in St. Paul and Minneapolis, the St. Louis Beacon and the nonprofit VoiceofSanDiego.org. The latter has reported on scandals that include members of the city council on the take from the owner of a dance club, and city bureaucrats covering up the problems of a pension fund that put the city's finances at risk—stories that forced the city's major newspaper to devote reporting resources to them. As the *New York Times* reported in its November 18, 2008 edition, the investigative reports of such Internet sites in cities that also include New Haven, Seattle, with "more . . . on the way," stand out in an Internet landscape long dominated by partisan commentary, gossip, vitriol and citizen journalism posted by unpaid amateurs.

"The fledgling movement has reached a sufficient critical mass, its founders think, so they plan to form an association, angling for national and foundation grants that they could not compete for singly. And hardly a week goes by without a call from journalists around the country seeking their advice about starting their own online news outlets."

Indeed, enterprising journalism pioneers, committed to the higher principles of journalism and the Fourth Estate—watchdog-reporter, information-provider, comfortable-afflicter—can find ways to disseminate news and information on Internet newspapers that offer all the best of our best newspapers and broadcast outlets: news, investigation, arts reviews, colorful features stories, and insightful commentary. All of these, or a cross-disciplinary platform of and by them, are sources of hope for the future of journalism.

As one of its practitioners from its past, I concluded some time ago that despite journalism's woes, I would as a young man do this again. It likely would involve a different kind of media platform, and the salary probably would be no more lucrative than what I earned as a newspaper reporter and then editor. It might even be less. But the potential rewards remain.

I remember just weeks into my first newspaper job, where I was responsible for covering sports and then county government but also for producing photos, the sentiment I experienced one day in the darkroom as I processed film for a picture spread. It was a feeling of satisfaction, of pleasure, as I realized that I was being paid to do what I enjoyed—like Roy Campanella had said of his job as a baseball player—to take pictures, to talk to people, to discover and make sense of information about government and society, to be curious about the world around me, and to write about it. This was no job, it was not necessarily a career; it was a mission. And if that feeling has come through somewhat in this book, along with a sense of what this nation is in danger of losing, then I have done my job as its author.

Index

Note: Page numbers in bold indicate primary discussions for each journalist.

About the Author

STEVEN M. HALLOCK is Assistant Professor of Journalism at Point Park University. After taking his PhD in journalism at the E. W. Scripps School of Journalism at Ohio University, he taught journalism at Southern Illinois University Carbondale. His newspaper experience of nearly 30 years includes national and regional award-winning editorial and column writing for many prestigious newspapers, including *The New York Times, Pittsburgh Post-Gazette, Philadelphia Inquirer, St. Louis Post-Dispatch, Dayton Daily News,* and *Denver Post*. He is the author of *Editorial and Opinion: The Dwindling Marketplace of Ideas in Today's News* (Praeger, 2007).